# Theoretical Health Economics

# Theoretical Health Economics

## Hans Keiding

### University of Copenhagen, Denmark

**World Scientific**

NEW JERSEY · LONDON · SINGAPORE · BEIJING · SHANGHAI · HONG KONG · TAIPEI · CHENNAI · TOKYO

*Published by*

World Scientific Publishing Co. Pte. Ltd.
5 Toh Tuck Link, Singapore 596224
*USA office:* 27 Warren Street, Suite 401-402, Hackensack, NJ 07601
*UK office:* 57 Shelton Street, Covent Garden, London WC2H 9HE

**British Library Cataloguing-in-Publication Data**
A catalogue record for this book is available from the British Library.

**THEORETICAL HEALTH ECONOMICS**

ISBN 978-981-3227-81-1

Desk Editor: Philly Lim

Typeset by Stallion Press
Email: enquiries@stallionpress.com

Printed in Singapore

# Preface

Health economics has had a relatively short, but very successful history as a university discipline. From rather humble beginnings in the 1970s and 1980s it has steadily gained importance, and nowadays most universities will have courses in health economics, addressing students in public health and in economics. This development is easily explained – the economic impact of healthcare in society, and the cost of healthcare to society, has been steadily increasing over the several decades, and by now it simply cannot be ignored when studying the economics of a modern society.

As a relatively young discipline, health economics as it appears today contains many particular features which can be traced back to its beginnings. Since it arose in the interface between the medical sciences and economics, the way of dealing with problems were often influenced by traditions which were well-established in the medical profession, while the classical way of thinking of economists came was filtering through at a slower pace. This means that much of both teaching and research in health economics puts the emphasis on collecting and analyzing data on health and healthcare as well as on public and private outlays on healthcare. This is definitely an extreme useful and worthwhile activity, and much new and valuable information is produced in this way, but occasionally there is a need for in-depth understanding of what is going on, rather than an estimated equation which comes from nowhere. This is where economic theory can offer some support.

The present book is an introduction to health economics where the emphasis is on *theory*, with the aim of providing explanation of phenomena as far as possible given the current level of economics.

The book has grown out of lecture notes from several different courses, with students having in some cases a rather humble background in economics, and in other cases with students at a more advanced level. This is reflected in the way in which the topics are treated, starting from an intuitive reasoning and then proceeding to a treatment of the same topic using more advanced economic theory. Users may then skip either the first or the second part according to their tastes. It has the consequence that some sections tend to use more formal reasoning than others, since the overall intention has been to keep the exposition self-contained, and with few exceptions all that is needed is some acquaintance with standard mathematical notation, and of course some willingness to accept a digression from time to another in order to build the theory on as solid foundations as possible.

The text has benefited greatly from the suggestions of many generations of students. In its final version, valuable assistance and advice was provided by Bodil O. Hansen, for which I am very grateful.

*Hans Keiding*

# Contents

# Chapter 1

# Health and healthcare: What is it?

## 1 Measuring health

Intuitively it is rather obvious that a closer analysis of the use of resources for improving health conditions, for society or for single individuals, will depend rather heavily on the way of measuring states of health. Clearly it would be very helpful for the analysis if a numerical measure of health was available, so that "marginal health effect" of each conceivable therapy might be computed as change in health per dollar spent in the treatment.

As already mentioned, there are considerable difficulties connected with such a measurement. There is no obvious unit of measurement for health, and even the concept of "health" as such is not terribly clear. This in itself should not be a cause of despair, since most of the economic disciplines run into similar difficulties. Even when seemingly exact measures exist, problems show up at a closer analysis – such as e.g. in national accounts: What does the GNP (Gross National Product) actually measure?. On the other hand, it is rather clear that the analysis improves with more precise measures of the consequences of economic choices. Therefore it is important to investigate how far one can get in measuring health.

At a closer sight this measurement problem pervades all of health economics. At the outset it is rather easily seen that there can be no measurement of health corresponding to those of the national accounts (where it makes sense to consider differences of two measured values as an expression of the magnitude of the improvement), but one might still hope for constructing a suitable scale and positioning different health states on this scale in such a way that higher scale value corresponds to better health. Next there is the problem of interpersonal comparisons – is it possible to compare the measures of health of two persons, concluding that one of them has a better state of health than the other? – and further on, can we aggregate the health of a whole society and then compare the overall state of health of two different countries?

**Box 1.1 The WHO definition of health.** According the the World Health Organization (WHO), 'health' is defined in the following way:

> Health is a state of complete physical, mental and social well-being and not merely the absence of disease or infirmity.

The definition was inserted in the preamble to the Constitution of WHO [WHO, 1946] and has not been changed since then. As it can be seen, health goes well beyond what is associated with good or bad health in common use of language. Also, it describes what we would call a state of perfect health but gives few if any hints to treating less-than-perfect health, with which we shall be primarily concerned in what follows.

Before we take up such theoretical aspects, we briefly consider methods for measuring health from a more intuitive angle. The approach is the following: First of all some fundamental characteristics of health of are isolated, so that each of them describes certain aspects of health, cf. Box 1.2. The degree of fulfillment of the demand for perfect health in each of these aspects is then measured on a scale from 0 til 1 (or rather, since the scores given are taken as integers, from 0 to 100). The difficult part of the measurement is then the weighing together of the scores in each of the health characteristics. For this a panel of individuals are questioned about there trade-offs between different states of health (where health is perfect in all except one of the aspects) and the average evaluation is then used for weighing the scorings of each of the aspects together to an aggregate health score.

The method has the advantage of being rather simple and easy to understand. The results show a considerable degree of coincidence in the answers of different individuals, which gives some promise that the measurement results are well founded. On the other hand it must be said that the measurement has no obvious theoretical foundation. If state of health is something to be measured in an objective way – which certainly is not to be excluded and indeed is the basic idea behind the measurements attempted – it would be comforting to have and least some conjecture of the reason why such a shared ranking of health states should exist. Indeed, the economist is accustomed to take the opposite viewpoint, namely that people apriori have very different tastes and desires (and this is indeed what makes trade possible), so that an observation of identical preferences would call

**Box 1.2  The dimensions of health.** Since a priori, health is something ranging from perfectness to total absence (death), a scale for measuring health states can naturally be chosen as the interval of real numbers from fra 0 to 1. Below we refer the work of Sintonen [1981] as an example of the construction of health measures.

A total of 11 characteristics were chosen, namely

- Ability to move around
- Ability to hear
- Ability to talk
- Sight
- Ability to work
- Breathing
- Incontinency
- Ability to sleep
- Ability to eat
- Intellectual and mental functioning
- Social activity

For each of these characteristics a numerical value is determined belonging to a precisely described state of imperfect functioning. For example, with first of the characteristics, ability to move around, the states are specified as follows:

- normal ability to walk, both outdoor and indoor and on stairs,
- normal ability for indoor movement, but outdoor movement and/or movement on stairs with trouble,
- can move around indoor (possibly using equipment), but outdoor and/or on stairs only with help from others,
- can move around only with help from others, also indoor,
- conscious, but bedridden and unable to move around; can sit in a chair if aided,
- unconscious,
- dead.

The people interviewed will be asked to assign numbers between 0 and 100 to each of the described situations, so that the most desirable state gets the value 100 and the least desirable 0; the remaining states should be evaluated so that if for example the number 75 is assigned to a state which is 3/4 as desirable as the best one, 33 to a state which is only 1/3 as desirable as the best one, etc. (whether it at all makes sense for the interviewed to desire something "3/4 as much" as something else is a question which is not posed in this context; we shall consider such questions later).

for a special explanation. So far it has been the other way around in health state measurement; preferences are for some unexplained reason assumed to be identical among individuals, what remains is only to reveal them.

We notice also, that the method assumes that the individual rankings made for each of the characteristics involved are independent of the state of events in the other characteristics. This assumption is dubious – if you happen to be in the unconscious state described above, you might well be pretty indifferent as to whether you can read a newspaper without glasses or whether you cannot move around without a dog. This is the property of *independence* which is at stake, and though not always reasonable it is often assumed in order to have a manageable preference relation in contexts of empirical investigations. As always, there is a trade-off between theoretical purity and practical applicability, and seen in this light the independence assumption is quite acceptable. Indeed, even stronger assumptions may be accepted if they open up for practical measurement of health status, a field which has so many potential applications. Therefore, the activity in this field has been growing in later years. In the next section, we give a short survey of the most important health status measures.

## 1.1 *Health indices and their foundation*

Measurement of health status has been carried through by several researchers over the years, and there is a steadily increasing activity in this field. This is partly explained by the fact that a measure of how patients consider their own situation – self-experienced health – is important also in medical research, and in particular it is important to have a method of measurement which is reasonably objective, so that improvement in health conditions may enter the medical documentation of new medicine or new methods of treatment. In this field there is need for documented effects of treatments, and the discussion of a suitable choice of "outcome" or "end points" of a medical intervention points to the need for such measurements. In many cases, the directly observable outcomes relate directly to treatment rather than to the effect on the general health condition of the patients, and this takes us back to health status measurement.

The need for establishing a standardized measurement of health status, in this case in the United States, is stressed by a law from 1989 (Patient Outcome Research Act), which initiates a broad research program in patient-oriented outcome research (meaning that outcome should not be measured as number of broken legs treated etc., but should pertain to the improvement of the health condition of the patients involved). The topic therefore has a high priority in contemporary medical research.

**Table 1.1.** Some commonly used health status measures

| | QWB | SIP | HIE | NHP | EuroQoL | SF-36 |
|---|---|---|---|---|---|---|
| **Aspects:** | | | | | | |
| Physical function | • | • | • | • | • | • |
| Social function | • | • | • | • | | • |
| Role function | • | • | • | | | • |
| Mental prob. | | • | • | • | | • |
| Self-experienced health | | | | • | • | |
| Pain | | | | • | • | • |
| Energy/fatigue | • | | | • | | • |
| Mental condition | | | | • | | • |
| Sleep | | • | | • | | |
| Cognitive functions | | • | | | | |
| Quality of life | • | | | | | |
| Reported change | | | | | | • |
| **Method:** | | | | | | |
| Administration | I,T | S,I,T | S,P | S,I | S | S,I,T |
| No. of questions | 107 | 136 | 86 | 38 | 9 | 36 |
| Scoring method | SI | P,SS,SI | P | P | SI | P,SS |

Abbreviations:
QWB = Quality of Well-Being Scale (1973) SIP = Sickness Impact Profile (1976) HIE = Health Insurance Experiment Surveys (1979) NHP = Nottingham Health Profile (1980) EQOL = European Quality of Life Index (1990) SF-36 = MOS 36-Item Short-Form Health Survey (1992)
Method of administration: S = Self, I = Interviewer, T = Third party
Scoring: P = Profile, SS = summarized scores, SI = Index
Source: Ware [1995]

The earlier mentioned definition of health adopted in WHO [1946] (cf. Box 1.1) is also here of little use, and therefore other approaches have been developed over time. Despite of the common objective these methods have emerged in a way as to display a considerable variability. The trend has been to include more and more aspects which involve "quality of life"; however, it should be added that even if quality of life is important, certain more general aspects of quality of life should be left out (social status, housing conditions, education), so that what is wanted is what should properly be called "health-related quality of life".

A survey of the aspects of health covered by the most commonly used health status measures is given in Table 1.1.

As it can be seen from Table 1.1, there are several approaches in the literature as to how health should be measured, which aspects of health should be included, which method of observation (administration of questionnaires) should be applied, and not the least, how the result of the measurement should be presented.

*Aspects:* At the general level there seems to be agreement that health – also when considered in its more narrow medical version – has both physical and mental aspects. Only few of the methods involve mental aspects, however, HIE and SF-36 include not only mental diseases but also general mental condition.

*Methods:* If a large-scale collection of data has to be carried through, the methods of measurement should be correspondingly simple. As the data collection in all the above methods consists in responses to questionnaires, which are filled out either by the person, the interviewer, or some third party observing the person, whose health status is going to be measured, it is rather important that these questionnaires have a suitable – and not too large – number of questions. The very comprehensive questionnaires employed in SIP or HIE (see Table 1.1) may be useful for occasional investigations but not as an instrument for general use.

The method described in the last column of the table, SF-36, has emerged from the research connected with the health insurance experiment, where there was a need for measuring health in order to test whether the different schemes covered by the experiment had different impacts for the health condition of the involved individuals. After the termination of the experiment other forms of medical research has been carried through based on the population involved (which therefore by now has been followed over a period of two-three decades so that they represent a valuable source of information), and this led to the construction in 1992 of a rather large questionnaire (MOS Functioning and Well-Being Profile) for measuring both mental and physical health. It actually included all the aspects mentioned in the table, but on the other hand used a questionnaire with 149 questions, considered as close to the limit of what is practically feasible. Consequently, a shorter version was constructed, leading to the so-called Short Form with only 3 36 questions, which, as it can be seen in the table, describe 8 aspects of health and checks for changes in self-experienced health.

*Presentation:* The result of a health status measurement may be presented either as a *health profile,* where the status within each of the aspects comprised by the method is described in suitable terms. This may either be a verbal description or it may be a number (a "score") for each aspect. Finally, these numbers may be weighed together into a single number as a health index.

An example of a health index presented in the table above is the EuroQoL, which is the result of a European project for construction of health status or quality-of-life measures. Here the assessment of the person results in a number for each of the aspects comprised, and this is followed by an automatic weighing, according to a given rule of these numbers into a single number between 0 and 1, which is then the value of the EuroQoL-index.

Throughout the chapter, we shall discuss this type of weighing together or aggregating profiles or vectors into single numbers, often presented as QoL or QALY-indices, and we shall argue that they will be meaningful only in very specific situations. Therefore, it might be much more fruitful to consider health status measures which avoid aggregation across aspects of health and present only a profile or vector of scores in these aspects. Among such methods we have the Nottingham Health Profile from 1980 and SF-36, which as already mentioned is distinguished by involving also the mental aspects of health. SF-36 has received widespread acceptance among medical researchers who look with some – justifiable – skepticism at the idea of presenting health conditions or quality of life as a single number.

## 1.2 *Numerical representation of health states*

Representing health states – or more precisely, the subjective evaluation of health states – by a numerical index takes us to a field which is well known to the economist, namely *utility representation of preferences*. What we have been dealing with in the previous sections corresponds rather closely – at least from a purely formal point of view – to the case of a consumer contemplating alternative bundles of goods. Just as in the latter case, we are dealing with a ranking of health states – some states being healthier than others – and given that this ranking of health states satisfies some consistency requirements, it can be represented by a numerical function in such a way that if one health state ranked higher than a second one, then the first is assigned a greater value than the second.

Technically, suppose that $H$ is a set of health states (with a structure yet to be specified), and that the ranking of health states is written as $h_1 \succsim h_2$ if $h_1$ is considered as representing at least as good health as $h_2$. A health index is then a function $u : H \to \mathbb{R}$ such that

$$h_1 \succsim h_2 \Leftrightarrow u(h_1) \geq u(h_2), \tag{1}$$

so that the ranking of health states is transformed into comparison of numerical values, an operation which is wellknown and in many cases looks simpler.

So far we have (deliberately) been rather nonspecific in our description of the "ranking" of health states. It is seen that if it is to have a representation, then it must be furnished with some structure which fits with the way in which numbers are ordered, in particular it must have the properties of

- *reflexitivity:* for all health states $h \in H$, $h \succsim h$,
- *transitivity:* for health states $h_1, h_2, h_3 \in H$, if $h_1 \succsim h_2$ and $h_2 \succsim h_3$, then $h_1 \succsim h_3$,

- *completeness:* for each pair $(h_1, h_2)$ of health states in $H$, either $h_1 \gtrsim h_2$ or $h_2 \gtrsim h_3$.

Some of these properties (presumably the first two of them) may be considered as being in reasonable agreement with our intuition about ranking of health states, but it may well be doubted that all health states can be readily compared so as to satisfy the third property. A ranking on $H$ (technically, a relation on $H$) satisfying the three above properties is called a *complete preorder*.

It is easily seen that if $H$ is a finite set, $H = \{h_1, \ldots, h_n\}$, then the three properties are not only necessary, but also sufficient for the existence of a representation. Indeed, the health states may be put into one finite sequence of the type

$$h_{i_1} \gtrsim h_{i_2} \gtrsim \cdots \gtrsim h_{i_n},$$

(why?) and the mapping taking the health state $h_{i_k}$ to the number $k$, for $k = 1, \ldots, n$, is a representation of $\gtrsim$.

If the number of health states is not finite, things are slightly more complex, and some structure on the set $H$ has to be assumed. We shall assume that $H$ is a topological space (that is, we may speak about open and closed subsets of $H$). In this case we shall look for a *continuous representation* of $\gtrsim$, that is a map $u : H \to \mathbb{R}$ which in addition to satisfying (1) also is continuous (so that $F^{-1}(G)$ is an open subset of $H$ for every open set $G$ in $\mathbb{R}$. The following result is a restatement of the classical result about utility representations, see e.g. Debreu [1959].

PROPOSITION 1 *Let $H$ be a topological space, which has a countable dense subset $I$. Then the following are equivalent:*

(i) $\gtrsim$ *has a continuous representation,*

(ii] $\gtrsim$ *is a complete preorder on $H$ which is continuous in the sense that for each $h \in H$,*

$$\{h' \in H \mid h' \gtrsim h\} \text{ and } \{h' \in H \mid h \gtrsim h'\} \tag{2}$$

*are closed sets in $H$.*

The countable and dense subset $I = \{h_1, h_2, \ldots\}$ will play a key role in the proof of Proposition 1. That $I$ is dense in $H$ means that for every $h \in H$ and every open $U$ set in $H$ containing $h$, there is some member of $I$ in $U$.

PROOF: (ii)$\Rightarrow$(i): First of all, we show that $\gtrsim$ has a representation on $I$. Let $u(h_1) = \frac{1}{2}$. If $h_2 \sim h_1$ (meaning that $h_1 \gtrsim h_2$ and $h_2 \gtrsim h_1$), then $u(h_2) = u(h_1)$. If $h_1 \succ h_2$ (that is $h_1 \gtrsim h_2$ and not $h_2 \gtrsim h_1$), then $u(h_2) = \frac{1}{4}$, and if $h_2 \succ h_1$, then $u(h_2) = \frac{3}{4}$. Following the same procedure, suppose that values have been assigned to $h_i$ for $i \leq n$, $n \geq 2$. Then either $h_{n+1} \sim h_i$ for some $i \leq n$, in which case we put $u(h_{n+1} = u(h_i)$, or one of the following cases must occur:

(a) $h_i > h_{n+1} > h_{i+1}$, put $u(h_{n+1}) = \frac{1}{2}u(h_i) + \frac{1}{2}u(h_{i+1})$,

(b) $h_{n+1} > h_i$ for all $i \leq n$, put $u(h_{n+1}) = \frac{1}{2}\min_{i \leq n} u(h_i)$,

(c) $h_i > h_{n+1}$ for all $i \leq n$, put $u(h_{n+1}) = \frac{1}{2}\max_{i \leq n} u(h_i) + \frac{1}{2}$.

Then $u$ will be defined for all $h_n \in I$ and take values in the interval $[0, 1]$.

Now, we extend the function $u$ from $I$ to $H$. Let $h \in H$ be arbitrary. If $h \in I$, then $u(h)$ has already been defined, so assume that $h \notin I$ and let $I^+(h) = \mathrm{cl}\{h' \in I \mid h' \gtrsim h\}$, $I^-(h) = \mathrm{cl}\{h' \in I \mid h \gtrsim h'\}$ (here $\mathrm{cl}\, A$ denotes the closure of the set $A$). Then clearly $I^+(h) \cup I^-(h) = H$ (otherwise the complement of $I^+(h) \cup I^-(h)$ would be open, and there would be an element of $I$ in this set, contradicting completeness of $\gtrsim$), and since both sets are closed and $H$ is connected, the intersection of $I^+(h)$ and $I^-(h)$ must be nonempty. Since this intersection consists of all $h'$ such that $h' \gtrsim h''$ for all $h'' \in I^-(h)$ and $h'' \gtrsim h'$ for all $h'' \in I^-(h)$, we get that $h \in I^+(h) \cap I^-(h)$ and $u(h) = \sup_{h' \in I^-(h)} u(h') = \inf_{h' \in I^+(h)} u(h')$. Since $h \in H$ was arbitrary, we have shown that $u$ can be extended to a representation of $\gtrsim$ on $H$.

It remains to show that $u$ is continuous. For this, we may restrict attention to sets of the form $u^{-1}(\{x \mid x \leq t\})$ and $u^{-1}(\{x \mid x \geq t\})$, for each $t \in \mathbb{R}$ such that $t = u(h)$, some $h \in H$. But this follows easily from (2), since $u^{-1}(\{x \mid x \leq t\}) = \{h \mid h^t \gtrsim h\}$ and $u^{-1}(\{x \mid x \geq t\}) = \{h \mid h \gtrsim h^t\}$ where $h^t$ is such that $u(h^t) = t$. It is easily seen that if there is no such $h^t$, then either $t < u(h)$ or $t > u(h)$ for all $h \in H$, and again $u^{-1}(\{x \mid x \leq t\})$ and $u^{-1}(\{x \mid x \geq t\})$ are closed. We conclude that $u$ is continuous. $\square$

## 1.3  *Properties of measurement scales*

Before proceeding we consider a somewhat more abstract version of our problem. We are concerned with measuring something, a property or a phenomenon, and a general approach to measurement can be found in Pfanzagl [1971], from which the following is taken.

In the general theory of measurement, we consider a *relation system* $\mathbf{A} = (A, (R_i)_{i \in I})$, consisting of a set $A$ together with a family $(R_i)_{i \in I}$ of relations on $A$. We consider only relation systems $(A, R)$ with a single relation $R$, which is binary, so that $R$ is a set of pairs $(a_1, a_2)$ of elements of $A$, for simplicity $(a_1, a_2) \in R$ is written as $a_2 R a_1$, with the interpretation that $a_2$ is as good as (as large as, as healthy as etc.) $a_1$.

There are two types of relation system which may interest us, namely (1) *empirical relation systems*, where $A$ consists of certain objects from the surrounding world, in our case alternative states of health, and $R_i$ is a relation satisfied by these objects, and (2) *numerical* relation systems, where $A = \mathbb{R}$ (the real numbers). Intuitively, designing a measurement consists in transforming *empirical* relation systems to numerical relation systems. We need some additional concepts.

A binary relation $\sim$ on $A$ is an *equivalence relation* if it is reflexive ($x \sim x$ for all $x \in A$), symmetric ($x \sim y$ implies $y \sim x$ for all $x, y \in A$), and transitive ($x \sim y$, $y \sim z$ implies $x \sim z$ for all $x, y, z \in A$). For a relation system $(A, R)$, an equivalence relation $\sim$ is a *congruency* if for all $a_1, a_2 \in A$,

$$a_2 \, R \, a_1 \text{ and } a_j \sim a'_j, \ j = 1, 2, \text{ implies } a'_2 \, R \, a'_1.$$

An equivalence relation $\sim_2$ is *coarser* than another equivalence relation $\sim_1$ if $a_1 \sim_1 a_2$ implies $a_1 \sim_2 a_2$; for every relation system $\mathbf{A} = (A, R)$ there is a coarsest congruency $\sim_\mathbf{A}$ on $A$ (which may possibly be the identity relation $=$).

For $\sim$ a congruency on $\mathbf{A}$, define $A/\sim$ as the set of equivalence classes

$$[a] = \{a' \in A \mid a' \sim a\},$$

where $a$ runs through $A$. Then $R$ gives rise to a relation $\tilde{R}$ on $A/\sim$ defined as

$$\tilde{R} = \{([a_1], [a_2]) \mid (a_1, a_2) \in R\},$$

and we get a relation system $\mathbf{A}/\sim = (A/\sim, \tilde{R})$, called the quotient relation system of $\mathbf{A}$ modulo $\sim$. This relation system is *irreducible* in the sense that $=$ is the only congruency on its underlying set.

Given an irreducible relation system $\mathbf{A} = (A, R)$ and a numerical relation system $\mathbf{B} = (B, S)$, a *scale* is a map $m : A \to B$ with the property that

$$(a_1, a_2) \in R \text{ implies } (m(a_1), m(a_2)) \in S.$$

The set of all admissible scales is denoted by $\mathcal{M}(\mathbf{A}, \mathbf{B})$. The ideal situation is that where only one scale is possible. In most cases there will be a large set of scales which are all equally good for the given problem. As a rule of thumb one has that the larger this set, the less information can one read out of the measurement data. A scale $m : A \to \mathbb{R}$ is *ordinal* if it is unique except for monotonically increasing and continuous mappings of $m(A)$ on $\mathbb{R}$. For an ordinal scale it is clearly the location of the measurement data with respect to the order relation $\geq$ that is relevant information; all other details (such as distance between measurement results, or comparison of distances) are irrelevant in the sense that they carry no information about the underlying phenomena. In many applications, including the one we have been developing in the previous sections, this is not quite enough, and we consider also *interval scales* which are unique except for positive affine transformations (adding an arbitrary number and multiplying by a positive number).

In general we say that a relation $T$ on the underlying set $B$ of the numerical relation system $\mathbf{B} = (B, S)$ (not necessarily belonging to the relation system itself, and not necessarily binary) is *meaningful* if for arbitrary scales $m, \hat{m} \in \mathcal{M}(\mathbf{A}, \mathbf{B})$ if

$$m^{-1}(T) = \hat{m}-1(T).$$

Here $m^{-1}(S) = \left\{(a_1, \ldots, a_k) \in A^k \mid (m(a_1), \ldots, m(a_k)) \in T\right\}$ is the inverse of $T$ under the map $m$. In words, for some relation in $\mathbf{B}$ (such as e.g. the relation consisting of all $(x, y, z) \in \mathbb{R}$ with $z = x - y$, then this relation is meaningful in $\mathbf{A}$ if for all scales from $\mathbf{A}$ to $\mathbf{B}$ the idea of a difference taken from the numerical relation system has a unique interpretation in terms of the relation $R$ on $A$.

There is a close connection between permissible transformations of a scale and the relations which are meaningful. The following is a simplified version of the result in Pfanzagl [1971], Theorem 2.2.9:

PROPOSITION 2 *A k-relation $T$ on $B$ is meaningful if and only if $T$ is invariant under the set*

$$\Gamma = \left\{m_1 \circ m_2^{-1} \mid m_1, m_2 \in \mathcal{M}(\mathbf{A}, \mathbf{B})\right\}$$

*of maps from $B$ to $B$.*

PROOF: If $T$ is meaningful and $m_1, m_2 \in \mathcal{M}(\mathbf{A}, \mathbf{B})$, then

$$(a_1, \ldots, a_k) \in m_1^{-1}(T) \Leftrightarrow (a_1, \ldots, a_k) \in m_2^{-1}(T),$$

so if $(b_1, \ldots, b_k) \in T$ and $a_i \in m_2^{-1}(b_i)$ for each $i$, then $(m_1(a_1), \ldots, m_1(a_k)) \in T$, so that $m_1 \circ m_2^{-1} \in \Gamma$,

Conversely, if $T$ is invariant under transformations from $\Gamma$, then for all $m_1, m_2 \in \mathcal{M}(\mathbf{A}, \mathbf{B})$ we have that

$$(b_1, \ldots, b_k) \in T, b_i' \in m_1(m_2^{-1}(b_i)), i = 1, \ldots, k \Rightarrow (b_1', \ldots, b_k') \in T,$$

so that if $a_i \in m_2^{-1}(b_i)$, $i = 1, \ldots, k$, with $(b_1, \ldots, b_k) \in T$, then also $a_i \in m_1(b_i')$ for $i = 1, \ldots, k$, where $(b_1', \ldots, b_k') \in T$. We conclude that $m_1^{-1}(T) = m_2^{-1}(T)$, so that $T$ is meaningful. □

The proposition tells us that there is a close relationship between the transformations of scales that can be made without changing the information transmitted, and the operations on measured date which make sense. Thus, if the magnitude of changes in health make sense, then the scales (health indices) should reflect this, and since arbitrary positive transformations would not keep differences intact, we can allow only affine transformations (adding a constant and multiplying by a positive constant) of the scales.

We shall see examples of scales allowing different classes of transformations as we proceed. While the general utility representation allowed all positive transformations, most of what we see from now one will be of the type which permits only affine transformations.

*QALYs.* A prominent example of a health state measure with additional properties is that of QALYs, Quality Adjusted Life Years. The rationale for using QALYs is that one wants to assess a *change* in health brought about be a particular treatment – so that differences play a central role – rather than a particular state of health, and in addition, this change of health state should be compared to a cost of the treatment, pointing to the need for assessing differences in money terms.

In their origin, the QALY measure was considered an extension to the then common way of measuring effects by life years gained, and the basic idea of QALYs is discounting the life years gained by the quality of life experienced in these years. So far this seems to be a fertile idea, since clearly the value of a life year gained depends on the ability to enjoy life during this year. Technically, the connection with life years gained is useful when defining QALYs; the fundamental idea of a QALY is that if the value of one year in perfect health is set to 1, then the value of one year in a described state of (less than perfect) health $h$ should be a number $q(h)$ between 0 and 1. The value of a number $T$ of years in a state $h$ of health is then

$$q(h)T.$$

This functional form may be used in practical assessments by the so-called *Time Trade-Off* (TTO) method. For each specified state $h$, the person investigated is asked to find the number of years in this state which is equivalent to one year in perfect health, and the result is then $1/q(h)$. Clearly, this presupposes the absence of discounting of future events, which may bias the assessment: if consequences in the distant future are unimportant, then the index value of bad states of health may be overvalued.

An alternative approach to the measurement of QALY values is the *Standard Gamble* (SG) method. Here the idea is to get a numerical evaluation through assessment of lotteries. More specifically, the person investigated is confronted with two prospects, namely (a) 1 year in the prescribed state $h$ of health, and (b) a lottery, giving 1 year in perfect health with probability $p$ and immediate death with probability $1 - p$. The person is then asked to state the value of $p$ for which the two prospects are equivalent; $p$ then is the value $q(h)$ of the QALY index.

As with the time trade-off method, there are some basic consistency assumptions behind this method; in particular, the attitudes towards risk may bias the results (if the persons questioned are risk averse, they may set the number $p$ close to 1 only due to this risk aversion, which means that the QALY index is overvalued; if the persons are risk lovers, it may go the other way). The use of the SG method points to the fundamental role of uncertainty in the assessment of health states, in particular of health states not actually experienced, where the person doing the assessment will have to consider both the likelihood of experiencing this state and the various further consequences which this state may or may not give rise to. We digress in the following subsection into the basics of assigning numbers to uncertain prospects, the theory of *expected utility*.

## 1.4  *Expected utility*

The theory of expected utility deals with situations where a decision maker must choose from a set of uncertain prospects formulated as *lotteries*, which to each of a given set of uncertain future states assigns an outcome. Choosing a particular uncertain prospect means that the actual outcome is determined by chance, indeed by the probabilities specified by these lotteries.

Formally, assume that set of uncertain future states is $S = \{s_1, \ldots, s_r\}$. A risky prospect over a set $X$ is a pair $(x, \pi)$, where $x : S \to X$ maps each state to an outcome, and where $\pi = (\pi_1, \ldots, \pi_r)$ is a probability distribution on $S$. A preference relation $\succsim$ on the set of risky prospects $(x, \pi)$ satisfies the *expected utility hypothesis* if there is a function $u : X \to \mathbb{R}$ such that

$$(x(s), \pi) \succsim (y(s), \pi') \iff \sum_{h=1}^{k} \pi(s_h) u(x(s_h)) \geq \sum_{h=1}^{k} \pi'(s_h) u(x(s_h)) \tag{3}$$

for all $(x(s), \pi), (y(s), \pi') \in \Xi$. The function $u$ is called a von Neumann-Morgenstern utility (after von Neumann and Morgenstern [1944]).

As it can be seen from this expression, the expected utility hypothesis amounts to the assumption that there exists a utility function $u$ defined on the "pure" (risk-free) outcomes, so that the utility $U$ of a risky prospect can be found by computing the mean value w.r.t. the probability distribution involved.

We shall restrict our discussion to a particularly simple case: We assume that there are only $r$ (not necessarily different) outcomes $x_1, \ldots, x_r$ available, each of which obtains in a specific uncertain state of nature, so that $X$ is the set $= \{x_1, \ldots, x_r\}$. In state $h$ the outcome $x_h$ will obtain; what can vary is the probability distribution $\pi$ over the states $1, \ldots, r$. The assumption of $r$, or, more generally, finitely many available outcomes is not crucial but facilitates the analysis, the results of which can be generalized to the case of infinitely many outcomes.

Thus, the choice problem under consideration in the remainder of this section is that of selecting a probability distribution $(\pi_1, \ldots, \pi_r)$ from the set of probability

**Box 1.3 The St. Petersburg paradox.** This is a classical paradox from the time when probability theory was young. A gambling house proposes to its costumers the participation in a game of throwing coins: a fair coin is tossed repeatedly, and the game stops when tails show up for the first time. The gains to be paid out are as follows, where $n$ denotes the number of times the coin was tossed:

| Number of rounds | Payment |
|:---:|:---:|
| 1 | 2 |
| 2 | $2^2$ |
| $\vdots$ | $\vdots$ |
| n | $2^n$ |
| $\vdots$ | $\vdots$ |

What would the gambler pay to participate in this game? A simple computation shows that the expected gain

$$\frac{1}{2} \cdot 1 + \frac{1}{2^2} \cdot 2^n + \cdots + \frac{1}{2^n} \cdot 2^n + \cdots$$

is infinitely large, so a gambler acting on expected gain would pay arbitrarily much to be allowed in. On the other hand, judging from one's own preferences the entrance fee would have a value less than 10. How can this be reconciled with probability theory?

The paradox was introduced by Nicolas Bernouilli in 1713 and a solution was proposed by his brother Daniel Bernouilli, arguing that what matters is not the money gain but the utility of this money gain. More specifically, he proposed to use the logarithm of the gain when taking expectations, giving the quantity

$$\frac{1}{2} \ln 2 + \frac{1}{2^2} \ln 2^2 + \cdots + \frac{1}{2^n} \cdot \ln 2^n + \cdots = \ln 2 \left( \frac{1}{2} + \frac{2}{2^2} + \cdots + \frac{n}{2^n} + \cdots \right)$$

which has a finite value.

The debate over possible resolutions of the St. Petersburg paradox has however continued to our days, following at least two different directions already outlined at that time: (1) people may disregard very unlikely events so that the large gains are not taken into consideration, or (2) it does not take into account that the gambling house has limited wealth.

distributions over $\{1, \ldots, r\}$, which we write as

$$\Delta = \left\{ (\pi_1, \ldots, \pi_r) \in \mathbb{R}_+^r \,\middle|\, \sum_{h=1}^{r} \pi_h = 1 \right\}.$$

The set $\Delta$ may be considered as the set of all lotteries with outcomes from the set $\{x_1, \ldots, x_r\}$. We assume – as usually – that the agent under consideration can order the alternatives in a consistent way, having a preference relation $\succsim$ defined on $\Delta$.

AXIOM 1 $\succsim$ *is a continuous total preorder.*

We know from the previous sections that continuous total preorders have utility representations, but this is not enough here; we are looking for a representation where the utility of a lottery is the expectation (with respect to the probabilities defined by the lottery) of the utility of outcomes. For this we use another assumption, which in its turn needs some motivating comments.

Given two probability distributions $\pi^0$ and $\pi^1$ and a number $\alpha \in [0, 1]$, define the *mixture* of $\pi^0$ and $\pi^1$ with weights $\alpha$ and $1 - \alpha$ as the probability distribution

$$\alpha\pi^0 + (1 - \alpha)\pi^1 = (\alpha\pi_1^0 + (1 - \alpha)\pi_1^1, \ldots, \alpha\pi_r^0 + (1 - \alpha)\pi_r^1)), \qquad (4)$$

that is the convex combination of $\pi^0$ and $\pi^1$. In our interpretation, the mixture corresponds to a lottery, which with probability $\alpha$ gives the right to participate in the lottery $\pi^0$ and with probability $1 - \alpha$ the right to participate in lottery $\pi^1$. This mixture lottery can be described in terms of the probabilities of each of the $r$ outcomes, which is exactly what happens in (4).

The next axiom states that the preference relation $\succsim$ respects the mixture operation:

AXIOM 2 *Let* $\pi^0, \widehat{\pi}^0, \pi^1, \widehat{\pi}^1 \in \Delta$ *with* $\pi^0 > \widehat{\pi}^0$, $\pi^1 \succsim \widehat{\pi}^1$, *and* $\alpha \in [0, 1]$, $\alpha > 0$. *Then* $\alpha\pi^0 + (1 - \alpha)\pi^1 > \alpha\widehat{\pi}^0 + (1 - \alpha)\widehat{\pi}^1$.

It may be noticed that we have allowed for indifference in one of the pairs; the other pair must enter into the mixture with a positive weight.

PROPOSITION 3 *Let* $\succsim$ *be a preference relation on* $\Xi$, *and assume that Axiom 1 and 2 are fulfilled. Then* $\succsim$ *satisfies the expected utility hypothesis.*

PROOF: For $\pi, \widehat{\pi} \in \Delta$ with $\pi > \widehat{\pi}$, let

$$c = \pi - \widehat{\pi};$$

Since the sum of the coordinates is 1 for both $\pi$ and $\widehat{\pi}$, it must be 0 for $c$. Now, let $\pi'$ and $\widehat{\pi}'$ be arbitrary lotteries, and suppose that $\pi' - \widehat{\pi}' = c$, see Fig. 1.1. We shall show that $\pi' > \widehat{\pi}'$.

Suppose to the contrary that $\widehat{\pi}' \succsim \pi'$. We use Axiom 2 on the pairs $(\pi, \widehat{\pi}), (\widehat{\pi}', \pi')$ with $\alpha = 1/2$ to get that

$$\frac{1}{2}\pi + \frac{1}{2}\widehat{\pi}' > \frac{1}{2}\widehat{\pi} + \frac{1}{2}\pi';$$

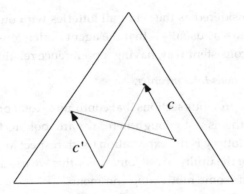

Fig. 1.1  Preferences over lotteries with three outcomes. The difference $c$ between two lotteries $\pi$ and $\widehat{\pi}$ play an important role.

furthermore, we have that

$$\frac{1}{2}\pi + \frac{1}{2}\widehat{\pi}' = \frac{1}{2}(\widehat{\pi} + c) + \frac{1}{2}(\pi' - c) = \frac{1}{2}\widehat{\pi} + \frac{1}{2}\pi',$$

which tells us that the two mixed lotteries are identical, so that one cannot be preferred to the other. From this contradiction we conclude that $\pi' \succ \widehat{\pi}'$.

It follows from this that if a vector $c \in \mathbb{R}_+^r$ with $\sum_{h=1}^r c_h = 0$ has a representation

$$c = \pi - \widehat{\pi} \text{ with } \pi \succ \widehat{\pi},$$

then $\pi' \succ \widehat{\pi}'$ holds for all pairs $(\pi', \widehat{\pi}')$ of lotteries with $\pi' - \widehat{\pi}' = c$. This property will come in useful below:

Define the set

$$C = \left\{ c \in \mathbb{R}_+^r \,\middle|\, \exists \pi, \widehat{\pi} \in \Delta, \pi \succ \widehat{\pi}, \pi - \widehat{\pi} = c \right\}.$$

Then $C$ is convex: if $c$ and $c'$ belong to $C$, then

$$\pi - \widehat{\pi} = c, \ \pi \succ \widehat{\pi},$$

$$\pi' - \widehat{\pi}' = c', \ \pi' \succ \widehat{\pi}',$$

and according to Axiom 2 we must have that $\alpha\pi + (1-\alpha)\pi' \succ \alpha\widehat{\pi} + (1-\alpha)\widehat{\pi}'$. But

$$\alpha\pi + (1-\alpha)\pi' - [\alpha\widehat{\pi} + (1-\alpha)\widehat{\pi}'] = \alpha c + (1-\alpha)c'$$

and the vector on the right hand side must belong to $C$.

Furthermore, we have that $0$ does not belong to $C$ (since $\succ$ is irreflexive). Consequently we can separate $0$ from $C$ by a hyperplane: There exists $u = (u_1, \ldots, u_r)$, $u \neq 0$, such that $u \cdot c > 0$ for all $c \in C$.

Writing this out in detail, we have that

$$\sum_{h=1}^{r} \pi_h u_h > \sum_{h=1}^{r} \widehat{\pi}_h u_h$$

for all $\pi, \widehat{\pi} \in \Delta$ with $\pi > \widehat{\pi}$. We leave it to the reader to check that conversely, if $\sum_{h=1}^{r} \pi_h u_h > \sum_{h=1}^{r} \widehat{\pi}_h u_h$ for some pair $(\pi, \widehat{\pi})$ of lotteries, then $\pi > \widehat{\pi}$. □

In the approach to expected utility taken here only two axioms have been used. This has the advantage of allowing for a rather simple derivation of the main result, but then we have the disadvantage of axioms which may be difficult to interpret. The crucial property of the preference relation on lotteries permitting an expected utility representation is that of *independence*: the ordering of alternatives in any given state is the same, independent of the state considered. Indeed, suppose that in state $s_1$, alternative $x_1$ is preferred to $x_2$, while in state $s_2$, $x_2$ is considered as good as $x_1$. Taking as $\pi^0$ ($\widehat{\pi}^1$) the lottery giving $x_1$ ($x_2$) in state $s_1$ with probability 1 and nothing in the other states, and as $\pi^1$ ($\widehat{\pi}^0$) the lottery giving $x_2$ ($x_1$) in state $s_2$ and 0 otherwise, then for $a = 1/2$ we would obtain that the lottery which gives $x^1$ with probability $1/2$ and $x_2$ with probability $1/2$ is preferred to itself, a contradiction.

The intuition behind the independence assumption, that the ranking of pure outcomes is independent of the uncertain state, gives us that for the application to uncertain health and lifespan prospects that there is a ranking of the health-lifespan combination that does not depend on the uncertain state. From this and to the QALY representation in (1.3) there is not far to go; we return to this at a later stage.

## 1.5 *Extensions of the expected utility approach*

The expected utility hypothesis has received much attention over the years – so much as to make it one of the single pieces of economic theory which has been most intensely debated. It is easy to find examples where decisions based on expected utility do not make sense, one of the more famous of these being the *Allais paradox* (see Box 1.3), and experimental tests of behavior under risk typically show that decision makers violate the hypothesis. Nevertheless, it is widely used in economic theory, since it captures at least some of the aspects of behavior under risk while still keeping the models manageable.

While some of the proposed improvements are too complex to be used in models where the object of study is not the very process of decision making, others have been considered in the context of health status measurement. One of the extensions of the expected utility hypothesis that have received considerable attention in

**Box 1.4 The Allais paradox.** The axioms of expected utility may or may not be satisfied in real world situations. The *Allais paradox* [Allais, 1953] exhibits two different cases of choice between lotteries, namely Case A:

|            | 89% | 1% | 10% |
|------------|-----|----|-----|
| Lottery A1 | 1   | 1  | 1   |
| Lottery A2 | 1   | 0  | 5   |

Here the first lottery represents a sure gain of 1, whereas the second lottery involves an element of gambling. It would seem reasonable – and indeed it is confirmed by many experiments – that lottery A1 is chosen.

Now, consider Case B of choosing between lotteries:

|            | 89% | 1% | 10% |
|------------|-----|----|-----|
| Lottery B1 | 0   | 1  | 1   |
| Lottery B2 | 0   | 0  | 5   |

Now both lotteries involve gambling, and in this situation the lottery B2 might well be chosen. However, if a decision maker satisfies the axioms of expected utility and has the von Neumann-Morgenstern utility function $u$, she cannot choose A1 in Case A and B2 in Case B. Indeed the first choice would imply that

$$u(1) > 0.89u(1) + 0.01u(0) + 0.1u(5)$$

or

$$0.11u(1) > 0.01u(0) + 0.1u(5), \tag{5}$$

whereas the choice of B2 occurs if

$$0.89u(0) + 0.11u(1) < 0.9u(0) + 0.1u(5),$$

which yields that

$$0.11u(1) < 0.01u(0) + 0.1u(5),$$

contradicting (5). This and other paradoxes have given rise to a voluminous literature on extensions of expected utility theory. We shall not pursue such extensions here, since much of what we shall be doing in the sequel relies rather heavily on expected utility theory.

the context of health economics is *prospect theory* put forward by Kahneman and Tversky [1979]: Instead of computing expected utility as in (3), the utility of an

**Box 1.5 Attitudes towards risk.** Once we have a von Neumann-Morgenstern utility, we may be interested in the shape of this function in cases where the outcomes are numbers (sums of money, life years etc.). The graph below presupposes a continuum of outcomes, which is natural in applications.

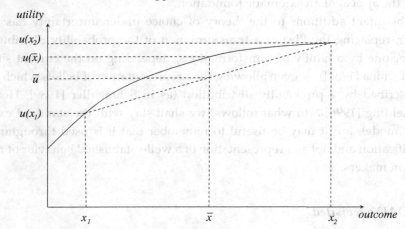

The function depicted is *concave*, showing that the decision maker is *risk averse:* In the figure, we have inserted a lottery with two possible prizes $x_1$ and $x_2$, each having probability 1/2. The expected value of the lottery is $\overline{x}$ (midway between $x_1$ and $x_2$), and the expected utility of the lottery is $\overline{u}$ (midway between $u(x_1)$ and $u(x_2)$), which is seen to be smaller than $u(\overline{x})$, the utility of getting the expected value in cash rather than taking the lottery ticket.

If the graph of $u$ had been a straight line, we would have a *risk neutral* decision maker, indifferent between the lottery and the cash value of its expectation.

uncertain prospect (with uncertain states numbered $1, \ldots, r$) is found as

$$V(\pi) = \sum_{i=1}^{r} p_i(\pi) v(x_i),$$ (6)

where $p : \Delta \to \Delta$ is a transformation sending the probability distribution of the uncertain prospect to a new probability distribution, and $v : \mathbb{R} \to \mathbb{R}$ is a *value function* corresponding to the utility function in our discussion above.

Except for the transformation of probabilities, the approach in (6) does not differ much from that of (3), at least from the formal point of view. However, prospect theory may account for deviations from what would result from expected utility maximization, for example if decision makers overestimate probabilities of very favorable or very unfavorable outcomes, something which seems to be the case in experiments. Also the value function may be source of under- or overestimation of the impact of extreme events. Such departures from "pure" expected utility maximization may account for much of what is not captured by the classical approach, but obviously at the cost of making the theory less simple, losing the appeal of an axiomatic foundation.

Subsequent additions to the theory of choice under uncertainty has moved further, replacing the idea of a transformation of the probability distribution to another one by a family of transformations, depending on the current situation (see Machina [1982]), or even allowing for a representation of beliefs which cannot be described by a probability distribution (as in Schmeidler [1989], Hougaard and Keiding [1996]). In what follows, we shall stay with the standard expected utility model, but it may be useful to remember that it is used throughout as a simplification and not as a representation of a well-established behavior of real-life decision makers.

## 1.6  *QALYs revisited*

With the expected utility model as theoretical basis, we may now reconsider the idea of an index of health related quality of life. In what follows, we use the approach of Bleichrodt et al. [1997]; for alternative ways of deriving a QALY index from expected utility theory, see e.g. Miyamoto [1999], Doctor et al. [2004].

The point of departure now is a set of *uncertain future prospects*, each described as a lottery with outcomes of the form $(h, T)$, where $h$ is a specific state of health and $T$ is a possible lifespan, each possible outcome having a certain probability. Clearly, future prospects could involve the passing over time from one state of health to another, but for our present purposes we may neglect this, since such more sophisticated setups could be encompassed easily once we know how to deal with the simple situation.

Assuming that the axioms of expected utility are satisfied, the individual preferences over uncertain future prospects can can be described by a utility function

$$U((h_i, T_i)_{i=1}^r) = \sum_{i=1}^r p_i u(h_i, T_i),$$

where we have assumed that there are $r$ possible outcomes with probabilities $p_1, \ldots, p_r$. Here $u$ is the (von Neumann-Morgenstern) utility defined on sure prospects $(h, T)$.

Assuming now that the set of prospects $(h, T)$ has the form $H \times \mathbf{T}$, so that all combinations of $h$ and $T$ are possible. In particular, we can combine each $T$ with all possible $h$. We now add an assumption about attitude towards risk (cf. Box 1.1.3).

AXIOM 3 *For any fixed state of health $h \in H$, the individual is* risk neutral *in lifespans T.*

With the assumption of risk neutrality, we get that for fixed $h$, $u$ is an affine function of $T$, so that

$$u(h, T) = u_1(h) + u_2(h)T \tag{7}$$

for some constants $u_1(h)$ and $u_2(h)$. To get some more knowledge of the constants, we add another axiom ( the 'zero hypothesis'):

AXIOM 4 *For $T = 0$, all prospects $(h, 0)$ are considered as equivalent.*

Interpreting $T = 0$, a lifespan of length 0, as death, the axiom will appear as uncontroversial. Applying the axiom to the expression in (7), we get that $u(h, 0) = u_1(h)$ must be independent of $h$, that is a constant. Since any affine transformation of a von Neumann-Morgenstern utility is again a von Neumann-Morgenstern utility representing the same preferences, we may assume that $u_1(h) = 0$, so that

$$u(h, T) = u_2(h)T,$$

giving us the functional form of QALYs with $u_2$ the index of health-related quality of life. We have thus shown the following proposition.

PROPOSITION 4 *Let $\succsim$ be a preference relation on lotteries over $H \times T$ satisfying the expected utility hypothesis. Then the following are equivalent.*

*(i) $\succsim$ satisfies Axioms 3 and 4*

*(ii) the von Neumann-Morgenstern utility function $u$ in the representation of $\succsim$ can be written as*

$$u(h, T) = q(h)T.$$

The QALY index $q(h)$ does not necessarily have the form which is assumed in practical applications, ranging from a minimum of 0 to a maximum of 1, and additional assumptions would be called for to assure these properties, but it is seen that the basic properties assumed in the practical approaches to QALY measurements (TTO, SG), can be given a theoretical basis.

This does not mean that QALYs are universally applicable as a representation of state of health, for individuals as well as populations. First of all, the very basis may be questioned (as in Gafni [1997]), but even if the axioms used so far are accepted, they deal with individual preferences, and going from individual preferences to a numerical representation of health states valid for all individuals is not without problems. We consider such problems briefly below.

## 1.7　*The aggregation problem in health status measurement*

Having considered the basics of setting up index values or assigning utilities to the health states of an individual, which in spite of some particularities comes close to what is known from representing utilities of consumption bundles for a consumer, we get to a point where the similarities end: in the approach to health state measurement using QALYs, it is usually postulated that the index value assigned to a given health state should be the same for all individuals – *a QALY is a QALY is a QALY*. This contrasts with the way in which economists treat utilities in general, where they represent the individual tastes or preferences for goods. Indeed, in the context of buying and selling commodities in the market, differences in taste is one of the prerequisites for trade, so if all individuals have identical preferences, only differences in endowments can give rise to economic activity. Thus, the idea of a unique QALY value of a given health state comes from another tradition, more close to the medical environment in which ideas have taken shape.

On the other hand, we should not reject the idea of one QALY value valid for all individuals right away, since such an equality might arise from the interaction of individuals in society, just as in the case of a market economy, where all agree on the assessment of a unit of one commodity against another one, since otherwise they would have engaged in further trading. It might be the case that a similar identity of marginal rates of substitution would hold when dealing with health, even though there are no markets where individual health be traded against some other commodities. After all, health is obtained as a result of carrying out other activities, many of which have a very direct relation to buying and selling goods and services in the market. We shall have more to say about this indirect way of achieving health in the next chapter. At present, we shall investigate only a simple – and rather abstract – model where health in its different forms is acquired as a result of a productive activity and check whether in such a world individuals with different preferences will end up having identical marginal rates of substitution between characteristics of health.

We consider an economy with $m$ consumers. There are $k$ different (health) characteristics $h_1, \ldots, h_k$ which matter for the consumer, and preferences $\succsim_i$ are defined on vectors $h_i = (h_{i1}, \ldots, h_{ik})$ specifying the level of achieving each of these characteristics. There are also $l$ ordinary goods, and the consumer can obtain a bundle of goods $x_i$ and use it to produce individual health; the technology available to consumer $i$ is given by a set $T_i$ consisting of pairs $(x_i, h_i)$ which indicate that the goods bundle $x_i$ can be transformed to the characteristics bundle $h_i$. To close the model we assume that there is an initial amount of goods $\omega$ from the beginning. As it can be seen, the model is rather simple (no production of goods, only ordinary goods in the market), but this is all that we need for our reasoning, and additional details could be inserted without changing the main points. We assume that preferences $\succsim_i$ are monotonous in the sense that if $h_{ij} > h'_{ij}$ for $j = 1, \ldots, k$, then $h_i \succ_i h*_i$, and that the technologies $T_i$ satisfy a monotonicity assumption: if $(x'_i, h'_i) \in T_i$ and $x_{ih} > x'_{ih}$ for $h = 1, \ldots, l$, then there is $(x_i, h_i) \in T_i$ for some $h_i$ with $h_{ij} > h'_{ij}$ for $k = 1, \ldots, k$.

An allocation in this economy is a pair $(x, h)$, where $x = (x_1, \ldots, x_m)$ consists of a goods bundle for each consumer, and where $h = (h_1, \ldots, h_m)$ specifies the final bundles of health characteristics. For an allocation $(x, h)$ to be feasible, each bundle of health characteristics $h_i$ should be producible with the goods bundle $x_i$, that is

$$(x_i, h_i) \in T_i, \text{ all } i,$$

and the goods bundles used should be available,

$$\sum_{i=1}^{m} x_i = \omega.$$

We proceed to consider equilibria obtained as a result of market activities: an array $(x_i, h_i, p)$, where $(x, h)$ is an allocation and $p = (p_1, \ldots, p_l)$ a price system, is an equilibrium if it satisfies the following (standard) conditions:

(1) $(x, h)$ is a feasible allocation,
(2) individual optimization: if $h'_i$ is a characteristics bundle obtainable from $x_i$ with $p \cdot x'_i \leq p \cdot x_i$, then $h_i \succsim h'_i$.

To facilitate the arguments below, we notice here that equilibria are Pareto optimal: If $(x, h, p)$ is an equilibrium and $(x', h')$ is another feasible allocation, then it cannot be the case that $h'_i$ is considered as good as $h_i$ by all consumers and better for some. Indeed, if this was to happen, then $p \cdot x'_i > p \cdot x_i$ for the consumers for whom $h'_i \succ_i h_i$, and if $p \cdot x'_i < p \cdot x_i$ for any of the other consumers, then by monotonicity of $T_i$ and of $\succsim_i$ there would be $x''_i$ with $p \cdot x''_i = p \cdot x_i$ and $h''_i$ with $(x''_i, h''_i) \in T_i$ such that $h''_i \succ_i h_i$, contradicting property (2) of the equilibrium. We conclude that $p \cdot \sum_{i=1}^{m} x'_i > p \cdot \sum_{i=1}^{m} x_i$ contradicting feasibility of $(x', h')$.

We show by an example that in general it is not to be expected that marginal rates of substitution between two health characteristics are the same for different consumers.

**Example 1** We simplify the model further, so that it has only two consumers; there are only one good and two characteristics. All consumers have the access to the same technology for producing health characteristics,

$$T = \left\{ (x, h) \mid (h_1^2 + h_2^2)^{1/2} \leq x \right\}.$$

Here the two health characteristics appear as a joint output, it is not possible to separate the production into two distinct processes each giving a single health characteristic as output. There is constant return in the production of health. We endow the consumers with preferences on characteristics bundles which can be represented by utility functions of the form

$$u_1(h_{11}, h_{12}) = \log h_{11} + 2\log h_{12},$$
$$u_2(h_{21}, h_{22}) = 2\log h_{21} + \log h_{22}.$$

The aggregate endowment of goods has the size of 1.

We examine the Pareto optimal allocations in this economy somewhat closer. A Pareto optimal allocation can be found by assigning a share $s$ of the endowment to the first consumer, leaving the remainder to the other one, letting the consumers use the technology to obtain the best possible characteristics bundle. The result will be that consumer 1 chooses $h_i$ from the set

$$\Xi_1 = \left\{ (h_{11}, h_{12}) \in \mathbb{R}_+^2 \,\middle|\, h_{11}^2 + h_{12}^2 = s \right\},$$

and if $h_1$ maximizes utility given $x_i = s$, we must have that

$$(h_{11}^0, h_{12}^0) = \left( \frac{s}{\sqrt{5}}, \frac{2s}{\sqrt{5}} \right).$$

Similarly, consumer 2 chooses from the set

$$\Xi_2 = \left\{ (h_{21}, h_{22}) \in \mathbb{R}_+^2 \,\middle|\, h_{21}^2 + h_{22}^2 = 1 - s \right\},$$

the resulting choice being

$$(h_{21}^0, h_{22}^0) = \left( \frac{2(1-s)}{\sqrt{5}}, \frac{1-s}{\sqrt{5}} \right).$$

Due to the simple structure of $\Xi_i$, $i = 1, 2$, we can readily find the marginal rates of substitutions as

$$\text{MRS}_i = \frac{h_{i2}}{h_{i1}},$$

so that

$$\text{MRS}_1 = 2, \quad \text{MRS}_2 = \frac{1}{2}.$$

We conclude that the marginal rates of substitution between the two characteristics is independent of the parameter $s$ and take different values for the two consumers in *all* Pareto optimal allocations. There is no hope of achieving equal assessment of characteristics through the intervention of the market.

It might be objected that what made this example work was the assumption of different preferences over characteristics bundles, that is a different assessment by the consumers of the health states. Although we should expect that consumers differ in this respect, we might consider the case where preferences are identical. Even in this case, we may construct a case where rates of marginal substitution never coincide, namely if we allow for non-constant returns to scale in the (common) technology:

Assume that the technologies are given by

$$\left\{ (x,h) \,\middle|\, (xh_1^2 + h_2^2)^{1/2} \leq x \right\},$$

while both consumers have the same utility function $u$ given by

$$u(h_1, h_2) = \log h_1 + \log h_2.$$

The Pareto optimal allocations can be found as before by choosing $s \in [0,1]$ and finding $h_1$ and $h_2$ by maximizing $u$ under the constraints

$$sh_{11}^2 + sh_{12}^2 = s^2,$$
$$(1-s)h_{21}^2 + h_{22}^2 = (1-s)^2,$$

respectively.. This will give characteristics bundles

$$(h_{11}, h_{12}) = \left( \sqrt{\frac{s}{2}}, \frac{s}{\sqrt{2}} \right), \quad (h_{21}, h_{22}) = \left( \sqrt{\frac{(1-s)}{2}}, \frac{(1-s)}{\sqrt{2}} \right).$$

Once again we have different marginal rates of substitution for the two consumers, namely

$$\frac{h_{11}}{h_{12}} = \frac{\sqrt{s_1}}{s_1}$$

for consumer 1 and

$$\frac{h_{21}}{h_{22}} = \frac{\sqrt{s_2}}{s_2}$$

for consumer 2, with the exception of the case $s = 1/2$, where the two consumers have been treated equally. In all the other Pareto optimal allocations, the individuals will assess the two characteristics differently against each other.

The examples show that in general, we cannot hope for agreement in the assessment of health characteristics, even when health is obtained as a result of some underlying market activities, where trading usually will proceed until such an agreement is obtained. The point is that the equality of marginal rates of substitution will pertain only to goods and does not translate to characteristics, except under special circumstances.

Returning to the general case, it can be shown (see Hougaard and Keiding [2005]) that if in the given economy, equality of marginal rates will obtain in all equilibria, and if the technology is the same for all but preferences are not identical, then the technology must be *separable* in the sense that each characteristics is produced separately. If both preferences and technologies are identical, then the latter must exhibit constant returns to scale.

## 1.8  DALYs

An alternative to the QALY index measuring health-related quality of life, and one which may overcome the aggregation problem discussed above, is the DALY measure of Disability Adjusted Life Years introduced by Murray [1994], see also Murray and Acharya [1997]. The DALYs appeared in the context of measuring the burden of disease and represented a qualification of the previously applied methods of computing lost life years due to illness: instead of displaying the burden as life years lost, thereby neglecting all aspects of illness except premature death, the DALY approach made it possible to account also for decreased ability to function in society.

Since DALYs are oriented towards burden of disease, the weight given to a life year in a given health condition varies from 0 (no disfunction = perfect health) to 1 (absolute disfunction = death), opposite of the variation in the QALY weight. But since the interpretation is different, one cannot get from one to the other by subtracting from 1. In principle at least, the DALY weight expresses a degree of functioning, not a quality of life, and numerical values of DALY weights are to be obtained in another way. Indeed, from the outset it has been emphasized that DALYs should be understood as assessments which can be used when making global decisions about reducing the burden of disease in the world, and consequently the basic tool for finding DALY weights, which then are marginal substitution rates between different diseases, are the so-called *Person Trade-Off* (PTO): For a given state of illness, the weight is found by asking a panel of interview persons to use a given sum of money for prolonging the life of a number of persons, and they must choose between two alternative approaches, either

- one additional life year of 1000 persons in the described state of functioning living one additional year, or
- one additional life year of $q \times 1000$ persons in perfect functioning.

If $q$ has been chosen so that the two alternatives are equally good, then the loss brought about by one person getting into the relevant state of functioning corresponds to the fraction $q$ of a lost life year, so that it may be added as a non-fatal loss caused by the illness considered.

In its basic orientation towards functioning rather than experienced quality of life, the DALY approach seems to get around the problems related to individual differences of preferences for health states, since it aims at finding societal marginal rates of substitution. When it comes to determining the numerical values of DALY weights through PTOs, individual preferences get back in, and we have again a problem of aggregation of preferences. However, other methods of determining

DALY weights are conceivable, for example using the money spent on combating different diseases as an indication of society's preferences. This would free the weight determination of its reliance on individual preference assessments, but it might also reduce the value of the computed burden of disease as a tool for decisions about which diseases to single out for a particular effort. For a more detailed criticism of DALYs, see Anand and Hanson [1997].

## 2  Healthcare expenditure

One of the more compelling reasons for studying the economics of healthcare is the large and growing size of healthcare expenditures. Measured in proportion to GDP, health expenditure has been increasing over the last decades and comes close 10% in most Western countries, with the US share well above 15%. Many reasons for this development have been put forward and intensely debated.

Among the explanations of steadily increasing healthcare cost, the aging of populations and appearance of many welfare-related diseases have been proposed most frequently, but it has also been a recurrent theme in the debate that rising healthcare expenditure has taken the form of a natural law, and that expenditure growth is unstoppable. Since our main interest is in detecting what may lie behind, we discard this idea and prefer to look at explanations based on economic theory, of which there are not so many, but which nevertheless mark the way towards a more profound understanding of the phenomena.

### 2.1  *Why does healthcare expenditure grow?*

There may be several reasons for the spectacular growth of healthcare spending over the last decades. First of all, it may be attributed to inefficiency, throwing away resources or misusing them on activities with little or no effect on the state of health of the population. Even if this argument is rarely put forward in such a direct way, it can be traced behind many of the complaints in the debate about unsatisfactory productivity growth and the consequent overuse of expensive labor power in healthcare.

The problem of a slower productivity growth in healthcare can be given a theoretical basis, as it was done by Hartwig [2008] using a simple model of unbalanced growth proposed by Baumol [1967]. Assume that there are two sectors in the economy, where the first sector is 'non-progressive', in the sense that labor productivity stays constant over time, whereas the second 'progressive' sector experiences

Box 1.6 **Health spending as percentage of GDP.** The outlays on healthcare in different countries is regularly published by OECD. The table below shows spending as a percentage of GDP, covering both total spending and public spending. It may be noticed that the US percentage is so high that even public spending has a size comparable to that of countries with a traditionally public health care system.

**Table 1.2.** Health spending in % of GDP 2014, selected OECD countries

| Country | Total | Public |
|---|---|---|
| Australia | 9.0 | 6.0 |
| Austria | 10.3 | 7.8 |
| Belgium | 10.4 | 8.1 |
| Canada | 10.0 | 7.1 |
| Costa Rica | 9.3 | 6.8 |
| Denmark | 10.6 | 8.9 |
| Finland | 9.5 | 7.2 |
| France | 11.1 | 8.7 |
| Germany | 11.0 | 9.3 |
| India | 4.7 | 1.4 |
| Ireland | 10.4 | 7.0 |
| Italy | 9.1 | 6.9 |
| Mexico | 5.7 | 2.9 |
| New Zealand | 9.4 | 7.5 |
| Russia | 5.9 | 3.7 |
| South Africa | 8.8 | 4.2 |
| Spain | 9.1 | 6.3 |
| Sweden | 11.2 | 9.3 |
| United KIngdom | 9.9 | 7.9 |
| United States | 16.6 | 8.2 |

Source: OECD [2015].

productivity growth at the rate $r$. Output in the two sectors is

$$Y_1(t) = aL_1(t),$$
$$Y_2(t) = bL_2(t)e^{rt},$$

where $L_i(t)$ is the labor input in sector $i$, $i = 1, 2$, and $a, b > 0$ are constants.

The cost of production is determined by the common wage rate $w(t)$, and the latter is assumed to increase with productivity in the progressive sector, so that

$$w(t) = w_0 e^{rt}.$$

There is no compelling reason that the wage rate should be determined in this way, but one may think of the progressive sector as subject to international competition, so that prices remain constant, and competitive wage rates reflecting value of marginal product would behave in this way. Unit cost in the two sectors will then be determined as

$$c_1(t) = \frac{w(t)L_1(t)}{Y_1(t)} = \frac{w_0 e^{rt} L_1(t)}{a L_1(t)} = \frac{w_0 e^{rt}}{a},$$

$$c_2(t) = \frac{w(t)L_2(t)}{Y_2(t)} = \frac{w_0 e^{rt} L_2(t)}{b L_2(t) e^{rt}} = \frac{w_0}{b}.$$

Thus, unit cost increases in the non-progressive sector whereas it remains fixed in the progressive sector. Under the additional assumptions that the proportion of output in the two sectors has a constant value $K$, we get that

$$\frac{L_1(t)}{L_2(t)} = \frac{Y_1(t)}{Y_2(t)} \frac{b e^{rt}}{a} = \frac{Kb}{a} e^{rt},$$

from which it is seen that the share of labor working in the non-progressive sector increases over time so that this sector eventually will absorb almost all labor power. Although the share of sector 1 in real GDP has remained constant, its share in nominal GDP grows towards 1.

While the model captures the feature of growing healthcare expenditure, the explanation in terms of inherent low productivity growth may be less appealing today than fifty years ago. After all, the technological progress in healthcare has been impressive and seems to be an ongoing process, so that the very nature of healthcare has changed its character. It might not be the aging population as such that causes the growth of expenditure but rather the availability of new cures for this aging population.

In the following, we expand on these, following the approach of Jones [2002]. We assume that individuals in society are afflicted by health problems, which can be characterized by a variable $x$ taking values in $\mathbb{R}_+$; we may think about $x$ as expressing the degree of complexity or severity (which amounts to the same in our model) of the health problem, so that at any time $t$, treatment has been developed only for health problems in the interval $[0, \bar{x}]$. The development of the medical services at time $t$ is given by an upper limit $\bar{x}(t)$ of complexity, and individuals with severity greater than $\bar{x}(t)$ cannot be treated and die. Due to technological progress, this limit is increasing at a constant rate $\alpha$, with initial value $\bar{x}(0)$ at $t = 0$.

The cost of treating an individual with health problem $x$ at time $t$

$$c(x, t) = c_0 e^{\beta x - \gamma(t - \alpha(x - \bar{x}(0)))} \tag{8}$$

where $\beta > 0$ is a constant reflecting the rate at which treatment cost increases with complexity of case, and $\gamma$ gives the rate of cost reduction due to technological progress. We may rewrite $c(x, t)$ introducing the variable $l(x, t) = \bar{x}(t) - x$ expressing the distance to the mortal case (or, assuming that individual health moves linearly over the states at rate 1, the life expectancy of the individual with health $x$). Since the limiting treatment has moved at rate $\alpha$ since $t = 0$, we have that $\bar{x}(t) = \bar{x}(0) + \dfrac{t}{\alpha}$, so that $x = \bar{x}(t) - l = \bar{x}(0) + \dfrac{t}{\alpha} - l$, and inserting in (8), we get

$$h(l, t) = c(\bar{x}(t) - l, t) = c_0 e^{\beta \bar{x}(0)} e^{\frac{\beta}{\alpha} - [\beta + \gamma \alpha]l} = h_0 e^{\mu t - \theta l},$$

where we have collected constants into a single one, $h_0$, and introduced new parameters $\mu = \dfrac{\beta}{\alpha}$, $\theta = \beta + \gamma \alpha$.

Assuming now that health states, or equivalently, life expectancies, are distributed uniformly in the population, which is taken to have the size $\bar{x}(t)$, we can find aggregate health expenditure $H(t)$ at time $t$ by integrating $h(l, t)$ over $[0, \bar{x}(t)]$,

$$H(t) = \int_0^{\bar{x}(t)} h(l, t) dl = h_0 e^{\mu t} \int_0^{\bar{x}(t)} e^{-\theta l} dl = \frac{h(0, t)}{\theta} \left[ 1 - e^{-\theta \bar{x}(t)} \right].$$

If individuals have identical incomes $y(t)$, then aggregate income is $Y(t) = \bar{x}(t) y(t)$, and the share of health expenditure in GDP at time $t$ becomes

$$\frac{H(t)}{Y(t)} = \frac{h(0, t)}{\theta \bar{x}(t)} \frac{\left[ 1 - e^{-\theta \bar{x}(t)} \right]}{y(t)}.$$

Having now an expression for the healthcare share of GDP at any given point of time, we may investigate its behavior as $t$ increases. For this, we need to know what happens with $y(t)$ over time, and we assume that it grows at the constant rate $g$, then we may write the fraction

$$\frac{h(0, t)}{y(t)} = e^{(\mu - g)t},$$

and we get (using also that $h(0, 0) = h_0$) that

$$\frac{H(t)}{Y(t)} = \frac{1}{\theta \bar{x}(t)} \frac{h_0}{y(0)} e^{(\mu - g)t} \left[ 1 - e^{-\theta \bar{x}(t)} \right].$$

To assess its value when $t$ increases, we note that the quantity in the last bracket becomes very close to 1 as $t$ increases; furthermore, $\bar{x}(t)$ increases linearly in $t$, but this growth is dominated by that of the exponential, so that $H(t)/Y(t)$ will increase when $\mu$ is greater than $g$. Now, $\mu = \beta / \alpha$ was the rate of cost increase caused by severity relative to the rate of extension of tractable cases, or alternatively formulated, the cost increase brought about by technological progress. When this rate exceeds the growth rate, a larger share of aggregate income must be used on healthcare.

This conclusion may not come as a complete surprise, since the pressure on health expenditure caused by the emergence of new medical technologies is well-known from the debate. Also, the model cannot be used for long term forecasts, since nothing prevent the share from rising above 1, something which happens since there healthcare expenditure emerges as a function of the health conditions of the individuals rather than as a result of a deliberate choice. These choices are what we shall be concerned about in most of what follows, but at this stage it is worthwhile noticing that even simple models of healthcare expenditure may put the current development in healthcare cost into a new perspective.

## 2.2   *Does health expenditure enhance growth?*

In the discussion so far, we have been concerned mainly with the rise in health-care expenditure brought about by economic development, but we might equally well be interested in the converse relationship, the effects of health expenditure on economic growth. There are several reasons why increased expenditure on health-care might foster economic growth (see e.g. Zhang et al. [2003]): longer lifespan increases the labor supply and induce people to save more, and reduced infant mortality may lead to lower birth rates and in perspective to a higher per capita GDP, and apart from these more technical arguments there is the very basic one relating health to productivity for the individual.

Here is a very simple model, due to Aghion et al. [2011], which captures the influence of health on growth. We assume that at any given point of time the per capita income $Y$ can be written as

$$Y = aH^\beta,$$

where $H$ is the stock of human capital, including health, also measured on per capita basis, and $a > 0$ and $\beta > 0$ are constants; here $a$ measures the productivity of $H$. Looking at the movement of $Y$ over time, the growth rate $y$ must satisfy

$$y = \alpha + \beta h,$$

where $h$ is the growth rate of health. It is now assumed that productivity changes over time according to the equation

$$\dot{a} = \theta(\overline{\alpha} - \alpha) + \alpha h + \delta.$$

Here $\overline{\alpha}$ expresses a benchmark productivity, $\theta$ and $\delta$ are constants. Combining the two expressions, we get that the change in the growth rate $y$ can be written as

$$\dot{y} = \theta(\overline{\alpha} - \alpha) + \alpha h + \beta \dot{h} + \delta = \delta + \theta\overline{\alpha} - \theta y + (\alpha + \beta\theta)h + \beta\dot{h}.$$

It is seen that per capita growth rates depend not only on current health but also on the growth rate of health. Assuming a linear relationship between health expenditure and health (something which of course is far from obvious and will concern us in the sequel) we get that increasing health expenditure indeed has a positive influence on economic growth.

## 3  Assessing healthcare services and healthcare systems

Looking at healthcare expenditure may give some impression of the weight put on matters of health and healthcare in a given country, but it is not the full picture – it matters quite as much what is obtained as a result of the expenditure. Large money outlays may conceal inefficiencies, and a relatively small percentage if healthcare expenditure can be a result of a very well-functioning healthcare sector but may as well occur if healthcare is not given due attention.

In order to assess the achievements of healthcare one must therefore include measures of output, something which is not easily done, in particular if the approach should be the individual self-estimated level of health and changes in this level. However, we might also use another approach, attempting to specify what *should* be criteria of a well-functioning healthcare system, and then assess the degree of attainment of the stated goals.

### 3.1  *The WHO report: ranking healthcare systems*

An important and at that time novel contribution in this direction was the World Health Report from the year 2000, [WHO, 2000], where an attempt was made to construct indices of both input and output, so that the healthcare systems of all member countries could be compared (and indeed ranked) according to the efficiency of their healthcare systems. In order to do so, the first step would be to clarify what actually constitutes the output of a healthcare sector.

Clearly, *health* is the most obvious and immediate output of a healthcare system, and any assessment of such systems would have to involve some measure of the health situation in the respective country. At this stage, it can come as no surprise that the choice of a performance measure for health is not an easy one. In the WHO report, it is constructed from data on survival at different ages and life expectancy at birth, together with a disability adjustment so as to obtain a measure of Disability Adjusted Life Expectancy (DALE). This is combined with a measure of health equity; the natural choice would be to use the distribution of DALE over the population of each country, but since data were not available for this, the distribution of child mortality was used instead.

Other output categories than health were considered: *Responsiveness* is a measure of how the health system performs with respect to non-health aspects, giving a numerical representation of the way in which the system treats the population, typically as providers of healthcare. Important aspects of responsiveness are *respect for persons,*

- respect for dignity of the patient,
- confidentiality, right to determine who has access to one's personal health information,
- autonomy to participate in choices about one's own treatment,

and *client orientation,*

- prompt attention in emergencies, reasonable waiting time otherwise,
- amenities of adequate quality (cleanliness, space, hospital food),
- access to support networks
- choice of provider, freedom to select person or organization delivering care.

---

**Box 1.7  Scores and weights of the aspects of responsiveness.** In the WHO report, the scores of each of the aspects of responsiveness were obtained by interviewing key informants (around 2000 in 35 countries), and weights of the aspects were obtained using an internet based survey with around 1000 participants. The weights obtained were as follows:

| | |
|---|---|
| Respect for persons | |
|     Respect for dignity | 16.7% |
|     Confidentiality | 16.7% |
|     Autonomy | 16.7% |
| Client orientation | |
|     Prompt attention | 20% |
|     Quality of amenities | 15% |
|     Access to support networks | 10% |
|     Choice of provider | 5% |

Source: WHO [2000]

---

In the *fairness* dimension, and more specifically in the analysis of *fair financing,* the approach taken is to measure to which degree the situation in each country approaches that of a perfect fairness, in the sense that the ratio of total health contribution to total non-food spending should be the same for all households, not depending on income, health state and use of health system.

Having now defined an aggregate measure of output, one may combine this with the expenditure side healthcare to obtain an *efficiency* measure, indicating how

Box 1.8 **Weights of the different aspects of goal attainment.** The WHO report used
the following weights:

| Health | |
|---|---|
| Overall | 25% |
| Distribution | 25% |
| Responsiveness | |
| Overall | 12.5% |
| Distribution | 15% |
| Fair financial distribution | 25% |

Source: WHO [2000]

well a country performs in providing healthcare from the available funding. Two
indices were computed, namely an index for performance taking only health level
(DALE) into account, and another one for overall performance.

The results of the WHO report were surprising and much debated in the years
following their appearance. Indeed, some countries which traditionally were considered as having a very well-functioning healthcare system were ranked rather
low, whereas many of the top-listed countries had attracted little previous attention. In some cases, a low ranking of countries with a large GDP share of healthcare
expenditure – USA ranking as number 37 – may fit reasonably well with intuition
(although it might be a surprise that its performance in pure health production
is even worse, ranking it as number 72), but a higher ranking of countries with
a traditional dedication to healthcare might have been disappointing (UK ranking only as number 18). Quite understandably, the approach taken in the WHO
report was criticized (see e.g. Richardson et al. [2003]) on several points. The
goals selected are debatable, and the weights assigned to the goals are in many
cases rather arbitrary. Further, the way of measuring inequality, both inequality in
health and inequality in healthcare financing, is far from being the only one possible. Finally, the approach to estimating the efficiency indices, which give rise to
the ranking of country healthcare systems, could also have been designed in many
other ways.

Notwithstanding the criticisms, the WHO report marked a new approach to the
assessment of healthcare systems, and it became a starting point for subsequent
comparisons of healthcare systems. Among the alternative approaches to the measurement of healthcare system performance, we select for further discussion one
which may be of particular interest in the context of theoretical health economics.

---

**Box 1.9 The top ten healthcare systems** according to the WHO report :

| Overall performance | | Health level | |
| --- | --- | --- | --- |
| 1 | France | 1 | Oman |
| 2 | Italy | 2 | Malta |
| 3 | San Marino | 3 | Italy |
| 4 | Andorra | 4 | France |
| 5 | Malta | 5 | San Marino |
| 6 | Singapore | 6 | Spain |
| 7 | Spain | 7 | Andorra |
| 8 | Oman | 8 | Jamaica |
| 9 | Austria | 9 | Japan |
| 10 | Japan | 10 | Saudi Arabia |

Source: WHO [2000]

---

### 3.2 *Using DEA to rank healthcare systems*

The DEA (Data Envelopment Analysis) method can be seen as consisting of two independent parts, namely

(i) measuring technical efficiency of a productive unit with reference to a given set of feasible productions, and

(ii) finding a representation of the set of feasible productions based on observation of other production plans.

For the solution to part (i), one chooses the Farrell index of output efficiency, introduced in Farrell [1957]. Considering as above a case with many outputs but only one input, and adding the assumption of constant returns to scale, then we may represent the feasible productions as a subset $Y$ of $\mathbb{R}^n_+$, where $y = (y_1, \ldots, y_n) \in Y$ represents the output obtainable using exactly 1 unit of input. A production plan $y \in Y$ is efficient if there is no production plan $y' \neq y$ such that $y'_h \geq y_h$ for all $h$. Clearly, efficiency is a property which a given production plan either has or does not have, so if we want to measure a degree of efficiency, we need some notion of distance of a feasible production to the set of efficient productions. In the standard case where $Y$ is a convex and compact set containing 0, this can be obtained using the *Farrell efficiency index*

$$e_Y(y) = \inf\{\lambda \mid \lambda y \notin Y\}.$$

The Farrell index is 1 if $y$ is efficient (but it can be 1 also for inefficient production plans) and less than 1 when the production is not efficient. It is only one among several possible measures of output efficiency, but it is very widely used, one of the reasons for its success being the simplicity of computing the value of this efficiency index in practice. We return to this and other similar measures of productivity in Section 4.3.

This takes us to part (ii) of the method, where we need to find some representation of the set $Y$ introduced above, which usually is not known, so it must be reconstructed from observation of either past productions or productions in other plants which may be assumed to have access to the same technology. Assume that these observations are $y^1, \ldots, y^r$, and that the unit whose efficiency must be investigated has carried out the production $y^0$; all these productions must belong to the (unknown) production set $Y$. Assuming convexity of $Y$, we know also that every convex combination

$$\mu_1 y^1 + \cdots + \mu_r y^r, \ \mu_i \geq 0, i = 1, \ldots, r, \ \sum_{i=1}^{r} \mu_i = 1, \tag{9}$$

must belong to $Y$, and we may then find the Farrell index value of $y^0$ as inverse of the maximal number $\lambda > 0$ such that $\lambda y^0$ can be written as in (9). This can be reformulated as solving the maximization problem

$$\max \lambda$$

such that

$$\sum_{i=1}^{r} \mu_i \leq 1, \ \lambda y_h^0 - \sum_{i=1}^{r} \mu_i y_h^i \leq 0, h = 1, \ldots, n, \tag{10}$$

$$\lambda, \mu_1, \ldots, \mu_r \geq 0.$$

It is seen that (10) is a linear programming problem, which is easily solved, meaning that measuring (Farrell) efficiency relative to the production set spanned by the data from other production plans is a relatively simple procedure.

It may be instructive to have a brief look at the *dual* problem of (10), which is

$$\min v$$

such that

$$\sum_{h=1}^{n} u_h y_h^0 \geq 1, \ v - \sum_{h=1}^{n} u_h y_h^i \geq 0, i = 1, \ldots, r,$$

$$v, u_1, \ldots, u_n \geq 0.$$

where we have introduced the (dual) variables $v$ and $u_1, \ldots, u_n$. The inequality in the first constraint may be replaced by a =, since equality can be obtained by choosing smaller values of all the $u_h$, all the other inequalities will still be satisfied and the value of $v$ will not increase. This gives us an interpretation of the variables $u_h$ as weights or prices of output commodities, with the property that the maximal output value computed at these weights of any of the reference units is as small as possible, given that it equals 1 for our unit. Or, otherwise put, the weights have been chosen as the most favorable for the unit to be compared, since it maximizes its output value given that the output values of the reference units should stay below 1. Thus, DEA can be seen as a comparison of output measured in prices which are not chosen arbitrarily but are found during the analysis as the most favorable to the productive unit considered, and consequently, if the results are not very good, they cannot be attributed to the weights used in aggregating all the different inputs to a single one.

---

**Box 1.10  The Euro health consumer index.** A comparison of European healthcare systems is performed on a yearly basis by Health Consumer Powerhouse. The method is based upon country ranking on a number of indicators which is considered as representing the consumer orientation of the system (patient rights, waiting times, range of services, availability of pharmaceuticals etc.). For each of these, a scoring is obtained, and the scorings are then aggregated using fixed weights.

For 2014, the resulting ranking gave the following top ten:

| Country | Overall ranking | Patient rights | Waiting time | Outcome | Range of services | Pharma-ceuticals |
|---------|---------|---------|---------|---------|---------|---------|
| Netherl. | 1 | 1 | 7 | 1 | 1 | 1 |
| Switzerl. | 1 | 12 | 1 | 3 | 14 | 9 |
| Norway | 3 | 22 | 22 | 1 | 3 | 7 |
| Finland | 4 | 6 | 10 | 6 | 4 | 1 |
| Denmark | 5 | 2 | 4 | 9 | 6 | 9 |
| Belgium | 6 | 22 | 1 | 9 | 4 | 9 |
| Iceland | 7 | 4 | 14 | 3 | 9 | 21 |
| Luxemb. | 8 | 17 | 7 | 6 | 6 | 16 |
| Germany | 9 | 10 | 7 | 3 | 21 | 1 |
| Austria | 10 | 9 | 4 | 16 | 11 | 9 |

Source: Björnberg [2016]

The Euro health consumer index gives an alternative viewpoint on the performance of healthcare sectors, but it can be criticized on several methodological aspects (choice of indicators and their measurement, aggregation using arbitrary weights etc.), cf. Cylus et al. [2016]

---

Applying the technique of DEA to the healthcare systems of different countries, we should use as output a selection of relevant outcome measures – which might be the same as those selected in the WHO 2000 comparison or others and then investigate whether a given country performs as well as the other countries with respect to the chosen output categories. This is so far as the DEA methodology can take us, in particular, it does not by itself yield a ranking of the national healthcare systems. Of course, the size of the efficiency indices computed may be compared, and if the healthcare systems of two countries are both efficient and are given the value 1, they may be given extended index values above 1 using the so-called superefficiency approach, which for efficient production plans amounts to finding the maximal proportional increase in output of all the other units for which the given unit will remain efficient. It should be remembered, however, that the way in which the output categories are aggregated changes with the choice of unit considered, so that a comparison of healthcare systems according to DEA score has no theoretical basis.

The investigation of efficiency of healthcare systems carried out by Retzlaff-Roberts et al. [2004] using OECD healthcare data refrains from setting up a ranking, which would anyway be difficult to interpret. The analysis extends that of WHO by considering also *health inputs* (we have discussed only output efficiency measurement using DEA, but a similar approach can be developed for efficiency in use of inputs), using categories as number of hospital beds available, number of physicians, aggregate health expenditure, adding also social categories as education, income distribution and number of smokers. Not surprising, it is found that countries may be efficient on the input side but not on the output side and vice versa.

## 4   Problems

**1.** In many of the approaches to the measuring of health, it is assumed that health has several dimensions which can be assessed separately, so that overall health can be found by combining the results from the separate dimensions in a suitable way.

In this case, the set $H$ of health states has the structure of a product, $H = H_1 \times \cdots \times H_d$ where $H_i$ for $i = 1, \ldots, d$ is the set of possible states of the particular type of health (such as e.g. physical function, social function, mental problems etc.).

Suppose that $H$ is ordered by the total preorder $\succsim$ interpreted as "as good as or better". For each health state $h = (h_1, \ldots, h_d)$ and each dimension $i$, a preorder $\succsim_{i,h}$ is then induced on $H_i$ by

$$h_i' \succsim_{i,h} h_i'' \Leftrightarrow (h_1, \ldots, h_{i-1}, h_i', h_{i+1}, \ldots, h_d) \succsim (h_1, \ldots, h_{i-1}, h_i'', h_{i+1}, \ldots, h_d).$$

The preorder is *independent* if $\succsim_{i,h}$ does not depend on $h$, meaning that

$$h_i' \succsim_{i,h} h_i'' \Leftrightarrow h_i' \succsim_{i,\hat{h}} h_i''$$

for all $h_i', h_i'' \in H_i$ and $h, \hat{h} \in H$, and in this case we write $\succsim_i$ instead of $\succsim_{i,h}$. Give an interpretation of independence.

Suppose that each $\succsim_i$ can be represented by a utility function $u_i$, and that $\succsim$ is represented by $u$. Show that if

$$u(h) = \sum_{i=1}^{d} u_i(h_i)$$

for each $h = (h_1, \ldots, h_d)$, then $\succsim$ is independent. Does the converse hold?

2. A patient is faced with the possibility of two different treatments for a serious life-threatening illness:

(a) Surgery, which, if successful, may give the patient 3 additional years of approximately full health, but there is a high risk, around 30%, of death following immediately after the operation.

(b) A cure with a new pharmaceutical drug, which is assumed to allow for a longer lifespan, namely 5 additional years, but with serious side effects, preventing the patient from many usual activities.

The patient chooses alternative (a). What can we infer from this about the QALY assessment of the health state resulting from the drug treatment?

3. Consider a QALY model $u(h, T) = V(h)T$, where $h$ is the health state, $T$ is duration (the length of life measured in years), and $V(h)$ is a quality-adjustment factor.

Assume that a healthcare provider adopts a policy of maximizing the sum of QALYs of all individuals in a given population. Discuss the pros and cons of such a policy. In particular, outline possible justifications and ethical objections.

Assume next that the health care provider does *not* wish to adopt a policy of the type outlined, that is the health care provider does not wish to maximize the sum of QALYs of all people in the population. Which other objectives could there be?

4. In the 2 consumer, one good, 2 characteristics model of Example 1 in Section 1.7, assume that the household technologies have the form

$$\left\{ (x, h) \,\middle|\, (vh_1^2 + h_2^2)^{1/2} \leq v,\ v \leq x \right\},$$

while the consumers have the same utility function $u$ given by

$$u(h_1, h_2) = \log h_1 + \log h_2.$$

Show in the consumers exhibit different marginal rates of substitution in all efficient allocations where the consumers use different exactly amounts of the good as input in their household technology.

5. Share of healthcare in GNP: When comparing the data for different countries, how are such differences influenced by family patterns, where the role of the family in caring for the sick at home is more important in some countries than in others?

Give other examples of healthcare which may not be properly reflected in statistics based on national accounts.

**6.** Consider the following simplified description of healthcare systems in selected countries: Each system is described by an input $x$ (total health expenditure in percentage of GDP) producing two outputs $y_1$ (the number of GP visits per capita) and $y_2$ (the number of outpatient hospital treatments per 100000 population). Consider the following data for five OECD countries from the year 2000.

| Country | $x$ | $y_1$ | $y_2$ |
|---------|-----|-------|-------|
| Denmark | 8.4 | 6.9 | 18813 |
| Italy | 7.7 | 5.9 | 14677 |
| Japan | 7.2 | 14.2 | 9522 |
| Poland | 5.7 | 5.3 | 12568 |
| UK | 6.9 | 4.4 | 23703 |

Comment on this model as a description of the workings of a healthcare system. In particular, comment on the differences between the five countries.

In a DEA framework, assume convexity and constant returns to scale in production and illustrate an output isoquant based on the above dataset. Which countries produce efficiently?

Using the Farrell efficiency index, calculate the efficiency score for Denmark and Japan. Comment on the result.

# Chapter 2

# Demand for health and healthcare

## 1  Health needs and healthcare

While economists have been trained to formulate social intercourse in the terminology of demand and supply, it should not be forgotten that demand arises from something more primitive, and in our context of health and healthcare, behind the observable demand there is a *need* which although less visible is still something which may be dealt with in a systematic way. Health is something which most people appreciate, in particular when it is beginning to deteriorate.

There is however a long way to go from the abstract recognizing of a need for healthcare to the practical and quantitative estimation of this need and its implication for delivery of healthcare. The concept of *needs assessment* appeared in the discussions of healthcare policy in the 1990s, where it was seen as an instrument for priority setting and planning in the healthcare sector. The approach to needs assessment was epidemiological, beginning with outlining the main health problems, based on available data for incidence and prevalence of diseases, and proceeding to an assessment of the services available and their cost; for a more detailed description, see Stevens et al. [2004]. At this stage, economic evaluation should enter the analysis to prepare for the final plans, which should then be used in contracting with providers of healthcare.

We shall return to the problems of priority setting in healthcare in a later chapter. At present, we are more interested in the economic aspects of health needs as seen from the perspective of the individual, and in our economic context, needs are relevant to the extent that they are expressed as a demand. In this context, one can meaningfully distinguish between a demand for healthcare here and now, often provoked by some unexpected event, and long time behavior, through which the individual may influence the need for future healthcare, either by building up resistance through healthy habits, or conversely increasing the future need for treatment by various forms of addictions. We deal with both at length in what follows, starting with the celebrated Grossman model of health demand and subsequently dealing with addictive behavior. But we shall also have a look at short-run aspects of demand, including the problems of queuing and waiting lists.

## 2  The problem of lifestyle selection

### 2.1  *Lancasterian characteristics*

We have already – in our discussion of health needs assessments – noticed that one must distinguish between *health* and *health care*, and this holds also when we consider questions of demand. While health as such cannot be purchased in a market, health care can, so one might be tempted to discard demand for health as meaningless, concentrating on the demand for healthcare, which makes sense immediately.

There is, however, good reason for dwelling at the seemingly meaningless demand for health: While health as such (or health in any of its many aspects, cf. our discussion in Chapter 1, Section 3) cannot be bought directly, the individual may certainly buy – and consume – goods and services which are conducive for good health. Thus, the individual may be thought of as buying *inputs* for a sort of home production, the *output of which* is health, or more precisely, some characteristics of health. Actually, this situation is not specific for health related consumption, and it has been dealt with in consumer theory by Lancaster [1966], giving rise to a general theory of characteristics.

To fix ideas, we begin by recalling the standard theory of consumer choices. Assume that there are $l$ goods available at prices $p_1, \ldots, p_l$, and the consumer is endowed with a certain budget (or income) $I$ designated for the purchase of the goods, so that the bundle $x = (x_1, \ldots, x_l)$ of goods bought by the consumer must satisfy the budget constraint

$$p \cdot x \leq I. \tag{1}$$

Under this constraint, the consumer will choose so as to achieve the highest possible level of satisfaction of needs. If the latter is formalized by a subjective preference relation $\succsim$ over goods bundles (say, all vectors $x$ in $\mathbb{R}_+^l$), then the consumer chooses the bundle $x^0$ satisfying (1) so that there is no bundle $x'$ better than $x^0$ and also satisfying (1). $x \succsim y$ means that the consumer is at least as well off with the bundle $x$ as with $y$. We illustrate this well-known situation in Fig. 2.1, where indifference curves have been drawn connecting all bundles that are considered as equally good by the consumer.

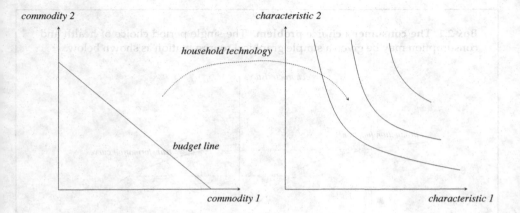

Fig. 2.1 Lancasterian consumer theory: The Lancasterian theory of consumption: Goods are bought subject to the budget constraint and then transformed into characteristics using the household technology. The bundle of goods to be purchased is selected so that the resulting characteristics bundle is the best possible.

The extension proposed by Lancaster addresses the problem that what the consumer really wants is not goods bundles but the individual and social well-being which can be obtained using these goods bundles. So what matters is not goods bundles $x = (x_1, \ldots, x_l)$ as above, but *characteristics bundles* $\xi = (\xi_1, \ldots, \xi_k)$, where each $\xi_j$ denotes the extent of satisfaction obtained of a specific type (social intercourse, power, sex etc. – or health of a certain type). These quantities cannot be obtained directly in the market, but must be produced using the goods bundles (which can be obtained in the market) as input.

Formally, we may describe this as a household production, where each consumer transforms goods to characteristics according to a *household technology*, which is a subset $T$ of $\mathbb{R}_+^l \times \mathbb{R}_+^k$, that is a set of admissible pairs $(x, \xi)$, where $x$ is a goods bundle ("input") and $\xi$ a characteristics bundle. The consumer's problem in this context will be to obtain the best possible characteristics bundle (assuming that the consumer has a given preference relation on characteristics bundles) within the constraints given by the household technology *and* the possibility of buying inputs with the given budget and at the given prices, that is satisfying the constraints

$$(x, \xi) \in T,$$
$$\sum_{h=1}^{l} p_h x_h \leq I.$$

The consumer's choices in the new model with characteristics can be illustrated as in Fig. 2.1. The preferences of the consumer are defined in coordinate system to

**Box 2.1 The consumer's choice problem.** The single period choice of health and consumption may be given a simple graphical representation as shown below.

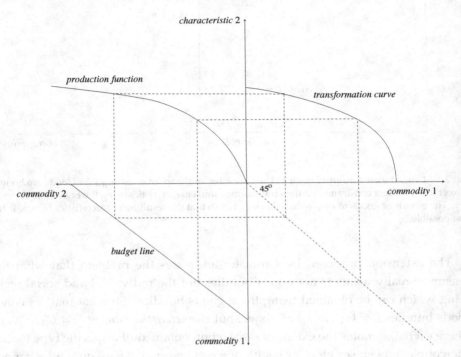

It is assumed here that one of the commodities bought in the market can enter directly into the final consumption bundle, whereas the other one must be transformed using the household technology (shown in the second quadrant). The first quadrant contains the final consumption bundles, whereas the third quadrant displays the budget line. A bundle on the budget line transforms to a bundle of commodity 1 and characteristic 2 situated in the first quadrant. Tracing the transformation of all bundles in the budget set, one gets a feasibility set in the first quadrant bounded by the transformation curve.

the right, whereas the budget constraint lives in that to the left. i The household technology does not really show up, being reduced to an arrow from one diagram to the other. Another commonly used illustration, directly related to health, is presented in Box 2.1.

The Lancasterian theory of demand can be analyzed further using the methods known from the standard theory of consumer demand. For example, a change in goods prices will have an impact on the set of achievable characteristics bundles, and the optimal choice will change accordingly, giving rise to a change in the demand in the goods market. Instead of going back and forth between characteristics and goods, one may transfer the preferences defined in the characteristics space back to the commodity space (one commodity bundle being as good as another if all the best characteristics bundle obtained from the first one is as good as the best achieved using the other bundle), and then we are back in the standard consumer theory. There are no specific properties of demand which can be traced to the origin of preferences as derived from production and consumption of characteristics.

## 2.2 *The Grossman model*

In the Lancasterian model of consumption characteristics outlined in the previous section, the characteristics, and in particular the characteristics pertaining to health, were something produced and consumed alongside with ordinary commodities. It might however be questioned whether this formulation is quite satisfactory, in particular since there is a long-run aspect of health which cannot reasonably be assumed away. When people quit smoking, it is usually not by fear of having a lung cancer at some instant in the evening, but in the course of 20 – 30 years from now, and the other way around: Eating a healthy diet will not improve your health today, but it will eventually. Certainly, much consumption related to health – indeed most of what is not treatment here and now, has a long-term aspect, and correspondingly the choice of consumption should be studied in the long perspective.

This is exactly what is done in one of the by now classical models in the field, the consumption choice model of Grossman [1972]. Before looking at the model in full detail, what we shall certainly do, it may be useful to outline its logical structure and main results, and this is what will be done in the present section.

The basic idea of the model is that health is a personalized capital good, which can be built up by the consumer through investment in own health, something which is certainly costly in terms of money and time; one may think of investment as healthy diet, recreational travels in the Caribbean, frequent visits in gyms and at the doctor (whereby it is understood that the consumer pays herself for most of this). The *health capital* is subject to a certain reduction being worn out by use (this rate of decrease may reasonably be assumed to be small in the consumers early life but increasing with age); its payoff is ability to work, measured in possible working hours – and with known money wages, directly in money. In our first (actually also in the more detailed) approach we may abstract from other payoffs such as the sheer pleasure of being healthy; here it is good to be healthy just because you can work more (or, slightly more sophisticated, because you have more time to be used either for work or for leisure, not wasted by illness).

To see by an intuitive argument what will come out of rational consumer choice in a world as the one sketched above, let us assume that the consumer wants to change the health capital stock at some time $t$ by a small unit. The gain to be achieved by this additional unit of health capital is the marginal product of health capital at time $t$, denoted $G_t$, which multiplied by the wage rate $w$ gives the increase in income in the next period. The cost is $s$ (the ratio between capital and investment), multiplied by the cost per unit health investment $C_{t-1}$ (the investment cost is dated one period earlier). In optimum we have

$$sC_{t-1} = wG_t$$

or

$$s = \frac{wG_t}{C_{t-1}}.$$

This was the period-$t$-optimization condition. In the longer run, there is one more consideration to be made, namely that the investment shall match the deterioration of health capital, which occurs at the *depreciation rate $d$*, as well as the time preference given by the discount rate of interest $r$. Consequently, on a steady-state path we must have that the rate of growth in capital $s$, must equal the rate of decrease, corrected by discounting, that is $d + r$. In total we therefore get

$$\frac{wG_t}{C_{t-1}} = d + r. \tag{2}$$

We see that the left hand side can be identified as the *marginal efficiency of investment* in health, the payoff per dollar invested in this particular type of capital. If we correct this by the rate of deterioration of the health capital, then it should equal the marginal efficiency of any other investment, in particular investment in the money market, which has the payoff $r$ per dollar invested.

## 2.3  *Derivation of the fundamental relation*

In this subsection we derive the fundamental equation (2) from a full model, basically following Grossman. We consider a single consumer facing an intertemporal choice problem, and the planning horizon consists of $n$ future periods, so time varies from $t = 0$ (today) to $t = n$. The size of the health capital in each of the periods is

$$H_0, H_1, \ldots, H_t, \ldots, H_n.$$

We assume now that there is a certain payoff connected with health capital, so that a stock $H_t$ of health capital at time $t$ gives rise to a flow $h_t$ of health capital services, interpreted as the benefits obtained from being healthy, at that time. There is a minimum size of the health capital, $H_{min}$. If the $H_t$ falls below $H_{min}$, then the consumer dies. Moreover, the existing stock of health capital is subject to depreciation, so that the stock is adjusted from one period to the next by

$$H_{t+1} = H_t + I_t - d_t H_t, \tag{3}$$

where $I_t$ is the investment in health at $t$ and $d_t$ the rate of depreciation effective for period $t$; as mentioned earlier, it seems reasonable that this rate of depreciation changes over time due to aging.

The consumer is endowed with a utility function of the form

$$U(h_0, \ldots, h_n, \xi_0, \ldots, \xi_n),$$

showing that consumer well-being depends on the current benefit derived from the health capital in each of the periods; the variables $\xi_t$ denote the consumption at time $t$ of other characteristics (in the Lancaster sense) than those related to health.

It is assumed that the consumer in each period produces both the health investments $I_t$ and the bundle of other consumption characteristics $\xi_t$ in a household technology, here given by production functions

$$I_t = G_H(m_t, T_t^H), \quad \xi_t = G_F(x_t, T_t),$$

assumed to be time independent. The variables entering as factors of production, are $m_t$, the amount of health related commodities and services purchased in period $t$, the bundle $x_t$ of ordinary consumption commodities bought in the market, whereas the two variables $T_t^H$ and $T_t$ denote the *time* used by the consumer in producing health investments and characteristics bundle, respectively. If it is assumed that the household production satisfies constant returns to scale, we may replace the production function $G^H$ by a function of only one variable,

$$I_t = m_t g_H(\tau_t^H), \quad \tau_t^H = \frac{T_t^H}{m_t}$$

where $g_H(\tau_t^H) = G_H(1, \tau_t^H)$ (production per unit of commodities inserted). Then the marginal products of time and of commodities in the household technology are

$$\frac{\partial I_t}{\partial T_t^H} = \frac{dg_H}{d\tau_t^H} = g_H',$$

$$\frac{\partial I_t}{\partial m_t} = g_H - \tau_t^H (g^H)'.$$

It remains to add the budget constraints: We assume that there is only a single budget restriction over the planning period (meaning that the consumer can borrow and lend at the interest rate $r$),

$$\sum_{t=0}^{n} [p_t m_t + v_t \cdot x_t](1+r)^{-t} = \sum_{t=0}^{n} w_t T_t^w (1+r)^{-t} + A_0, \tag{4}$$

where $w_t$ is the wage rate at time $t$, and $T_t^w$ is the time expenditure in the labor market.

Since the use of time is explicitly taken care of in the model, we need budget restrictions also here, indeed one for each time period,

$$T_t^w + T_t^H + T_t + T_t^L = \Omega, \ t = 0, 1, \ldots, n \tag{5}$$

where the first three variables have already been introduced, and $T_t^L$, denotes loss of time due to illness. We assume that it depends on the current size of health capital,

$$T_t^L = L(H_t),$$

satisfying the condition $dL/dH_t < 0$ – the more health, the less time is wasted due to illness. The constant $\Omega$ denotes the total time available in the period.

We may now derive first order conditions for a utility maximum under the constraints (4) and (5). We eliminate the constraint (5) by inserting $T_t^w = \Omega - (T_t^H + T_t + T_t^L)$ into (4), so as to obtain a Lagrangian of the form

$$U(h_0, \ldots, h_n, \xi_0, \ldots, \xi_n) - \lambda \sum_{t=0}^{n} \left[ v_t \cdot x_t + C_t + w(T_t^H + T_t + T_t^L) \right](1+r)^{-t},$$

where $C_t = p_t m_t - w T_t^H$ is the health expenditure of the period, that is purchase of commodity inputs and use of time evaluated at opportunity cost (which is the wage rate); we have left out all constants, which will disappear anyway in the first order conditions. Differentiating with respect to $I_{t-1}$, health investment at time $t-1$, we obtain

$$U_t' \frac{\partial h_t}{\partial H_t} \frac{\partial H_t}{\partial I_{t-1}} + \cdots + U_n' \frac{\partial h_n}{\partial H_n} \frac{\partial H_n}{\partial I_{t-1}}$$

$$- \lambda \left[ \pi_{t-1}(1+r)^{-(t-1)} + w \frac{\partial T_t^L}{\partial H_t} \frac{\partial H_t}{\partial I_{t-1}}(1+r)^{-t} + \cdots + w \frac{\partial T_n^L}{\partial H_n} \frac{\partial H_n}{\partial I_{t-1}}(1+r)^{-n} \right] = 0.$$

There are three different types of members in this expression; the first type (indexed from $t$ to $n$) emerges from differentiating the utility function w.r.t. the health components ($U$ depends on $h_t$ which depends on health capital at time $t$, and the latter is influenced by $I_{t-1}$). After this come the members derived from the constraint; first we have an expression which gives us the effects at $t - 1$, when the investment is carried out; $\pi_{t-1}$ denotes the marginal cost in production of health investment, and they can be found from the expressions $w = \pi_{t-1}g_H'$ (price of a factor equals the value of the marginal product of that factor) or alternatively $p_{t-1} = \pi_{t-1}(g_H - g_H')$. Following this we have members showing the effects on the budget constraint of these investments in the years to follow; this effect is indirect and stems from the effect of the health capital stock on the time available to the consumer.

It remains to rewrite the expressions $\dfrac{\partial H_\tau}{\partial I_{t-1}}$ for $\tau = t, \ldots, n$ slightly. For this we use the relation (2) connecting investment and capital. For $\tau = 1$ the partial derivative equals 1, since all of the investment is carried over as health capital in the next period. For the following periods the depreciation of health capital has to be taken into account, so that

$$\frac{\partial H_{t+1}}{\partial I_{t-1}} = 1 - d_t, \quad \frac{\partial H_n}{\partial I_{t-1}} = (1 - d_t)\cdots(1 - d_{n-1}).$$

We insert these expressions in the first order condition as derived above, and move the members around, isolating the expression $\lambda\pi_{t-1}(1+r)^{-(t-1)}$ on the left hand side, and inserting

$$\frac{\partial h_\tau}{\partial H_\tau} = -L'(H_\tau) = \gamma_\tau, \quad \tau = t, \ldots, n.$$

Here $L'$ is the derivative of the function determining the dependence of healthiness on health capital. It is seen that it is also the derivative of health consumption w.r.t. health capital, and that could not have been derived from what has been assumed so far, but amounts to a new assumption, saying that healthiness is important because (and, to be sure, only because) it makes more time available. Whether this assumption is a plausible one, is another matter.

Be this as it may, we end up with the expression

$$\pi_{t-1}(1 + r)^{-(t-1)} = w\gamma_t(1 + r)^{-t} + (1 - d_t)w\gamma_{t+1}(1 + r)^{-(t+1)}$$
$$+ \cdots + (1 - d_t)\cdots(1 - d_{n-1})w\gamma_n(1 + r)^{-n} + \frac{U_t'\gamma_t}{\lambda}$$
$$+ \cdots + (1 - d_t)\cdots(1 - d_{n-1})\frac{U_n'\gamma_n}{\lambda}.$$

We now have a formula for the discounted marginal cost of investment in health at time $t - 1$. To get on to something useful we reduce the expression by finding the similar expression for marginal cost one period later, that is $\pi_t(1 + r)^{-t}$, which of course looks much like the former one, namely as follows,

$$\pi_t(1 + r)^{-t} = w\gamma_t(1 + r)^{-(t+1)} + \cdots + (1 - d_{t+1})\cdots(1 - d_{n-1})w\gamma_n(1 + r)^{-n}$$
$$+ \frac{U_{t+1}'\gamma_{t+1}}{\lambda} + \cdots + (1 - d_{t+1})\cdots(1 - d_{n-1})\frac{U_n'\gamma_n}{\lambda}.$$

Now we subtract the latter from the first, which means that several of the members cancel each other; what is left is only

$$\pi_{t-1}(1+r)^{-(t-1)} = w\gamma_t(1+r)^{-t} + \frac{U_t'\gamma_t}{\lambda} + (1-d_t)\pi_t(1+r)^{-t}.$$

Isolating the two members containing $\gamma_t$ on the right hand side and multiplying by $(1+r)^t$, this side of the equation becomes

$$\gamma_t[w + \frac{U_t'}{\lambda}(1+r)^t].$$

On the other side we are left with

$$\pi_{t-1}(1+r) - \pi_t(1-d_t) = \pi_{t-1} + \pi_{t-1}r - \pi_t + \pi_t d_t,$$

a somewhat messy expression, which however may be improved by some cosmetic changes: We introduce the quantity

$$\tilde{\pi}_{t-1} = \frac{\pi_{t-1} - \pi_t}{\pi_{t-1}}$$

which is the percentual change in marginal cost from $t-1$ to $t$; from this we obtain $\pi_{t-1} - \pi_t = \pi_{t-1}\tilde{\pi}_{t-1}$. Next we cheat slightly and put $\pi_t d_t = \pi_{t-1}d_t$, and we get the fundamental equation

$$\frac{\gamma_t[w + U_t'\lambda^{-1}(1+r)^t]}{\pi_{t-1}} = r - \tilde{\pi}_{t-1} + d_t. \tag{6}$$

Comparing with the intuitive derivation of the fundamental relationship of the Grossman model presented in the previous section, we see that we have obtained basically the same formula; the added difficulties of the present approach has the advantage of giving a better understanding of the relationship. On the left hand side we still have marginal payoff of health investment (but now we have also the "pure" consumption effect of health in the formula), and on the right hand side we have the quantities which relate to the time aspect, whereby the correction term $\tilde{\pi}_{t-1}$ has been added; this term is not an inessential one since it expresses the effects of the structure over time of the investment and its effects over the periods to follow.

### 2.4  *Applying the model*

This rather simple version of the Grossman model may now be supplemented with further assumptions, mainly of a very conventional type. This will give us a possibility of doing comparative statics, which may give insights into the reaction of the public to changes in either the health-related data of the situation or in the economic conditions for intertemporal choice.

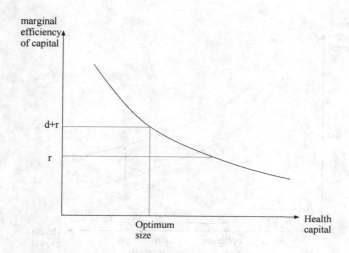

Fig. 2.2 Decreasing marginal efficiency of health investment with the size of the health capital. When the rate of depreciation increases, e.g. due to aging, the optimal size of the health capital is reduced.

Thus it sounds quite plausible that there should be a decreasing relationship between size of health capital and *marginal efficiency of health investment*, the payoff per dollar of additional investment in health. The more healthy one becomes, the less will be the payoff from having even better health; the relationship is illustrated in Fig. 2.2, which also shows how the consumer adapts in her optimization to changes in the depreciation rate. If it is assumed that the rate of depreciation increases with age, then optimal choice will lead to a reduction over time of the size of the health capital, since it will not be optimal to keep up the previous state of health as it becomes too costly to replace all the capital which is worn out. In its consequence, this means that health capital will decrease over the years and eventually hit the level of 0, presumably to be interpreted as death. It should be remembered, however, that the model is one of fixed horizon and no uncertainty, so that death does not come as a surprise, but as a planned final state (if terminal size of health capital does not matter for the utility of the consumer).

A more interesting consequence of the same type of analysis will emerge if we assume that the payoff of investment in health capital is changed, something that may happen as a result of new medical technology. When it becomes easier to acquire new units of health capital ($C_{t-1}$ decreases), then the value of $G_t$, which will equalize the left- and right-hand sides in (6), will become smaller. Inserting this into the decreasing relationship between the size of the health capital and its marginal efficiency of investment will tell us that optimal size of health capital increases.

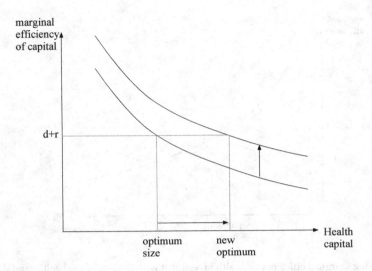

Fig. 2.3 The effects of an increase in the wage rate. Since the change affects both numerator and denominator, but the latter less than the first, the overall effect will be an increase in the marginal efficiency of health investment at any level of health capital, so that the curve shifts upwards. For fixed $r$ and $d$ the new optimum will be reached at a higher value of the health capital.

We can also follow the effects of a change in the wage rate $w$ on the optimal stock of health capital. The wage rate appears explicitly in the numerator of the fundamental expression for optimal choice of health capital, so it would seem obvious that an increased wage rate makes health investment more attractive and therefore shifts the optimal size of the health capital in the upwards direction. However, this effect will have to be modified due to the fact that the wage rate does enter also in the denominator, even if not with the same weight: An increase in the wage rate of 10% appears in the numerator with the full 10% , while the denominator increases only to the extent that the expenditure on health investment contains labor cost (of others such that medical professionals, personnel attending the machines in the gymnasium etc., and own time evaluated at opportunity cost, i.e. the wage to be earned in alternative occupation) rather than remuneration of other factors of production. In an extreme case the labor content of health investment might be 100%, in which case changes in the wage rate would leave the optimal amount of health capital unchanged, but under ordinary circumstances it is to be expected that the value of the expression on the left hand side will be reduced, and in order to retain equality with the right hand side, the amount of health capital "installed" must be increased. Thus, a rise in wages entails an increase in the general state of health, perhaps not a very shocking new piece of insight, but at least an illustrative example of the way in which a precise model of optimizing behavior, in casu the Grossman model of long term choices of consumption and health, can be used to produce forecasts of aggregate behavior.

## 2.5 *Extensions of the model*

Since its appearance, the Grossman model of health capital construction has remained the main building block in any theory of demand for health and health services. Subsequent contributions to the literature have refined the approach and added some new features, but the basic structure remains more or less the same. We consider some of the refined versions of the model.

One such version obtains if time is continuous rather than discrete. In itself, this changes very little, but it opens up for another addition to the model, namely replacing the rigid horizon to one determined by health conditions: life terminates if the size of the health capital falls to a critical level $H_{min}$, but the length of life will then be determined by the optimality conditions. This extension was introduced by Muurinen [1982] and used also in Ehrlich and Chuma [1990]. Below we give a simple version of the continuous time model, following Liljas [1998].

As before, we are considering a consumer wanting to maximize utility over the lifetime, and to deal with the problem in continuous time we assume that this utility has a simple form, namely

$$U = \int_0^T u(h(t), z(t))e^{-\sigma t}dt, \tag{7}$$

where $h(t) = \varphi(t)H(t)$ is the flow of health derived at time $t$, obtained from the health capital $H(t)$ available at $t$, $z(t)$ is a vector of other goods entering the utility function (and since we are not particularly interested in this component, we assume that there is only one such good), and $\sigma$ is the subjective rate of time preferences. The consumer has a budget constraint of the form

$$\int_0^T \left[ \pi(t)d_t(H(t))H(t) + \pi(t)\dot{H}(t) + q(t)z(t) + w(T)T^L(t) \right] e^{-rt}dt = R, \tag{8}$$

where $d_t(H)$ is the depreciation rate for health capital at date $t$, $\pi(t)$ and $q(t)$ are prices of health investment (which is written as $\dot{H}$, the time derivative of $H$) and consumption good, respectively, $w(t)$ is the wage rate, $T^L(t)$ the time loss due to illness, and $r$ is the capital market rate of interest. It is seen that we have simplified the production of health investment somewhat, but the basic structure has been kept.

The problem of the consumer is to find a path $H(\cdot)$ of health capital (and consumption) so as to maximize $U$ subject to the budget constraint (8) and the time constraint, which now has the form

$$h(t) + T^L(t) = \Omega, \tag{9}$$

since we interpret $h(t)$ as healthy time, and with an initial condition $H(0) = H_0$. The upper bound $T$ is not fixed but will be determined as $T = \inf\{t \mid \min H(t) = H_{\min}\}$, where $H_{\min}$ is the threshold level of health capital, below which the individual is no longer alive.

To find necessary conditions, we insert $T^L(t) = \Omega - h(t)$ in (7) and define the Lagrange function of the problem,

$$L = \int_0^T \left[ (u(h, Z)e^{-\sigma t} + \lambda \left( \pi d(H)H + \pi \dot{H} + qz + w(\Omega - h) \right) e^{-rt} \right] dt, \tag{10}$$

where we have omitted explicit reference to the dependence on $t$ to facilitate reading. Maximizing $L$ by suitable choices of $H(\cdot)$ and $Z(\cdot)$ is a problem in the calculus of variations, and first order conditions w.r.t. health capital are given by the Euler-Lagrange equation

$$\frac{\partial F}{\partial H} - \frac{d}{dt}\frac{\partial F}{\partial \dot{H}} = 0,$$

where $F$ is the integrand in (10). Performing the derivations, we obtain the expression

$$\frac{\partial u}{\partial h}\frac{\partial h}{\partial H}e^{-\sigma t} - \lambda \left[ \pi d(H) + \pi \frac{dh}{dH}H - w\frac{dh}{dH} \right] e^{-rt} - \lambda e^{-rt}(\dot{\pi} - r\pi) = 0,$$

which can be reduced to the following expression,

$$\frac{\frac{dh}{dH}\left( w + \frac{u_h' e^{(r-\sigma)t}}{\lambda} \right)}{\pi} = r + d + H\frac{dh}{dH} - \frac{\dot{\pi}}{\pi}. \tag{11}$$

which is largely the same as (6) which was derived in the original Grossman model, although with some differences, since righthand side of (11) has a new member which describes the change in depreciation arising from changes in health capital.

Further extension of the Grossman model can be built upon the version outlined here, for example adding a random disturbance to $H(t)$ at each $t$. The reader is referred to Liljas [1998] for details.

## 3  Other models of demand for healthcare

While the classic Grossman model focusses on the investment aspects of health behavior, other models of demand for health have emphasized the short run, where health expenditure has to do with actual illness and these expenditures compete with other consumption goods for the short term budget of the consumer. Nevertheless, some of the characteristic features of the Grossman model may be found also here, such as the idea that health is a consumption characteristic which must be produced by the household on the basis of commodities bought in the market as well as the time given up by the household.

### 3.1 The Newhouse-Phelps model

An example of this kind of models is provided by Phelps and Newhouse [1974], where the health expenditure $C$ of a consumer is supposed to consist of direct outlays to the amount of $cP$, where $P$ is the price of health care services and $c$ the part of this price left for the consumer (the rest is covered by an insurance or another scheme for health care financing), and a time use $t$ which may be evaluated in money terms at the price $W$, which expresses the value of one hour for a consumer. Altogether we have a budget constraint

$$C = cP + Wt \qquad (12)$$

for health expenditures. This is not a standard budget constraint, since the amount $C$ may depend on the remaining choices of the consumer as well as on the income, but even though overly simplified the model may still be used to illustrate some peculiarities of the demand for health care services:

First of all we see that given (12) it is conceivable that the demand for health care may depend only weakly on prices, since the consumer pays only the part $c$, and – what is more important – the substitution effect of a change in price may lead to a considerable shift in the time use and only a minor change in the demand for health care.

Secondly, the share which is reimbursed by the health insurance scheme, will often vary with the size of the consumption. Typically, there is a certain initial use which is not refunded at all or where the reimbursement is very small, whereas further consumption is reimbursed at a higher rate. The budget constraint corresponding to (12) will no longer be a straight line but will display a kink at the level where the higher reimbursement rate comes into force. This is illustrated in Fig. 2.4.

The kinked budget line gives rise to a particular pattern of behavior with the consumer, obviously depending on the shape of the indifference curves. If the indifference curves are smoothly curved, the consumer will never have her optimum in the kink, but rather at some distance to the right or to the left; it may even happen that there are two optima on the same indifference curve situated at each side of the kink. If the curvature of the indifference curves is small enough, the optimum

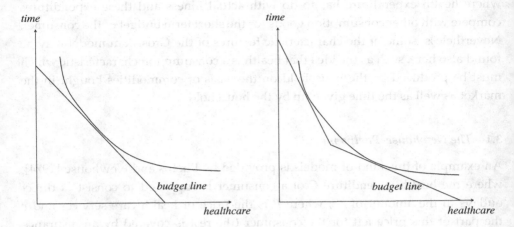

Fig. 2.4   The Phelps-Newhouse model: In the figure at the left there is a usual budget line corresponding to the expression (12), which however is quite sharply sloped since the share $c$ is low and time is considered as very important. In the figure to the right the budget constraint shown is one arising from a scheme for reimbursement of health expenditure where the percentage reimbursed increases after a certain level of expenditure has been reached.

will be rather far away from the kink point, meaning that consumers will either use very little health care or conversely use very much, but that there will be few or no consumers close to the consumption given by the kink point.

It may be debatable whether much can be learned from this model which was not known at the outset, but at least the model gives some useful hints about the adjustments which will necessarily follow from the introduction of a particular rule for own payment versus reimbursement; it may as suggested by the model result in a polarization of behavior such that some consumers reduce their use of healthcare while others increase it.

In some cases, the reimbursement depends on consumption also in previous periods, negatively if a heavy use of the insurance means that the coverage will be reduced, or positively if the reimbursement comes into function only after a certain cumulated expenditure. In such situations a dynamic approach is needed: Increased expenditure today will entail either smaller or greater expenditures in future periods since todays expenditure is added to the cumulated use of the insurance. We shall not develop such models (which anyway are not very much developed in the literature; the basic reasoning, namely that consumption should be seen in close connection with the health plan of the consumer, is important, and we shall return to this again and again).

## 3.2 Elasticity of healthcare

It may be argued that the demand for the services of the health care sector is determined directly by an underlying physical need for treatment rather than by prices as discussed hitherto. The basis for such an argumentation is that a service often has a definite and very limited character; an individual suffering from a particular disease usually needs particular and well-defined treatments in a similarly well-defined quantity (visits to the doctor, treatment in hospital, medicin etc.). If the price of this well-defined treatment is raised or lowered, it only means that the consumer will have to part with a greater or smaller part of her consumer surplus, possibly even all of it. In the worst case the price may be so high that it deters consumption, but as long as this has not happened, the same service will be delivered. This means that demand is inelastic up to a certain limit.

If this can be shown to be the case, it would mean that the classical argument against providing the services free of charge to the consumers would lose power. According to this argument, goods and services delivered free of charge will be demanded and used in surplus of what was economically rational (in terms of the consumers' own preferences) as illustrated in Fig. 2.5. If the consumer has a decreasing demand curve and the price is 0, then demand will surpass the level where the corresponding price equals marginal cost. This in its turn means that services are delivered beyond the point where the cost for society of delivering them balances the value for the individual of receiving them, so that the allocation is inefficient.

If demand is inelastic, so that the demand curve is horizontal, then this argument is clearly of no impact, and in this case the idea of providing services free of charge looks attractive. However, the argument is based on the assumption that the services provided by the health care sector are distinct and well-defined in relation to the need of the individual. The important part of this is that the quantity demanded should be something determined already by medical considerations independent of any economic data. As long as these assumptions hold, the principle of free delivery is welfare superior to selling in a market, at least if welfare depends on equality in health, since too high a price may leave some people untreated.

However, some care must be taken; it may well be the case that the demand for treatment for a particular disease is inelastic, but treatment as a whole will involve several different types of treatment, corresponding to different diseases, and since the latter may be of greater or smaller importance for the everyday situation of the individual, a certain sensitivity to prices will result: If a leg is broken, not many options are left open with respect to treatment, but it is less clear whether we want to go to the dentist every time we have some unpleasant sensations in the teeth.

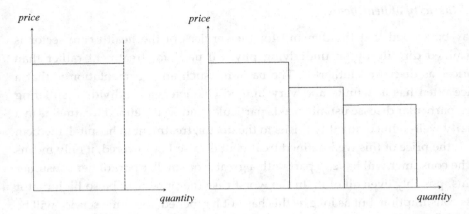

Fig. 2.5   Inelastic demand: In the figure to the left we have the typical inelastic demand for treatment of an acute disease. The quantity of treatment demanded is the same at all prices up to a certain level, where the patient can no longer afford to be treated. In the figure to the right the demand of the patient consists of several distinct demands for the service, corresponding to all the diseases from which the patient may suffer at a given time. While each of these demands fits with the figure to the left, the total demand for service will be more elastic.

To this should be added the time and uncertainty aspects of demand. There is a marked difference between the demand which stems from a disease which is present on one side and the demand connected with a health insurance on the other side. The considerations related to insurance and health service of non-insurance type are postponed to a more thorough treatment in Chapter 5, but it should be noticed that a discussion of the elasticity of demand for health with respect to price cannot be separated from the discussion of the methods for financing health expenditure.

# 4   Health and rational addiction

The model of lifestyle choice which has concerned us over the last many pages is actually only a special case of a consumer choice in situations where previous consumption matters. In the Grossman model, this has taken the form of investment in health capital, but one may imagine many other situations where the consumption choices of the past influence the utility of consumption today. We shall take a closer look at this more general version, known in the literature as "rational addiction" (as introduced in Becker and Murphy [1988] following Stigler and Becker [1977]).

### 4.1 *The rational addiction model*

We are dealing with a consumer who at any moment of time $t$ between 0 and $T$ must choose consumption $y(t)$ and $c(t)$ of two different goods. The first of the two goods is a standard commodity (which will be used as numeraire in the following), whereas consumption of the second commodity matters not only for current but also for future utility, since it gives rise to a "consumption capital" denoted by $x$. The consumption at time $t$ builds up future consumption capital, which in its turn may depreciate at a given rate $\delta$ but may also be reduced as a result of activities $D(t)$ which reduce or increase the capital. The dynamics of consumption capital is

$$\dot{x}(t) = c(t) - \delta x(t) - h(D(t)). \tag{13}$$

The consumer chooses $y$ and $u$ so as to maximize discounted future utility

$$U(0) = \int_0^T e^{-\sigma t} u(y(t), c(t), x(t)) dt, \tag{14}$$

so in this sense we may consider the consumer as "rational". The addiction inherent in the model comes from (13) since the value of $u(\tau)$ for $\tau < t$ matters for the instantaneous utility $u(y(t), c(t), x(t))$ through its influence on $x(t)$.

The consumer must choose under a budget constraint, namely

$$\int_0^T e^{-rt} \left[ y(t) + p(t)c(t) + q(t)D(t) \right] dt \leq W_0 + \int_0^T e^{-rt} w(x(t)) dt, \tag{15}$$

where $p$ is the price of the consumption which creates addiction (the standard good is numeraire so that its price is 1), and $q$ is the price of activities changing the consumption capital.

The optimization problem of the consumer consists in finding consumption paths $y$ and $u$ maximizing (14) under the constraint (15). An optimal consumption path must be a solution to the problem of maximizing

$$L(y, c, x, D) = \int_0^T \left[ e^{-\sigma t} u(y(t), c(t), x(t)) + \mu e^{-rt} \left( w(x(t)) - y(t) - p(t)c(t) - q(t)D(t) \right) \right] dt$$

subject to the dynamics in (13), where the multiplier $\mu$ is the marginal value (in terms of $U(0)$) of a change in the budget constraint. We use the necessary conditions for an optimum derived from Pontryagin's maximum principle: Define the Hamiltonian of the problem,

$$H(y, c, x, D, t) =$$
$$\left[ e^{-\sigma t} u(y(t), u(t), x(t)) + \mu e^{-rt} \left( w(x(t)) - y(t) - p(t)c(t) - q(t)D(t) \right) \right]$$
$$+ \psi(t) \left[ c(t) - \delta x(t) - h(D(t)) \right],$$

---

**Box 2.2 Coffee addiction.** The rational addiction model of consumer choice has been given empirical verification in several different contexts. Olekalns and Bardsley [1996] consider the consumption of coffee from this perspective. To test whether consumer behavior follows the prescriptions of the theory, the model must be modified so as to replace consumption capital, which cannot be observed, by something else, and the authors propose the model

$$C_t = \beta_0 + \beta_1 P_t + \beta_2 P_{t-1} + \beta_3 P_{t+1} + \beta_4 C_{t-1} + \beta_5 C_{t+1},$$

where $C_t$ is coffee consumption and $P_t$ price of coffee at date $t$. The future consumption comes in as a representative of consumption capital, and rationally addicted consumer will react on expected future price changes. Estimation of the model on US data from the period 1967-92 yields the result

$$C_t = -0.353 - 2.887 P_t + 1.684 P_{t-1} + 1.531 P_{t+1} + 0.523 C_{t-1} + 0.473 C_{t+1},$$

and the signs of the coefficients are in accordance with the predictions of the rational addiction model – current consumption is positively related to previous consumption as a proxy for consumption capital.

---

then

$$\psi(t) = -\frac{\partial H}{\partial x} \tag{16}$$

and $y(t), c(t)$ and $D(t)$ maximize $H(y, c, x, D, t)$ at each $t$, so that

$$\frac{\partial H}{\partial y} = 0, \ \frac{\partial H}{\partial c} = 0, \ \frac{\partial H}{\partial D} = 0, \text{ each } t. \tag{17}$$

Inserting in (16), we get the differential equation

$$\dot{\psi}(t) = -e^{-\sigma t} u'_x - \mu e^{-rt} w'(x(t)) + \psi(t)\delta,$$

with solution

$$\psi(t) = e^{\delta t}\left[\int_t^T e^{-(\sigma+\delta)\tau} u'_x(\tau) d\tau + \mu \int_t^T e^{-(r+\delta)\tau} w'(x(\tau)) d\tau\right]. \tag{18}$$

It is seen that $\psi(t)$ may be interpreted as the marginal value of stock of consumption capital. We now obtain first order conditions w.r.t. $y(t), c(t)$ and $D(t)$,

$$e^{-\sigma t} u'_y(t) - \mu e^{-rt} = 0,$$

$$e^{-\sigma t} u'_c(t) - \mu e^{-rt} p(t) + \psi(t) = 0, \tag{19}$$

$$\psi(t) h' - \mu q(t) e^{-rt} = 0.$$

Defining the undiscounted costate variable as $\alpha(t) = e^{\sigma t}\psi(t)$ and rearranging in (19), we get the equations

$$u'_y(t) = \mu e^{(\sigma-r)t},$$ (20)

$$u'_c(t) = \mu e^{(\sigma-r)t} p(t) - \alpha(t),$$ (21)

$$\alpha(t)h'(D(t)) = \mu q(t)e^{(\sigma-r)t}$$ (22)

Here the equation (20), for the consumption which does not create any consumption capital, is entirely standard: marginal utility of consumption at date $t$ must equal the marginal utility of wealth (the price of this good is always 1) multiplied with gain or loss due to differences between subjective time preference and market interest rate. In (21), marginal utility of consuming an additional unit should balance not only the instantaneous marginal cost, measured in utility, which is the first member on the righthand side, but also the long-term effect of this consumption, captured by $\alpha(t)$. Finally, (22) deals with instantaneous changes in consumption capital, showing that in optimum, the long-term effects of such a change should equal the marginal cost.

If we consider the second consumption good as harmful if $u'_x$ and $w'$ are negative, so that the consumption capital reduces the enjoyment of consumption or the ability to obtain the funds for consumption, then the $\alpha(t) < 0$ by (18), and the righthand side in (21) exceeds the price. Conversely, if consumption is beneficial with $u'_x$ and $w'$ positive, then marginal utility of momentaneous consumption is smaller than its price.

## 4.2 A simplified example

Even if the first order conditions provide useful knowledge about the optimal consumption paths, they are not easy to visualize due to the complexity of the dynamical model, and in order to get a somewhat closer feeling of what is involved, we consider here a simplified version of the model. First of all, we leave out the numeraire good, which anyway does not participate in creating consumption capital, and we abstract from the negative effect of $x$ on the budget constraint as well as the possibility of changing $x$ by specific activities, that is we assume that $D(t) = 0$ for all $t$. We specify the instantaneous utility as

$$u(c, x) = cx - c^2 - \gamma x^2$$

with $\gamma > 1$, so that $u$ is concave and the marginal utility of the consumption good increases with the stock of consumption capital. This is one but not the only way of specifying an addiction: instead of having the enjoyment of the good increasing with the record of past consumption, it might also decrease, so that still larger amounts of the good is needed when the amount of past consumption becomes larger. We assume that the rate of subjective time preference $\sigma$ coincides with the market interest rate $r$.

To make the analysis as simple as possible, we assume an infinite horizon, so that the rational consumer must choose a consumption path maximizing

$$\int_0^\infty e^{-\sigma t}\left[c(t)x(t) - c(t)^2 - \gamma x(t)^2 - \mu p c(t)\right]dt \tag{23}$$

where $\gamma > 0$ is a constant, subject to the dynamics

$$\dot{x}(t) = c(t) - \delta x(t). \tag{24}$$

Since we are now working with an infinite horizon problem, we need a so-called transversality condition to prevent solutions from growing without bounds, the one that fits for our purpose is that

$$\lim_{t\to\infty} e^{-\sigma t}\|x(t)\|^2 = 0.$$

Substituting from (24) into (23) we get a classical problem of the calculus of variations, maximizing

$$\int_0^\infty e^{-\sigma t}\left[x\dot{x} + 2\delta x - \dot{x}^2 - 2\delta x\dot{x} - \delta^2 x^2 - \gamma x^2 - \mu p\dot{x} - \mu p\delta x\right]dt.$$

The Euler-Lagrange equation, which, if the expression is written as $\int_0^\infty L(t, x, \dot{x})dt$, takes the form

$$\frac{\partial L}{\partial x}(t, x, \dot{x}) - \frac{d}{dt}\frac{\partial L}{\partial \dot{x}}(t, x, \dot{x}),$$

reduces to

$$\ddot{x} - \sigma\dot{x} - \left(\delta^2 + \sigma\delta + \gamma - \sigma - 2\delta\right)x = (\sigma + \delta)\mu p. \tag{25}$$

This is a second order differential equation, and for its analysis, we begin by looking for steady state solutions $x^*(t) = x^*$, where $\dot{x}^*(t) = \ddot{x}^*(t) = 0$. Clearly, the steady state value must be

$$x^*(t) = \frac{(\sigma - \delta)\mu p}{\delta^2 + \sigma\delta + \gamma - \sigma - 2\delta}.$$

To find all solutions of (25), we add all solutions of the homogeneous equation, and to this end we must find the roots of the characteristic equation

$$\lambda^2 - \sigma\lambda - \left(\delta^2 + \sigma\delta + \gamma - \sigma - 2\delta\right) = 0,$$

which are

$$\lambda = \frac{\sigma}{2} \pm \sqrt{\frac{\sigma^2}{4} + \delta^2 + \sigma\delta + \gamma - \sigma - 2\delta}.$$

The expression under the square root can be written as

$$-\frac{1}{4}\Big[(\sigma + 2\delta)^2 \cdot (-1) + 4 \cdot (-\gamma) + 4(\sigma + 2\delta) \cdot 1\Big],$$

and the expression in the bracket is negative by our assumption on $\gamma$, since the Hessian of $u$ is negative definite for $\gamma > 1$, and the expression can be recognized as the quadratic form arising from multiplying the Hessian from both sides by the vector $(\sigma + 2\delta, 2)$. Consequently, the characteristic equation has two roots $\lambda_1 < \lambda_2$, and the complete solution to (25) has the form

$$x^* + A_1 e^{\lambda_1 t} + A_2 e^{\lambda_2 t}.$$

The larger root $\lambda_2$ is greater than $\sigma/2$, so a solution which grows at the rate $\lambda_2$ will violate the transversality condition, and therefore we may restrict attention to solutions of the form

$$x(t) = x^* + A e^{\lambda_1 t}, \quad \lambda_1 = \frac{\sigma}{2} - \sqrt{\frac{\sigma^2}{4} + \delta^2 + \sigma\delta + \gamma - \sigma - 2\delta}, \quad A = x_0 - x^*,$$

where $x_0$ is an arbitrarily chosen initial value of $x$. It may be noticed that $\lambda_1 < 0$ when $\delta^2 + \sigma\delta + \gamma - \sigma - 2\delta > 0$, and in this case, the steady state $x^*$ is stable in the sense that an optimal path $x(t)$ will converge towards $x^*$ for $t \to \infty$ independent of the initial state $x_0$.

From the dynamics of $x(t)$ we can find that of $c(t)$ using (24), and we get that

$$c(t) = (\delta + \lambda_1)x(t) - \lambda_1 x^*, \tag{26}$$

showing that the consumption-and-capital path moves on a straight line in a $(x, c)$-diagram, depending on the steady-state value, as shown in Fig. 2.6. The slope of the line, $\delta + \lambda_1$, is positive, so that $c$ and $x$ are positively related, if $\lambda_1 > -\delta$ (and this happens if $\sigma + 2\delta > \gamma$) and negative if $\lambda_1 > -\delta$ ($\sigma + 2\delta < \gamma$).

The positive relation between $c$ and $x$ means that an increase in current consumption leads to an increase in future consumption as well, which is the key property of *addiction*. We have seen that for addiction in this sense to occur, the marginal utility of consumption must be increasing in consumptiom capital, but even so the optimal consumption choice may decrease if the marginal cost of future consumption capital (see (21)) is large enough. The slope in (26) depends also on the other parameters of the model.

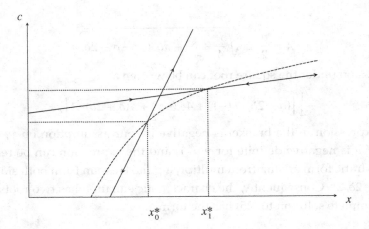

Fig. 2.6  Dynamics in the simple rational-addiction model: steady states are determined by the value of $\lambda_1$, and consumption varies linearly with $x$ in a neighborhood of the steady state. Two alternative steady states are shown, $x_0^*$ is unstable whereas $x_{*1}$ is stable.

## 4.3  *Cigarette smoking*

The main reason for discussing rational addiction in the context of health economics is of course that several forms of addiction have severe health consequences, eventually turning the individual choice problems to one which involves the national healthcare systems. Not surprisingly, tobacco addiction has attracted considerable attention, but many other problems related to lifestyle have similar character: consumers make decisions which have unpleasant future consequences, even being fully aware of the latter. The rational addiction model puts these choices into the standard framework of economic theory.

The following simple model of cigarette consumption (due to Suranovic et al. [1999]) is a version of the rational addiction model focussed on cigarette smoking. We work here in discrete time, where the units are chosen as rather small. A cigarette smoker at age $A$ attains an immediate benefit $B_A(s)$ from smoking $s$ cigarettes, and $B_A$ is assumed to have the standard properties of positive but decreasing marginal benefits. There is however a disutility as well, which in the model arises from the reduced life expectancy caused by smoking: if $T(A)$ is life expectancy of a non-smoker at age $A$, then a smoker will have a reduced life expectancy taking the form

$$\lfloor T(A) - \alpha(S_A + s) \rfloor,$$

(the notation $\lfloor a \rfloor$ stands for the smallest integer $\leq a$), where $S_A = \sum_{t=0}^{A-1} s_t$ is the stock of previous cigarette consumption, and $\alpha$ is a constant between 0 and 1. If utility at a future date $t$ to be enjoyed is $W_t$, then the discounted future utility is

$$V_A(s) = \sum_{t=0}^{[T(A)-\alpha(S(A)+s)]} e^{-rt} W(t) \, dt,$$

where $r$ is the subjective discount rate and $W(t)$ is the utility obtained at time $t$. The loss due to shorter life expectancy of choosing consumption $s$ rather than 0 is then

$$L_A \approx V_A(s) - V_A(0) = \sum_{t=T(A)-\alpha(S(A)+s)}^{T(A)-\alpha S(A)} e^{-rt} W(t).$$

So far we have dealt only with direct benefit and loss, but we should also take into account that changing habits (quitting or even reducing the smoking) is connected with disutility. In the model this is covered by a term $C_A(s, s_H^A)$, where $s_H^A$ is a variable subsuming the history of smoking; it might be taken as $s_{A-1}$, last period's choice of smoking, or as $\frac{1}{A} S_A$, average smoking, or it may be something else, but in any case it may be taken as given when making the choice of current consumption. We omit reference to $s_A^H$ in the sequel.

To complete the model, we need also to take into consideration the other parts of the consumption bundle to be chosen by the consumer. Assuming for simplicity that all other goods are represented by a single commodity $y$, then the choice of the consumer at age $A$ in the current period is assumed to maximize

$$W_A = B_A(s) - L_A(s) - C_A(s) + U(y),$$

where $U$ is the benefit derived from consumption of $y$, subject to the budget constraint

$$p_s s + p_y y = I_A,$$

where $I_A$ is current period budget of the consumer and $p_s, p_y$ the prices of cigarettes and the consumption good, respectively.

It may be noticed that the model is concerned only with single period choices, which must satisfy the standard conditions

$$B_A' - L_A' - C_A' = \mu p_s,$$
$$U' = \mu p_y.$$

The first order conditions may be used to illustrate what may be considered as typical choice patterns: For young persons with no record of smoking, the reduction of life expectancy caused by the first cigarette consumption is quite small, and there is no adaptation cost connected with changing from 0 to any positive amount. The optimal consumption bundle may therefore be one with $s > 0$. At higher values of

*A*, the loss of life years per extra cigarette consumed today is the same, but these lost years are closer if $S_A$ ia larger, so that the discounted utility loss is larger. Keeping adjustment cost low is therefore very important, fitting with observed behavior: changing the smoking habits are very difficult and becomes more so over the years.

Since we are considering only the one period maximization problem, the utility of consumption in future years is assumed constant, something which clearly is not quite consistent as overall utility will decline over the life years due to the increase in smoking capital. For a full model, we should choose consumption plans covering all future periods and taking into account that the life time itself is endogenous.

The separation of current decisions and long run decisions might however be a realistic feature of actual behavior. Indeed, some doubt may be raised against the rationality of smoking decisions – and even of long term consumer behavior in general – and other approaches may be useful if decisions about smoking are looked at from another angle. One such alternative approach assumes that the consumer has *time inconsistent* preferences (cf. e.g. Gruber and Köszegi [2001]) so that the weights of consumption at different future dates may change over time. An application of this idea to cigarette consumption is given in Kan [2007].

Consider a consumer who can choose between two different programs, namely

(a) continue smoking, giving payoffs $u_S$ today and in all future periods, and
(b) quit smoking, giving payoff $u_Q$ today and $u_N$ in all future periods,

whereby $u_Q < u_S < u_N$. With time inconsistent preferences, present day utility of program (a) is

$$u_S + \beta \left( \delta u_S + \delta^2 u_S + \cdots \right) = u_S + \frac{\beta \delta}{1 - \delta} u_S,$$

so that the utilities obtained at future dates, discounted at the rate $\delta < 1$, are further discounted by a factor $\beta < 1$. Similarly, program (b) yields the present day utility

$$u_Q + \beta \left( \delta u_N + \delta^2 u_N + \cdots \right) = u_Q + \frac{\beta \delta}{1 - \delta} u_N$$

Clearly, if $u_S - u_Q$ (the cost of quitting smoking) is smaller than the gain as considered today, which is $\frac{\beta \delta}{1 - \delta}(u_N - u_S)$, then program (b) is better than program (a) and smoking is quitted.

Alternatively, the smoker may postpone the decisions to the next period, giving rise to the utility stream $u_S$ today, $u_Q$ in the following period, and then $u_N$ in all future. This program is better than (a) if

$$u_S + \beta \delta u_Q + \beta \left( \delta^2 u_N + \delta^3 u_N + \cdots \right) > u_S + \beta \left( \delta u_S + \delta^2 u_S + \cdots \right),$$

which can be simplified to the inequality

$$u_S - u_Q < \frac{\delta}{1-\delta}(u_N - u_S).$$

Since $\beta < 1$, a smoker who would prefer quitting to smoking, would prefer the latter option of postponing the decision, and if

$$\frac{\beta\delta}{1-\delta}(u_N - u_S) < u_S - u_Q < \frac{\delta}{1-\delta}(u_N - u_S), \tag{27}$$

then the smoker will be caught in a perpetual wish to quit smoking tomorrow, without ever getting it done.

To overcome the dilemma and induce the smoker to quitting today rather than postponing, an additional cost should be imposed if smoking is not quitted in the next period. This will change the present day utility of the postponement program to

$$u_S + \beta(u_Q - c) + \beta\left(\delta^2 u_N + \delta^3 u_N + \cdots\right),$$

which will be better than (a) if

$$u_S - u_Q - c < \frac{\beta\delta}{1-\delta}(u_N - u_S).$$

This type of economic quitting support may be considered as executing of self-control, forcing a cost upon one self in the case of not carrying out the promised smoking cessation.

## 5 Queuing and demand for healthcare

### 5.1 *Classical queuing theory*

The theory of queues can be traced back to the first years of telephone communication and the development of telephone exchanges, but the classical queuing theory is mainly inspired by work of Kendall in the 1950s (see e.g. Kendall [1953]). In later years, the classical theory has been under rapid development and transformation following the emergence of new fields of application such as computer systems, where the emphasis is on *networks of queues*. Also, the interpretation of what is in the queue has undergone changes. Originally conceived as individuals (costumers), what is queuing may as well be information packages, or claims on an insurance company which must be served by the assets available. To get some feeling of what queuing theory can deliver, it remains useful to begin with the classical theory.

The fundamental characteristics of a queue are:

*Input or costumer arrivals.* Here it is specified how the arrivals to the queue occur, usually given as the time between two consecutive arrivals, which may be deterministic, but in most models are random, subject to a given probability distribution.

*Service pattern.* Here it is specified how the queue is served, individually or in bundles, and how long time it takes to carry out the service, this may also be subject to randomness.

*Number of servers.* If there are more than one server, we have a case of parallel service. There may be specific rules about the sequencing of service, either with separate lines at each server or with one common line, from which the costumer goes to the first non-occupied server.

*Capacity.* A queue may have restricted capacity, so that costumers arriving when the system is at capacity limit are rejected.

*Queuing discipline,* understood as the priority rules for servicing costumers in the line. The standard rule is FIFO (First In, First Out), others may occur (Last In First Out). In application to healthcare, *priority queues* are of special interest: here the costumers are separated upon arrival into two or more lines such that the first line is serviced first, the next line serviced only when the first line is empty etc.

In the classical queuing theory as well as in many later extensions the most important parameters for describing the queue are *average rate of arrival* $\lambda$, average rate of service $\mu$, and the number of servers $c$. In many cases, it suffices to know the *traffic intensity* (or service rate)

$$\rho = \frac{\lambda}{\mu}$$

for queues with a single server, and the corresponding quantity $\rho = \frac{\lambda}{c\mu}$ for queues with $c$ servers.

Intuitively one would say that if $\lambda$ and $\mu$ are known, the behavior of the queue is largely understood: if $\rho > 1$, the queue will increase beyond limits and will stop functioning according to its purpose, and if $\rho < 1$, then costumers will be served but there will be costumers waiting for service in the fraction $\rho$ of each time unit. However, for a thorough understanding of queues more details are needed, many of which will depend on properties of the arrival and service processes. Before we introduce such queuing models, we notice that there is one useful result, known as Little' formula (Little [1961]), of queuing theory which does not demand more information that we have at present.

PROPOSITION 1 *For a given queue, let $\lambda$ be average rate of arrival, and let L and W be expected number of costumers in the system and expected waiting time, respectively, when the system is in a steady state (that is when the system has been at work for a long time). Then*

$$L = \lambda W. \tag{28}$$

PROOF: Let $A(T)$ be the number of arrivals from time 0 to time $T$, and let $B(T)$ be total waiting time experienced by all costumers arrived between 0 and $T$, so that $B(T) = w_1 + w_2 + \cdots$ with $w_i$ waiting time for costumer $i$. Vi let $\lambda(T)$ be average rate of arrival in the period from 0 to $T$, that is

$$\lambda(T) = \frac{A(T)}{T},$$

and $W(T)$ average waiting time in the system from 0 to $T$,

$$W(T) = \frac{B(T)}{A(T)}.$$

Finally, $L(T)$ is the average number of costumers in the system during the period,

$$L(T) = \frac{B(T)}{T}.$$

We then have

$$L(T) = \frac{B(T)}{T} = \frac{B(T)}{A(T)} \frac{A(T)}{T} = W(T)\lambda(T).$$

Assuming that the limits for $T \to \infty$ are well-defined and given by $\lim_{T\to\infty} \lambda(T) = \lambda$, $\lim_{T\to\infty} W(T) = W$, then $L = \lim_{T\to\infty} L(T)$ exists and satisfies

$$L = \lambda W,$$

which is Little's formula. $\square$

If we want to make use of more detailed information about the queue, we need some general concepts from the theory of stochastic processes, more specifically about *Markov processes*. Since we shall use Markov processes also in later chapters, we digress briefly to treat this topic. We are dealing with a system which can be in one of a set $S$ of possible *states*, and we observe it at time $t = 0, 1, 2, \ldots$. For the moment, we assume that $S$ is finite.

Let $X_0, X_1, X_2, \ldots$ be random variables describing the state of the system at time $t$, $t = 0, 1, 2, \ldots$, and let $S = \{0, 1, \ldots, m\}$. This gives us a stochastic process with discrete parameter space $t = 0, 1, \ldots$ and finite state space $S$. The process is a Markov chain, if for each $t$,

$$P\{X_t = x_t \mid X_{t-1} = x_{t-1}, \ldots, X_0 = x_0\} = P\{X_t = x_t \mid X_{t-1} = x_{t-1}\}. \tag{29}$$

The conditional probabilities $p_{jk}(t) = P\{X_t = k \mid X_{t-1} = j\}$ are called the *transition probabilities*, and the Markov chain is (time-)*homogeneous* if $p_{jk}(n) = p_{jk}$ is independent of $t$.

Writing the transition probabilities in matrix form as

$$P = \begin{pmatrix} p_{11} & \cdots & p_{1m} \\ \vdots & & \vdots \\ p_{m1} & \cdots & p_{mm} \end{pmatrix},$$

one may find the probability $p_{jk}^{(n)}$ of passing from state $j$ to state $k$ in $n$ periods as the $(j, k)$ element in $P^n$ (the matrix $P$ multiplied by itself $n$ times. In particular, one has the equation

$$p_{jk}^{(m+n)} = \sum_{r=0}^{k} p_{jr}^{(m)} p_{rk}^{(n)}, \tag{30}$$

known as the *Chapman-Kolmogorov equation*, here in the version applicable to Markov chains.

It is of special interest to see what happens after many periods, in particular it is convenient that the probability of being in a particular state stabilizes over time. Using the matrix notation, this means that there should be a (column) vector $x$ such that

$$x^t P = x, \quad x^t e = 1$$

(here $x^t$ is the transpose of $x$, and $e = (1, \ldots, 1)^t$. The last equation shows that $x$ defines a probability distribution over the states, called the *stationary probability distribution*. For such a distribution to exist, the Markov chain, or rather its matrix $P$ must satisfy some regularity conditions; we shall assume in the following that the stationary distribution exists. Also, the above reasoning may be extended to Markov chains with a countably infinite state space $S = \{0, 1, 2, \ldots\}$, which is the case which interests us.

In our applications, we have continuous rather than discrete time, and the approach outlined above must be slightly modified, since transition probabilities $p_{ij}(h)$ then depend on the interval $h$ during which transition can take place. However, there is a way of returning to almost the same framework defining "momentaneous" transition probabilities

$$q_{ij} = \lim_{h \to 0} \frac{p_{ij}(h) - p_{ij}(0)}{h},$$

or in matrix notation,

$$Q = \lim_{h \to 0} \frac{1}{h} [P(h) - I]$$

where $I$ is a unit matrix. Then $\sum_{j \neq i} q_j = -q_{ii}$ for each state $i$. The matrix $Q$ is called the *infinitesimal generator* of the Markov process. There is a similar way of getting to a stationary probability distribution over states, namely if for each state $j$, $\lim_{t \to \infty} p_{ij}(t)$ exists and is independent of initial state $i$. In this case, it is denoted by $u_j$, and the vector $(u_j)_{j \in S}$ solves the equation system

$$u^t Q = u, \; u^t e = 1.$$

In the queues which are most often encountered in applications, and also are the simplest to deal with, the Markov chain is a *birth- and death process*: all transitions are from one state to a neighboring one, so that you can go either from $i$ to $i + 1$ or $i - 1$ (or stay where you are). We introduce the notation

$$q_{i,i+1} = \lambda_i, \; q_{i,i-1} = \mu_i,$$

and we get that $-q_{ii} = -(\lambda_i + \mu_i)$, $q_{ij} = 0$ for $j \notin \{i - 1, i, i + 1\}$. It is assumed that $\mu_0 = 0$. To find a stationary probability distribution (provided that it exists), we may use (30), which takes the form

$$-(\lambda_j + \mu_j)p_j + \lambda_{j-1}p_{j-1} + \mu_{j+1}p_{j+1} = 0$$

for $j \geq 1$ (where $p_j$ is the stationary probability of state $j$), and

$$-\lambda_0 p_0 + \mu_1 p_1 = 0.$$

Defining

$$\pi_j = \frac{\lambda_0 \lambda_1 \cdots \lambda_{j-1}}{\mu_1 \mu_2 \cdots \mu_j} \tag{31}$$

for $j \geq 1$ and $\pi_0 = 1$, we get that $p_1 = \pi_1 p_0$, and in general, that $p_j = \pi_j p_0$. We then have that if $\sum_{k=0}^{\infty} \pi_k < \infty$ (a condition which in this case also guarantees the existence of the stationary probability distribution), then

$$p_j = \frac{\pi_j}{\sum_k \pi_k}. \tag{32}$$

The simplest queue in the classical theory is M/M/1, where both arrival and service times have an exponential distribution. This is a birth- and death process, where the states are the number of costumers in the system (queuing up or being served) and where $\lambda_i = \lambda$, $\mu_i = \mu$ for all $i$. We may now use (32) to get

$$p_j = (1 - \rho)\rho^j, \ j = 0, 1, 2, \ldots, \tag{33}$$

where $\rho = \lambda/\mu$ is the traffic intensity.

---

**Box 2.3 Ambulance service and queuing theory.** Singer and Donoso [2008] consider the case of an ambulance service. Considered as a queuing system, the service process is quite complex, since the arrivals take the form of contacts to a call center, which passes the requests to a control room, deciding whether or not to send an ambulance. If an ambulance is required, the contact will join the queue for a vehicle, which then will go to the address requested and from there to a hospital, after which the vehicle returns to the base.

We consider here only the first subsystem, that is the call center. Seen from the point of view of the patient, this is a queue with $c$ servers (operators). Assuming exponential arrival and service, we have an M/M/c model. This model can be analyzed as a birth-and-death process where the arrival rate $\lambda$ is independent of the number of individuals in the queue, but where the service rate is $n\mu$ if there are $n \leq c$ individuals in the queue and $c\mu$ otherwise (empty servers are filled up immediately). We we can use the formula (31) and (33) to get

$$p_n = \frac{\rho^n}{n!}p_0, n \leq c, \ \ p_n = \frac{\rho^n}{c!c^{n-c}}p_0, n \geq c, \ \ p_0 = \left[\sum_{n=0}^{c-1} \frac{\rho^n}{n!} + \frac{\rho^c c\mu}{c!\,(c\mu - \lambda)}\right]^{-1},$$

and average waiting time for service in the queue is

$$W = \frac{\mu\rho^{c+1}}{(c-1)!(c\mu - \lambda)^2}p_0.$$

The parameters are subject to choice depending on the time of the day as well as other circumstances. The total waiting time of a patient consists of waiting times in each of the subsystems. Having estimates of the parameters, it may be investigated how the waiting time depends on number of calls, number of vehicles, operators etc., for details, see Singer and Donoso [2008].

---

The average number of costumers in the system can now be found as

$$E[N] = \sum_{n=0}^{\infty} np_n = \sum_{n=1}^{\infty} n(1 - \rho)\rho^n = \frac{\rho}{(1 - \rho)}.$$

Using Little's formula (28), we get that average waiting time in the system is

$$E[W] = \frac{E[N]}{\lambda} = \frac{1}{\mu(1 - \rho)}.$$

**Box 2.4** Wang [2004] considers emergency treatments and the role of waiting times. We consider here a simplified version to see how queuing theory may be used to assess the capacity of an emergency ward treating patients for whom a waiting time before treatment of more than a given amount of time may be lethal.

Let $w_q$ be the (random) waiting time in the queue. Obviously $w_q = 0$ exactly when the system is empty, so the probability of $w_q = 0$ is $p_0 = 1 - \rho$. If the costumer finds $n$ others in the system, the waiting time is

$$s_n = v_1' + v_2 + \cdots + v_n,$$

where $v_1'$ is remaining service time for the costumer being served and $v_2, \ldots, v_n$ are serving times of the costumers in the queue. This means that $s_n$ is the sum of $n$ exponentially distributed variables with the gamma density

$$\frac{\mu^n x^{n-1} e^{-\mu x}}{\Gamma(n)}.$$

We now use that $h(x)dx = P\{x \leq w_q \leq x + dx\}$ for small intervals $dx$, and we get that

$$h(x)dx = \sum_{n=1}^{\infty} P\{x \leq w_q \leq x + dx \mid \text{state} = n\} \times P\{\text{state} = n\}$$

$$= \sum_{n=1}^{\infty} \frac{\mu^n x^{n-1} e^{-\mu x}}{\Gamma(n)} p^n dx = \mu \rho (1 - \rho) e^{-\mu(1-\rho)x} dx,$$

so that the density function is $h(x) = 1 - \rho$ for $x = 0$ and $\mu \rho(1 - \rho)e^{-\mu(1-\rho)x}$ for $x > 0$. We can now find the probability that the waiting time in the queue exceeds $t$ as

$$P\{w_q > t\} = 1 - \left[ (1 - \rho) + \rho(1 - e^{-\mu(1-\rho)t}) \right] = \rho e^{-\mu(1-\rho)t}.$$

If average arrival is 10 per minute and service is 11, then the probability of waiting in the queue more than $t$ minutes can be seen from the table:

| $t$ | 1/2 | 1 | 2 | 3 | 4 | 5 |
|---|---|---|---|---|---|---|
| Probability | 0.56 | 0.33 | 0.12 | 0.05 | 0.02 | 0.01 |

## 5.2 *Waiting lists as demand regulators*

Queuing in the healthcare sector can take several different forms, from waiting lines in the emergency ward to waiting lists for surgery. However, the basic mechanisms are largely the same, and the resulting waiting time in the queue has a negative value to the patient, whether it is a question of hours in a waiting room or months at home waiting for a call. Actually, the disutility of waiting has economic consequences, as pointed out by Lindsay and Feigenbaum [1984]. We outline their model in the following.

Assume that people join a waiting list in order to obtain a particular good. Each person gets a fixed amount of the good at a fixed price, presumably lower than the market clearing price. There may be a cost $c$ of joining the waiting list, but the main obstacle is the process of waiting: we assume that the instantaneous value to the individual of obtaining the good, $v$, decays over time at a rate $g$, so that after a waiting time of $W$ this value is only

$$ve^{-gW}. \tag{34}$$

The decision about whether or not to join the queue must be taken before observing the length of the waiting list (which in may cases may remain hidden to the individual), so what matters is the *expected* waiting time. To decide whether or not to join the waiting list, the individual must compare the cost $c$ of joining and the value of getting the good, so that the optimal decision is

$$\text{join} \ \text{if} \ ve^{-gW} \geq c,$$
$$\text{stay out} \ \text{if} \ ve^{-gW} < c.$$

This can also be rephrased as a statement involving the expected waiting time, using that there is a critical value $W^*$ such that $ve^{-gW^*} = c$ or

$$v = ce^{gW^*}, \tag{35}$$

so that the individual will join the queue if the expected waiting time is smaller than $W^*$ and stay away if it exceeds $W^*$.

If $v$ varies among the individuals, distributed according to a probability distribution function $F$ with density function $f$, then (35) can be used to define a demand relationship between the number of individuals entering the queue and the expected waiting time. If we assume that all individuals are exposed to the same risk of needing the good, expressed by the rate of infliction $\lambda$, then arrival rate to the queue when expected waiting time is $W$ will be given by

$$D(W) = \lambda N(1 - F(ce^{gW})), \tag{36}$$

where $N$ is the number of individuals in society. The demand is a decreasing function of waiting time, conf. Figure 2.7.

Having a demand function, we naturally want to find also a supply relationship between expected waiting time in the queue and number of individuals which can be accommodated in the system. If we assume that the this number is kept within the limit of what the system can handle without breaking down, then we assume that a higher arrival rate with a fixed service rate will result in a longer waiting time (and this is what happens in the simple case M/M/1, considered above). Multiplying

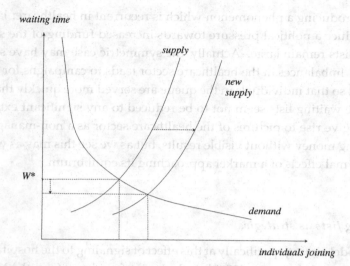

Fig. 2.7   Rationing by waiting lists: If patients' demand for healthcare depend negatively on the length of the queues, then this may be used to reduce pressure on the delivery of healthcare.

the arrival rate with $N$, we get the supply function $S(W)$ which can be used together with the demand to determine an equilibrium in the market.

What are the main insights to be obtained from this model? The main point in the design of the model was that arrival rates are not given and fixed, but depend on the characteristics of the queuing system. Individuals' decisions about joining the queue or staying away will depend on the expected waiting time, an in the equilibrium the resulting arrival rate fits accurately with the expected time of waiting. The number $L^*$ of individuals in the queue (or written into the waiting list) is determined as a by-product: by Little's formula (28), we have that this number equals $\lambda(W^*)W^*$, where

$$\lambda(W^*) = \frac{D(W)}{N} = 1 - F(ce^{gW^*})$$

is the arrival rate determined by the waiting time $W^*$.

An increase in the capacity of the server, illustrated by an outward movement of the supply schedule in Fig. 2.7 will reduce the waiting time, but the effect on the length of the waiting lists is less obvious, since

$$\frac{d}{dW^*}(\lambda(W^*)W^* = 1 - F(ce^{gW^*} - W^*(f(ce^{gW^*})cge^{gW^*}),$$

which can be positive or negative depending on parameter values. Thus, it is perfectly possible that waiting lists are unchanged or increasing even after a capacity increase, reproducing a phenomenon which is recurrent in healthcare: large wait-ing lists produce a political pressure towards increased funding of the sector, but the waiting lists remain large. Actually, the symmetric case may have some real-istic content: Imbalances in the healthcare sector leads to campaigns for increased productivity, so that individuals in the queue are served more quickly than before, but again the waiting lists seem not to be reduced to any significant extent. Such phenomena give rise to pictures of the healthcare sector as a non-manageable en-tity devouring money without visible results, but as we see this may as well be the perfectly normal effects of a market approaching its equilibrium.

## 5.3  *Waiting lists as strategies*

A simple model aiming specifically at this effect of signaling to the hospital owners, has been proposed by Iversen [1993] on the basis of evidence from the Norwegian hospital sector. In its very basic version we have a hospital which takes an interest both in the waiting time $t$ of a patient and the number of patients which are registered as potential users of this hospital, $\lambda$. There is only a single waiting list corresponding to a unique treatment delivered by the hospital; this may be somewhat primitive, but since our main interest is in the mutual relationship between hospital owners and hospital management, we need not get into details of deciding the length of several waiting lines, each for a particular treatment; the simplistic situation will do.

If the hospital management has an objective function of the form $u(t, \lambda)$ (in-creasing in $\lambda$ but decreasing in $t$), and if it is included that the hospital is subject to technological constraints in the relationship between $t$ and $\lambda$, determined by capacity and in particular by its budget $s$, we obtain a budget constraint of the form

$$C(t, \lambda) = s,$$

where $C(t, \lambda)$ is the cost function of the hospital, and in total we get an optimiza-tion problem defined as maximization of the objective subject to the constraint as described.

On the opposite side we have the hospital owner with a utility (or social welfare) function of the form $W(t, \lambda)$ defined on $t$ and $\lambda$. It is seen that what emerges is a game between hospital management and hospital owner, where the hospital management chooses $t$ and the hospital owners $s$; the last variable of interest, $\lambda$, is then determined by the budget constraint.

In a Nash equilibrium $(t^0, s^0)$ the hospital management has chosen the combi-nation of $t$ and $\lambda$ which is best given the budget constraint at the level $s^0$, while the hospital owners have chosen a budget which appears as acceptable and responsible given the actual waiting lines for treatment (since in our model, a smaller budget means that less patients are treated, a somewhat dubious assumption in the context of hospitals). Alternatively one may assume with Iversen that a Stackelberg equilibrium is established with the hospital management as leader and the owners as follower, meaning that the hospital takes the reaction of the owners on the choice of waiting lines into their account (these reactions would amount to suitable budget increases when waiting lines are long), and then choose a value of $t$ which with the calculated response from the owners $\lambda(t)$ gives the best result evaluated in the terms of $u$.

The hospital management has in its power to convince the owners about the necessity of budget increases, so to say by taking the patients as hostages, may well correspond to a viewpoint taken by the public authorities but probably much less to reality. But it does emphasize that the waiting lines play an important role in the hospital sector, and not only as a natural part of the capacity choice but also as signal between different decision makers in the sector (as we have seen here) and as an instrument for allocation of health care (as we shall see later). A more realistic treatment of the relationship between owners and management, also in the provision of health care, must wait until we have had a more detailed discussion of agency related to situations in the health care sector.

Before we leave the problems of waiting lists, it should perhaps be noticed that waiting lines may be useful not only for signaling to owners but also as a parameter in the mutual competition between hospitals. Suppose that patients have some freedom of choice with respect to the hospital in to be treated, and that the payment is mainly taken care of by other organizations than the patient itself (state or insurance company), so that payments to hospitals follow the patients. In this case the length of the waiting line, that is $t$, can be applied as a parameter to control demand, which may be assumed to depend on the waiting lists $t_1, \ldots, t_n$ announced by all the hospitals providing treatment of the disease concerned. For given waiting lines of the others, the hospital faces an optimization problem of the following type:

$$\max u_i(t_i, D(t_1, \ldots, t_i, \ldots, t_n))$$
over $t_i$ satisfying
$$pD(t_1, \ldots, t_i, \ldots, t_n) - C(t_i, D_i(t_1, \ldots, t_i, \ldots, t_n)) = s.$$

Here $D_i(t_1, \ldots, t_i, \ldots, t_n)$ is demand for treatment in hospital $i$ (with the previous notation this equals $\lambda_i$), and $s$ is the budget which at present is a fixed parameter; the financing organization is not involved in the competition for costumers.

The purpose of competition among hospitals is of course that it shall result in shorter waiting lists, and with the assumptions on $u_i$ stated above this is what should happen. In order to analyze the model we must know something more about demand; if it is assumed that the hospital having shortest waiting lists gets all patients (with equal division among hospitals in the case of identical waiting lines) we have a situation of Bertrand competition (though not in prices but in other decision parameters, here waiting lines). In the logic of Bertrand competition, the equilibrium would be one where the waiting lists are reduced to the minimal possible size.

On the other hand, as in the theory of industrial organization we have to consider whether Bertrand competition is to be expected in the given case, or whether the conflict between hospitals for patients should rather be treated as a repeated game, for which the equilibrium solutions are less obvious and well-defined, but where the optimistic predictions about the reduction of waiting lists to a "competitive" level cannot be expected to obtain.

## 6  Problems

**1.** In a debate about the increasing public expenditure caused by an aging population it has been argued that property incomes should be subject to a higher tax rate than other incomes, since a taxation of this type might improve the overall health state of the population and through this reduce healthcare expenditure.

Explain how this argumentation can be based on economic theory, and give a critical assessment together with suggestions for other economic means of improving the health of the aging population.

**2.** A country has a healthcare system based on large out-of-pocket payments for all kinds of medical service. In connection with a restructuring of healthcare it is proposed to invest in a considerable expansion of both hospitals and primary healthcare. To finance this very large investment it is proposed to sell healthcare investment certificates with a yearly interest payment determined as current central bank interest rate plus 2%. In addition to the interest payment, owners of the healthcare investment certificates are entitled to a 50% reduction in out-of-pocket payments for all kinds of healthcare.

Give an assessment of the workings of this arrangement in the long run. Could the funding of the large investments have been organized in a way which would be more beneficial for the overall health conditions in the country, given that it is not an option to increase taxes for this purpose?

**3.** As a result of economic crisis and fear of unemployment, private consumption has fallen to a low level while savings have increased considerably, and the level of interest rates has stabilized on a level close to 0.

In the ongoing debate on these matters, it has been argued, with reference to the Grossman model of consumer behavior, that the low interest rates will have a positive effect on the overall level of health in the population. On the other hand, it is observed that the impact of health problems which can be related to lifestyle has increased somewhat.

Explain how the two phenomena can be reconciled within the same model of economic behavior.

**4.** It is well documented in the medical literature that a high level of the Body Mass Index (BMI) is connected to an higher risk of diseases which are costly for both the patient and society, and the average cost of treatment has been assessed to have a magnitude of around €100,000. It is therefore suggested that individuals with BMI> 30 should be offered a loan of this size, to be renewed yearly with an interest rate of 8 pct. per year as long as BMI remains above 25 and repaid fully after 10 years. If BMI falls below 25, the loan is cancelled with no repayment.

Give an assessment of this proposal based on economic theory.

**5.** Activities in a small specialized clinic can be described approximately by an exponential distribution, where an average of two patients can be treated per hour. Patients are called in for treatment in the morning, and after surgery they are then transferred to a ward, where they lie down and are observed until they can be discharged safely. The time spent here also follows an exponential distribution, with an average duration of 28 minutes.

There are only four beds available, and surgery will be paused if all beds are occupied. How often does this happen?

**6.** A pension fund servicing the upper middle class in society introduces two new supplementary schemes for individuals in the age group between 35 and 45:

(i) a scheme which entitles the costumer to a treatment over 8 weeks each year in a health resort at the French mediterranean coast,

(ii) a 50% discount on all services in a fitness center from the age of 45 to 65.

Both schemes must be funded by yearly payments over 5 years, and for each of them, payments and outlays must be balanced. After the introduction, it turns out that many costumers choose (ii) whereas the demand for (i) is rather small.

After several years with very low interest rates there is a general increase in the level of interest rates. Since the discounted value of future gains will is diminished, it is expected that there will be no demand for scheme (i). However it turns out that costumers move from (ii) to (i). Give a theoretical explanation.

# Chapter 3

# Supply of healthcare

## 1   The triangle of healthcare markets

The supply side of the healthcare markets is composed of a wide variety of health-care providers, from hospitals and doctors to psychoanalysts and physiotherapists, covering also the market for pharmaceutical drugs. It goes without saying that all these healthcare providers have very little in common.  Some of them are in the market for profits, others are non-profit businesses with a philanthropic purpose. The underlying technology varies from personal service to highly industrialized production.

It appears that the only common feature of all the different versions of healthcare provision is that it deals with 'healthcare', not much of a unifying criterion from the point of view of economic theory.  However, for a very considerable part of the sector, there is a phenomenon of economic nature which they share, namely the presence of a third party in the market relationship between supply and demand: due to the organization of healthcare financing, payment for healthcare delivery is shared between patient and the relevant healthcare organization, which depending on the country may be a private health insurance company or the government institutions taking care of healthcare provision. The situation is usually illustrated by the triangle shown in Fig. 3.1.

Given this triangle, both the demand decisions of the consumer/patient and the supply decisions of the provider will be affected. The natural reaction from the part of the patient takes the form of increased demand as compared to the situation of full out-of-pocket payment (the fact that in some cases full out-of-pocket payment is beyond the reach of the patient is often, but not always, overlooked in the discussion, cf. Nyman [1999]). For the provider taking the interests of the patient into consideration, supply may also be more different if not too tightly restricted by the possibilities of payment, so that both have a common interest in a high level of activity. The financing part, on the other side, has an obvious interest in keeping

Fig. 3.1    The fundamental triangle of healthcare provision: The patient receiving is either not paying at all or paying only a part of the expenses.

cost as low as possible, and it will try to curtail the activities correspondingly. In various versions, this interrelationship will concern us in all the subsequent chapter, and we shall deal with different aspects of it as we proceed. At present, we focus on the behavior of the healthcare provider.

In the following, we formally split the discussion according to type of healthcare service or product delivered, dealing in turn with doctors, hospitals, and the pharmaceutical industry. It should however be emphasized that the economic models considered are applicable beyond the strict limitations given by type of provision. Also, we shall return to each of these types later when considering regulation of the healthcare sector, where the distinction is more clear.

## 2    Healthcare supply and supplier-induced demand

The decisions of a healthcare provider offering services, typically of a personal character, to patients, can in principle be analyzed in the same way as that of any producer, that is by specifying the production and cost functions, the market structure and the objective of the producer, and then proceeding to a characterization of optimal decisions. However, what is of interest when dealing with supply decisions in healthcare is the special features derived from the nature of the services delivered and from the particular market, with the third participating agent paying at least partially for the services delivered.

One of the specific aspects of service provision, and one which traditionally has attracted much attention, is the possibility of the provider to influence the consumer (patient) and her demand for services. This phenomenon of *supplier induced demand* (known in the literature as SID) is not restricted to doctors and not to healthcare providers in general, rather it may occur whenever a consumer demands a service with limited information about its quality, but traditionally, SID has been discussed in connection with the supply decisions of physicians. In the following, we shall therefore treat the physicians and their decisions in considerable detail, using first a standard economic approach and subsequently going into more detail.

## 2.1 *Advertising and the Dorfman-Steiner results*

The simplest way of treating the phenomenon of supplier induced demand (known in the literature as SID) is to consider this activity as just one out of many possible forms of *advertising*. Most advertising contains an element of persuasion, of convincing the consumer that purchasing the particular good or service will increase utility. It may be argued that there are many crucial differences between advertising and SID, but even so it makes sense to have a brief look at the classical theory of advertising, introduced in Dortman and Steiner [1954].

We are here dealing with a monopolist selling a single good produced with constant unit cost $c$ and facing a consumer demand $D(p, A)$ which depends on the price of the good and the volume of advertising $A$ measured in money terms. The profit-maximizing monopolist will solve the problem

$$max_{p,A} \left[ (p - c)D(p, A) - A \right].$$

and the first order conditions for a maximum are

$$D(p, A) + \frac{\partial D}{\partial p}(p - c) = 0$$

$$\frac{\partial D}{\partial A}(p - c) = 1. \tag{1}$$

The first condition in (1) may be rewritten as

$$\frac{p - c}{p} = -\frac{1}{\varepsilon_p}, \tag{2}$$

where $\varepsilon_p = \frac{\partial D}{\partial p} \frac{p}{D}$ is the price elasticity of demand, and this is recognized as the standard condition for a profit maximizing monopolist: the quantity on the left-hand side is the *Lerner index* giving the mark-up as percentage of price, and on the right-hand side we have the inverse elasticity which is standard in monopoly pricing. The second condition in (1) may be rearranged and multiplied by $A/D$ so as to become

$$\varepsilon_A = \frac{p}{p - c} \frac{A}{pD}, \tag{3}$$

where $\varepsilon_A = \frac{\partial D}{\partial A} \frac{A}{D}$ is the elasticity of demand with respect to advertising expenditure. Combining the two expressions (2) and (3) and assuming $\varepsilon_p \neq 0$, we finally get the Dorfman-Steiner condition

$$\frac{\varepsilon_A}{-\varepsilon_p} = \frac{A}{pD}. \tag{4}$$

The condition says that the optimal advertising expenditure relative to total revenue is determined by the relative elasticities. Other things being equal, if the price elasticity is (numerically) small, as we would rather expect it to be for the services of a healthcare provider, the fraction on the left-hand side would be large and advertising would play an important role. This might of course be counterbalanced by a small value of $\varepsilon_A$, something which does not look plausible if we identify $A$ with provider activities directed towards increasing the demand of the patient. Thus, the classical profit maximizing provider might well be engaged in activities related to SID.

In the case where the provider is constrained in the choice of $p$, in particular if the price charged either to the patients or to the insurance organization paying for the patient is rigidly fixed at some $p = \bar{p}$ (which is referred to as the 'rate' paid to the provider), the maximization of profits can be achieved only through $A$, and we focus on the condition (4), which can be rewritten as

$$\varepsilon_A \frac{\bar{p} - c}{\bar{p}} = \frac{A}{\bar{p}D},$$

connecting the share of advertising in total revenue with elasticity of advertising *and* the Lerner index. Alternatively, we may look directly at the first order condition taking the form

$$\frac{\partial D}{\partial A}(\bar{p} - c) = 1.$$

If we assume diminishing marginal effect of advertising, then a reduction in $\bar{p}$, which reduces the margin for the provider, must be counterbalanced by an increase in $\frac{\partial D}{\partial A}$, which can be obtained only by a reduced amount of advertising. This gives us the somewhat counterintuitive result that a rate reduction will diminish rather than increase the advertising activities of the provider. We should however remember that the identification of $A$ with activities related to SID, should be taken with some reservations, since in our model, $A$ is also a cost, and the rate reduction induces a cost curtailment which counteracts the intuitive tendency towards an increase in $A$.

We return later to the effects of a rate reduction. At this stage, we notice that the standard model of a profit maximizing enterprise may not be quite satisfactory as a model of e.g. physician behavior, and therefore we turn to models which are constructed specifically for this case.

**Box 3.1** Among the models of price determination specifically created to explain phenomena in the healthcare sector, the following one is very simple yet rather suprising in its conclusions.

We consider a very rigid form of the so-called literal target income hypothesis, where physicians aim at attaining a specific income level. If this level of income is $R^*$, the doctor must set prices such that when cost is covered, the resulting profit is exactly $R^*$. Assuming that cost $C(q)$ depends on the activity level (which here is the number of patients treated) $q$, the connection between quantity and price determined by the supply side is

$$pq = C(q) + R^* \text{ or } p = \frac{C(q)}{q} + \frac{R^*}{q},$$

which gives us a downward-sloping curve as shown in Fig. 3.2.

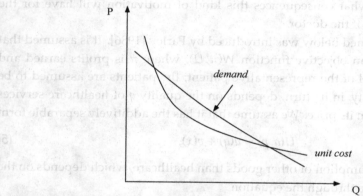

Fig. 3.2 The two qualitatively different equilibria for the doctor choosing under the literal target income hypothesis.

Inserting also a demand curve of the patients for the services of the doctor, we find equilibria where the two curves intersect. The case of two intersections, as shown in the figure, is the most interesting one. As it can be seen, the model can explain different types of "classical" physician behavior, namely both the expensive doctor treating a selected upper-class clientele and the poor people's doctor treating a large number of patients for next to nothing, both are equilibrium outcomes under exactly the same conditions!

It should of course be taken into account that the model is very simple indeed, but it indicates that seemingly fundamental different types of behavior may emerge as equally likely solutions to the same underlying conditions.

## 2.2   *An economic model of the physician*

Even if the decisions of a healthcare provider, say a physician, in the context of a
system where patients pay for the service out of their own pockets, can be analyzed
using the standard apparatus of economic theory, there may be many reasons for
not being entirely satisfied with this. After all, in the profession of a healthcare
provider, and in particular of medical doctors, the motivation behind the activities
carried out are not entirely concentrated on earning profits. The same may be
said about other professions, where goals may be many and often conflicting with
that of maximizing profits, but when dealing with doctors, there are rather strong
indications as to what may be the other goals. Indeed, it is rather to be expected
that the doctor is concerned about the patient's wellbeing, and therefore it seems
reasonable to see what consequences this kind of motivation will have for the
optimizing choices of the doctor.

The model outlined below was introduced by Farley [1986]. It is assumed that
the physician has an objective function $W(\pi, U)$, where $\pi$ is profits earned and
$U$ is the utility level of the representative patient; the patients are assumed to be
identical. This utility, in its turn, depends on the quality $q$ of healthcare services
received, but also on its price. We assume that it has the additively separable form

$$U(q, p) = u(q) + v(x), \tag{5}$$

where $x$ is the consumption of other goods than healthcare, which depends on the
price $p$ of healthcare through the equation

$$x = I_0 - \beta p q,$$

where $I_0$ is the income of the patient and $\beta \in [0, 1]$ is the share of healthcare cost
paid by the patient. From this we get that

$$\frac{\partial U}{\partial q} = u' - v'\beta p, \quad \frac{\partial U}{\partial p} = -v'\beta q.$$

The profit function of the physician has the form

$$\pi = (p - c)Nq, \tag{6}$$

where $N$ is the number of patients being treated by the physician, and $c$ is unit
cost, assumed here to be constant. The number of patients depends on the patient
utility achieved, that is

$$N = f(U),$$

where $f$ is assumed to be monotonically increasing, so that higher patient utility,
obtained as a result of quality of service delivered and/or price charged for this

service, will result in a larger number of patients choosing to be served by the physician.

Since quality $q$ and price $p$ of healthcare service is chosen by the physician, we may consider first order condition for maximizing

$$W(\pi, U) = W((p - c)f(U)q, u(q) + v(I_0 - \beta pq))$$

with respect to $q$ and $p$, which in view of (5) and (6) take the form

$$\frac{\partial W}{\partial q} = W'_\pi(p - c)[N + qf'(u' - v'\beta p)] + W'_U(u' - v'\beta p) = 0,$$

$$\frac{1}{q}\frac{\partial W}{\partial p} = W'_\pi(p - c)f'v'\beta q - W'_\pi f + W'_U\beta v' = 0. \tag{7}$$

The conditions may not be quite easy to interpret in their present form, so we consider some alternative versions: The second equation may be rewritten as

$$\frac{p - c}{p} = \left[1 - \frac{W'_U\beta v'}{W'_\pi f}\right]\frac{f}{f'v'\beta(pq)}. \tag{8}$$

Here the last fraction on the right-hand side may be interpreted as an inverse elasticity. Indeed, if we introduce the variable $e = pq$ as the payment for a whole treatment (consisting of $q$ units at the cost $p$ per unit), then the number of patients obtained depends on $e$, and we may define the elasticity of this dependence as

$$\varepsilon_f = \frac{\partial f}{\partial e}\frac{e}{f} = \frac{f'\beta v'e}{f},$$

and (8) can then be reformulated as

$$\frac{e - cq}{e} = \left[1 - \frac{W'_U\beta v'}{W'_\pi f}\right]\frac{1}{\varepsilon_f}. \tag{9}$$

On the left-hand side, we have the Lerner index, formulated for treatments rather than consultations (the unit cost of a treatment is $cq$), and the inverse elasticity on the right-hand side corresponds to the expression in the formula (2) for the profit maximizing monopolist. The expression in the bracket thus acts as a modifier, reducing the monopolistic markup due to the regard for patients' utility and the influence of patient utility on demand. Indeed, if $W'_U = 0$ so that the doctor pays no attention to the patient's wellbeing, then this expression is 1 and the formula reduces to that in (2).

Another special case worth considering occurs if $f' = 0$ so that the number $N$ of patients is constant and does not depend on $U$. In this case $\varepsilon_f = 0$ and (9) is not welldefined, but working instead with (7), we get that

$$W'_\pi N = W'_U\beta v',$$

showing that prices are set so that marginal utility of extra income equals marginal disutility of lost patient satisfaction. The marginal rate of substitution between own money gain and patient satisfaction is constant,

$$\frac{W'_\pi}{W'_u} = \frac{\beta v'}{N}. \tag{10}$$

This case is often identified with the so-called *target income hypothesis*, according to which the physician finds a compromise between income considerations, which would indicate SID activities, and the care for patients' wellbeing. It is seen that the fixed marginal rate of substitution depends on the number of patients. If for some reason this number of patients is reduced, the physician will reconsider the price decisions so as to increase the marginal rate of substitution, so that the patients will have to pay more, a phenomenon which has been observed in some studies, cf. [Newhouse [1970b]].

The first equation in (7) show that a similar compromise between income considerations and regard for patient wellbeing is achieved in the choice of quality. In the case where $N$ is fixed and $f' = 0$, it reduces to

$$\frac{W'_\pi}{W'_u} = \frac{v'\beta p - u'}{p - c} \frac{1}{N'} \tag{11}$$

indicating that the physician will reduce quality if $N$ is reduced. Combining (10) and (11), we get that under the target income hypothesis,

$$c = \frac{u'}{\beta v'},$$

so that cost per unit of quality equals the patient's marginal rate of substitution between income and quality, that is her marginal money value of quality.

While introducing the professional ethics of the physician in the economic model, we have been rather vague on the role of advertisement or demand inducing activity. The latter phenomenon enters only through the dependence of $N$, the number of patients, on the utility obtained by the representative patient. In subsequent elaborations of the model, see e.g. Jaegher and Jegers [2000], this approach is retained, and it may be questioned whether the phenomenon of demand inducement is really captured by these models.

## 2.3 *Demand inducement*

Another version of the model of a utility maximizing physician, and one which comes closer to the problems of demand inducement, can be found in McGuire and Pauly [1991]. Here it is assumed that the doctor has an objective function

$W(\pi, \tau, I)$ depending on income $\pi$ and on leisure time $\tau$, and in addition on $I$, which denotes the amount of activities which the doctor carries out in order to increase the demand for her services. The exact nature of these activities are not specified, and for the purpose of the analysis this is less important, what matters is that $W'_I$ is assumed to be negative, so that the inducement of demand is considered as something unpleasant, which should not be used unless considered necessary. However, these activities have an effect: Demand $q(I)$ is assumed to depend on $I$; the income $\pi$ is found as

$$\pi = mq(I), \tag{12}$$

where $m$ is the service fee of the doctor, assumed to be given, either through a previous agreement between doctors and payment organizations, or directly by government decision.

In addition to this, the variable $\tau$ is connected to the other variables by a time constraint

$$\tau = 24 - tq(I), \tag{13}$$

where $t$ is the duration of a consultation. It is assumed that the objective function $W$ is separable in its three arguments, so that it can be written $W(\pi, \tau, I) = w_1(\pi) + w_2(\tau) + w_3(I)$; one of the consequences of this assumption is that all the mixed partial second derivatives are 0, something which will be used below.

The point of the analysis is that although the outlays of the health insurer can be controlled directly through $m$, one has to pay attention to the secondary effects, since the doctors adapt to the new rates. In order to obtain first order conditions we find the derivative of the objective function (after inserting (12)) with respect to $I$, and we get

$$w'_1 q' m + w'_2 - w'_3 q' t = 0. \tag{14}$$

To find the effect on $I$ of a change in the price paid for a consultation, we use the implicit function theorem on the optimality condition (14), considered as an equation $F(m, I) = 0$, for which we have that

$$\frac{dI}{dm} = -\left(\frac{\partial F}{\partial I}\right)^{-1} \partial F \partial m.$$

Applied to (14) this gives

$$\frac{dI}{dm} = -\frac{w''_1 q(q'm) + w'_1 q'}{w''_1 (q'm)^2 + w''_3 + w''_2 (q't)^2}. \tag{15}$$

If as usual we assume decreasing marginal utilities, then all the second derivatives, and consequently the denominator on the right-hand side of (15) are negative. The numerator on the other hand has both negative and positive terms, so nothing can be said in general about the sign of the derivative.

Assume now that marginal utility of income is rapidly decreasing ($w_1''$ is negative and numerically large), so that the sign of the numerator is dominated by this term. Then the right-hand side in (15) is negative, and we get that reduced payment gives rise to increased activity to obtain customers. The authors identify this case with what is called the LTI (Literal Target Income) hypothesis on the behavior of doctors, striving to attain a definite level of income. A change in the remuneration rates must then be counteracted by a change in number of consultations, so that the desired income level can be maintained.

An opposite case, that of $w_1'' = 0$, may also be considered. Here only the second term in the numerator, which is positive, will remain, and the right-hand side becomes positive, so that reduced rates give rise to reduced volume of consultations. The underlying reasoning is as follows: When the second derivative is 0, the marginal utility of income is constant. Therefore the loss in utility due to reduced income cannot be compensated by an increase in $I$, which not only has a negative effect in itself but also reduces leisure time. Therefore the optimum must be reestablished through increased free time which means that fewer patients are treated.

It may be argued that the insights derived are not very far-reaching, since it captures only the relationship between remuneration rates and the demand-augmenting activities, but it may be seen as a first step towards a better understanding of the agency situation involved in the relation between doctor and patient.

## 3   Agency and common agency

### 3.1   *The principal-agent model*

In order to approach the discussion of provider behavior and to deal with the phenomena of supplier-induced demand, we now introduce the basic principal-agent model, which considers a case of contracting with an agent who is supposed to perform a certain action, which unfortunately cannot be observed directly. The model applies to many different cases of provision of healthcare, and also to many other cases which have no relation to healthcare. It deals with the design of a contract which is as good as possible for both parties, in particular as good as possible for the principal given that some crucial information is unavailable.

We begin the discussion with a very simple example, where we want to design a contract between a firm owner, in the following called the *principal,* and an individual, called the *agent,* who is engaged to perform some activities which matter for the outcome of the firm. The result of the activities of the agent is a money outcome, which can take the values $b_1$ and $b_2$, where $b_2 > b_1$. The agent chooses an effort level $e$, and the probability of the good result $b_2$ is a function $\pi(e)$ of the effort. The agent is paid some amount $r$ which may depend on the uncertain outcome. It is assumed that the principal is risk neutral whereas the agent is risk averse. The effort matters for the agent in the sense that it enters the utility function $u^A(r, e)$, where $r$ is the remuneration paid by the principal to the agent.

What is important here is that the effort level $e$ chosen by the agent cannot be observed by both parties and therefore it cannot be made part of the contract about the agent's payment. What can be observed is the final outcome, which is subject to random shocks so that the effort cannot be inferred by reasoning backwards from the observed outcome. Consequently, the payment $r$ can depend only on outcome, so that in our context it takes the form $r_1$ if $b_1$ and $r_2$ if $b_2$. Given the effort $e$ the expected utilities of the two parties will be

$$U^P = (1 - \pi(e))(b_1 - r_1) + \pi(e)(b_2 - r_2)$$
$$U^A = (1 - \pi(e))u^A(r_1, e) + \pi(e)u^A(r_2, e).$$

A contract, thus, is given by a pair $r = (r_1, r_2)$ of payments to the agent. Given the contract $r$, the rational agent must find the effort level which maximizes expected utility $U^A$, and we may consider the resulting choice of effort as the reaction of the agent on $r$ and treat it as a function $e^*(r)$. This reaction pattern of the agent can then be used by the principal when deciding about the optimal contract.

By now we have described what is going on in the model. The principal solves the problem of maximizing expected revenue choosing among different contracts $r$ and regarding $U^P$ as the result of $r$ and the agent's reaction $e^*(r)$, possibly under a constraint with regard to the expected utility obtained by the agent, which should be as large as what could be obtained by alternative employment. As we shall see later, the first order conditions derived from this optimization problem are not as intuitive as one might wish. At present, we look at a very simple case so as to obtain some qualitative insights which may be useful in further elaborations of the subject.

We therefore assume that the choice of the agent is restricted to two levels of effort, $H$ (high) og $L$ (low). The utility of the agent has the form

$$u^A(r, e) = v(r) - w(e),$$

so that it is separable in money and effort. Here $v(\cdot)$ is concave, so that the agent is risk averse, and $w(e)$ is the utility of effort, or rather the disutility since it is assumed to be negative.

In Fig. 3.3 we have drawn indifference curves in an $(r_1, r_2)$-diagram for the agent, illustrating the evaluation by the agent of contracts $(r_1, r_2)$, each indifference curve consisting of contracts giving the same expected utility with a fixed level of effort (for example, for $e = H$). With two possible effort levels there will be two systems of indifference curves. It is possible to say something about the relation between $L$- and $H$-indifference curves; indeed, if we look at their intersection with the diagonal, which gives us all the contracts where the agent gets the same payment in each state (so that the contract is risk-free, the principal carries all risk), then the slope of the $L$-indifference curve, which gives the marginal rate of substitution between payment in the good and bad states, will be numerically larger than the slope of the $H$-indifference curve, intuitively since low effort means that the bad state occurs relatively often, so that the agent will be willing to exchange a rather large amount of money in the bad state in order to get one more unit in the good state. This can also be seen directly: since an indifference curve has the equation

$$F(r_1, r_2) = (1 - \pi(e))v(r_1) + \pi(e)v(r_2) - w(e) - C = 0,$$

where $C$ is a constant determining the position of the indifference curve in the diagram, we can find the slope using implicit function theorem, getting

$$\frac{dr_2}{dr_1} = -\frac{F_1'}{F_2'} = -\frac{1 - \pi(e)}{\pi(e)} \frac{v'(r_1)}{v'(r_2)},$$

and assuming that high effort has a positive effect on the probability of the good result, we get that the numerator in the first of the two fractions gets smaller when we insert $H$, from which the result follows.

For any given point on the 45° line the $H$-indifference curve through this point correspond to a lower level of utility than the similar $L$-indifference curve, this follows from what be considered as the basic assumption in the model, namely that a fixed, state-independent remuneration of the agent will induce the agent to choose low effort. It follows that the intersection of $L$- and $H$-indifference curves corresponding to the same utility level must occur to the left of the 45°-line. Connecting all these intersection points, we get a curve $AA'$ in Fig. 3.3 moving upwards towards northeast; to the left of the curve, the agent chooses $H$, and to the right, $L$ is chosen. This means that the actual indifference curve, which takes into account what the agent will choose, has two parts, shifting from one to another when it passes the curve $AA'$.

For the graphical illustration of the optimal contract we need also the indifference curves of the principal, and for this it is convenient to change the variables,

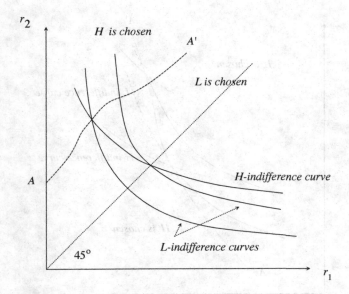

Fig. 3.3    Indifference curves for the agent.

describing the variables as pairs $(y, z)$, where $z$ is the maximal obtainable payment and $y$ is a reduction in payment, so that $(r_1, r_2) = (z - y, z)$. We redraw the indifference curves of Fig. 3.3 in an $(y, z)$-diagram as shown in Fig. 3.4. The slope of the agent's indifference curves for given $e$ are found as

$$\frac{dz}{dy} = -\frac{\partial U^A/\partial y}{\partial U^A/\partial z} = \frac{v'(z)}{v'(z - y) + \dfrac{\pi(e)}{1 - \pi(e)}v'(y)},$$

and here the denominator is larger for $e = H$ than for $e = L$, so the $L$-indifference curves has the higher slope. In Fig. 3.4 the curve $AA'$ separating $L$ (to the left) from $H$ (to the right), is still heading towards northeast.

The advantage of the $(y, z)$-diagram emerges when we draw indifference curves for the principal (which are curves connecting the same level of expected profits since the principal is risk neutral), as shown in Fig. 3.5, since these indifference curves are straight lines for both choices of effort by the agent. From the equation

$$(1 - \pi(e))(b_1 - z + y) + \pi(e)(b_2 - z) - D = 0,$$

where $D$ is a constant, we use the implicit function theorem to find that

$$\frac{dz}{dy} = -\frac{\partial U^P/\partial y}{\partial U^P/\partial z} = 1 - \pi(e),$$

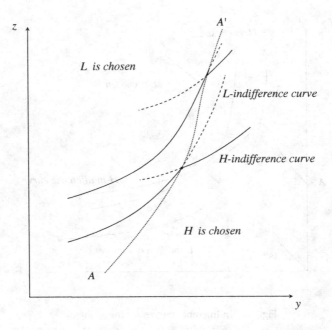

Fig. 3.4   The principal-agent model: change of variables.

so that the indifference curves for the principal are steeper for $e = L$ than for $e = H$. At each level of expected profits the two indifference curves (lines) corresponding to this level intersect in a point where $y = b_2 - b_1$: If the principal leaves every surplus profit from the good state to the agent, then the agent's choice of effort becomes irrelevant.

The choice of effort made by the agent again determines which branch of the indifference curve that will be activated, and by our construction, this choice is determined by the position of the curve $AA'$. To the left of $AA'$ the agent has chosen $L$, so that the relevant indifference curve is the steep line; to the right of $AA'$ it will be the less steep indifference curve, so the actual indifference curve will have a jump at $AA'$.

Now the two systems of indifference curves can be collected in one diagram, so that one can study the optimal contracts, which are such that none of the parties can obtain a better result without the other one being worse off. With the indifference curves derived the diagram becomes rather complex, and the main information can be obtained from the figures already drawn. The optimal contracts must be situated either on the curve $AA'$, so that the indifference curve of the agent has a kink and that of the principal a jump, or they must be on the vertical axis where $y = 0$. This conclusion comes from looking at the slopes: for a given value of $e$ the

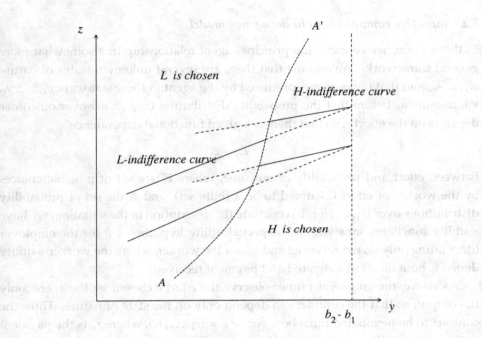

Fig. 3.5 The principal's indifference curves.

indifference curve of the agent is steeper than that of the principal unless $y = 0$. Since an optimum in the interior, where the indifference curves are smooth, would imply that their slope should be identical, we can have optima only at the boundary or at $AA'$.

This geometric insight gives us some useful hints to properties of optimal contracts: they must either be of the type where the agent is given a fixed, state-independent payment, but where the effort is always low ("the agent pretends to work and the principal pretends to pay for it"). Such a contract may be optimal if the additional payment in the case of the good outcome, needed to induce the agent to overcome the risk aversion and to put up more effort, is too large to be profitable for the principal. The alternative, contracts on the curve $AA'$, gives the right incentives for high effort, but the additional payment is as small as possible with this property.

These conclusions are perhaps not overly surprising and could perhaps have been obtained by other reasoning, but then the model was a very simple one and only the first step towards an understanding of the problems of incentives and the connection between the contracts agreed upon and the resulting supply of effort. We consider an extension of the model in the following.

## 3.2   *Incentive compatibility in the agency model*

In this section, we consider the principal-agent relationship in a somewhat more general framework. We assume that there are several unknown states of nature $s_1, \ldots, s_r$, and that the outcome produced by the agent in these states are $y_1, \ldots, y_r$. We assume as before that the probability distribution $(\pi_1, \ldots, \pi_r)$ over outcomes depends on the effort $e$, so that there is a given functional dependence

$$\pi : E \to \Delta$$

between effort and probability of outcome, where $E$ is a set of possible choices by the worker of effort (assumed to be a finite set), and $\Delta$ the set of probability distributions over $\{b_1, \ldots, b_r\}$. To conclude the description of the situation, we have a utility functions, satisfying the expected utility hypothesis, $u$ for the employer (depending only on net revenue) and $u^A$ for the worker, where the worker's utility depends both on effort delivered and payment received.

As above, the employer cannot observe the effort $e$ chosen by the agent, only the output, so that the contract can depend only on the state of nature. Thus, the contract to be negotiated must be a vector $r = (r_1, \ldots, r_r)$, where $r_h$ is the payment to the worker if the employer gets the revenue $b_h$.

Consider a contract $r^0$ which is optimal in the sense that it is the best possible for the employer given that the worker must be guaranteed a certain (expected) utility payoff which for convenience we have normalized to 0. Such a constraint can be explained by the opportunities of the worker to get employment elsewhere. In other words, $(r^0, e^0)$ must maximize the employer's expected utility

$$U^P(\pi(e), t) = \sum_{h=1}^{r} \pi_h(e) u(b_h - r_h)$$

over all $r = (r_1, \ldots, r_r)$ and $a$ such that the worker's utility satisfies

$$U^A(\pi(e), r, e) = \sum_{h=1}^{r} \pi_h(e)(v(r_h) - w(e)) = 0.$$

If $\pi(e^0)$ is an interior point of $\Delta$, so that $\pi_h(e^0) > 0$ for all $h$, we get from differentiating the Lagrangian

$$U^P(\pi(e), r) + \lambda U^A(\pi(e), r, e)$$

with respect to $r_1, \ldots, r_r$ that

$$-u'(b_h - r_h^0) + \lambda v'(r_h^0) = 0, \ h = 1, \ldots, r, \tag{16}$$

which may be reformulated as

$$\frac{u'(b_h - r_h^0)}{u'(b_k - r_k^0)} = \frac{v'(r_h^0)}{v'(r_k^0)},$$

$h, k \in \{1, \ldots, r\}$, $h \neq k$. This expression has a rather straightforward interpretation: the marginal rate of substitution between income in the various states of nature must be the same for both agents.

In the special case where the employer is *risk-neutral*, with $u(b) = b$ for all $b$, we get that

$$U^P(\pi(e), r) = \sum_{h=1}^{r} \pi_h(e)(b_h - r_h),$$

and (16) can be written as

$$\frac{1}{v'(r_h^0)} = \lambda, \; h = 1, \ldots, r. \tag{17}$$

Now we return to what was said above: the employer cannot control the actual choice of effort by the worker; the worker must be assumed to choose $a$ so as to maximize *his* expected utility *given the contract* $r^0$, and the resulting level of effort $e^*$ is typically another one than $e^0$ found in the employer's maximization problem treated above. The employer will have to take this reaction of the worker on any proposed contract $r$ into account when solving his maximization problem.

This new maximization problem may also be reformulated as follows: For each possible level $e$ of effort, let $t(a)$ be determined so that $R(e) = \sum_{h=1}^{r} \pi_h(e)r_h(e)$ is the smallest (expected) sum of money necessary to induce the worker to choose $e$ (assuming that such a number $R(e)$ exists). The employer has solved his original problem if he chooses $e^*$ such that with the associated $r(e^*)$ and $\pi(e^*)$, his expected utility is maximal.

In the first step of this procedure (where we determine $t(a)$ for each $e$), we solve the problem of maximizing

$$\sum_{h=1}^{r} \pi_h(e)r_h$$

over all $(r_1, \ldots, r_r)$ such that

$$\sum_{h=1}^{r} \pi_h(e)(v(r_h) - w(e)) = 0,$$

$$\sum_{h=1}^{r} \pi_h(e)(v_h(r_h) - w(a)) \geq \sum_{h=1}^{r} \pi_h(e')(v(r_h) - w(e')), \text{ all } e'.$$

Here the first of the constraints is the same as in our initial maximization problem; the worker must have at least what he can obtain in other employment. The second condition is *incentive compatibility*: The expected utility of the effort level $a$ should be as high as that of any other level; otherwise we cannot expect the worker to put forward this effort.

Let $r^* = (r_1^*, \ldots, r_r^*)$ be a solution, and let $K(e)$ be the subset of $A$ consisting of all $e'$ such that the last condition is fulfilled with equality. Then the last inequality transforms to $|K(e)|$ equations, and we get from the necessary conditions for a maximum (assuming, as previously, that the functions are differentiable) that

$$\pi_h(e) + \lambda v'(r_h^*) + \sum_{e' \in K(e)} \mu(e') v'(r_h^*)(\pi_h(e) - \pi_h(e')) = 0,$$

or

$$\frac{1}{v'(r_h^*)} = -\lambda - \sum_{e' \in K(e)} \mu(e') \frac{\pi_h(e) - \pi_h(e')}{\pi_h(e)}, \tag{18}$$

for $h = 1, \ldots, r$, where $\lambda$ and $\mu(e')$, $e' \in K(a)$, are Lagrangian multipliers.

The expression in (18) should be compared with (17). It gives an evaluation of the deviation from Pareto-optimality, namely the second member on the right hand side, which can be written as a weighted sum of the relative changes in probability of state $h$ by a change of effort from $a$ to $a'$ which is as good as $a$ for the worker but not necessarily for the employer. This deviation can be considered as the cost incurred by the need for an incentive compatible contract, that is the cost of asymmetric information.

### 3.3  *Common agency*

The agency models considered so far have had a general perspective, and they do not immediately fit with agency situations in healthcare. For one thing, the problem of whether the agent, here the provider of healthcare, puts up enough effort may be less interesting than the question of overprovision, with which we have already been concerned in the form of supplier-induced demand. This is however largely a question of applying the model in the right way, and other shortcomings are more fundamental. Among these, the problem that the provider must satisfy the demands not only of the patient but also of the paying organization, so that in our new terminology, the agent has more than one principal.

The theory of agency has taken this into account in the form of *common agency* as introduced by Bernheim and Whinston [1986]. Instead of a single principal, there are now $m$ principals, each paying a remuneration to the agent. As previously, the agent has utility $U(r, e) = V(r) - K(e)$, but now $r$ is the (aggregate) remuneration from the principals, and $e$ is an effort variable. The agent's choice is relevant for the payoffs of the principals: there are $n$ possible outcomes $b_1, \ldots, b_n$ subject to uncertainty. Here each outcome $b_h$ is a vector $(b_h^1, \ldots, b_h^m)$ of outcomes for each principal, and the effort $e$ chosen by the agent determines a probability distribution $\pi(e)$ over $\{b_1, \ldots, b_n\}$. Principals are as before assumed to be risk neutral so that their payoff given $e$ is $\pi(e) \cdot b^i = \sum_{h=1}^n \pi_h(e) b_h^i$, $i = 1, \ldots, m$.

Each of the $m$ principals wants the agent to choose an action which maximizes expected outcome $\pi(e) \cdot b^i$ among all $e$. In order to achieve the best possible result, the principal should choose a remuneration scheme depending on outcome (since, as before, only outcomes are observable to both principal and agent), that is a vector $r^i = (r_1^i, \ldots, r_n^i)$, where $r_h^i$ is the payment from principal $i$ to the agent contingent on observation of outcome $b_h^i$. Since the interests of the principals may be conflicting, we cannot expect one choice of $e$ to satisfy all principals simultaneously, so we consider situations where each principal selects the remuneration scheme given those of the other principals: An *equilibrium* in the common agency model is an effort $\hat{e}$ and an array of remuneration schemes $\hat{r}^1, \ldots, \hat{r}^m$ such that for $i \in \{1, \ldots, m\}$, $(\pi(\hat{e}), \hat{r}^i)$ solves the problem

$$\max_{e, r^i} \pi(e) \cdot (b^i - r^i)$$

subject to (19)

$$\pi(e) \cdot v\left(r^i + \sum_{j \neq i} \hat{r}^j\right) - w(e) \geq \pi(e') \cdot v\left(r^i + \sum_{j \neq i} \hat{r}^j\right) - w(e'), \text{ all } e',$$

and satisfies *individual rationality* in the sense that

$$\pi(\hat{e}) \cdot (b^i - \hat{r}^i) \geq 0, \ i = 1, \ldots, m. \tag{20}$$

Here the condition (19) requires that the remuneration scheme is as good as possible given the remunerations offered by the other principals and the dependence of the agent's choice on all these remunerations. The condition (20) makes sure that the optimal choice of a principal according to (19) is no worse that what would be the outcome if the agent does not participate, here assumed to be 0.

For later use, we notice that we can write (19) as

$$\max_{e, r} \pi(e) \cdot \left(b^i - r + \sum_{j \neq i} \hat{r}^j\right)$$

subject to (21)

$$\pi(e) \cdot v(r) - w(e) \geq \pi(e') \cdot v(r) - w(e'), \text{ all } e',$$

where we have only substituted maximization in $r = r^i + \sum_{j \neq i} \hat{r}^j$ for maximization in $r^i$. The new version has a useful interpretation: when solving the incentive problem principal $i$ may undo the offers of the other principals, replacing them with an aggregate offer to the agent. If we consider only the overall payment from principals to the agent, which after all is what matters to the agent, then we are interested in pairs $(\hat{e}, \hat{r})$ which can be implemented in equilibrium, meaning that there are $\hat{r}^1, \ldots, \hat{r}^m$ such that $(\hat{e}, \hat{r}^1, \ldots, \hat{r}^m)$ is an equilibrium.

PROPOSITION 1 *The following properties are equivalent:*

  (i) $(\hat{e}, \hat{r})$ *can be implemented in equilibrium,*

  (ii) $(\hat{e}, \hat{r})$ *satisfies* $\pi(\hat{e}) \cdot (b - \hat{r}) \geq 0$ *and solves the problem*

$$\max_{e,r} \pi(e) \cdot (b - mr + (m-1)\hat{r})$$

  *subject to*

$$\pi(e) \cdot v(r) - w(e) \geq \pi(e') \cdot v(r) - w(e'), \text{ all } e'.$$

PROOF: (i) $\Longrightarrow$ (ii). Let $(\hat{e}, \hat{r}^1, \ldots, \hat{r}^m)$ be an equilibrium. Adding all the inequalities in (20), we get that

$$\pi(\hat{e}) \cdot \sum_{i=1}^{m} (b^i - \hat{r}^i) = \pi(\hat{e}) \cdot (b - \hat{r}) \geq 0.$$

Since $(\hat{e}, \hat{r})$ solves (21) for each $i$, it will also maximize the sum over all $i$ of the objective functions subject to the incentive constraint, and this sum is

$$\pi(e) \cdot \sum_{i=1}^{n} \left( b^i - r + \sum_{j \neq i} \hat{r}^j \right) = \pi(e) \cdot (b - mr + (m-1)\hat{r}),$$

which gives us (ii).

  (ii) $\Longrightarrow$ (i). Define individual remuneration schemes $\hat{r}^1, \ldots, \hat{r}^m$ by

$$\hat{r}^i = \frac{1}{m} \left[ (m-1)b^i + \hat{r} - \sum_{j \neq i} b^j \right].$$

Then $\sum_{i=1}^{m} \hat{r}^i = \hat{r}$, and

$$b^i - r + \sum_{j \neq i} \hat{r}^j = b^i - r + \frac{1}{m} \sum_{j \neq i} \left[ (m-1)b^j + \hat{r} - \sum_{h \neq j} b^h \right] = \frac{1}{m} b^i - r + \frac{m-1}{m} \hat{r}.$$

It follows now from (ii) that $(\hat{e}, \hat{r})$ maximizes $\pi(e) \cdot \sum_{i=1}^{m} (b^i - r - \sum_{j \neq i} \hat{r}^j)$ over all $e$ and $\hat{r}$ satisfying the incentive compatibility condition, and since the optimal effort $\hat{e}$ is determined only by $\hat{r}$ and does not depend on its distribution among principals, we conclude that $(\hat{e}, \hat{r}^1, \ldots, r^m)$ solves also the problem (21) and hence is an equilibrium. □

We can use the result of Proposition 1 to compare the equilibria in common agency with what would result if the principals were to cooperate fully, acting as a single principal to achieve an efficient outcome $(\bar{e}, \bar{r})$. We first define an aggregate remuneration scheme to be *cost minimizing* at $e$ if it solves the problem

$$\min \pi(e) \cdot r$$

under the constraints $\hspace{4cm} (22)$

$$\pi(e) \cdot v(r) - w(\hat{e}) \geq \pi(e') \cdot v(r) - w(e), \text{ all } e'.$$

Equilibrium remuneration schemes are cost minimizing:

PROPOSITION 2 *Let* $(\hat{e}, \hat{r}^1, \ldots, \hat{r}^m)$ *be an equilibrium. Then* $\hat{r} = \sum_{i=1}^m \hat{r}^i$ *minimizes* $\pi(\hat{e}) \cdot r$ *over all r with*

$$\pi(\hat{e}) \cdot v(r) - w(\hat{e}) \geq \pi(e) \cdot v(r) - w(e), \text{ all } e. \hspace{2cm} (23)$$

PROOF: By Proposition 1, we must have that

$$\pi(\hat{e}) \cdot (b - m\hat{r} + (m-1)\hat{r}) \geq \pi(\hat{e}) \cdot (b - mr + (m-1)r)$$

for all $r$ satisfying the incentive constraint, and this implies that $\pi(\hat{e}) \cdot \hat{r} \leq \pi(\hat{e}) \cdot r$ for all such $r$. □

The proposition may be applied when considering solutions to the incentive problem where principals act cooperatively. For any value $e$ of the agent's effort, we may define $\tilde{r}(e)$ as the cost minimizing remuneration scheme for given $e$ (taking a suitable selection if more than one remuneration scheme is cost minimizing). Since cost minimization involves only aggregate remuneration, it defines also an incentive compatible remuneration scheme in the single-principal problem which emerges when all principals act cooperatively. We then have that $(\hat{e}, \tilde{r}(\hat{e}))$ can be implemented as an equilibrium if $\hat{e}$ maximizes

$$\pi(\hat{e}) \cdot [b - m\tilde{r}(e) + (m-1)\tilde{r}(\hat{e})].$$

In some particular cases, the results above can be used to show that the single-principal optimal contract $(\bar{e}, \bar{r})$ which maximized $\pi(e) \cdot (b - r)$ under the incentive constraint (23), can be implemented as an equilibrium. Implementability in equilibrium of $(\bar{e}, \bar{r})$ requires that $\bar{e}$ maximizes

$$\pi(\bar{e}) \cdot [b - m\tilde{r}(e) + (m-1)\bar{r}].$$

Assuming for example that all cost-minimizing remuneration schemes are identical, we get that $\bar{e}$ must maximize $\pi(e) \cdot (b - \bar{r})$.

Although it is possible to establish a correspondence of this type between single- and multiple-principal problems under specific assumptions, there are other and perhaps more realistic assumptions under which the single-principal solution cannot be implemented in equilibrium in the multiple-principal case. For this we shall use the best response correspondence of the agent,

$$E(r) = \{e \mid \pi(e) \cdot V(r) - K(e) \geq \pi(e') \cdot V(r) - K(e'), \text{ all } e\}.$$

PROPOSITION 3 *Assume that the function $\tilde{e}(\cdot)$ is a selection from $E(\cdot)$ such that $\tilde{e}(\bar{r}) = \bar{e}$, and such that the map $\pi \circ e$ from aggregate remuneration schemes to probability distributions over outcome is differentiable at $\bar{r}$. If $V'(\bar{r}_s) \neq V'(\bar{r}_t)$ for any pair $(s, t)$ of states with $\pi(\bar{e})_s > 0, \pi(\bar{e})_t > 0$, then $(\bar{e}, \bar{r})$ cannot be implemented in any equilibrium.*

PROOF: Suppose to the contrary that $(\bar{e}, \bar{r})$ can be implemented. Then by (ii) of Proposition 1, $\bar{r}$ must maximize

$$\pi(\tilde{e}(r)) \cdot (b - r) + (m - 1)\pi(\tilde{e}(r)) \cdot (\bar{r} - r) \tag{24}$$

over all the aggregate remunerations that may occur at some effort level. Assume that $\pi(\bar{e})_1 > 0, \pi(\bar{e})_2 > 0$ and $V'(\bar{r}_1) \neq V'(\bar{r}_2)$. If at $\bar{r}$ the remunerations in states 1 and 2 are changed slightly while keeping the agent at the indifference surface, we have that

$$\frac{dr_2}{dr_1} = -\frac{\pi(\bar{e})_1}{\pi(\bar{e})_2} \frac{v'(\bar{r}_1)}{v'(\bar{r}_2)}. \tag{25}$$

If $\bar{r}$ maximizes (24), then there must be a neighborhood $U$ of $\bar{r}_1$ such that $\bar{r}_1$ maximizes

$$\pi(\tilde{e}(r^1)) \cdot (b - r^1) + (m - 1)\pi(\tilde{e}(r^1)) \cdot (\bar{r} - r^1) \tag{26}$$

on $U$, where $r^1 = (r_1, r_2(r_1), \bar{r}_3, \ldots, \bar{r}_n)$ and $r_2(r_1)$ is the value of $r_2$ for which $r^1$ remains at the same indifference surface as $\bar{r}$. But then its derivative must be 0 at $\bar{r}_1$. Computing the derivative, we have that

$$\frac{d}{dr_1}\pi(\tilde{e}(r^1)) \cdot (b - r^1) = 0$$

since $\bar{r}$ solves the one-principal problem. For the second part of (26), we get that

$$\frac{d}{dr_1}\left[\pi(\tilde{e}(r^1)) \cdot (\bar{r} - r^1)\right]_{r_1 = \bar{r}_1} = -\pi(\bar{e})_1 + \pi(\bar{e})_2\frac{dr_2}{dr_1}(\bar{r}_2) = -\pi(\bar{e})_1\left[1 - \frac{v'(\bar{r}_1)}{v'(\bar{r}_2)}\right],$$

which is $\neq 0$ since $v'(\bar{r}_1) \neq v'(\bar{r}_2)$, giving a contradiction. We conclude that $(\hat{e}, \hat{r})$ cannot be implemented.                                                                                     $\square$

The result of Proposition 3 shows that with many principals it may be less easy to implement the desired incentives than if there had been only one principal. The intuition behind this shortcoming relates to free-rider problems: each principal takes the contracts of the others as given and may therefore be less willing to remunerate the agent for choosing the right amount of effort.

## 4  Hospital management and objectives

### 4.1  *A model for the choice of quality*

There is a rather voluminous literature pointing to a certain inherent tendency for over-treatment in the sense that more sophisticated, and therefore also more expensive, treatment is chosen instead of basic treatments for which there is a large unsatisfied demand. We take a well-known work of Newhouse [1970a] as our point of departure.

We are considering a model describing behavior of non-profit private organizations (most of the American hospitals belong to this category). It is assumed that such organizations are mainly interested in two aspects of their productive activity, namely the quantity and the quality of output (but, as we see, not the realized surplus however measured). The quantity aspects are important since size, power and prestige are mutually connected. Quality, on its side, matters partly due to the ethical demands for high-quality treatments of patients, partly since such a production will carry prestige in the eyes of the profession and the general public, something which again enhances possibilities of fund-raising, attracts the best professionals, the best research etc. For the hospital manager to find the optimal decision is therefore a question of striking the right balance between quality and quantity, since as always you cannot have both – the hospital must make sure that its activities can be financed by the sources available.

To have a model which allows for some conclusions, we shall accept several rather drastic simplifications; instead of the rather imprecise categories "quantity" and "quality" we shall assume that there is a unique variable $q$ describing the quantity aspects of the activity of the hospital (such as numbers of patients treated, or alternatively number of bed-days), and – what is perhaps worse – that all relevant aspects of quality can be subsumed in a single variable $s$. The assumption may be justified by the fact that $s$ could have been replaced by a vector of quality parameters, what would have seemed more acceptable, and the only change would be that the formal analysis would look slightly more complicated. Also, this simplistic way of representing quality in economic models is rather standard and widely used in models of industrial organization where choice of quality matters, as it does in quite a number of contexts.

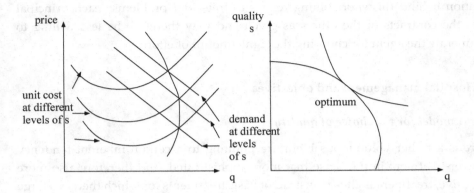

Fig. 3.6    Deriving the feasible boundary in the Newhouse model.

From this point, our model becomes rather standard: The firm faces a demand relationship, here formulated as a function $P(q, s)$, which to each level of production and quality gives the price which makes the costumers buy exactly this amount of the good at this quality. Further, the firm has a cost function $C(q, s)$ of usual form, so that cost depends on quantity as well as on quality.

To see how a model with such ordinary ingredients can turn into a model for over-provision of quality, it is convenient to start with a geometric analysis, based on Fig. 3.6. At each level of the quality variable $s$ one can draw the demand curve $P(q, s)$ as well as the curve of average cost $C(q, s)/q$ (considered as functions of $q$). If we assume that the hospital has a budget constraint which sets a limit to the permissible deficit to be financed by the owners (and for simplicity we may as well assume that this limit is 0) then the choice of $q$ must be determined by the intersection of average cost and demand. Any production level higher than this $q$ will entail deficits, that is it will violate the budget constraint.

We then change $s$ repeatedly and get corresponding values of the optimal choice of quantity $q(s)$. If the graph of this function is drawn in a coordinate system with $q$ and $s$ on the axes, we get a kind of transformation curve between quantity and quality, as it presents itself to the firm. What remains for the hospital manage-ment is to pick the most desired combination of quantity and quality from this transformation curve, and the final choice must reflect the preferences of the hos-pital management with respect to combinations of quantity and quality. These preferences are illustrated by indifference curves in the figure.

Optimum in this model may be expected to be situated at some other point than the one which maximizes the first coordinate, the pure quantity-maximizing choice. In Newhouse [1970a], this is taken as an illustration of the inherent tendency towards over-provision of quality: Less than the maximal possible number of bed-days are produced since management has substituted quality for quantity.

This conclusion is however heavily depending on the assumption that the quality parameter s does not enter, or it enters only with a very small weight in the demand of the consumers (patients). This seems strange, at least compared to standard approaches to consumer demands: independent of initial reasons for introducing new treatments, they tend to be demanded by the general public after a rather short time. The identification of one variable ($q$) with "what people want" and another one ($S$) with whims of management, which are irrelevant for the consumers, takes us to a model of managerial misbehavior which is rather irrelevant in our context. Rather, the Newhouse model should be taken as an indication that decisions about production will differ dependent on the objectives of management, and other decisions would have been made with other objectives.

A classical model of Spence [1975] treats the problem of choice of quality in a rather general setting (the model can be found also in Tirole [1988]). The slightly older Newhouse model should probably be seen in the light of the Spence model, which is briefly recapitulated below.

The starting point is the same as ours, namely the functions $P(q,s)$ and $C(q,s)$. We begin with a consideration of the socially optimal choice; in a partial model of this kind, maximizing social welfare amounts to maximization of the consumer surplus derived from the demand function together with the profit of the producer. Thus, we have to look for the maximum taken over all values of $q$ and $s$ of

$$\int_0^q P(x,s)dx - C(q,s).$$

The first order conditions are

$$P(q,s) - C_q'(q,s) = 0,$$

$$\int_0^q P_s'(x,s)dx - C_s'(q,s) = 0.$$

Next we look at the behavior of a monopolist; here the objective is to maximize

$$qP(q,s) - C(q,s),$$

and the first order conditions for maximum become

$$qP_q'(q,s) + P(q,s) - C_q'(q,s) = 0$$

$$qP_s'(q,s) - C_s'(q,s) = 0.$$

Looking at the second equation in each of the two sets of first order conditions, we obtain that

$$\frac{\int_0^q P_s'(x,s)dx}{q} = \frac{C_s'(q,s)}{q} \text{ respectively } P_s'(q,s) = \frac{C_q'(q,s)}{q},$$

from which it is seen that both right hand sides have the same form; the left hand sides may be interpreted as average willingness to pay for additional quality respectively the marginal costumer's willingness to pay for additional quantity. Thus, it is the marginal costumer that is decisive for the level of quality at monopoly whereas for the social optimum, all the costumers matter[1]

If we now to the two types of objectives studied in the Spence model add the non-profit organization with a managerial utility function $U(q,s)$ we shall have an objective amounting to choosing $q$ and $s$ such that $U(q,s)$ is maximized under the constraint

$$qP(q,s) - C(q,s) = 0$$

(cost should be covered by revenues). To derive first order conditions we introduce the Lagrangian

$$U(q,s) + \lambda(qP(q,s) - C(q,s),$$

and get after taking derivatives, that the conditions for optimal choice in the non-profit organization are

$$U_q'(q,s) = -\lambda(qP_q'(q,s) + P(q,s) - C_q(q,s))$$
$$U_s'(q,s) = -\lambda(qP_s'(q,s) - C_q(q,s)).$$

Rewriting the second equation so that it gets the same form as the previous first order conditions w.r.t. quality, we get

$$P'(q,s) + \frac{U_s'(q,s)}{\lambda q} = \frac{C_s'(q,s)}{q}.$$

Due to the additional member it is not quite as straightforward to interpret this condition as it was in the previous cases. The ratio $U_s'(q,s)/\lambda$ can be interpreted as the marginal rate of substitution between achieving quality and keeping the budget (as always the Lagrange multiplier is the value, measured in terms of the objective function, of a marginal relaxation of the constraint), and this has to be counted as per unit of quantity produced. We can see that also here attention is paid to the marginal costumer rather than to their average when the willingness

---

[1]Strictly speaking this comparison of first order conditions presupposes that the quantity is the same in the two cases, something which would not be the case in our application; the intuition may be useful anyhow.

to pay for additional quality has to be computed. The first order condition may now be read as a condition that taken per unit, the willingness to pay for quality of the marginal costumer together with the willingness to pay of management shall match the cost of additional quality.

This may not be a very clear picture of whether management chooses more or less quality than society wants, but they can be used in the case where the level of production is the same (as mentioned in the footnote, this is not exactly the situation of the Newhouse model); if we know how $C'_s$ varies in $s$ for fixed $q$ then conclusions can be made about the dependence of quality on market structure and organizational form. Clearly, the quality oriented non-profit organization will supply a higher value of $s$ than the monopolist. Whether this level of $s$ even exceeds the socially optimal depends on the amount to which the utility function of the decision maker exaggerates or underplays the judgement of the public as measured by average willingness to pay among the costumers of the firm.

This conclusion – over-provision of quality occurs if the management puts more weight on quality than its costumers – are almost demonstratively self-evident, and one may of course ask whether the analysis was worth the trouble. It should however be added that the model does other things as well, and that it is open for analysis of the consequences of other objectives than the three which were considered above. It may rather easily be extended to cases of under-provision of quality (such as cases where management is confined to maximizing quantity under a budget constraint). The precise conditions derived from the maximization problems may have other useful applications as well.

## 4.2 *Supply from private and public healthcare providers*

With the appearance in the recent years of private hospitals in Denmark we have a situation where the supply of health care of a given type is composed of both a publicly and a privately produced part. This has been a commonplace situation in many other countries, where the co-existence of private and public providers is considered as the normal state of affaris. However, this coexistence gives rise to a certain differentiation in supply, and many of the differences to be observed between behavior in public and private organizations are consequences of adjustment to the different conditions under which the two types of organizations operate.

An analysis of some consequences of the coexistence of the two types of providers was presented in Schweitzer and Rafferty [1976]. In the model there are two types of producers (to be called type I and II in the following); both provide treatment of two different diseases, and they have access to the same technology, as described in Fig. 3.7 by isoquants for production of each treatment. For geometrical

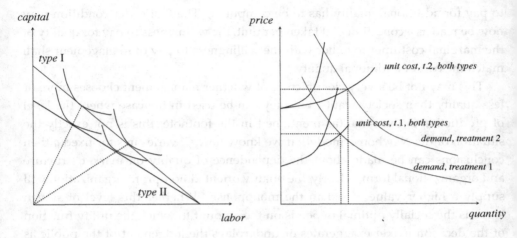

Fig. 3.7  Public and private providers.

reasons we have chosen the standard two-dimensional framework of our analysis, restricting the choice of input to a combination of labor and capital.

The basic difference between the two types of providers is (in the model) to be found in the prices of the factors. One of them, here type I, has access to capital at a lower price than the other. The reason for this may be that type I is a publicly owned hospital which is not subject to the same demands with respect to interest payments on the capital installed as type II assumed to be private. This may be a reasonable assumption, in particular referring to the coexistence of public and private providers as it used to be, but another and alternative interpretation would turn the situation around, letting the private providers be those having easier access to factor markets, whereas the public providers nowadays are subject to budgetary controls and restrictions in the possibilities of acquiring new equipment, so that the shadow prices of capital and/or labor may well be considerably higher than the market prices at which the private providers can buy. Be this as it may, the model will work in any case.

In the isoquant diagram to the left we see that the isocost lines for providers of type I are more steep than those of type II, so that type I providers will choose more capital intensive ways of production than type II, and of course will experience lower unit cost than type II. This in itself is not at all surprising given that type II providers experience higher prices on capital services than does type I. But more importantly, we notice that one of the treatments, here treatment 2, is more labor-intensive and uses less capital than treatment 1 (at all levels of production and all factor prices), which means that the differences in unit costs are much smaller for treatment 2 than for treatment 1. Translated to average cost curves this means that a given level of unit cost is reached at almost the same level of output in treatment 2, while for treatment 1 the output corresponding to any given level of unit cost is markedly greater for type I than for type II.

Adding a demand schedule for each treatment and assuming for simplicity that price equals average cost in equilibrium (both private and public providers are non-profit organizations), we get that the two types will produce more or less the same amount of treatment 2 while treatment 1 will be provided predominantly by type 1.

The result is, as it can be seen from the figure, a tendency towards specialization – providers of type II will be particularly active in the labor-intensive treatment, where the conditions for the two types are almost equal. One may recognize here something here close to the main result in the Heckscher-Ohlin theory of international trade; if we had assumed a fixed assignment of factors and more capital available for type I, then this theory could have been applied directly: The types will specialize in the treatments in which they have a comparative advantage.

Whether this description of the situation fits well with what actually happens when several types of providers coexist, is however debatable. It is evident that the private hospitals in Denmark have conquered a part of the market for smaller surgical operations, but this cannot directly be attributed to any advantageous treatment in the factor markets; what matters in the Danish context is the fact that there is no reimbursement from the state-financed health insurance for treatments in private hospitals whereas treatment in the public sector is fully paid. Consequently, the private providers will have an advantage only in such treatments, where there is rationing in the public system, so that the shadow price generated is higher than the ("true") price to be paid for treatment in the private hospital.

## 4.3 *Productivity in healthcare provision*

The concept of technical efficiency in production is of central importance, but measurement of efficiency is a more recent development. As we have briefly methioned in Chapter 1, Section 3.2, quantitative assessments of efficiency, or rather, lack of efficiency, were considered by Farrell [1957] elaborating on ideas of Debreu [1951]. Since then, a separate field of research has appeared, dealing with the construction and interpretation of indices of technical efficiency. In the following, we give a very brief survey of the field, see also Christensen et al. [1999].

We begin by establishing some terminology:

A *technology* is a subset $L$ of $\mathbb{R}^n_+$ with the following properties:

   (i) $L \subseteq \mathbb{R}^n_+$ is non-empty and closed (relative to $\mathbb{R}^n_+$),

(ii) $L$ is comprehensive level, i.e. $x \in L$ and $\tilde{x} \in \mathbb{R}^n$, $\tilde{x} \le x$ implies $\tilde{x} \in L$.
Here $L$ is interpreted as a set of output vectors $x \in \mathbb{R}_+^n$ that can be produced from a given and fixed input vector. The (output) frontier given $L$ is he set

$$I(L) = \{x \in L \mid \forall \lambda \ge 1, \lambda x \notin L\},$$

and the efficient subset is defined as

$$S(L) = \{x \in L \mid [x' \ge x, x \ne x'] \Rightarrow x' \notin L\}.$$

Finally, for $x \in L$, the dominating set is $D(x, L) = \{x' \in L \mid x' \ge x\}$.

We denote by $\mathcal{L}$ a given set of admissible technologies, and we assume that it contains some particular technologies: A technology $L$ is a Leontief technology if

$$L = \{x \in \mathbb{R}_+^n \mid x \le a\}$$

for some $a \in \mathbb{R}^n$. We write $L = L_a$ if reference to the point $a$ matters.

An *index of technical output efficiency* (in the sequel: an efficiency index) is a function $E : \mathbb{R}_+^n \times \mathcal{L} \to [0, 1]$ from the set of pairs $(x, L)$, where $x \in \mathbb{R}_+^n$ is an output vector, $L \in \mathcal{L}$ a technology, and $x \in L$, to $[0, 1]$.

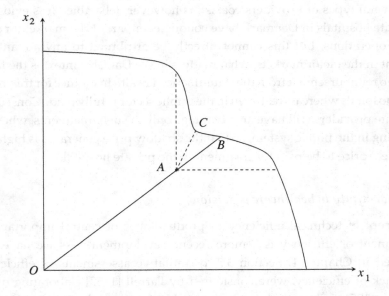

Fig. 3.8  Efficiency indices: The Farrell index value in $A$ is computed as $|OA|/|OB|$, showing how far the point $A$ falls short of reaching the frontier when all outputs must be increased in the same proportion. The Färe-Lovell index finds the shortest distance from $A$ to the frontier allowing for movement in all positive directions.

Here are some examples, among them the one that we know already: The *Farrell index* $E_F$ is given by

$$E_F(x, L) = \inf\{t > 0 \mid t^{-1}x \in L\}$$

for $x \in L$. The Farrell index is radial in the sense that it compares an output combination with the vector obtained by intersecting the ray from the origin to the output combination with the frontier, cf. Fig. 3.8. Thus, $E_F(x, L) = 1$ if and only if $x$ belongs to the frontier $I(L)$, and since $S(L)$ may be a proper subset of $I(L)$, there can be inefficient points $x$ with Farrell efficiency 1.

The *Färe–Lovell index* is defined by

$$E_{FL}(x, L) = \min\left\{\frac{1}{n}\sum_{i=1}^{n} v_i \,\middle|\, (v_1^{-1}x_1, ..., v_n^{-1}x_n) \in L, \ 0 < v_i \leq 1, \ i = 1, ..., n\right\}.$$

when $x \in L$, $x_h > 0$, all $h$. For $x$ not in the interior of $\mathbb{R}^n_+$, let $S(x) = \{h \mid x_h > 0\}$ be the non-zero coordinates of $x$, and define the Färe-Lovell index as

$$E_{FL}(x, L) = \min\left\{\frac{1}{|S(x)|}\sum_{i \in S(x)} v_i \,\middle|\, (v_1^{-1}x_1, ..., v_n^{-1}x_n) \in L, \ 0 < v_i \leq 1, i = 1, ..., n\right\}.$$

In the case where $v_i = t$ for all $i$, the Färe–Lovell and the Farrell indices coincide, but they may differ for example if there are inefficient points on the isoquant. Instead of comparing a vector in the output set to the "best" vector on the ray through the origin (which, as we saw above, may itself be inefficient), the Färe–Lovell index compares the vector to a particular efficient vector in $D(x, L)$. To perform this comparison, the coordinates of the given vector may have to be reduced in different proportions, making the Färe-Lovell index non-radial.

The Zieschang index $E_Z(x, L)$ is computed by taking first the Farrell index, and then multiplying by $E_{FL}(z, L)$, where $z$ is the vector $tx$ with $t = E_F(x, L)$, i.e.

$$E_Z(x, L) = E_F(x, L)E_{FL}(E_F(x, L), L).$$

Thus, the fact that non-efficient output combinations may get the value 1 by the Farrell index is resolved by the subsequent application of the Färe-Lovell index.

*An axiomatic approach to efficiency indices.* Below we consider a list of axioms, each of which states a property of an abstract output efficiency index, starting with axioms which are as intuitive and uncontroversial as possible, in order to establish what could be considered as a common foundation for efficiency indices. Our first two axioms are the most easily acceptable.

AXIOM 1 (Dominance) *If $L_1, L_2 \in \mathcal{L}$ and $x \in L_1 \cap L_2$ are such that $D(x, L_1) = D(x, L_2)$, then $E(x, L_1) = E(x, L_2)$.*

The dominance axiom asserts that the assessment of output efficiency depends only on the set of dominating output combinations. This seems reasonable enough taken isolated. If domination is violated, then efficiency of an output combination depends upon what could be achieved if some additional amounts of an input commodity were made available. Even if such considerations might be relevant in some situations, it would take us outside the field of output efficiency indices in their usual interpretation.

The next axiom states that the simple operations of changing labels of output commodities or changing their units of measurement should not have any influence on the degree of efficiency of a given output combination.

AXIOM 2 (Commensurability *Let $A \in \mathcal{A}$ be an $(n \times n)$ matrix corresponding to a change of units or a permutation of commodity labels (or both). Then for all $x \in \mathbb{R}^n_+$ and $L \in \mathcal{L}$:*

$$E(x, L) = E(Ax, AL).$$

The axiom combines the two properties of symmetry and scale invariance. The index of technical efficiency should not depend on the numbering (or the "labels") of the commodities, nor should it be possible to change the index just by changing units of these commodities. This axiom can hardly be contested.

The following axioms are more open to debate than the previous two. We shall need a monotonicity axiom which specifies the consequences of varying either the technology with given output or the output with given technology.

AXIOM 3 (Weak monotonicity in technology) *If $L_1, L_2 \in \mathcal{L}$, $L_1 \subset L_2$ and $x \in L_1 \cap L_2$ then*

$$E(x, L_2) \leq E(x, L_1)$$

*with strict inequality if $L_1$ is contained in the interior of $L_2$.*

If $L_2$ is larger than $L_1$, meaning that the technology $L_2$ gives more possibilities of producing the given output than does $L_1$, then the efficiency of the given output combination cannot be larger at the big technology set than at the small one.

To see that the axiom is not beyond dispute, consider the following example: Let $n = 2$ and let $L_1 = L_{(2,1)} \cup L_{(1,2)}$, that is the union of two Leontief technologies. For $x = (3, 3)$, the Zieschang index is

$$E_Z((3,3), L_1) = E_F((3,3), L_1)E_{FL}((2,2), L_1) = \frac{2}{3} \cdot \frac{3}{4} = \frac{1}{2}.$$

Now let $C$ be a convex cone containing $\mathbb{R}^2_+$ in its interior, and let

$$L_2 = [(\{(2,1)\} - C) \cup (\{(1,2)\} - C)] \cap \mathbb{R}^n_+.$$

Clearly, $L_1 \subset L_2$, but $L_2$ has no boundary segments parallel to the axes, so

$$E_Z((3,3), L_2) = E_F((3,3), L_2),$$

and for $C$ sufficiently close to $\mathbb{R}^2_+$ we get that $E_Z((3,3), L_2) \geq E_Z((3,3), L_1)$ violating weak monotonicity in technology.

The advantage of having a property such as monotonicity in technology is that it allows us to restrict attention to a smaller and more tractable set of technologies. The family of Leontief technologies rather suggests itself in this context.

AXIOM 4 *(Finite union property) Let $L_{c_1}, \ldots, L_{c_r}$ be Leontief technologies, and let $x \in L_{c_i}$, $i = 1, \ldots, r$. If for all $i$, $E(x, L_{c_i}) = \lambda$, then $E(x, \cup_{i=1}^r L_{c_i}) = \lambda$.*

We may think of the finite union as arising when a firm has access to several production processes (of the Leontief type) but must use only one of them. If an output combination is equally efficient in each of the processes, it seems reasonable to define its degree of efficiency in the overall technology as this common degree of efficiency in each of its constituent processes.

Examples of efficiency indices which do not satisfy Axiom 4 are easily constructed: Let $\mu^k$ be Lebesgue measure in $\mathbb{R}^k$, and define the Lebesgue efficiency index by

$$E_{Leb}(x, L) = 1 - \frac{\mu^{|S(x)|}(D(x, L) \cap [0, x])}{\mu^{|S(x)|}([0, x])}.$$

It is fairly obvious that $E_{Leb}$ does not satisfy Axiom 4.

The fifth axiom to be considered is a weak continuity property:

AXIOM 5 (Diagonal continuity) *For each $k$, the index $E(x, L_{e_k})$ is a continuous function of $x$ when restricted to the ray through $e_k$.*

This axiom together with Axiom 2 tells us that $E(\lambda e_k, L_{e_k})$ is a continuous function of $\lambda$ for $\lambda \geq 1$ (recall that $e_k$ is the diagonal unit vector in the $k$-dimensional face of $\mathbb{R}^n_+$. The reason that we assume continuity in $x$ only for particular Leontief technologies and restrict the domain considered to the diagonal is that some of the indices in the literature display discontinuities. Therefore, we use as little continuity as possible, and Axiom 5 is sufficient for our purposes.

The axioms introduced above are satisfied by the Farrell and the Färe-Lovell indices, so they are not contradictory. Actually, there are rather many efficiency indices which satisfy the axioms, and this is indeed one of the points in our approach, since we look for the general functional form of an efficiency index.

Let $f : [0,1]^n \to [0,1]$ be a function which is

(a) strictly increasing: $z, z' \in [0,1]^n$, $z_h \geq z'_h$, $z \neq z'$ implies $f(z) \leq f(z')$, and $z < z'$ implies $f(z) < f(z')$,

(b) symmetric: $f(Az) = f(z)$ for all $(n \times n)$ permutation matrices $A$.

(c) continuous on the diagonal $\{z \in [0,1]^n \mid z_1 = \cdots = z_n\}$.

A function with these properties will be called an $n$-dimensional *performance evaluation*. We may think of $f(z)$ as an efficiency index for the Leontief technology $L_{(1,\ldots,1)}$, a measure of the nearness of an output combination $z \in [0,1]^n$ to the output combination $(1,1,\ldots,1)$. In particular, if $(1,1,\ldots,1) \in L$ and $z \in S(L)$, then $f(z)$ is a measure of lack of efficiency of $z$.

Given a performance evaluation $f$, we may define an associated efficiency index $E^f$ for output combinations in the interior of $\mathbb{R}^n_+$ by

$$E^f(x, L) = \inf\{f(z) \mid (z_1^{-1}x_1, \ldots, z_n^{-1}x_n) \in L, 0 < z_1 \leq 1, i = 1, \ldots, n\}. \tag{27}$$

To extend the definition to outputs in all of $\mathbb{R}^n_+$, we need $k$-dimensional performance evaluations $f^k$ for each $k = 1, \ldots, n$, and for $F = (f^k)_{k=1}^n$, we have an efficiency index $E^F$ given by

$$E^F(x, L) = E^{f^k}(x, L)$$

where $k = |S(x)|$.

Now we are ready for the first main result of this section:

PROPOSITION 4  *If $F = (f^k)_{k=1}^n$ is a family of performance evaluations, then $E^F$ satisfies the Axioms 1 – 5. Conversely, if an efficiency index $E$ satisfies Axioms 1 – 5, then $E = E^F$ for some family of performance evaluations.*

PROOF: It is clear from the definition of $E^F$ that it satisfies Axioms 1 and 2. To prove Axiom 3, let $x^*$ be a point in $D(x, L_1)$ such that $E^F(x, L_1) = f^k(x^*)$. If $L_1 \subset L_2$, then $D(x, L_1) \subset D(x, L_2)$, whence $E^F(x, L_1) \geq E^F(x, L_2)$. If $L_1 \subset \text{int} L_2$, then $D(x, L_2)$ contains points smaller in all coordinates than the point

$$\left( \frac{x_1^*}{x_1}, \ldots, \frac{x_k^*}{x_k} \right),$$

and by strong monotonicity of $f^k$, we have $E(x, L_2) < E(x, L_1)$.

If $L_{c_i}$ for $i = 1, \ldots, r$ are Leontief technologies with $E(x, L_{c_i}) = \lambda$, all $i$, then $f(z) = \lambda$ for each point $z = (x_1'/x_1, \ldots, x_k'/x_k)$ with $x' \in D(x, L_{c_i})$ and minimizing $f$. In particular, the minimal value of $f$ on points $z = (x_1'/x_1, \ldots, x_k'/x_k)$ with $x' \in D(x, \cup_{i=1}^r L_{c_i})$ must also be $\lambda$, and we have that Axiom 4 is satisfied. Finally, Axiom 5 follows directly from the continuity properties assumed on the performance evaluations $f^k$.

To prove the converse, let $E$ be an efficiency index satisfying the Axioms $1 - 4$. Choose $L \in \mathcal{L}$ and $x \in L$ arbitrarily, and let $\mathbb{R}_{++}^S$ be the face of $\mathbb{R}_{++}^n$ containing $x$; renumbering if necessary and applying Axiom 2, we may assume that $S = \{1, \ldots, k\}$. Also, and by the same argument, we may assume that $x = e_S$, the vector with $x_h = 1$ for $h \le k$, $x_h = 0$ otherwise.

Define the mapping $f^k : [0, 1]^k \to [0, 1]$ by

$$f^k(z) = E(x, L_z), \; z \in [0, 1]^k \subset \mathbb{R}_+^S$$

where $L_z$ is the Leontief technology $L_z = \{z\} + \mathbb{R}_+^n$. Then $f^k$ is symmetric by Axiom 2, and $f^k$ is strictly increasing by Axiom 3.

Let $\lambda = \min\{f^k(z)|z \in D(x, L)\}$, and suppose that the minimum is attained at some $z^* \in D(x, L)$. By the monotonicity Axiom 3, we have $E(x, L) \le E(x, L_{z^*}) = \lambda$. To finish the proof, we must show that $E(x, L) \ge \lambda$. For this, we let $\varepsilon > 0$. Using Axiom 5, we choose a family $(z_i)_{i=1}^r$ of points in $[0, 1]^k$ with $E(x, L_{z_i}) = \lambda - \varepsilon$ and such that

$$(D(x, L) + \mathbb{R}_+^n) \subset L_{z_1} \cup \cdots \cup L_{z_r}$$

(this is possible since the set $\{z \in [0, 1]^k | f^k(z) \ge \lambda - \varepsilon\} + \mathbb{R}_+^n$ may be approximated arbitrarily close by finite families of Leontief technologies). We get by Axioms 3 and 4 that

$$E(x, L) \ge \lambda - \varepsilon,$$

and since $\varepsilon > 0$ was arbitrary, we obtain that $E(x, L) = \lambda$ as desired. $\square$

This theorem tells us that efficiency indices satisfying Axioms 1-5 have a common functional form, since the value of the index is found my minimizing a suitable function on the dominating set. It is rather straightforward that both the Farrell index and the Färe-Lovell index have this form.

We should comment briefly on what the theorem does not tell us: It does not endow the inherent performance evaluations $f^k$ with any structure apart from monotonicity, symmetry, and continuity on the diagonal. In order to proceed from the general characterization given in Proposition 4 to specific functional forms, further properties must be assumed.

## 5 The market for pharmaceutical drugs

The market for drugs, whether prescribed by the doctor or sold over the counter, is a richfield of study for the economist, since it displays a variety of pathologies in the sense that the economic functioning of this market differs widely from that of standard markets, and attempts at regulation often fall short of achieving their goals, while giving rise to side effects that are often unexpected.

**Box 3.2 The Malmquist index.** In order to measure how the efficiency indices are affected when the technology is subject to changes over time, one makes use of the Malmquist index (Malmquist [1953]). Suppose that the technology is $L_0$ at $t = 0$ and $L_1$ at $t = 1$. If the output combination $x_0 \in L_0$ has efficiency score $E(x_0, L_0)$ at $t = 0$, and the output combination $x_1$ at $t = 1$similarly has obtained a score of $E(x_1, L_1)$, then these scores convey information about the situations with given technologies but do not immediately tell something the degree of technological progress experienced.

One may measure a *catch-up effect* by

$$\frac{E(x_1, L_1)}{E(x_0, L_0)}$$

showing how the static efficiency has moved with the shift in technology, and to obtain a numerical assessment of technological change one needs to look at efficiency of a given output combination when technology changes, that is

$$\frac{E(x_0, L_0)}{E(x_0, L_1)} \text{ or } \frac{E(x_1, L_0)}{E(x_1, L_1)},$$

which is based on either one of the output combinations; a compromise is attained using a geometric average

$$\sqrt{\frac{E(x_0, L_0)}{E(x_0, L_1)} \frac{E(x_1, L_0)}{E(x_1, L_1)}},$$

which may be considered as a measure of the *frontier shift*. Now we obtain the Malmquist index as the product of catch-up effect and frontier shift

$$M(x_0, x_1, L_0, L_1) = \frac{E(x_1, L_1)}{E(x_0, L_0)} \cdot \sqrt{\frac{E(x_0, L_0)}{E(x_0, L_1)} \frac{E(x_1, L_0)}{E(x_1, L_1)}} = \sqrt{\frac{E(x_1, L_0)}{E(x_0, L_0)} \frac{E(x_1, L_1)}{E(x_0, L_1)}}.$$

For practical uses, the frontiers have to be estimated, and this is usually done using DEA (cf. 1.3.2). Below is an example of a calculation, performed for 20 hospitals in Oman and related to the period 1999-2000 (see Ramanathan [2005]). Output categories were outpatient visits, inpatient services and surgical operations. We show the results for the first five hospitals.

| Hospital no. | Catch-up | Frontier shift | Malmquist index |
|:---:|:---:|:---:|:---:|
| 1 | 0.939 | 1.050 | 0.985 |
| 2 | 1.010 | 1.272 | 1.285 |
| 3 | 1.000 | 0.656 | 0.656 |
| 4 | 1.000 | 1.038 | 1.038 |
| 5 | 0.998 | 1.022 | 1.020 |

It is seen that decline in productivity according to the Malmquist index may occur when efficiency in the given technology has deteriorated although technical changes have moved in the opposite direction.

Already from the most casual observation, one must expect deviation from textbook models of markets. We are dealing with markets where the consumers do not choose the commodities themselves, since this is done by their doctors, and they do not pay for them, at least not fully, as the healthcare system steps in with partial or total reimbursement of the outlays. On the other side of the market, we have the pharmaceutical industry, consisting of "big pharma" with operating under patent protection, together with a wide variety of generic producers supplying the drugs which are no longer protected by patents. Producers sell to wholesalers and they further sell to pharmacies, and all the way downstream there are tendencies towards monopolistic behavior as well as government regulation with the aim of keeping prices low. The sector is subject to a slow process of liberalization, and new types of regulation are developing continuously. To make matters more complicated, the methods of regulation differ among countries.

## 5.1 *The use of patents*

The problem of finding the right economic incentives for the promotion of new inventions has received particular attention in the later decades. In particular, the patent system, which creates distortion of the free markets to protect the innovator against competitors, needs some theoretical foundation. The following simple model, taken from Wright [1983], can be used to present some basic arguments for the use of patents.

We consider a world where research is carried out by small independent firms. Each firm carries out one (small) unit of research, and the amount of research carried out with $m$ active firms is therefore $m$. The researchers may have different cost for carrying out their projects, and assuming that the firms with lower cost will be active before those with higher cost, we obtain an aggregate cost function $c(m)$ which is increasing in $m$.

The probability that the invention will come through, so that at least one out of the $m$ projects is successful, is denoted $P(m)$. If this happens, society obtains a benefit $v$, so that the expected value of a research activity of size $m$ is $vP(m)$.

From the point of view of society, the optimal level of research activity $m_0$ is found where expected marginal social benefits equals marginal cost,

$$vP'(m_0) = c'(m_0).$$

We now consider some alternative ways of organizing research in society.

*Research contracts.* In order to achieve the social optimum, research firms may be offered a fixed amount $w = vP'(m_0)$ if they deliver their unit of research. The

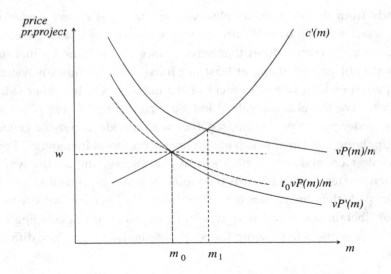

Fig. 3.9   Optimal volume of research: From the point of society, marginal cost of research should equal marginal benefits, resulting in $m_0$. If financed by patents, only the succesful project is remunerated, and the equilibrium choice is $m_1$. Social optimum may then be recovered by suitable taxation.

researchers will then turn active as long as this payment exceeds their individual cost, meaning that exactly $m_0$ researchers will be active. This arrangement seems quite straightforward and effectively implements the optimal research level, so that at this point it would be the best possible, at least in our very simple setup. However, as we shall see below, things are not that simple.

*Patents or prizes.* Suppose that instead of paying each researcher, only the projects which result in an invention are awarded, getting the value of the succesful invention. In this case each project can be considered as a ticket to the award lottery, with expected return $\frac{1}{m}vP(m)$. Firm $i$ will then equate marginal cost to this expected return,

$$c'(m) = \frac{1}{m}vP(m).$$

Assuming that $P'(m)$ is decreasing (the probability of success increases with the number of projects but clearly not in a linear way), we have that $P(m)/m$ is greater than $P'(m)$, and with increasing marginal cost we get that too many resources are allocated to research, see Fig. 3.9.

In our simple setup, where no distinction is made between patents and prizes (the latter being equal to the discounted gains from the patent), we see that both result in suboptimal allocation, a version of the tragedy of the commons, since each firm neglects its effect on total cost (subjective cost is smaller than true cost, so

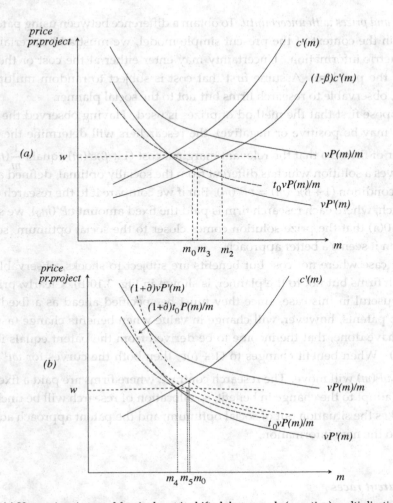

Fig. 3.10  (a) Uncertainty in cost: Marginal cost is shifted downwards (negative) multiplicative shock, so that the new optimum is $m_0$. Under research contracts, optimum is $m_2$, whereas the prize method yields a research of size $m_3$ closer to optimum. (b) Uncertainty in benefit: When benefit is subject to a positive multiplicative shock, the baseline research level $m_0$ remains unchanged under research contracts (and prizes), but social optimum changes to $m_5$. The patent approach allows equilibrium research production to adapt to the situation, attaining the level $m_4$.

that too many firms enter). This can be remedied by reducing the payment offered through patent or prize by a fraction $t_0$ so as to achieve

$$c'(m_0) = \frac{1}{m}(t_0 v)P(m_0).$$

In the case of a patent, such a reduction is achieved by shortening the duration of the patent.

*Patents and prizes with uncertainty.* To obtain a difference between using patents and prizes in the context of the present simple model, we must add uncertainty and asymmetric information. Uncertainty may enter either at the cost or the benefit side of the problem. Assume first that cost is subject to random multiplicative shocks, observable to research firms but not to the social planner.

Suppose first that the method of prizes is used. Having observed the shock $\beta$ (which may be positive or negative), the researchers will determine the optimal number of firms so that the relevant marginal cost $(1 + \beta)c'(m)$ equals $\frac{1}{m}(t_0 v)P(m)$. This gives a solution which is different from the socially optimal, defined as above by the condition $(1 + \beta)c'(m) = vP'(m)$. But if we compare it to the research contract approach, where each research firm is paid the fixed amount $vP'(m_0)$, we see from Fig. 3.10(a) that the prize solution comes closer to the social optimum, so in this situation it seems a better approach.

The case where not cost but benefits are subject to shocks, observable to the research firms but not to the planner, is shown in Fig. 3.10(b). Clearly, prizes will not be useful in this case, since they must be specified ahead as a fixed sum of money; patents, however, will change in value when benefits change (assuming, as we have done, that the income to be derived from the patent equals its social benefit). When benefit changes to $(1 + \delta)v$, then both the curves for $wP'(m)$ and for $\frac{1}{m}t_0 vP(m)$ will move. The research contract, where firms are paid a fixed price, cannot adopt to the change in benefit, so allocation of research will be unchanged. This takes the situation out of social optimum, and the patent approach adapts far better to the new information.

## 5.2   Patent races

One of the principal distinctions between research contracts and patents (or prizes) is that under the first arrangement all researchers receive payment, whereas patent is obtained only by a single successful research firm. The firm which takes out the patent has a guaranteed monopoly over a certain number of years (we return to this patent period below), and in this monopoly period it can secure that development cost is covered together with an additional profit. The less successful contestants will get nothing, so that their research outlays on this project remains uncovered. Since it is quite customary that several firms are engaged in largely similar research projects, where at most one of them will even obtain patent rights, there will in many cases be much at stake for the firms.

This phenomenon, several research firms competing to obtain a single patent, occurs not only in the pharmaceutical industry but is quite widespread, and indeed may be considered to be a fundamental aspect of the patent system: it encourages the competing researchers to put more effort into their activity.

Returning to our situation of several firms engaged in research pointing towards the same patent, this may be characterized as a *patent race*, which may be modeled as follows:

Assume that $n$ firms are doing research which aims at obtaining a patent. The probability of obtaining the patent depends on the effort that the firms choose to invest in the project. In our model we describe this effort by the amount of money used $r_i$, $i = 1, \ldots, n$. If firm $i$ obtains the patent, the income derived from the latter is $W$, giving a net income of $W - r_i$. If it does not obtain the patent, net income is $-r_i$, and in the case where several firms reach the patent stage simultaneously, they share the patent income. As usually, the reward $W$ is taken as the discounted present value of future incomes to be derived from sales of the patented drug.

The way in which effort matters in our model is through the time $T(r)$ to a finished invention, where $T$ is decreasing in the variable $r$ denoting research outlays. Clearly, the use of a simple functional relationship between intervention and money devoted to it is simplistic, neglecting efficiency considerations in the research activity. On the other hand, since we at present are interested in the competition between research firms, we refrain from introducing further complications in the model.

We have now formulated the patent race as a game, where strategies are research outlays in the firms, and outcome is a patent assignment $I(r_1, \ldots, r_n)$ defined as

$$I(r_1, \ldots, r_n) = \begin{cases} \{i \mid T(r_i) \leq T(r_j), \ j = 1, \ldots, n\} & \text{if } r_i > 0 \text{ for some } i, \\ \emptyset & \text{otherwise,} \end{cases}$$

from which the payoff of firm $i$ is found as

$$\pi_i(r_1, \ldots, r_n) = \begin{cases} \dfrac{W}{|I(r_1, \ldots, r_n)|} - r_i & \text{if } i \in I(r_1, \ldots, r_n) \\ -r_i & \text{otherwise.} \end{cases}$$

We are interested in Nash equilibrium strategies in this game, that is research outlays in the firms at which no firm can obtain a better result by any change. At a first sight, this does not seem to be a fruitful approach, since for any $(r_1, \ldots, r_n)$ there will be some firm which could benefit from changing its strategy. Indeed, if it does not get the patent, outlays should be at most 0 if optimal, meaning that only winning firms use money on research, and then clearly they all use the same amount. However, if there is more than one winning firm, any one of them could improve by a slight change of $r$, and if there is only one winning, this firm should decrease its outlay to the actual size.

What this argumentation tells us is that the game has no Nash equilibrium in *pure strategies*. It does, however, possess equilibria when we allow for *mixed strategies*. Since the game is symmetric, we look for symmetric equilibria, where all choose the same probability distribution function $F$ over research outlays. It is obvious that the probability of choosing research outlays $r$ greater than $W$ must be 0. If firm 1 chooses research outlays $r$ in the interval $[0, W]$, the expected net income is

$$W \cdot \text{Prob}\{r_2 \le r, \ldots, r_n \le r\} - r = WF(r)^{n-1} - r.$$

Assuming that the support of $F$ is all of $[0, W]$, we may exploit that the expected value at any pure strategy should be the same, and since $r_1$ can be chosen arbitrarily small, this value must be 0. We can then solve for $F(r)$ to get

$$F(r) = \left(\frac{r}{W}\right)^{\frac{1}{n-1}}$$

for $r \in [0, W]$ and $F(r) = 1$ for $r \ge W$.

The fact that there are only equilibria in mixed strategies is not surprising given the structure of the conflict (technically it has to do with the nature of the payoff which is discontinuous in research effort), and we may also be confident that actual behaviour of pharmaceutical research firms are in line with this finding (in the sense that their decisions to engage in any given research project cannot be anticipated with certainty). It may be worth noticing that the patent race gives rise to *excessive use of research outlays:* In the equilibrium, the average outlay is

$$\mathsf{E}r = \int_0^W r\,dF(r) = \frac{1}{n-1} \int_0^W \left(\frac{r}{W}\right)^{\frac{1}{n-1}} \, dr = \frac{W}{n},$$

so that the total expected research outlays equals the value of the patent. This in itself does not provide an assessment of social losses, since the value of the patent may not correspond to its value to society, and in addition, the incentive problem has not been addressed properly in the model, but it does point to an objection against the patent system, namely its inherent tendency towards duplication of effort.

The model considered here is obviously only a first step in understanding patent races. For a more detailed treatment, see the survey in Reinganum [1989].

## 5.3   *Market size and research*

While in many contexts, innovation and the investment in research is taken as given, it appears as plausible that investment should be related to the market in which the new drugs are to be sold, so that research is directed towards products with large market share or profitability. A much discussed example of the direction of research towards profitable markets is that of cosmetic products which are given preferential treatment in the research portfolio as against development of vaccination drugs which combat the great killers, malaria or tuberculosis. Although the number of potential users of the latter type of drugs is very large, expected profitability is low since the medical industry will be subject to severe price controls, something which will not happen for cosmetic medicin.

A model which explicitly involves the market size in the research activity was developed in Acemoglu and Linn [2003]. We have here a large set $I$ of individuals, who at $t = 0, 1, \ldots$ consume two types of goods. The first type is a basic good which can be consumed directly or used as input in the production of the other goods. These other goods take the form of medical drugs of $J$ different types. Each individual consumes at most one type of drug, so that $I$ can be partitioned in $J$ sets $G_j$ with individual $i \in G_j$ consuming drugs of type $j$. The utility functions of individuals $i \in G_j$ are specified as

$$\sum_{t=0}^{\infty} \left[ c_i(t)^{1-\gamma} (q_j(t) x_{ji}(t))^{\gamma} \right] (1 + r)^{-t}$$

where $r$ is the subjective discount rate, $c_i(t)$ the consumption of the basic good at time $t$, $x_{ji}(t)$ the consumption of drug $j$ at $t$, and $q_j(t)$ a variable expressing the quality of the drug $j$ at $t$. Finally, $0 < \gamma < 1$ is a constant.

We choose the basic good as numeraire at each $t$, so that the price $p_j(t)$ of drug $j$ at time $t$ is expressed in terms of units of the basic good at $t$. The individual $i$ has a given endowment $y_i(t)$ of the basic good in each period, and the demand at date $t$ can be found as

$$x_{ji}(t) = \gamma \frac{y_i(t)}{p_j(t)}$$

for $j$ such that $i \in G_j$, and $x_{ji}(t) = 0$ otherwise (the time $t$ utility is Cobb-Douglas, so the demand has a simple functional form).

Looking at the drug of type $j$, we assume that at each $t$ there is a best-practice technology for its production, and the firm using this technology can produce one unit of drug with quality $q_j(t)$ using one unit of the basic good. The technological progress takes the form of quality improvements, an innovation in the type $j$ drug means that it can now be produced in quality $\lambda q_j(t)$ with $\lambda > 1$. We postpone for the moment a description of the technology behind innovations.

In the market for pharmaceutical drugs at time $t$, there is a firm selling the highest-quality drug of type $j$. We assume that this market leader chooses its price

$p_j(t)$ such that the producers with output of lower quality cannot sell with positive profits. To find this price, we first notice that consumer $i$ buying drug $j$ obtains a utility at time $t$ which is

$$[(1 - \gamma)y_i(t)]^{1-\gamma} \left[\frac{y_i(t)}{p_j(t)}\right]^{\gamma} = (1 - \gamma)^{1-\gamma} \left[\frac{\gamma}{p_j(t)}\right]^{\gamma} y_i(t).$$

Buying instead with the next-best producer of type $j$, who sells drugs of quality $q_j(t)/\lambda$ and charges a price equal to marginal cost, which is 1, so that no positive profit is earned, then utility would be

$$(1 - \gamma)^{1-\gamma} \left[\frac{\gamma}{\lambda}\right]^{\gamma} y_i(t).$$

It follows that the limit price which makes it unprofitable for competitors to enter the market is

$$p_j(t) = \lambda.$$

Profits of the high-quality producer are then

$$\pi_j(q_j(t)) = (\lambda - 1)\gamma Y_j(t),$$

where $Y_j(t)$ is aggregate income of the consumers in the segment $G_j$ at time $t$.

Now we turn to the research activities. We assume that innovation in the production of type $j$ follows a Poisson process with intensity $\delta_j z_j(t)$, where $z_j(t)$ is the amount of the consumption good used on research. The units of time is taken so short that at most one event can happen in the interval between every $t$ and $t + 1$. If $V_j(t, q_j(t))$ denotes the value of the top-quality firm at $t$ when quality is $q_j(t)$, then using one unit of the consumption good any individual firm can obtain an expected value of $\delta_j V_j(t, q_j(t))$, and assuming free entry into research, we get that if $z_j(t) > 0$, then

$$V_j(t, q_j(t)) = \frac{1}{\delta_j}, \tag{28}$$

in particular, $V_j(t, q_j(t))$ is constant over time. Also, the firm value must satisfy the following equality,

$$rV_j(t, q_j(t)) = \pi_j(\delta_j(t)) - \delta_j z_j(t) V_j(t, q_j(t)), \tag{29}$$

saying that the value must be such that the capital gain of having a firm in any period equals the profits derived from its operation adjusted for the expected loss due to emergence of a new competitor with a higher level of quality.

For the full specification of the equilibrium path, we should also add a balancing condition

$$\sum_{i \in I} c_i(t) + \sum_{j \in J} z_j(t) = \sum_{i \in I} y_i(t).$$

The more interesting part of the equilibrium allocation is the determination of $z_j(t)$, which, if nonzero, is determined by (28) and (29) as

$$z_j(t) = (\lambda - 1)\gamma Y_j(t) - \frac{r}{\delta_j}.$$

As it can be seen, the research activity is largely determined by the market size. If a particular type of drug has a small market, an increased market share of the same drug would entail that also the research activity in this field would be larger.

As is often the case, the conclusions of a model may seem little surprising, but here as in other situations, the confirmation of what would otherwise be intuition or hunches, by a formal model which uses as simple a setup and as few assumptions as possible, gives confidence in this particular way of visualizing what goes on in the sector.

---

**Box 3.3 Orphan drugs.** The long development period of a drug and the high cost of bringing it to the market is taken into account by the regulating authorities at least in some of its aspects. The development procedure as sketched above certainly presupposes that in the end there will be sufficient sales to recover the cost and secure a profit to the developer, and this may not be the case if the drug is intended for an illness which is not widespread. Among such illnesses there are several which attract much public attention, and for which there may even be a public demand for action, even though the number of patients is small. Many of these are well described in the medical literature, such as cystic fibrosis, hemophilia, Huntington's chorea, and severe acute respiratory syndrome (SARS). They qualify as "rare diseases" under the current European definition, which demands under one affected person per 2000 citizens.

To encourage the development of orphan drugs, several countries have taken specific action, starting with the Orphan Drug Act passed in the USA in 1983. This act offers several benefits to developing firms, including quick review by the administration, short approval time, tax credits, and 7 years of market exclusivity for orphan indications. The act has been reasonably successful in the sense that quite a number of orphan designations have been accepted (meaning that the drug in question qualifies as orphan drug and receives the according treatment) and some 250 new drugs have been developed. Other countries have followed the US, with a European Orphan Drug Regulation being approved in 1999.

## 5.4 *The life cycle of a drug*

In the considerations above, we have treated research and innovation as an activity leading to a patent which then secures a monopoly position in the market for the new product over a considerable span of time. The reality of medical innovation does not quite take this form, or rather, research and innovation is a lengty process rather than a one-shot event, by which the new medicin comes around momentarily. Actually, the process of introducing a new medical drug is time and resource consuming, as indicated in Fig. 3.11. The research process is usually at a very early stage at the time when the patent is taken out – if the innovator waits too long, other firms may take out a patent which stops the whole project.

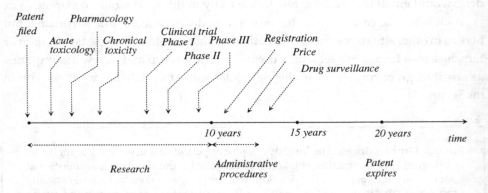

Fig. 3.11  The life cycle of a drug. cf. Moors and Faber [2007]. Research must be carried on well into the patent period, followed by clinical trials, so that in most cases a rather modest part of the 20 year patent period remains when sales have started.

Once the medicin has taken its final form – and many projects are never carried so far – it can be subjected to the *clinical trials,* which follow specific rules and which are mandatory for the marketing permit. The trials are divided into four types: in Type I trials the new medicin tested for possible toxic effects on the patient, and Type II trials checks whether the drug works in accordance with its what it was designed to achieve; both of these tests can be carried out in laboratory conditions. Then Type III trials tests the drug on real patients in sufficient number so as to obtain statistically valid results on the effects of the drug. Only now the innovator can apply for marketing permit; Type IV trials test the drug when it is actually marketed. It goes without saying that the new drug can fail at any point during the procedure. There are several spectacular cases of drugs which have been withdrawn from the market at the very start since unexpected side effects were revealed late in the test or even after marketing had started.

**Box 3.4 Follow-on drugs.** A "follow-on" or "me-too" drug differs only slightly from another one already approved for marketing. It belongs to the same therapeutic class but has with a slightly different active component, and it competes in the market for the same customer segment. The number of instances where a follow-on drug appears has increased in recent years, and more importantly, the time between approval of first drug and appearance of the first follow-on drug had decreased. An investigation of follow-on drugs in the US market was done by DiMasi and Paquette [2004], from which the table below is taken.

DiMasi and Parquette selected therapeutic groups where a first approval of a drug had occurred, given a total of 72 groups. These groups contained an average of 4.3 types of drugs each, showing that the phenomenon of closely related drugs is quite widespread. Table 3.1 shows average period of marketing exclusivity for first entrants to a therapeutic class (number of years from first approval to first follow-on approval) in different periods:

**Table 3.1.** Period of market exclusivity

| | |
|---|---|
| 1960s | 7.2 |
| 1970s | 8.2 |
| 1980-84 | 5.9 |
| 1985-89 | 5.1 |
| 1990-94 | 2.8 |
| 1995-98 | 1.8 |

Source:DiMasi and Paquette [2004], p.5

While the appearance of follow-on drugs intensifies competition in the market and potentially lowers the prices of drugs, it may be argued that the duplication of research represents an efficiency loss for society. However, new drugs closely related to already existing drugs may be useful since the side effects can be different. Excluding approval of other drugs once the first one has been accepted for marketing may be even be disastrous for society if the first drug turns out to be poisonous and is withdrawn from the market.

Since most of the research on follow-on drugs is carried out while the first drug is not yet ready for approval, it would be difficult to avoid inefficiencies in this way.

As it can be seen from the figure, which depicts the average case, much of the patent period, usually 20 years, is used for research, clinical trials, and bureaucracy, so that when marketing permit is at last granted, not so many years are left. In the average, the effective patent period of medical drugs is around 8 years. This means that all the outlays on the project, plus a share of the cost of all the projects that were never carried through, must be recovered in this shorter time span, if the innovator's business must be profitable.

Taken as a whole, innovations in the pharmaceutical industry have been quite profitable. According to Joglekar and Paterson [1986], the internal rate of interest of medical investment projects was 6.1% on the average, which seems quite acceptable. However, this average covered quite considerable differences among individual projects. It turned out that for the sample of projects considered, the median (characterized by the property that half of the projects were less profitable, half of them more) was $-5,5\%$. Thus, bad projects alternate with good ones, and since the project period is long and the investment costly, only firms of a certain size can take on such projects. The mergers of smaller pharmaceutical companies into larger and larger ones, which has been characteristic for the last decades, has its background in the cost structure of producing new drugs.

## 5.5 *Drug price comparisons*

The comparison of drug prices between countries has become increasingly important in recent years, both in Europe, where national regulation of drug prices is slowly changing into a common European system of regulation, and in the US, where the debate often focusses on instances of drugs with prices that are lower in neighboring countries. For a comprehensive survey of the problems involved in such comparisons, briefly outlined below, the reader is referred to Danzon and Chao [2000], Danzon and Kim [1998].

*Choice of index formula:* Most index computations are based on weighting the individual price changes according to their importance in the consumption either in the base country (in which case we have a Laspeyres index) or in the countries with which we compare (giving us a Paasche index). We briefly recall the basic facts about price indices:

Consider a consumer with consumption set $\mathbb{R}^n_+$ and utility function $u$ in two alternative situations, characterized by price vectors $p^0, p^1 \in \mathbb{R}^n_+$. Let the consumer's income be $I$. In the initial situation she would buy $x^0 = \xi(p^0, I)$ (where $\xi$ is the ordinary demand function of the consumer), thereby attaining a utility level $r = u(\xi(p^0, I))$. Suppose that the change from $p^0$ to $p^1$ represents a rise in some or all prices. By how much should we compensate our consumer if he is to maintain the same level of satisfaction or utility?

Standard consumer theory has the answer: The consumer should buy $h(p^1, r)$, where $h$ is the compensated demand, giving the bundle which minimizes expenditure at the prices $p^1$, and for this she would need an income of $e(p^1, r) = p^1 \cdot h(p^1, r)$ (thus, $e$ is the consumer's expenditure function). Therefore, compensation should be paid to the amount of $e(p^1, r) - I$.

**Box 3.5  Early European price comparisons.** Sermeus and Adriaenssens [1989] report on a European price comparison of selected drugs in 1988 for the (then) 12 EU member countries. A total of 125 different drugs were selected in such a way that the 25 most important drugs in each country were represented. The drugs selected represented about 15% of total sales. Of the 125 drugs, 43 were found in 11 countries when only molecule and method of dispensation was demanded to be identical. When package sizes differed, the price was taken as weighted average of nearest package sizes. When the drug was not found, a synthetic price bases on average conditions was inserted instead.

The results are shown below in Table 3.2.

**Table 3.2.** Price of selected bundle in 11 European countries, European Currency Units (ECU) and index numbers, 1988.

|  | Total cost ECU | Index: EU-average= 100 |
|---|---|---|
| Spain | 1105,2 | 70 |
| Portugal | 1126,5 | 71 |
| Greece | 1149,5 | 73 |
| Italy | 1206,8 | 76 |
| France | 1252,1 | 79 |
| Belgium | 1381,9 | 88 |
| U.K. | 1735,2 | 110 |
| Ireland | 1871,1 | 118 |
| Netherlands | 2087,6 | 132 |
| Denmark | 2216,0 | 140 |
| Germany | 2289,3 | 145 |

Source: Sermeus and Adriaenssens [1989], s.412.

The prices used are the retail prices of pharmacies in January 1988. Prices in Southern European countries are considerably lower than those of Northern countries. However, the results should be seen in relation to the methods used, both with respect to choice of drugs and to the use of total sales as weights in the index formula, which means that new and expensive drugs may matter more than drugs which are in universal use but have very low prices.

Casual observations will tell us that this is not the way in which such problems are solved in practice. Actually, it is a theoretical solution only, since neither $h(p^1, r)$ nor $e(p^1, r)$ can be observed. Practical compensation measures involve the computation of some price index $\text{In}(p^0, p^1)$ using observable data, and the compensation is then $(\text{In}(p^0, p^1) - 1)I$.

Examples of index formula are the *Laspeyres* index

$$\text{La}(p^0, p^1) = \frac{p^1 \cdot x^0}{p^0 \cdot x^0},$$

the *Paasche* index

$$Pa(p^0, p^1) = \frac{p^1 \cdot x^1}{p^0 \cdot x^1},$$

where $x^1 = \xi(p^1, I)$. Note that $Pa(p^0, p^1) = 1/La(p^1, p^0)$. Another index formula is *Fisher's "ideal" index*

$$Fi(p^0, p^1) = \sqrt{La(p^0, p^1)Pa(p^0, p^1)},$$

and several other formula have been proposed. However, most price index computations are based on one of the above three formulas.

It is well-known that compensation for a price increase using a Laspeyres index will overcompensate since it does not take the substitution effect into account. In most cases, Paasche indices will result in lower index values for the foreign countries as compared to the base country.

*The sample of drugs to be used in comparisons:* The choice of basic bundle of pharmaceutical drugs, the prices of which are compared across countries, is important for the representativity of the results obtained, since a small selection of drugs may introduce a bias in the comparison. It is however not easy to obtain a large, representative sample of drugs, since the drugs considered should be available in the market in each of the countries for which prices are to be compared. This condition turns out to be very restrictive. Drugs are marketed in some countries and not in others, and even when they are in all countries, they are marketed under different brands and by different companies. This does not in itself preclude comparison, as long as the same drug is there, but even so the drugs are not quite the same: They may have the same active component, but then the strength may be different, and the package may contain different numbers of pills, all circumstances which make price comparisons less simple. The problems are aggravated by the nature of the drug market – prices change often, large packages may be cheaper than small packages, etc. As a result, starting out with a selection of drugs in the base country and moving to otherwise similar countries, one may quickly lose more than half of the drugs originally in the sample.

*Prices:* For a consistent comparison of prices, the level in the vertical structure at which the price is quoted, should be the same throughout. Usually the drug passes from industry through wholesalers to the pharmacy, and from the pharmacy to the patient. This opens up for country differences which are related to wholesalers' and pharmacies' markups rather than to prices as charged at factory level. Moreover, the different levels of value-added taxes may contribute to the picture of country differences which are not closely related to the fundamental problem. Therefore safer to prices charged by the producer are used in price comparisons.

**Box 3.6** A comparison of drug prices in Denmark and selected neighboring countries (unpublished) was carried out in 1997 based on data from 1996. A representative basket of drugs was selected, and corresponding drugs were searched for in the other countries. The identification in other countries was based on active component, method of dispensing, dosage, and package size. Table 3.3 below shows the final sample sizes obtained depending on the criterion for matching.

Table 3.3. Number of items in original sample of 100 drugs which were matched, depending on criterion for matching

| Country | Active component | same, plus NFC | same, plus strength | same, plus package size |
|---|---|---|---|---|
| Belgium | 87 | 62 | 48 | 18 |
| Finland | 89 | 77 | 68 | 53 |
| France | 84 | 59 | 42 | 8 |
| Greece | 83 | 58 | 49 | 9 |
| Holland | 86 | 73 | 61 | 29 |
| Ireland | 85 | 69 | 58 | 30 |
| Italy | 83 | 59 | 44 | 6 |
| Portugal | 77 | 51 | 38 | 16 |
| Spain | 85 | 53 | 39 | 16 |
| Germany | 88 | 77 | 65 | 35 |
| U.K. | 88 | 71 | 59 | 37 |
| Austria | 85 | 67 | 51 | 21 |

The price comparisons depending on different degrees of tolerance in identifying drugs can be seen from Table 3.4:

**Table 3.4.** Price index for drugs in selected countries 1996. Denmark = 100.

| Country | tolerance in package size(%) | | | | |
|---|---|---|---|---|---|
| | 0 | 10 | 15 | 20 | 50 |
| Belgium | 83,48 | 83,07 | 83,07 | 83,82 | 84,59 |
| Finland | 91,58 | 92,36 | 92,36 | 92,14 | 92,84 |
| France | 84,22 | 87,58 | 87,58 | 87,58 | 81,68 |
| Greece | 70,13 | 70,13 | 70,13 | 70,13 | 99,31 |
| Holland | 89,24 | 90,57 | 93,55 | 96,02 | 95,53 |
| Ireland | 86,25 | 89,24 | 89,11 | 89,28 | 92,48 |
| Italy | 49,11 | 49,11 | 49,11 | 49,11 | 69,11 |
| Portugal | 84,98 | 82,69 | 82,69 | 82,76 | 92,64 |
| Spain | 57,43 | 58,37 | 58,37 | 58,52 | 68,84 |
| Germany | 101,71 | 100,23 | 100,07 | 100,50 | 102,74 |
| U.K. | 82,92 | 85,57 | 85,12 | 85,77 | 86,95 |
| Austria | 92,61 | 92,59 | 92,50 | 92,38 | 93,16 |

The price differences increase when the number of matches gets large.

The next problem to be faced is related to the way in which the drug is marketed. As long as only presence of the same active component is demanded, it is relatively easy to find a counterpart. With a finer classification (so-called NFC classification at 5th level[2]), and with additional criteria, this becomes more difficult. Adding to this the differences in dosage and in package size, it becomes increasingly problematic to find similar products to compare in different countries, as shown in Box 3.6. Clearly, correction for dosage and package size may be done according to simple rules, but it should be remembered that such synthetic prices do not correspond to real prices observed in the market. Moreover, actual pricing in any single country of the same molecule marketed in different packages and dosages do not fit with the simple rules.

*Exchange rate:* As the drug prices are reported in national currency, they must be recalculated in a common currency unit. For this one may use the standard exchange rate, but it is often recommended to use Purchasing Power Parities (PPP) which are artificial exchange rates that take into account the purchasing power of the national currency. Clearly the use of ordinary exchange rates will give rise to changes in relative drug prices which have very little to do with the drug market but reflects changes in balances of payments and international creditworthiness. Using PPP does however not mean that a higher degree of objectivity is achieved, since the PPP once again is an index calculated to show what the national currency can buy for the average consumer, and this may not be the relevant point of view in the context of drug prices, since the buyers of drugs are not necessarily typical consumers. There is no easy way out of these problems.

## 6   Problems

**1.** In the quantity-quality models of hospitals (Section 4.1), the manager decides about a quality level and has then a given cost structure. Construct a model of a doctor who chooses quantity of patients and the quality of services along the same lines as in the Newhouse model, and who is subject to market conditions in the form of demand curves depending on level of services. The doctor has a double objective of obtaining a target income and delivering a high level of service.

---

[2]NFC (abbreviation of New Form Codes) is a classification system for active components of pharmaceutical drugs based on the Anatomical Therapeutic Classification (ATC) system initiated by EphMRA, the European Pharmaceutical Market Reseach Association. The classification uses five levels:

1:  code of anatomical main group,
2:  therapeutic main group,
3:  therapeutic/pharmacological subgroup,
4:  chemical/therapeutic/pharmacological subgroup,
5:  chemical substance.

Sketch the model graphically and in equation form. What kind of conclusions can be obtained in this model?

**2.** A firm produces muesli for sale in health food stores. The production is based in quinoa which is transformed and flavored, and the production process is carried out by natives of Peru with a special eduction needed to prepare the correct mixtures of ingredients. Due to national immigration rules the firm cannot get as many workers as it wants. Although the product is unique, there are other health food products which compete for the same segment of consumers.

Give an analysis of the production and pricing of the firm, using standard tools of economic analysis (isoquants, demand functions).

Some public attention has been given to the fact that the wages of the Peruvian workers are rather low. The firm argues that increased wages will lead to higher prices, something which the firm cannot allow due to the competition from other health food producers. Discuss this argument.

**3.** Some service contracts contain a "no-cure-no-pay" clause, which means that if the buyer is not satisfied with the service delivered, then she may deny payment. Are there cases of no-cure-no-pay in healthcare?

Can an optimal mechanism in the principal-agent model be interpreted as a no-cure-no-pay contract? If not, which kind of additional features of the model would be called for?

**4.** A pharmaceutical company has patented several new products and must now select one of these for marketing. Before the marketing permit can be obtained, the drug must be subject to clinical trials which are time consuming and expensive, so the choice is one which matters for the company.

Give a description of the market for a patented drug when the marketing permit has been granted. How can the company estimate future sales and how should the drug be priced?

Assume that the final choice is between two drugs, one of which is a cosmetic drug to be used against wrinkles, whereas the the other one is an antibiotic to be used in cases of penicillin resistance. Discuss the demand elasticities and use this to give a suggestion for the company's choice.

**5.** When the patent on a drug expires, other producers may enter the market, selling the drug under another name,. Describe the market which results from this appearance of competitors. What (if anything) limits the entrance of new producers of the drug?

In many cases, the original patent producer will continue marketing the drug. Why will this be possible? In addition, the producer will enter the market for copy producers, selling the original drug under a new name and to a lower price. Give an explanation in terms of price discrimination.

**6.** Horizontal structure in the drug market: On its way from producer to patient, the drug passes the *pharmacy,* which introduces a markup on the drug price set by the producer. Give a description of the pharmacy market and the extent of competition in this market.

In many countries, the pharmacies are subject to regulation with an upper bound on their percentage markup on producer prices for prescription drugs. What are the consequences for prices of other goods sold in the pharmacies, such as over-the-counter (OTC) drugs?

Liberalization of the pharmacy sector in recent years have led to the formation of pharmacy chains, where one firm has several pharmacies. Discuss the possible consequences of this development. What will happen if the pharmaceutical drug producers enter the market as owner of pharmacy chains?

# Chapter 4
# Paying for healthcare

## 1  Introduction

It seems natural that our previous discussion of demand and supply conditions should be followed up by a treatment of price formation in the markets considered, following the usual pattern of economic texts. On the other hand, both supply of and demand for healthcare is different in nature from the counterparts in standard textbooks, and the markets for healthcare are particular, since in many cases no payment is collected at delivery. Nevertheless prices have a role to play, and setting the right prices is not a trivial matter.

Actually the importance of pricing tends to be understated in the discussion of health care provision, since they do not give rise to payments. But prices have important signalling functions which if neglected or misused can have negative effects, as it has been seen when all types of hospital treatments were evaluated at a uniform bed-day price. Such practices led to the restriction of pricing to an accounting convention with no important functions, and many of the attempts in recent years to improve the economic functioning of the health care sector can be seen as projects for a better price formation.

In the following we look closer at prices in the health care sector, taking as point of departure the classical economic welfare theory. The treatment of the benchmark cases of a competitive economy, with suitable types of market failure added, will give us some principles for price formation and insight in the role that prices play. It may not be easy to transform the general principles to exact rules specifying who should pay and how much, but – as always with theory – knowing the background may prevent wrong decisions from being taken and inspire the ongoing work on improving the rules governing the sector.

The chapter is organized as follows: We begin by considering the classical welfare economics, after which we turn to cases of market failure, namely external effects, public goods, and increasing returns to scale in production, adapted so as to incorporate healthcare provision. In each of these cases theory comes up with a suggestion as to what should be done (even if not equally effective in all the cases); typically, the workings of the standard market has to be modified to a greater or lesser degree, in some cases indeed to such a degree that the market can no longer be recognized. We follow up on this by considering practical applications, where the informational requirements for following the prescriptions of theory may be too heavy, so that the rules followed have character of ad-hoc conventions.

---

**Box 4.1 NHS,** The National Health Service, is the public health system in England (and Scotland, Wales and Northern Ireland). It was established after World War II together with other social reforms, and formally began is work in 1948. The basic principles at its foundation was those of universal health care covering all citizens and being delivered without payment. The system is funded through income taxes and the National Insurance, which is a system of specific taxes paid by workers and employers and to cover (part of) the social security services of the country. England, Scotland, Wales and Northern Ireland all have separate versions of NHS.

In recent years, the NHS has underwent several major organizational reforms, where the emphasis has went back and forth between local and central influence, and where the fundamental decisions at some moment have been delegated to the general practitioners (the fundholding GPs of the 90s) but are now taken by local CCGs (clinical commissioning groups) which decide on about 60% of the NHS budget.

The principle that treatment should be free at the point of delivery has been upheld and covers most of the services with the exception of a fixed prescription fee and payment for optical and dental care.

---

## 2  Welfare economics and the market mechanism

Since we shall be dealing in this chapter with cases where the market does not work optimally, it seems natural to begin the discussion with the case where the market *does* work well. This is the standard general equilibrium model of welfare economics, where it is shown that equilibria are Pareto optimal and Pareto optimal allocations can be obtained as equilibria at suitable prices and after suitable income redistributions. Since this is standard textbook material, we shall be brief and use the description mainly for the purpose of introducing the notation and concepts.

*Classical welfare theory.* We consider an economy with $m$ consumers and $n$ producers. There are $l$ commodities, and each of the $m$ consumers $i = 1, \ldots, m$ is characterized by a consumption set $X_i \subset \mathbb{R}^l$ consisting of all the feasible consumption bundles, and a preference relation $\succsim_i$ defined on the consumption bundles $x_i \in X_i$.

At this point, we might wonder what became of the distinction introduced earlier (in Chapter 1, Section 1.7, and in Chapter 2, Section 2) between consumption goods available in the market, and *health characteristics* which are individual and cannot be transferred from one consumer to another, but should be produced in the individual household or health technology. Actually, it has not been forgotten, and we return to it below, but at present our notation will be less burdensome if we abstract from it.

Each of the $n$ firms $j = 1, \ldots, n$ has a production set $Y_j \subset \mathbb{R}^l$. As usual, for $y_j \in Y_j$, $y_{jh}$ is the net output by firm $j$ of commodity $h$, so that $y_{jh}$ is negative if $h$ is an input and positive if it is an output.

We assume that there is an initial endowment $\omega \in \mathbb{R}^l$ of the $l$ commodities available. This endowment may be distributed initially among consumers, but we shall not need this feature at present. We can now define an *allocation* in the economy considered as an array $z = (x_1, \ldots, x_m, y_1, \ldots, y_n)$ consisting of a consumption plan for each consumer and a production plan for each producer. The allocation is said to be feasible if

$$x_i \in X_i, \ i = 1 \ldots, m, \ y_j \in Y_j, \ j = 1, \ldots, n, \ \text{and} \ \sum_{i=1}^{m} x_i = \sum_{j=1}^{n} y_j + \omega.$$

It remains now to introduce the notions of Pareto optimum and equilibrium in the context of this model. A feasible allocation $(x_1, \ldots, x_m, y_1, \ldots, y_n)$ is *Pareto optimal* if for any other feasible allocation $(x_1', \ldots, x_m', y_1', \ldots, y_n')$ it must be the case that $x_i' \prec_i x_i$ for some $i$. The pair $(z, p)$ consisting of an allocation $z = (x_1, \ldots, x_m, y_1, \ldots, y_n)$ and a price $p \in \mathbb{R}_+^l$, $p \neq 0$, is an equilibrium if

   (i) $(x_1, \ldots, x_m, y_1, \ldots, y_n)$ is feasible,

   (ii) for each $i$ and $x_i' \in X_i$, if $x_i' \succ_i x_i$, then $p \cdot x_i' > p \cdot x_i$,

   (iii) for each $j$, $p \cdot y_j \geq p \cdot y_j'$, all $y_j' \in Y_j$.

To establish the two main theorems of welfare economics, we need some conditions of well-behavedness of the characteristics of the economy. We state them in the theorems since we shall be concerned later with situations in which these conditions might not be satisfied.

PROPOSITION 1 (1st fundamental theorem of welfare economics) *Suppose that consumers' preferences satisfy local non-satiation (for each bundle $x_i$ and every neighborhood $U$ of $x_i$, there is some $x_i'' \in U$ with $x_i'' \succ_i x_i$). If $(x_1, \ldots, x_m, y_1, \ldots, y_n, p)$ is an equilibrium, then the allocation $(x_1, \ldots, x_m, y_1, \ldots, y_n)$ is Pareto optimal.*

PROOF: Assume to the contrary that there is a feasible allocation $(x_1', \ldots, x_m', y_1', \ldots, y_n')$ such that $x_i' \succsim_i x_i$ for all $i$ and $x_i' \succ_i x_i$ for some $i$. Then $p \cdot x_i' > p \cdot x_i$

---

**Box 4.2 The healthcare system of France.** The French healthcare system is based on *mandatory insurance* provided by non-for-profit insurance companies (there are several but the largest of them serves about three-fourth of the population). Payment is levied as fixed percentages of earned incomes (the percentage depends on the type of income), so that the system is basically tax financed.

The has traditionally been several different schemes (specifying the reimbursements in case of illness) so that there is a certain element of choice between insurance schemes, and the basic scheme can be supplemented by voluntary insurance which reduces the element of coinsurance of the basic schemes.

To obtain reimbursement, the individual is supposed to have chosen a *family doctor* which works as gatekeeper and refer to subsequent visits to specialists or hospital if necessary. There is copayment for visiting the doctor (to the amount of €1) and for hospital stays amounting to around €20, considered as being the 'hotel cost' of the stay, which the individual would have had to pay if not hospitalized.

For further information, see e.g. Sandier et al. [2004], Rodwin [2003].

---

for all $i$ with $x_i' \succ_i x_i$; if $p \cdot x_i' < p \cdot x_i$ for some of the remaining consumers, then by local non-satiation there would be $x_i'' \succ_i x_i$ close enough to $x_i'$ so that $p \cdot x_i'' < p \cdot x_i$, a contradiction. It follows that $\sum_{i=1}^m x_i' > \sum_{i=1}^m x_i$. On the other hand, $p \cdot y_j' \leq p \cdot y_j$ since $y_j$ maximizes profits, so

$$\sum_{i=1}^m p \cdot x_i - \sum_{j=1}^n p \cdot y_j > \sum_{i=1}^m p \cdot x_i' - \sum_{j=1}^n p \cdot y_j'.$$

However, by feasibility of allocations both sides are equal to $p \cdot \omega$, so we have a contradiction. □

The following theorem is the more important one for our purposes, since it pertains to decentralization of decisions through the market.

PROPOSITION 2 (2nd fundamental theorem of welfare economics) *Suppose that for each consumer $i$, $X_i$ is convex and $\succsim_i$ is monotonic ($x_{ih}' > x_{ih}$, all $h$, implies $x_i' \succsim_i x_i$) and has convex and closed upper contour sets $\{x_i' \mid x_i' \succsim_i x_i\}$, and for each producer $j$, $Y_j$ is closed, convex and satisfies free disposal ($y_j \in Y_j$ and $y_{jh}' \leq y_{jh}$, all $h$, implies $y_j' \in Y_j$).*

*If $(x_1, \ldots, x_m, y_1, \ldots, y_n)$ is a Pareto optimal allocation such that $x_i \in \mathrm{int} X_i$ for each $i$, then there is $p$ such that $(x_1, \ldots, x_m, y_1, \ldots, y_n, p)$ is an equilibrium.*

PROOF: For each consumer $i$, we define first the set $X_i^\circ$ of bundles that are as good as or better than $x_i$ (or, equivalently, the upper contour sets of $\succsim_i$ at $x_i$). These sets are closed and convex by assumption. Next, we construct the set

$$Z = \left\{ z = \sum_{i=1}^{m} x'_i - \sum_{j=1}^{n} y'_j - \omega \,\middle|\, x'_i \in X_i^\circ, i = 1, \ldots, m, y'_j \in Y_j, j = 1, \ldots, n \right\}.$$

This set is easily seen to be convex.

We claim that $Z$ contains no vectors $u$ with $u_h < 0$ for all $h$. Indeed, suppose that some such $u$ belongs to $Z$, so that $u = \sum_{i=1}^{m} x'_i - \sum_{j=1}^{n} y'_j - \omega$ for some $x'_i \in X_i^\circ$, $i = 1, \ldots, m$, $y'_j \in Y_j$, $j = 1, \ldots, n$. Then the allocation where consumer 1 gets $x'_1 - u$, and consumers $i = 2, \ldots, m$ get $x'_i$, is feasible (the sum of what is consumed equal the total production plus the endowment), each consumer is at least as satisfied with her bundle as with $x_i$, and consumer 1 is more satisfied, since the bundle $x'_1 - u$ has more of each commodity than $x'_1$ which was already as good as $x_1$. But then we have a contradiction, since $(x_1, \ldots, x_m, y_1, \ldots, y_n)$ is Pareto optimal.

Since the convex sets $Z$ and $\{u \in \mathbb{R}^l \mid u_h < 0, \text{ all } h\}$ are disjoint, there is a linear function $p \in \mathbb{R}^l$, $p \neq 0$, such that

$$p \cdot z \geq 0 \text{ for } z \in Z,$$
$$p \cdot z \leq 0 \text{ if } z_h < 0, \text{ all } h.$$

It follows that $p_h \geq 0$ for each $h$, so that $p$ may be interpreted as a price vector, and trivially 0 minimized $p \cdot z$ on $Z$. Since $0 = \sum_{i=1}^{m} x_i - \sum_{j=1}^{n} y_j - \omega$, and minimizing a linear function on a sum of sets is equivalent to minimizing on each of the sets then take the sum, we get that

(1) for each $i$, $x_i$ minimizes $p \cdot x'_i$ over $X_i^\circ$, meaning that $p \cdot x'_i \geq p \cdot x_i$ for each $x'_i \in X_i$ with $x'_i \succsim_i x_i$. If $x'_i \succ_i x_i$ and $p \cdot x'_i = p \cdot x_i$, then by continuity of preferences there must also be $x''_i \in X_i$ with $x''_i \succ_i x_i$ and $p \cdot x''_i < p \cdot x_i$, a contradiction, and we conclude that $x'_i \succ_i x_i$ implies $p \cdot x'_i > p \cdot x_i$.

(2) For each $j$, we have that $-p \cdot y_j \leq -p \cdot y'_j$, all $y_j \in Y_j$, which means that $p \cdot y_j \geq p \cdot y'_j$, all $y_j \in Y_j$.

We have thus shown that $(x_1, \ldots, x_m, y_1, \ldots, y_n, p)$ satisfies all the conditions of a market equilibrium. □

In the benchmark case of classical economic welfare theory, the market may be used to decentralize decisions. First of all, allocations obtained via the market are Pareto optimal, and secondly, the market mechanism is sufficiently flexible to allow for all the Pareto optimal allocations, at least when supported by a suitable redistribution of incomes (in our market equilibrium, we did not care about the source of consumer income but assumed it sufficient for acquiring the equilibrium bundle).

*Efficiency and market with health characteristics.* We now return from classical economic theory to the context of health economics. As mentioned above, we should

**Box 4.3 The healthcare system of Germany.** The German healthcare system is based on national health insurance and is indeed the historically first system of this type, dating back to Bismarck's social legislation in 1883–89. The current system consists of two types of insurance schemes, the national sickness fund ('Krankenkassen'), to which most of the population belongs, which is financed by contributions from employers and employees together with government subsidies. Individuals are automatically enrolled in this scheme unless their income is above a certain (high) level. There is a possibility of opting out of the scheme (with a tax payment remaining) for high-income citizens, who then use the private insurance scheme.

Copayments are small in the sickness fund scheme, and copayment for hospital stay depends on length of stay and not on procedure.

take into consideration that the consumer is concerned not only with standard commodities which can be bought in a market and transferred from one individual to another, but also with purely individual health characteristics. A consumption bundle of consumer $i$ then takes the form of a vector $(x_{i1}, \ldots, x_{il}, h_{i1}, \ldots, h_{ik})$, where $x_{ih}$ for $h = 1, \ldots, l$ is individual $i$'s consumption of the ordinary good $h$ and $h_{ij}$ is the level of the $j$th health characteristic obtained the individual, and consumption bundles are now taken from $\mathbb{R}^l_+ \times [0,1]^k$, where we have assumed that health characteristics are given values between 0 and 1. The connection between consumption goods and health characteristics is provided by the health technology $T_i \subset \mathbb{R}^l_+ \times [0,1]^k$ transforming goods bundles to vectors of health characteristics, and individuals have preferences $\succsim_i$ over consumption bundes $(x_i, h_i)$.

This seemingly complicating feature can actually be dealt with by the theory considered above. There are two ways of doing this:

(1) The discussion can be reduced to one which concerns only bundles of consumption goods, namely by defining individual preferences over goods bundles taking into account the health characteristics which can be obtained with such goods bundles: Let $\succsim_i'$ be given by

$$x_i >_i' x_i' \text{ iff } \forall (\hat{x}_i, h_i') \in T_i, \hat{x}_i \leq x_i' \, \exists (\bar{x}_i, h_i) \in T_i, \bar{x}_i \leq x_i : (x_i, h_i) >_i (x_i', h_i').$$

Thus, the goods bunde $x_i$ is better than the goods bundle $x_i'$ if for all household productions of health possible with $x_i'$ there is a household production made from $x_i$ which is better. Under weak assumptions on $T_i$ the derived preference relation $\succsim_i'$ will have the properties needed for the two fundamental theorems of welfare theory. Notice that with this approach, the goods bundle $x_i$ is considered as the bundle delivered to individual $i$ *before* any household production.

(2) An alternative, and perhaps more appealing, approach is to *interpret* the bundles $x_i$ in the classical welfare theory as goods-and-characteristics bundles $(x_i, h_i)$. The household technologies $T_i$ for $i = 1, \ldots, m$ become ordinary production sets

$$Y^{T_i} = \{(-x_i, h_i) \mid (x_i, h_i) \in T_i\}$$

once the correct signs have been introduced. There is only one caveat here: Since characteristics are non-transferable, there should be no summations in the conditions for feasibility of allocation, but this is achieved easily if we consider the health characteristics of each individual as separate commodities, so that the total number of commodities becomes $l + mk$ instead of $l$. When writing a commodity bundle as $(x_i, h_i)$, it should be understood that zeros are inserted in all the irrelevant coordinates, and similarly, the ordinary consumption sets involve only vectors with zeros at the places corresponding to health characteristics.

Having individual household production transforming goods to characteristics, we may also additional producers of individual health characteristics, to take care of special forms of healthcare. Comparing with the previous approach, it is seen that a consumption bundle now is a *final* consumption bundle, household production has been taken care of.

Given this interpretation of the classical model, we obtain that Pareto optimal allocations can be decentralized using markets. This goes not only for ordinary goods but also for health characteristics, something which may surprise at a first look. However, nothing new is obtained here, since anyway only consumer $i$ is present in the "market" for health characteristics of individual $i$, so that no transactions between individuals take place. The insight is however not entirely valueless, it shows that in Pareto optimal allocations there is an implicit valuation of individual $i$'s health characteristics, which is the same whether production occurs in the household or elsewhere, and this insight will be useful in Chapter 6.

## 3 Externalities

When *market failure* occurs, the two fundamental theorems of welfare economics cannot be upheld any more, and the question then arises of whether market mechanism may be complemented by some additional device so as to restore the possibility of decentralizing Pareto optimal allocations. We shall have a closer look at this – of course with special emphasis on what is relevant for healthcare – below. As it may be recalled, an externality or an external effect is present whenever the acts of one economic agent influences the possibilities of choice or the consequences of choice of any other agent in a way which is over and above the mutual influence

**Box 4.4 Medicare,** the US social insurance system for elderly (people aged 65 or more, together with certain groups of disabled individuals), was introduced in 1966. The funding comes from the federal budget, together with some payments from the members, and one of the reasons for tax financing was that before its introduction, health insurance was often not available to the elderly since the price of such insurance depended on age and therefore was considerably higher for the elderly.

The has four parts: Part A is hospital insurance covering inpatient hospital stays up to 60 days, with a fixed deductible in form pf a once-and-for-all payment by the patient. Additional days requite copayment. Part B is medical insurance paying for some services not covered by Part A, mainly on outpayment basis, and it covers physician services, visiting nurse, and covers some of the cost of durable medical equipment. Part B is optional, and individuals covered otherwise through their workplace may choose to wait in joining it.

In addition to these two parts, there are also a Part C, which deals with health plans, to which the individuals can subscribe, obtaining additional coverage against a more limited choice (substituting health plan adherence for fee-for-service), and Part D deals with additional coverage of medical drugs.

brought about by the market (this latter qualification explains why the effects are "external").

External effects have increasingly been the object of study of theoretical and applied economists, since some very important external effects have profound consequences for our everyday life; among those in particular effects related to the environment and its deterioration. The external effects which are operative in the health care sector are perhaps less spectacular, and they are most certainly of another nature, but they are nevertheless widespread and important. The most immediate examples are related to the functioning of society as a whole which depends on the state of health of the population. Considerations of such mutual relationships led to the first government promoted schemes of social security, and they are behind the discussion of the harmful effects of reducing hospitalization of mentally ill, leaving them to the streets of the large cities.

One of the objectives of the national care systems in most countries – and one which is rarely if at all debated, possibly because it is usually formulated in a rather vague and undemanding way – is that everyone should be entitled to medical treatment. In official documents it is often stated in as the "Samaritan principle" of health care. According to traditional economic thought this might be achieved in the simplest possible way by income transfers; people are then able to decide for themselves how much and how expensive health care they want, and they might use their money for other purposes if they wished to do so. This however is not in accordance with the Samaritan principle as this is usually understood. Indeed, it seems to include some constraints on the consumers' free choices, so that they are not allowed to prefer other consumption to health care. This means that there is an externality in consumption, since the general opinion does not permit individuals to receive less treatment than what is considered right. In other words, we are so worried about the welfare of other individuals (interpreted in our way) that we find it reasonable that the free choice of consumption is restricted.

The presence of this form of additional preferences on consumption of other people has as a consequence that ordinary welfare theory has to be reconsidered – not surprisingly of course since we are discussing market failures. The problem is not unsurmountable in the sense that the decentralization of decisions, which is the main message of welfare theory, can still be obtained, at least partially, but the price system is less neat than in classical welfare theory. This is the topic of the subsection to follow.

### 3.1  *Allocation with paternalistic preferences*

A first approach, tailored to the specific case of health-related external effects, would be to consider the choice of allocation, as a situation with *paternalistic preferences*, where society rank allocation in a way which may or may not be in accordance with individual preferences.

As before, we have $l$ commodities, $m$ consumers, and $n$ producers. Each of the $m$ consumers $i = 1, \ldots, m$ are characterized by a consumption set $X_i \subset \mathbb{R}^l$ consisting of all the feasible consumption bundles, and a preference relation $\succsim_i$ defined on the consumption bundles $x_i \in X_i$. Further, we have $n$ firms, each with a production set $Y_j \subset \mathbb{R}^l$, and there is an initial endowment $\omega \in \mathbb{R}^l$ of the $l$ commodities available.

So far, everything is as before, but now we introduce the new aspect in the form of a preference relation $\succsim_S$ ("society's preferences") over allocations; the statement $(x_1, \ldots, x_m, y_1, \ldots, y_n) \succsim_S (x_1', \ldots, x_n', y_1', \ldots, y_n')$ means that society considers the allocation $(x_1, \ldots, x_m, y_1, \ldots, y_n)$ to be at least as good as the allocation $(x_1', \ldots, x_m', y_1', \ldots, y_n')$; in our context of treatments for all in case of illness, allocations which do not provide for such treatment may be considered as inferior to other allocations which do take this into consideration.

With our new concept of an overall preference relation on allocation, we may define a *social optimum* as a feasible allocation $(x_1, \ldots, x_m, y_1, \ldots, y_n)$ which is maximal for the social preference relation $\succsim_S$ on the set of feasible allocations (in the sense that there is no feasible allocation $(x'_1, \ldots, x'_m, y'_1, \ldots, y'_n)$ which satisfies

$$(x'_1, \ldots, x'_m, y'_1, \ldots, y'_n) >_S (x_1, \ldots, x_m, y_1, \ldots, y_n).$$

A social optimum is not necessarily a Pareto optimum; this will depend on the degree of coincidence between social and individual preferences (allocations allowing for smoking behavior may be socially inferior to allocations with less smoking but still be preferred by many individuals). We note in passing that if there is coincidence, then the social optimum can be attained using the market, what is needed is only a suitable redistribution of income:

PROPOSITION 3 *Under the assumptions of Proposition 2, suppose that $\gtrsim_S$ is compatible with $(\gtrsim_i)_{i=1}^m$ in the sense that for all feasible allocations $(x_1, \ldots, x_m, y_1, \ldots, y_n)$, $(x'_1, \ldots, x'_m, y'_1, \ldots, y'_n)$, if $x_i \gtrsim_i x'_i$, all i with $x_{i^0} >_{i^0} x'_{i^0}$ for some $i^0$, then*

$$(x_1, \ldots, x_m, y_1, \ldots, y_n) \gtrsim_S (x'_1, \ldots, x'_m, y'_1, \ldots, y'_n).$$

*If $(x_1, \ldots, x_m, y_1, \ldots, y_n)$ is a social optimum such that $x_i \in \mathrm{int} X_i$ for each i, then there is p such that $(x_1, \ldots, x_m, y_1, \ldots, y_n, p)$ is an equilibrium.*

PROOF: It suffices to show that under the conditions of the theorem, the social optimum $(x_1, \ldots, x_m, y_1, \ldots, y_n)$ is Pareto optimal. Indeed, if there were a feasible allocation $(x'_1, \ldots, x'_m, y'_1, \ldots, y'_n)$ with $x'_i \gtrsim_i x_i$, all i and $x'_{i^0} >_{i^0} x_{i^0}$ for some $i^0$, then

$$(x'_1, \ldots, x'_m, y'_1, \ldots, y'_n) >_S (x_1, \ldots, x_m, y_1, \ldots, y_n)$$

contradicting that $(x_1, \ldots, x_m, y_1, \ldots, y_n)$ was a social optimum. The conclusions follow now from Proposition 2.                                                             □

The result is of course not surprising given the standard welfare theorems, which tell us that every Pareto optimal allocation, and in particular the social optimum, can be decentralized. In this decentralization, we needs that the consumers' incomes are redistributed in the right way, and achieving this in practice is of course no simple matter.

Another obvious weakness is the assumption of Pareto compatibility of the paternalistic preferences, since in realistic cases maximizing an overall social preference relation may not yield a Pareto optimum. Thus we need a result which can be obtained without this assumption. For this we shall need a modification of the definition of an equilibrium. We want to find out how far it is possible to decentralize decisions in an economy with external effects, and of course we have to be prepared for some complications in the sense that a single price system will carry too little information to the agents. Therefore we introduce an equilibrium with taxes and subsidies as an allocation $(x_1, \ldots, x_m, y_1, \ldots, y_n)$ together with

> **Box 4.5 Medical Savings Accounts.** This particular method of financing healthcare was established in Singapore in the 1990s. The basic idea is that each individual sets aside an amount on an earmarked account which can be used only for healthcare payments, with preferential treatment from government in the form of tax exemptions. The main point here is that the when healthcare is needed, the individual pays with money which is her own, and consequently she is expected to be more careful and avoid unnecessary expenditure. In this way, the medical savings accounts (MSA) have been seen as the ultimate way of abolishing moral hazard.
>
> Clearly, MSA cannot stand alone since healthcare needs will arise for persons who have not yet obtained the necessary savings. And indeed, the healthcare system in Singapore has three distinct components: The first one, MediSave, consists of the medical savings accounts, whereas the second component, MediShield, is an insurance for catastrophic illness (such events will typically be very costly but the individual influence on cost is minor). Finally, a traditional, tax-financed third component Medifund pays for healthcare of persons who are not able to pay for themselves.
>
> The contributions to the medical savings accounts come from an overall payroll tax, of which a part is directed towards the savings accounts. The accounts can be used to pay for hospitalization and other healthcare, and the balance on the account can be bequeathed upon death to children or relatives.
>
> The crucial question of whether the MSA system allows for a more efficient alliocation of healthcare ressources than the tax-financed or insurance-based systems remains largely open, since many other factors have intervened, cf. e.g. Dixon [2002]. The system may have certain weaknesses, such as treatment of chronic diseases, which does not fit well into the three-component system.
>
> Variations of the MSA system have been introduced in USA, China and South Africa.

a price system $p \in \mathbb{R}^l_+$ *and* systems of commodity taxes or subsidies $s_i \in \mathbb{R}^l$ for each consumer, such that

(i) $(x_1, \ldots, x_m, y_1, \ldots, y_n)$ is feasible,

(ii) for each consumer $i$, $x_i$ is $\succsim_i$-maximal in the set

$$\left\{ x'_i \in X_i \,\middle|\, \sum_{h=1}^{l} (p_h + s_{ih}) x'_{ih} \le \sum_{h=1}^{l} (p_h + s_{ih}) x_{ih} \right\},$$

(iii) for each producer $j$, $y_j$ maximizes the profit $\sum_{h=1}^{l} p_h y'_{jh}$ over all $y'_j \in Y_j$.

PROPOSITION 4 *Let* $(x_1, \ldots, x_m, y_1, \ldots, y_n)$ *be a social optimum allocation such that* $x_i$ *belongs to the interior of* $X_i$, *all* $i$. *Assume moreover that the allocation is Pareto optimal among all those allocations which are as good as* $(x_1, \ldots, x_m, y_1, \ldots, y_n)$ *in terms of society's preferences.*

*Then there is a price system p and individualized taxes/subsidies on all commodities $(s_i)_{i=1}^m$, so that the allocation together with these constitutes an equilibrium with taxes and subsidies.*

PROOF: For the given allocation $(x_1, \ldots, x_m, y_1, \ldots, y_n)$ we define for each $i$ the sets $X_i^\circ = \{x_i' \mid x_i' \in X_i'', x_i \gtrsim_i x_i'\}$ of bundles at least as good as $x_i$ for consumer $i$ (here $X_i''$ is the subset of $X_i$ defined by the allocation $(x_1, \ldots, x_m, y_1, \ldots, y_n)$ according to our assumption on $P$); the sets $X_i''$ are convex by our assumptions. Also, for each $j$ the set $Y_j$ is convex.

Next, we look at the set

$$V = \sum_{i=1}^m X_i^\circ - \sum_{j=1}^n Y_j - \{\omega\}$$

where addition of sets is performed by taking the set of all vectors that can be written as a sum of vectors from each of the sets, the so-called Minkowski-addition of sets. It is easily seen that the set $V \subset \mathbb{R}^l$ is convex. Moreover it is constructed in such a way that $0 \in V$ (the zero vector can be written as $\sum_{i=1}^m x_i - (\sum_{j=1}^n y_j) - \omega$, since the allocation $(x_1, \ldots, x_m, y_1, \ldots, y_n)$ is feasible).

From our assumptions on $(x_1, \ldots, x_m, y_1, \ldots, y_n)$ we get that the set $V$ cannot contain vectors with only negative coordinates. Indeed, if such a vector $v$ belonged to $V$, we might write

$$0 > v = \sum_{i=1}^m x_i' - \sum_{j=1}^n y_j' - \omega$$

for suitable $x_i' \in X_i^\circ$, $i = 1, \ldots, m$, $y_j' \in Y_j$, $j = 1, \ldots, n$, and this tells us that the allocation $(x_1', \ldots, x_m', y_1', \ldots, y_n')$ is feasible and at least as good for everyone as $(x_1, \ldots, x_m, y_1, \ldots, y_n)$. Since clearly it does not use up all the ressources, there is something left of everything, and if we give this to any one of the consumers, she has become better off than in $(x_1, \ldots, x_m, y_1, \ldots, y_n)$, and consequently we have made a Pareto-improvement, a contradiction.

Using separation of the convex set $V$ from the set of all vectors with only negative coordinates we get that there exists a vector $p \neq 0$, such that $p \cdot v \geq 0$ for all $v \in V$, and $p \cdot v < 0$ for all $v$ with only negative coordinates, the latter property being equivalent to $p_h \geq 0$ for all $h$.

We need only to establish the properties (i) to (iii) of an equilibrium; property (i) holds trivially, and since $0$ minimizes the linear function $p \cdot v$ on $V$, it minimizes the same linear function on each of the summands of $V$; in particular, $-y_j$ minimizes $p \cdot (-y_j')$ on $-Y_j$, or, otherwise put, $y_j$ maximizes $p \cdot y_j$ on $Y_j$.

For each consumer $i$ choose a supporting price system $\pi_i$ of $\{x_i' \mid x_i' \succsim_i x_i\}$ at $x_i$, and define the system of taxes/subsidies $s_i$ by $s_i = p - \pi_i$. This gives us condition (ii), and we are done. $\qquad\square$

The result shows that if the externalities in consumption has the type of stating a correct way of allocating in society (correct in the sense that it expresses accepted social norms), then optimal (in terms of the social preferences) allocations can be decentralized if we are willing (and able) to use a system of personalized taxes or subsidies on the commodities in the market (whereby the equilibrium tax may be 0 for a large number of commodities so that they are not taxed or subsidized).

There are two obvious objections against this approach. The result does not point in the direction of the way in which healthcare is financed in real life. There may be several causes for this: The consumption externality experienced in connection with healthcare may not be of this type, or the real world healthcare systems just didn't implement this decentralization scheme. But there may have been good reasons for this, namely that personalized taxes and subsidies give rise to several problems, mainly of informational character, which we shall consider closer in the sequel.

On the other hand, using taxation to correct externalities is a classical approach, dating back to Pigou, so as a first hint to an approach to decentralizing healthcare decisions in society it should not be discarded altogether.

### 3.2 *External effects and Arrow commodities*

In this subsection we return to our benchmark economy and look at the modifications that has to be made due to the presence of externalities. The fundamental problem is intuitive enough: When the acts of one agent influences the possibilities of choice of other agents or their assessments of the outcomes, then choices made solely according to individual utility may not result in Pareto optimal allocation any more. We need to reestablish the concern for the situation of other individuals in the market situation if we will uphold the connection between efficiency and decentralization via markets.

In the general treatment of externalities – without explicit reference to health – there is a classical way of extending the welfare economic notion of decentralizing via the market to the case considered. The inspiration comes from specific examples, where the externality can be easily tracked to a specific origin, as is for example the case in many cases of polution. Assume for example that a firm produces an output $y$ of a commodity and in the course of production gives rise to a negative external effect. If this external effect is closely connected with the output, then we may consider this very $y$ as an input in consumer's utility functions or the production function of other firms. There are then two classical approaches towards making prices work as decentralizing devices, namely

(1) creating artificial markets, where an externality-creating commodity is bought and sold,

(2) taxing the externality so as to make prices be an expression of social rather than individual cost and social marginal utility (the so-called Pigovian taxes)

Each of these approaches have their pros and cons. The artificial markets can typically not rely on voluntary participation, but if participation is secured, they may find the right equilibrium values which makes the final allocation efficient; taxing the externality seems to be a more secure way of setting the price signals right, but here there is no simple way of adding a mechanism for setting the right taxes, so that in the end the economy may again get an inefficient allocation.

Below we shall expand on alternative (1), which, even if unrealistic, gives some useful hints to what should be done to neutralize (or "internalize") the external effects. The two alternatives are, when properly adapted to meet reality, not fundamentally different.

*Arrow commodities.* Using the inspiration from simple models of (mainly production) externalities, Arrow suggested (cf. e.g. Arrow [1970]) that the approach could be used in much wider generality, namely by introducing specific commodities which capture the external effect. These commodities, of the type "firm $j$'s acceptable level of pollution caused by firm $k$", or "level of healthcare delivered to consumer $i$ in case of a disease as wished by consumer $h$". With Arrow commodities for all the cross-influences in the economy, we can then consider the resulting economy, which has a vastly expanded number of commodities but otherwise looks like the economy considered above, and then discuss decentralization in this new economy.

The Arrow commodities will all take the form $x_{i,h}^{j}$, interpreted as a $h$th type of influence from agent $j$ to agent $i$. If we deal with a production externality, then the amount of external effect depends on the production at firm $j$ and enters in the production set of firm $i$, in the case that $i$ is a consumer it enters the utility function.

Once the relevant commodities have been introduced, the economy works as before, at least formally. The originator of the external effect "sells" it (or, if it is a negative effect, buys the right to it) and the receiver "buys" the effect (or sells rights if the effect is negative). In the equilibrium, each Arrow commodity has a price, which can be interpreted as the cost to the originator and compensation to the receiver (if the effect is negative) or conversely as a subsidy to the originator of a positive external effect, paid by the receiver.

It should be mentioned at this stage – even though it has limited relevance for our main theme, the external effects in healthcare – that this approach has some limitations, even formally (the practical limitations will be commented on later), since we cannot always be sure that (1) all externalities can be equivalently explained by the presence of Arrow commodities, and (2) that the standard assumptions of the benchmark economy will be satisfied. For (2) it was pointed out that the convexity assumptions on production sets may be violated if Arrow commodities are introduced, typically in cases where limiting cases of environmental pollution may either be very costly or cause the polluting firm to close down, that is producing nothing [Starrett, 1972]; subsequently this was modified by Boyd and Conley [1997], see also Murty [2006]. Since we are dealing with consumption externalities, this may not worry us unduly.

There is however another detail to which we should pay some attention: The kind of externality that we are investigating will typically reach all consumers to an equal level, in the sense that the treatment given to some person $i$ in case of illness matters for all consumers and not just for some of them. The above description of Arrow commodities focussed on effects originating with some agent and received by another agent, but we may as well have effects originating with a single agent but received by many agents. This means that the relevant external effect takes the form of a *public good* (where everyone consumes the same amount), and to see what the result of decentralization will be, one needs a closer look at the possibilities of decentralizing allocations with public goods.

## 4 The public goods problem in healthcare

### 4.1 *Free riding and Lindahl equilibria*

A particular form of mutual dependence of the individual agents, consumers and producers, in an economy arises when there are commodities which are used simultaneously by everyone. Public (or collective, as they are also named) goods have the property called *non-exclusivity in consumption:* the particular units of the commodity available may be used by any individual without excluding that other individuals can use exactly the same units of the commodity.

Classical examples of public goods are street lightening, availability of parks and recreational areas, provision of law and order, education in the sense of general educational level. Of immediate relevance for a discussion of health economics are public goods as the containment of infectious diseases, general sanitary conditions etc. Going to more mixed cases, where there is an element of public good in commodities which otherwise are used in the usual sense (such goods are here called "private" to distinguish them from public goods), one has the general level of health in the population, and there are many others. It is seen already from this list that public goods tend to be somewhat abstract ("sanitary conditions, fighting infections"), and that they are intermingled with ordinary services provided to the individual. Therefore, it is not easy to transform general principles about pricing of public goods to practically feasible payment rules. Unfortunately, this is only the beginning of our troubles. As we shall see, the principles themselves have inherent weaknesses which make them suffer to a degree of becoming almost meaningless at a confrontation with reality.

*Lindahl-equilibria.* Faithful to our already well-established tradition we start with an investigation of the possibilities of decentralizing decisions in an economy with public goods. To do so, we need some notation pertaining to public goods. We assume that there are (as always) $l$ private goods, together with $k$ public goods; with this convention the consumption sets $X_i$ are subsets of $\mathbb{R}^{l+k}$, and the consumers' preferences $\succsim_i$ are of course defined on these sets. It will be convenient to describe the bundles of the consumers as $(x_i, z_i)$, where $x_i$ is a bundle of $l$ private goods, $z_i$ a bundle of $k$ public goods.

We assume that the public goods are produced in one or several firms. Since we are not particularly interested in the production side of the economy, there is no need for distinguishing between different firms, so we assume that there is only one, with a production set $Y \subset \mathbb{R}^{l+k}$. Finally we have as usual the total endowment of the economy, now a vector in $\mathbb{R}^{l+k}$. It is usually assumed that public goods are not initially available but have to be produced if they are desired. This means that the endowment vector can be written $(\omega, 0)$ with 0 in all coordinates belonging to public goods.

An allocation is what it has been all the time, that is an array $((x_1, z_1), \ldots, (x_m, z_m), y)$ which specifies the consumption $(x_i, z_i)$ (now of both private and public goods) for each consumer and the production in the single firm. But the definition of feasibility of allocations has to be adapted to the situation: $((x_1, z_1), \ldots, (x_m, z_m), y)$ is feasible if

- $(x_i, z_i) \in X_i$, $i = 1, \ldots, m$, $y \in Y$,
- $\sum_{i=1}^{m} x_{ih} = y_h + \omega_h$, $h = 1, \ldots, l$, (private goods),
- $z_{1j} = \cdots = z_{mj} = y_j$, $j = 1, \ldots, k$, (public goods)

The allocation $((x_1, z_1), \ldots, (x_m, z_m), y)$ is Pareto optimal if it is feasible and there is no other feasible allocation $((x'_1, z'_1), \ldots, (x'_m, z'_m), y')$ which is as good for all consumers and better for at least one consumer.

Are Pareto optimal allocations obtainable as equilibria? Generally not: If there were prices on the $l + k$ commodities, so that each consumer would buy the bundle $(x_i, z_i)$, which is specified in the Pareto optimal allocation, then the relation between prices of two arbitrary commodities, public or private, would equal the marginal rate of substitution for this consumer, and in particular, all these marginal rates of substitutions would be equal for all individuals. Otherwise put, all consumers would agree on the amount of a private good (or in practice, money) that should be given up by each consumer in order to have one more unit of the public good. It does not seem reasonable that there should be this kind of consensus, in particular since everyone has to use exactly the same amount of the public good. The equality certainly does hold when we deal with only private goods, but here it obtains by individual adjustment through the consumed quantities of the goods.

The logical consequence of the fact that consumers tend to have different marginal rates of substitution between public and private goods is to choose different prices for the individual consumers, corresponding to what came out of our consideration in the previous section of consumption externalities – not too surprising since at a closer look, public goods are also a form of consumption externalities. Formally this is done by introducing individual prices $q_1, \ldots, q_m$ on the public goods. Here the price system $q_i = (q_{i1}, \ldots, q_{ik})$ is a vector with $k$ coordinates, so that agent $i$'s payment for public goods is found by multiplying each of the last $k$ coordinates in $z_i$ by the corresponding prices and then add to obtain $\sum_{h=1}^{k} q_{ih} z_{ih}$. The total value of the bundle $(x_i, z_i)$ at the price system $(p, q_i)$ consisting of the common price vector $p$ for private goods and the system of individual prices $q_i$ is then

$$(p, q_i) \cdot (x_i, z_i) = p \cdot x_i + q_i \cdot z_i = \sum_{h=1}^{l} p_h x_{ih} + \sum_{h=1}^{k} q_{ih} z_{ih}.$$

We may now define what is to be understood by an equilibrium in this setup. An allocation $((x_1, z_1), \ldots, (x_m, z_m), y)$ and a price system consisting of a price vector $p$ for private goods and a family $(q_i)_{i=1}^{m}$ of systems of individual prices for public goods is a *Lindahl equilibrium*, if

(i)  the allocation $((x_1, z_1), \ldots, (x_m, z_m), y)$ is feasible,

(ii)  for all $i$, $(x_i, z_i)$ is $\succsim_i$-best in the "budget set"

$$\{(x_i', z_i') \mid p \cdot x_i' + q_i \cdot z_i' \leq p \cdot x_i + q_i \cdot z_i\}$$

(better bundles are more expensive), and

(iii)  $y$ maximizes the profit $(p, (\sum_{i=1}^{l} q_i) \cdot y')$ over all $y' \in Y$ (the producer receives the sum of the individual payments for public goods).

Thus we have here that the private goods have a common price whereas public goods have individual prices. The price which the producer of the public good faces equals the sum of the individual prices of the public good.

The Lindahl equilibrium (Lindahl [1919]), is a market-like arrangement which indeed decentralizes decisions. Indeed, a Pareto optimal allocation can be obtained as a Lindahl equilibrium, or, more precisely:

PROPOSITION 5 *Assume that consumers have convex and monotonic preferences, and the producer has a convex technology. If* $((x_1, z_1), \ldots, (x_m, z_m), y)$ *is a Pareto optimal allocation, then there are private goods prices p and individual prices on public goods* $(q_i)_{i=1}^m$ *such that the allocation together with these prices is a Lindahl equilibrium.*

The proof of this result exploits a classical trick, whereby the given economy with public goods is transformed to an ordinary one, though with a much larger number of private goods. The idea is to define a new private commodity for each consumer and each public good, so that "consumer $i$'s use of public good $j$" is a new commodity. This yields many new commodities in the economy, but that does not bother us, since we are never explicit on this number. The obvious advantage of this new convention is that we can omit the public goods; they are taken care of by the new wealth of private goods.

This does not by itself solve the problem, but actually not much more is needed. In the new economy with only private goods we specify consumption sets for the individual consumers so that they have exactly the relevant commodities, and this again does not really change anything. The only new aspect of our formalism is that we have to redefine the production set in our new economy: For every old production plan, specifying for example an output $y_h$ of a public good, we introduce a production plan with output $y_{ih} = y_h$ for each of the newly defined private goods related to the former public good $h$ (this just corresponds to the fact that the amount $y_h$ of public good $h$ corresponds to amount $y_h$ available to each consumer $i = 1, \ldots, m$. Thus, from a technical point of view, we have inserted the special characteristic of a public good, namely that everybody consumes the same amount, into the production by specifying that the same amount is available as output of distinct, personalized output commodities.

Though simple, this transformation of the old economy into a new one is very useful. The new economy is of the standard type, for which the main results of welfare theory hold. It is easily seen that an allocation which was Pareto optimal in the old economy, is transformed to one which is Pareto optimal in the new one. Applying the second main theorem, we get prices on all the commodities of the new economy such that the allocation together with these prices is an equilibrium. All that remains is to identify the prices in the new economy with the individual prices on public goods in the old one[1].

---

[1]There is a small detail about monotonicity of consumer preferences which has to be formulated slightly stronger than we have done, but we shall not go into this.

We have now obtained some insight into the possibilities of decentralization via prices in an economy with public goods; the point is that prices have to be individualizes so that they can reflect the marginal rates of substitution of the consumers which are not necessarily equal. This marginal rate of substitution may also be interpreted as the willingness to pay of the individual for the particular public good. With this interpretation the Lindahl equilibrium becomes quite intuitive: Everyone pays according to individual willingness, and the sum of these contributions is used for producing public goods (we shall see in a short while that this intuitive interpretation is not to be taken too literally).

In order to find the right individual prices on the public goods some information about the consumer's marginal rate of substitution (willingness to pay) is needed. This marginal rate of substitution is private information; none except the individual herself knows it. Unfortunately, the individual may well be aware that the information desired is used for computing a payment, something which would make it tempting to state a lower willingness to pay than what is actually true. Indeed, as the good is a public one, from the viewpoint of the individual it will be provided anyway, and a lower payment gives immediate gains. Once the information has become unreliable, the Lindahl equilibrium does no longer perform in the desired way. It has become victim of the so-called "free-rider" problem of public goods.

As it can be seen, the Lindahl equilibria are of interest from a theoretical point of view but not practically viable. They are rather the ideal to be approached by mechanisms for allocation of public goods, and they will be used as such in the sequel.

## 4.2 Willingness to pay

At this point where the distance from our theoretical point of departure to the actual reality seems very large, we insert a discussion of measurement of willingness-to-pay, which is a field characterized by a considerable activity in recent years. The interest in measuring the willingness to pay of the citizens for different services provided by the public sector has several sources; first of all, information on such matters is generally lacking, also for politicians involved in formulating public policy; secondly, a disclosure of a public willingness to pay for particular projects (for example projects related to infrastructure, building of new roads etc.) will improve their chance of being carried out, something that the involved organizations have been well aware of. The reason that investigations of willingness to pay for health care are not very common should probably be found in the absence of suitable sponsors willing to finance such investigations.

It is common to distinguish between two methods for measuring willingness to pay, namely (1) *revealed preference methods,* and (2) *stated preference methods.*

In type (1) the fundamental idea is to discover the willingness to pay of the individual investigated from observations of the economic decisions and choices which has been made by the individual. In its simplest version, where all goods are private goods available in the market, this boils down to the classical revealed demand analysis: It is indeed possible to reconstruct the preference relation of the individual from her actual behavior, at least if there are enough observations. In a less classical framework, where some goods are not available in the market (and this is of course the practically relevant framework, since otherwise there would be no need for a willingness-to-pay analysis), one has to reconstruct the preferences from choices of commodities and services which are perhaps not the same but which are technologically and preferentially related.

A health-related example of revealed preferences could be to estimate the willingness to pay for a longer life by the differences in the cost of junk food and a healthy diet; unfortunately, many other things are at stake, people do not choose their life style in such a simple way (as we know from Chapter 2), and indeed the healthy diet is in many cases no more expensive than junk food. Other cases (not related to health) are easier: An estimate of the willingness to pay for reducing the risk of fire could be concerned with what people can do themselves (smoke alarms, fire extinguishers etc.). In investigations of traffic safety the amount paid for equipment as airbags, helmets for bicyclists etc. are important.

In general it is seen as a weakness of this type of investigations that they are rather imprecise as they have to be in view of the data available. It is not easy to deduct behavior and preferences from actual choices pertaining to other goods, since the mutual relationship differs from one person to another. To this comes some problems connected with the empirical research design – it is difficult to avoid a bias in the direction of getting persons that are already more concerned about the effect under study than the general population, so that the revealed willingness to pay will become too high.

The second type (2) of methods consists of several different types of investigations. Here the involved individuals may be asked to rank several descriptions (including quantities and payments) of the goods to be evaluated – something not too different from the previously considered methods of measuring health status. This is called *contingent ranking.*

Alternatively the respondents may be asked for a direct statement of the amount to be paid (which in an interview is often formulated as maximal willingness to pay supplemented by some questions for a description of important properties of the good).

Investigations of type (2), which are based on direct questions and answers, can be criticized for opening up for several possible errors and biases deriving from the interview situation. The following sources of errors are often mentioned:

The first problem is *strategic behavior* as mentioned at the end of the previous section; if the information on willingness to pay are to be used for determining actual payment, there is an incentive for giving incorrect answers. This possibility should however not be overestimated: In the concrete investigations it is usually rather obvious that the answers given by the single individual will have no effect whatsoever on an eventual payment of that individual (even in cases where it may be a part of the interview design that the person is asked to react "as if" there was a real payment connected with the stated willingness to pay). Moreover, the strategic behavior is clearly less important, the more payers there are, something which will also emerge from our formalism on public goods (if the number of consumers increases, then incentive to give wrong information diminishes).

The next problem is that of *hypothetical answers*, which has already been touched upon, and which has to do with the fact that the interviewed is not involved in a real decision problem but takes part in an investigation which does not compel in the same way. The answers given can possible be surrogate reactions on quite different matters. In connection with this there may also be a problem related to the *moral satisfaction* that the interviewed may derive from giving "positive" or "politically correct" answers to the questions posed.

Further it has been argued that a so-called *embedding effect* can be observed: People may give quite different answers depending on how the good under consideration is presented, whether it is considered as a single good or as part of a bundle of services. In an investigation carried out by Kahneman and Knetsch [1992], three groups of people were asked about their willingness to pay for certain environmental programs. The first group had a choice between three different types of environmental policy, the second group had only the choice between the two last, the third group could have only the third one. The result was that the total amount which the groups were willing to pay for environmental policies was more or less the same in all the groups, whereas the groups evaluated environmental measure three very differently, much lower when there were other measures available than when it was the only one.

The whole situation, where basically individuals are asked about their choices in situations which have never been tried by these individuals, and often involving goods and services about which they have little if any knowledge, has also been object of criticism. This is of course difficult to change, and similar situations occur in other types of empirical investigations. The borderline between what is reasonable and what is not is however somewhat unclear; it may well be a problem to carry out willingness-to-pay investigations about "risk" as if it was potatoes or street lightening. In our formal world risk is not a commodity in itself, rather a property of lotteries among which the consumer can choose, and it might make sense to ask about the evaluation of lotteries and the willingness to pay for changing one lottery to another with lower risk. Unfortunately, almost no matter which formal model is chosen, this willingness to pay will depend on other properties of the lotteri (for example its mean value), and therefore we are back in the problem that "risk" as such cannot meaningfully be evaluated.

To all this may be added a more practical problem: The reason that we are interested in willingness to pay is that the total willingness to pay is crucial for optimal allocation. However, standard statistical procedures go for the mean value, assuming that everyone has the same mean value but that the observation is subject to random noise. This is exactly what is *not* the case in connection with public goods; we assume here that all people have different willingness to pay, so we should base the investigation on another statistical model. Technically, it means that we should work with samples which are stratified in such a way that we may expect the willingness to pay to be the same within strata even though they differ between strata. So far no willingness-to-pay investigations have faced this problem in a satisfactory way.

*Mechanisms for revelation of willingness to pay.* The Lindahl equilibria had, as we saw, mainly theoretical interest, but they do not furnish us with any hints as to how to find an optimal allocation of and payment for public goods. We have to do this using other considerations, some of which will be sketched below.

In the following discussion we simplify somewhat, assuming that there are only two commodities, one public and one private good. The firm producing the public good has constant returns to scale, and choosing suitable units we may assume that one unit input of the private good yields one unit public good.

Among the many ways in which the decision may be made about (a) production of and (b) payment for the public good, there are two extremes, namely
   (1) both (a) and (b) are chosen decentrally, and
   (2) both (a) and (b) are subject to central decision.

*Voluntary contributions:* We begin with alternative (a). Each consumer $i$ donates $t_i$ units of her endowment of private goods, $\omega_i$ to production of public good; in total $\sum_{i=1}^{m} t_i$ units are used as input, which by our convention gives an output $\sum_{i=1}^{m} t_i$ of the public good. The consumer is left with $\omega_i - t_i$ units of the private good. Her bundle then becomes $(\omega_i - t_i, \sum_{i=1}^{m} t_i)$. If she has chosen $t_i$ such that the utility of

$(\omega_i - t_i, \sum_{i=1}^{m} t_i)$ is maximal, given the other individuals' choices, then

$$\frac{d}{dt}u_i(\omega_i - t_i, \sum_{i=1}^{m} t_i) = -u'_{i1} + u'_{i2} = 0,$$

from which we get that

$$\frac{u'_{i1}}{u'_{i2}} = 1, \, i = 1, \ldots, m.$$

In her optimum the consumer will demand one additional unit of the public good in order to give up one additional unit of the private good. But then it follows that the allocation obtained in this way cannot be Pareto optimal. If namely everyone gives up only $1/m$ additional unit of the private commodity, then already one additional unit of the public good emerges, and this is an improvement for all consumers, who individually were ready to offer up to a whole unit of the private good in order to get this unit of the public good. Thus, the voluntary principle is no good (as we more or less knew already).

*Foley equilibrium* [Foley, 1970]. Consider now alternative (b). First of all we have to specify, what the decisions are about, so we define a *budget* as

$$B = (z, t_1, \ldots, t_m)$$

where $z$ is the amount of public good to be produced, $t_1, \ldots, t_m$ the amounts of private good to be collected from the consumers (or, if we assume that the price of the private good is 1, the tax collected). Clearly, we need the constraint $z \leq \sum_{i=1}^{m} t_i$ (no budgetary deficits).

When the budget $B$ has been decided, every consumer $i$ can find her bundle as $(\omega_i - t_i, z)$. She can therefore evaluate different budgets: Consumer $i$ likes $B^0 = (z^0, t_1^0, \ldots, t_m^0)$ at least as much as $B^1 = (z^1, t_1^1, \ldots, t_m^1)$, if $u_i(\omega_i - t_i^0, z^0) \geq u_i(\omega_i - t_i^1, z^1)$. It is now natural to define the budget $B^0$ as optimal if there is no other budget $B'$ which is as good as $B^0$ for all consumers and better for at least one consumer.

A choice of an optimal budget (together with normal market activity for all the private goods, something that we do not need to consider here where there is only one such good) yields a Pareto optimal allocation and thereby a Lindahl equilibrium: When $B^0$ satisfies the above criteria the corresponding allocation $((x_1^0, z^0), \ldots, (x_m^0, z^0))$ is given by $x_i^0 = (\omega_i - t_i^0, z^0)$, $i = 1, \ldots, m$. If there were another feasible allocation $((x_1', z'), \ldots, (x_m', z'))$, such that all consumers were at least as well off and some better off, then one could construct a budget, namely $B' = (z', \omega_1 - x_1', \ldots, \omega_m - t_m')$, that would be as good as $B^0$ for all consumers and better for at least one, contradicting the optimality of $B^0$.

This way of solving the matter is however not quite satisfactory: The criterion for the choice of a budget $B^0$ is that there cannot be unanimous decision in favor of another budget. This criterion puts almost no limitation on what can be chosen, in particular it may be quite far from what a majority of the consumers would consider as desirable. To this should be added that the original problem – that of finding a feasible way of getting the economy into a Lindahl equilibrium – has only been transformed into a similar one, namely that of finding an optimal budget. Unfortunately there is no standard way of solving this problem.

*The Groves-Ledyard mechanism* [Groves and Ledyard, 1977]. We shall now consider a procedure which may be seen as a compromise between (a) and (b): (a) is taken care of in a decentralized way, while (b) is institutionalized. More specifically the procedure is as follows:

Each consumer $i$ sends a signal, which here is just a number $b_i$, to a central authority. Given signals $b_1, \ldots, b_m$ the production of the public good is fixed at

$$z = \sum_{i=1}^{m} b_i,$$

and consumer $i$'s payment (in terms of private goods) is

$$t_i = \frac{1}{m} \sum_{k=1}^{m} b_k + \left[ \frac{m-1}{m}(b_i - \mu_i)^2 - \sigma_i^2 \right],$$

where

$$\mu_i = \frac{1}{m-1} \sum_{k \neq i} b_k, \quad \sigma_i^2 = \frac{1}{m-2} \sum_{k \neq i} (b_k - \mu_i)^2.$$

There is an important difference between this procedure and the totally decentralized voluntary contributions: The quantity $z$ is found in the same way, but the payment now depends on the signals of the others: The more consumer $i$'s signal differs from that of the others the greater is her tax. This reduces the incentive to let $b_i = 0$ just to get rid of tax payments. We shall see that the procedure actually does lead to Pareto optimal allocations.

Before doing so we ought to make sure that the procedure is well-defined in the sense that the payments cover the outlays, $\sum_{i=1}^{m} t_i = \sum_{i=1}^{m} b_i$, or, what amounts to the same,

$$\sum_{i=1}^{m} \left[ \frac{m-1}{m}(b_i - \mu_i)^2 - \sigma_i^2 \right] = 0.$$

We have

$$\sum_{i=1}^{m} (b_i - \mu_i)^2 = \sum_i b_i^2 + \sum_i \mu_i^2 + \sum_i 2 b_i \mu_i$$

$$= \sum_i b_i^2 + \frac{1}{m-1}\left(\frac{m-2}{m-1}\left(\sum_i b_i\right)^2 + \frac{1}{m-1}\sum_i b_i^2\right) - \frac{2}{m-1}\left(\sum_i b_i\right)^2 + \frac{2}{m-1}\sum_i b_i^2,$$

so that

$$\frac{m-1}{m}\sum_i (b_i - \mu_i)^2 = \frac{m}{m-1}\sum_i b_i^2 - \frac{1}{m-1}\left(\sum_i b_i\right)^2$$

and

$$\sum_{i=1}^m \sigma_i^2 = \frac{1}{m-2}\left[(m-1)\sum_i b_i^2 - \frac{\sum_i(\sum_i b_i - b_i)^2}{m-1}\right]$$

$$= \frac{1}{m-2}\left[(m-1)\sum_i b_i^2 - \frac{m\left(\sum_i b_i\right)^2 + \sum_i b_i^2 - 2\left(\sum_i b_i\right)\left(\sum_i b_i\right)}{m-1}\right] = \frac{m}{m-1}\sum_i b_i^2 - \frac{1}{m-1}\left(\sum_i b_i\right)^2.$$

This gives us the desired equality.

Let $((x_1^0, z^0), \ldots, (x_m^0, z^0))$ be an allocation such that for each consumer $i$, given the signals of the others there is no other choice of signal $b_i'$ that would give her a better final result (that is, $(b_1^0, \ldots, b_m^0)$ is a Nash equilibrium).

Consider now consumer $i$. If she wishes to increase the amount of public goods by a (small) unit, then she has to pay

$$q_i = \frac{\partial t_i}{\partial b_i} = \frac{1}{m} + \frac{m-1}{m}2(b_i - \mu_i).$$

Notice that $\sum_{i=1}^m q_i = 1$.

Given the signals $b_h^0$ from the other consumers $h \neq i$, consumer $i$ has chosen $b_i^0$ so that $u_i(\omega_i - t_i, \sum_{h \neq i} b_h^0 + b_i)$ is maximized. This means that

$$\frac{\partial u_i}{\partial b_i} = -u_{i1}' q_i + u_{i2}' = 0$$

or

$$\frac{u_{i1}'}{u_{i2}'} = \frac{1}{q_i}.$$

The ratio $1/q_i$ is the marginal rate of substitution in the point $x_i^0$, which again means that it is the slope of the tangent to the indifference curve through the point. If therefore $x_i'$ is another bundle with $u_i(x_i') > u_i(x_i^0)$ we must have

$$x_i' + q_i z' > x_i^0 + q_i z^0.$$

Now we can use the technique from the discussion of Foley equilibria: Let $B^0 = (z^0, t_1^0, \ldots, t_m^0)$ be the budget which belongs to the equilibrium $(b_1^0, \ldots, b_m^0)$, and let $B' = (z', t_1', \ldots, t_m')$ be another budget. If $B'$ were as good as $B^0$ for all and better for some $i$, then for all $i$ we would have $u_i(\omega_i - t_i', z') \geq u_i(\omega_i - t_i^0, z^0)$, and from this we could conclude that

$$x_i' + q_i z' \geq x_i^0 + q_i z^0$$

or

$$(t_i^0 - t_i') + q_i(z' - z^0) \geq 0$$

with strict inequality for some $i$, from which

$$\sum_{i=1}^{m} (t_i^0 - t_i') < (z^0 - z') \sum_{i=1}^{m} q_i,$$

or, since $\sum_{i=1}^{m} q_i = 1$ and $\sum_{i=1}^{m} t_i^0 = z^0$,

$$\sum_{i=1}^{m} t_i' < z'$$

contradicting that $B'$ was a budget.

It follows from this that $B^0$ is optimal, and as we have seen, this implies that the associated allocation is Pareto optimal. Thus we may conclude that an allocation $((x_1^0, z^0), \ldots, (x_m^0, z^0))$, which is an equilibrium for the Groves-Ledyard mechanism, is Pareto optimal.

The ideas behind the Groves-Ledyard mechanism has a much longer range than the case considered above – also when we take into account that we might have had more than one private and one public good. We have here a mechanism which gives something desirable (in this case Pareto optimality, or equivalently Lindahl equilibria), even though the involved agents act strategically (in our case by not naively sending the $b_i$ which corresponds to their wishes concerning the production of public goods, but looking for a signal which gives the best final position in terms of public goods and tax payments). The importance of such mechanisms is obvious, since they open up for decentralization without loosing the overall goals for society.

## 5   Pricing in healthcare provision

Most of the economics of healthcare revolves around payments, by patients or insurance companies, and to providers of all types. Since the total amount of all these payments constitutes the aggregate healthcare cost in a country, it can come as no surprise that there is considerable interest around the form that these payments assume, and the incentives that may or may not be created by the rules that they follow. What is paid for is of course determined both by quantity and by price, but the two things are usually closely connected, and when we consider payment rules with some kind of welfare-maximizing properties, they will typically be determined together.

In this section, we take a closer look at some pricing rules related to welfare maximization. As we have seen, the presence of market failure in some version or another means that ordinary markets cannot be relied upon, and there is a need for regulation. The nature of this regulation will depend on the type of market failure; we have already considered externalities and public goods, and we turn now to cases of increasing return (natural monopolies) and to asymmetric information which is an important factor in the economic activities related to healthcare.

## 5.1 Pricing under increasing returns to scale

The last of the three classical types of market failure is the one which has given rise to public intervention long ago, since the conditions for a smooth functioning of the market mechanism is violated to an extent where the market literally breaks down. Technically, the problems are caused by nonconvexities in the production sets of the firms: if profits are positive at some production, then it will be more than doubled if all proportions are multiplied by 2, so that there is an inherent tendency to overproduction making market prices shrink to a level where the firms cannot survive.

Since the technology points towards to a situation with only one producing firm, this is a reasonable point of departure for a discussion of what to do to reestablish efficient allocation. Unfortunately, this single firm cannot be left to itself, since being a monopolist it will be tempted to select a production plan which is not sustained in a competitive equilibrium. Consequently, the firm must be supervised or regulated, so that it is either told what to produce and which price to charge, or it must be subsidized in a particular way so as to induce the correct decisions.

In the following we look at two classical ways of selecting optimal production (and the corresponding prices) in public entreprises, namely (a) marginal cost pricing and (b) Ramsey pricing. Following this, we consider the other approach, which consists in allowing the firm to select production according to its own choices but restricting the revenues in a suitable way.

## 5.2 Marginal cost pricing

The simplest way of restoring allocative efficiency is to select allocations where the standard conditions of a competitive equilibrium are fulfilled, just as it was done when selecting Lindahl equilibria when allocating public goods. This amounts to selecting prices and quantities produced so that price equals marginal cost for each commodity, not only those produced under standard circumstances, but also when production exhibits increasing returns to scale (or presence of very large fixed costs).

If prices are set according to marginal cost one may end up with a deficit, and this will typically be the case if there are increasing returns to scale in production, as shown in Fig. 4.1. Here prices set according to marginal cost cannot cover average cost.

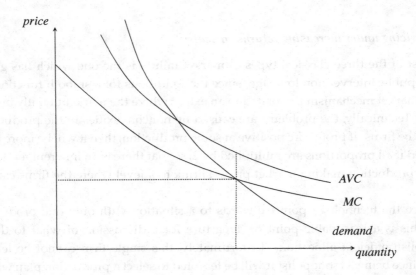

Fig. 4.1 Marginal cost pricing: optimal quantity is determined by the standard condition *marginal cost = inverse demand*. The resulting price falls short of average cost when there are increasing returns to scale.

There is nothing intrinsically wrong with deficits in firms producing in accordance with marginal cost pricing. Prices can be seen as *signals* about resource use, and low prices indicate that the consumers get their share of the returns to scale in the form of a large consumer surplus. The deficit only indicates that the firm must be compensated in another way, if the production cost should be fully covered by the firm. However, when applying this principle in practice, it will be confronted with the common viewpoint that a firm which cannot obtain a nonnegative profit is fundamentally unsound, and traditionally, the political system has been reluctant in accepting marginal cost pricing with all its consequences.

It must be admitted that the reluctance against public organizations running a deficit may have a rational origin: If the cost structure is private information of the organization, then the unqualified acceptance of deficits may well result in gross inefficiency. Indeed, regulating a firm, public or private, with an unknown cost function is a classical problem in the theory of regulation. We postpone a discussion of this situation for the moment and consider now the case where deficits are not acceptable, so that prices must cover cost.

## 5.3 *Ramsey pricing*

When prices are set so as to cover cost, but with the objective of maximizing welfare retained under this constraint, the problem to be solved is to determine how much of the aggregate cost should be recovered through the price of each good or service. Intuitively one might be tempted to choose a proportional rule, but this rule neglects the underlying details of consumer satisfaction as weighted against cost, indicating that demand elasticities might play a role, as indeed they do.

Formally, we face the task of choosing prices $p_1, \ldots, p_m$ of the $m$ commodities marketed by the firm or the healthcare organization, so that consumer welfare is maximized under a profit constraint (here taken to be zero profits, but the argument works with any other predetermined level of profits). It turns out to be convenient to work with the consumer's *expenditure function*, $e(p, r)$ which indicates the smallest outlay for the consumer if she wants to attain the utility level $r$ by purchasing commodities at the prices $p = (p_1, \ldots, p_m)$. Now the problem of finding the welfare maximizing prices under the profit constraint can be written as

$$\max_{p,r} e(p_1, \ldots, p_m, r)$$

subject to (1)

$$\pi(p_1, \ldots, p_m) = 0.$$

Here $\pi$ is the profit function, $\pi(p)$ depends on the prices of the commodities sold, the quantities being given by the market demand function.

In order to find necessary conditions for an optimum in (1) we define the Lagrangian of the problem,

$$L(p_1, \ldots, p_m, r, \lambda) = e(p_1, \ldots, p_m, r) + \lambda \pi(p_1, \ldots, p_m),$$

and setting the partial derivatives of $L$ w.r.t. $p_h$, $h = 1, \ldots, m$, equal to zero gives the expressions

$$\frac{\partial e}{\partial p_h} = -\lambda \frac{\partial \pi}{\partial p_h}, \quad h = 1, \ldots, m. \tag{2}$$

We now recall that the vector of partial derivatives of the expenditure function with respect to prices $p_i$, $i = 1, \ldots, m$, at $(p, r)$ is the (Hicksian or compensated) demand $q = h(p, r)$ at prices $p$ and utility level $r$, that is the expenditure minimizing bundle achieving utility $r$. We therefore have that (2) can be rewritten as

$$q_h = \lambda \frac{\partial \pi}{\partial p_h}, \quad h = 1, \ldots, m. \tag{3}$$

To get on from here we assume that there is no substitution in the consumption of the commodities considered, so that the firm faces $m$ different demand functions of the type $q_h = f_h(p_h)$, where each $f_h$ is differentiable with $f_i' \neq 0$. Writing

$$\frac{\partial \pi}{\partial p_h} = \frac{\partial \pi}{\partial q_h} \frac{dq_h}{dp_h}$$

for each $h$ and using that $f_h$ is invertible, we get the expressions

$$q_h \frac{dp_h}{dq_h} = -\lambda \frac{\partial \pi}{\partial q_h}, \quad h = 1, \ldots, m. \tag{4}$$

Since the profit function can be written as $\pi = \sum_{h=1}^{m} p_h q_h - c(q_1, \ldots, q_h)$, where $c(q_1, \ldots, q_m)$ is the cost of producing $(q_1, \ldots, q_m)$, we get by differentiating that

$$\frac{\partial \pi}{\partial q_h} = p_h + q_h \frac{dp_h}{dq_h} - c_h', \tag{5}$$

with

$$c_h' = \frac{\partial c(q_1, \ldots, q_m)}{\partial q_h}$$

being the marginal cost of producing commodity $h$.

Inserting (5) into (4) and rearranging, we get

$$(1 + \lambda) q_h \frac{dp_h}{dq_h} = -\lambda (p_h - c_h'), h = 1, \ldots, m.$$

Dividing by $p_h$ and $\lambda$ on both sides, using that the numerical demand elasticity of commodity $h$ with respect to its price is

$$\varepsilon_h = -\frac{dq_h}{dp_h} \frac{p_h}{q_h},$$

we finally get the expression

$$\frac{p_h - c_h'}{p_h} = \frac{1 + \lambda}{\lambda} \frac{1}{\varepsilon_h}, \quad h = 1, \ldots, m. \tag{6}$$

The expression in (6), derived by Ramsey [1927] in the context of optimal taxation rules, tells us that prices should be set so that the Lerner index on the left-hand side is proportional to the inverse elasticity, a phenomenon which is wellknown from many other cases of pricing, including monopoly pricing and price discrimination. In particular, if we assume that medical services, which are strictly necessary for survival, have a very small elasticity of demand, then such services would be subject to a larger markup than those services which could be easily discarded. This may look counterintuitive, since the pricing rule was derived so as to maximize consumer welfare under the no-subsidy constraint. However, it does make sense: the low price for consumers for whom price matters means that they will participate in covering the overhead which should otherwise be paid by the low-elasticity costumers alone.

What might bother us in applying the Ramsey rule and charging high prices to the needing and low prices to people from whom the service is largely unnecessary is probably the implication of high prices when incomes are too low. This is a problem from which we have largely abstracted here, considering only a single consumer, or alternatively considering only the consumption sector as a whole. But then we have also disregarded income transfers here, looking only at allocative efficiency, which can be achieved by pricing rules, whereas distributional fairness would need other instruments such as income transfers.

## 5.4  Cost allocation

An alternative approach to the pricing of products and services, which does not depend on details of demand elasticity etc., and which by its very nature guarantees that all costs are covered, is to compute unit costs of delivering the services and then charge these unit costs as price. Unfortunately, simple as it sounds, this approach quickly gets into problems: When goods and services are produced in a joint production process, there is no correct way of assigning the total cost to each of the goods or services. There are two ways out of this dilemma, namely (1) a practical approach, using ad hoc criteria for allocating cost to products, or (2) an axiomatic approach, specifying properties of the cost allocation procedure and then deriving explicit formula when possible. We review the two approaches briefly below.

Given the production $q = (q_1, \dots, q_n)$ and the cost $c(q_1, \dots, q_n)$, we are searching for unit costs $(c_1, \dots, c_n)$ such that $\sum_{i=1}^{n} c_i = c(q)$. In practical applications, some of the cost items are *direct* in the sense that they are attributed in a unique way to a particular product. The remaining cost is *overhead* and this is what should be allocated to the individual products. For simplicity, we shall assume here that the direct costs have already been subtracted, so that $c(q)$ represents the overhead to be distributed.

*Activity based costing (ABC).* If cost is not attributable to products, one may look for a next-best solution, and among these a method widely used in practice consists in assigning cost to *activities*, writing

$$c(q) = c^{a_1}(q) + \cdots + c^{a_r}(q),$$

where $a_1, \ldots, a_r$ are suitable ways of splitting the production process into parts, and their nature will depend heavily on the application at hand. The idea behind the identification of key activities in the production is that each activity should be linked to a *cost driver*, which should be quantifiable and which can be related to products, and then the cost will be assigned to products in proportion to the allocation of the cost driver.

We may formalize a cost driver for an activity $a$ as a function $\zeta^a(q)$ which has an additively separable function form, so that

$$\zeta^a(q_1, \ldots, q_n) = \zeta^a_1(q_1) + \cdots + \zeta^a_i(q_n)),$$

and the cost $c^a$ of the activity is attributable to the cost driver $\zeta^a$ in the sense that $c^a(q) = g^a(\zeta^a(q))$ for every $q$ for some function $g^a$. Assuming linearity of this unknown $g^a$, we can write the activity cost as

$$c^a(q) = g^a \cdot \left[ \zeta^a_1(q_1) + \cdots + \zeta^a_n(q_n) \right],$$

and if also the functions $\zeta^a_i$, for $i = 1, \ldots, n$ are assumed linear, we can allocate $c^a(q)$ to individual unit costs

$$c^a_i(q) = \frac{\zeta^a_i(q_i)}{\sum_{i=1}^{n} \zeta_i(q_i)} c^a(q_1, \ldots, q_n), i = 1, \ldots, n. \tag{7}$$

Clearly, the success of this approach depends on whether such cost drivers can be found, as well as on the reasonableness of the linearity assumptions.

In practical applications of activity based costing the above procedure of determining activities and the related cost drivers is often carried out in several steps, giving rise to a hierarchy of activities: There are basic activities, which contribute to the final delivery of the products and services, but these activities in their turn depend on other, assisting activities, ending with the upper level of management. The ABC approach will then consist in first allocating the top activities to all lower level activities, then allocating next layer cost, including those allocated in the first step, to all activities below, etc., ending with an allocation of cost to the final products.

The widespread application of the ABC method makes it tempting to appoint it as *the* method of cost allocation. This is however not entirely correct, since there are many other ways of assigning unit costs to products, and none of the methods can have a claim to be the correct one without further qualifications. Indeed, the choice of an appropriate method presupposes that an objective of the cost allocation procedure has been declared, since then it will be possible to determine one, perhaps even a unique, method as the one which achieves the stated objective. This changes the perspective of cost allocation somewhat, as we shall see below.

*Axiomatic cost allocation.* The approach to cost assignment working from general principles to concrete methods is inspired from the consideration of specific cases, where the assignment of some overall sum of cost to separate entities, which could be departments of the organisation or services delivered by the organisation. The specific solutions proposed were found by applying solution concepts from cooperative game theory, and with this followed the reliance on axiomatic foundations of the solutions, or, in this case, cost assignments.

Cooperative game theory deals with problems of assigning payoffs to individuals based on the potential gains of groups of individuals that may or may not materialize. In our present case, where the total cost of a bundle $q = (q_1,\dots,q_n)$ should be assigned to individual products, we work with cost instead of gains. The relevant identification of coalitions can be obtained in several ways.

One approach could be that coalitions are identified with groups $S \subseteq \{1,\dots,n\}$ of products, giving rise to cost functions $c_S$ defined by

$$c_S(q_1,\dots,q_n) = c(q_S; 0),$$

where $(q_S, 0)$ is the vector with $i$th coordinate equal to $q_i$ if $i \in S$ and 0 otherwise. Using the Shapley value (see Box 4.6) as a solution concept for cooperative games, one may define the cost share of product $i$ as

$$\varphi_i(q_1,\dots,q_n) = \sum_{S:i\in S} \frac{(|S|-1)!(n-|S|)!}{n!} \left[ c_S(q_1,\dots,q_n) - c_{S\setminus\{i\}}(q_1,\dots,q_n) \right], \qquad (8)$$

with resulting unit costs

$$c_i(q) = \frac{\varphi_i(q_1,\dots,q_n)}{q_i}, \quad i = 1,\dots,n. \qquad (9)$$

This method is known as the *Shapley-Shubik* method for cost allocation (after Shubik [1962]). What should interest us here is not so much the formula as the properties of the method, of which the following should be mentioned:

(i) *Additivity:* If production can be split into two separate processes with cost $c^1(q)$ and $c^2(q)$, respectively, then allocating cost for $c^1$ and $c^2$ separately and adding the results will yield the same unit costs as allocation $c^1 + c^2$,

---

**Box 4.6 Cost allocation and cooperative game theory.** The simplest case of cost allocation occurs when the cost of a certain activity must be allocated to a set $N = \{1, \ldots, n\}$ of individuals (or firms, or organizational units). Suppose that we know the cost $c(S)$ arising if each subset $S$ of $N$ carries out the activities by themselves, neglecting the rest. Presumably, it is cheaper to work in common, but the cost $c(N)$ must be paid, and the task consists in finding cost shares $c_i$, for $i \in N$, such that $\sum_{i \in S} c_i$ (the classical case was that of an airport, where different aircrafts use runways of different length, and this should be reflected in the payment for use of the airport, cf. Littlechild and Thompson [1977]).

The situation can formally be identified as a *cooperative game*, where $N$ is the set of players. Subsets are here called coalitions, and each coalition $S$ can obtain a certain gain $v(S)$ for themselves. A solution is a vector $x = (x_1, \ldots, x_n)$ with $\sum_{i \in N} x_i = v(N)$. There several suggestions as to what constitutes a useful solution. One of these is the *Shapley value* with

$$x_i = \frac{1}{2^n} \sum_{S \subset N} [v(S) - v(S \setminus \{i\})] = \sum_{S:i \in S} \frac{(|S| - 1)!(n - |S|)!}{n!} [v(S) - v(S \setminus \{i\})].$$

for $i = 1, \ldots, n$. Here the $i$th individual is assigned the average of her marginal contribution to the coalitions, a principle which seems quite reasonable. However, this would be a rather weak argument, since many other solution concepts would appear as equally attractive. Therefore solutions are typically selected according to their *properties*.

The Shapley value can be characterized as the only solution which satisfies

- additivity: for two games with the same players, it makes no difference whether a solution is found for each of them and then added, or a solution is found to the sum of the games,
- symmetry: individuals with the same influence on outcome get the same in the solution,
- dummy-property: individuals with no influence in any context get nothing.

For more details on the Shapley value and other solutions to cooperative games, see e.g. Keiding [2015].

The Shapley value was among the first solution concepts to find application in cost allocation (one has to replace gains expressed through $v$ by cost given by $c$), but subsequently it turned out that other solution concepts might as well be useful in cost allocation.

---

(ii) *Average cost compatibility:* If the cost function has the simple form

$$c(q_1, \ldots, q_n) = \hat{c}\left(\sum_{i=1}^{n} q_i\right),$$

(so that all products have identical influence on cost), then each of the resulting unit costs must equal average cost $\hat{c}\left(\sum_i q_i\right) / \sum_i q_i$.

The two properties may seem quite reasonable and intuitively not very restrictive. It may therefore be surprising that they can be used to characterize the Shapley-Shubik method in a unique way, so that if we insist on properties (i) and (ii), then we must necessarily use the method given in (8) and (9).

An alternative method, which uses another identification of coalitions, this time less intuitive, replaces the property in (ii) by another one, namely

(iii) *Monotonicity:* If for two cost functions $c^1$ and $c^2$ and some $i \in \{1, \ldots, n\}$

$$\frac{\partial c^1(q)}{\partial q_i} \geq \frac{\partial c^2(q)}{\partial q_i} \text{ for all } q,$$

then $c_i^1(q) \geq c_i^2(q)$ for all $q$.

The monotonicity property links the unit cost of $i$ to the impact of product on cost. It can be shown that property (iii) together with a symmetry property leads to the *Aumann-Shapley* method, which finds the unit cost of commodity $i$ as

$$c_i(q) = \int_0^1 \frac{\partial c}{\partial q_i}(tq)\mathrm{d}t. \tag{10}$$

As it can be seen from (10), the Aumann-Shapley unit cost is found by averaging marginal cost when production moves from 0 along the ray determined by the actual production. This procedure is intuitive also without recourse to game theory, which in the present case is less immediate.

The obvious next step would be to look at methods which compute unit cost by integration of marginal cost along another path than the one used in (10), and this will indeed give rise to other allocation methods with other characterizing properties. The exact nature of these are not so interesting for us at this point, but the general approach to cost allocation, namely a characterization by desirable properties, provides an alternative to the traditional cost accounting methods with their inherent lack of transparency.

## 6  Paying the doctor

The way in which patients – and particularly health insurance companies or government healthcare institutions – pay the doctors for their services has been object of debates for many years. The traditional way of paying for the services is inherited from ordinary markets, where each type of service has a specific price which is paid after delivery, in the debate known as *fee-for-service*. At the other end of the spectrum one finds *capitation*, a fixed payment per patient assigned to the doctor's practice.

Each of the two systems have their built-in weaknesses. With fee-for-service we expect a certain inflation in the number of consultations given or other services provided by the doctor, as already discussed in the context of supplier-induced demand. Capitation, on the other hand, can be expected to have a negative impact on the quality of the services delivered. In many countries, healthcare organizations use combinations of the two systems, trusting that a mixture will reduce the negative side effects of the pure versions. Still another approach, introduced in later years, is *bundled payment*, where payment follows the delivery of whole episodes or treatments rather than isolated consultations or treatments.

In the following, we look into payment rules which are designed so as to give the right incentives to the providers. Since both price and quantity matter, what we look for is not so much a rule for setting prices as a mechanism that determines how much should be delivered and to which payment.

## 6.1  *Regulating a monopoly with unknown cost*

Regulation of a monopoly has been investigated by several authors, in particular by Baron and Myerson [1982]; here we shall work with a simplified version of their model.

We consider a firm which operates under increasing returns to scale, producing a single good in the quantity $q$ and having a cost function of the form $\theta C(q)$, which depends on a multiplicative productivity parameter $\theta$. The productivity parameter $\theta$ of the firm, also to be mentioned as its type, is observed only by the firm itself. It is assumed to be randomly distributed in an interval $\Theta = \left[\underline{\theta}, \overline{\theta}\right] \subset \mathbb{R}_+$, with probability distribution function $F$ and density $f$. The demand side is described by an inverse demand function $P(q)$, which is non-increasing in $q$ and such that for each $\theta \in \Theta$, there is a unique $q$ such that $P(q)q = \theta C(q)$. Consumer satisfaction at production $q$ is given by

$$V(q) = \int_0^q P(s)\mathrm{d}s, \tag{11}$$

and consumer surplus is $S(p) = V(q) - P(q)q$.

In a regulated monopoly, the regulator will collect a message from the firm about productivity $\theta$, and given this signal, the regulator decides whether to produce at all, and if so, how much to produce. Moreover, a reward is paid to the firm for delivering the quantity ordered. Formally a regulatory policy is a triple $(\delta, q, r)$ of functions of $\theta$, where

    (a) $\delta(\theta)$ is the probability that the firm is allowed to market a nonzero output,

    (b) $q(\theta)$ is the output which the firm should produce, and

    (c) $r(\theta)$ is the revenue assigned to the producer.

We assume that productivity is private information of the firm, so the productivity signaled by the firm may be the true one or it may be false. It may be noticed that we assume that the messages to be sent are values of the productivity mechanism, meaning that we are treating a *direct mechanism*; also, we shall be interested in equilibria where truth-telling is the optimal choice of the firm. This may look restrictive, but in fact it is not, a consequence of the *revelation principle* in mechanism design, cf. Myerson [1981].

Before dealing with the objectives of the regulator, we consider some properties which a regulatory policy must have independent of the objective: Since $\theta$ cannot be observed by the regulator, the mechanism must be incentive compatible. For each pair $(\hat{\theta}, \theta)$ let

$$\pi(\hat{\theta}, \theta) = \delta(\hat{\theta})\left[r(\hat{\theta}) - \theta C(q(\hat{\theta}))\right], \tag{12}$$

be the net income of the producer of type $\theta$ who states the type $\hat{\theta}$, given the regulatory policy $(\delta, q, r)$. The incentive compatibility constraint is then

$$\pi(\theta, \theta) \geq \pi(\hat{\theta}, \theta), \text{ all } \theta, \hat{\theta} \in \Theta. \tag{13}$$

Also, the mechanism is voluntary in the sense that it satisfies the participation constraint

$$r(\theta) \geq \theta C(q(\theta)), \text{ all } \theta \in \Theta. \tag{14}$$

It is convenient to reformulate the participation and incentive compatibility constraints using the following result, where $\pi(\theta) = \pi(\theta, \theta)$ denotes the net income of the producer announcing true type. A regulatory policy $(\delta, q, r)$ is *feasible* if it satisfies the constraints (13) and (14).

PROPOSITION 6 *Let $(\delta, q, r)$ be a feasible regulatory policy. Then*

$$\pi(\theta) = \pi(\overline{\theta}) + \int_{\theta}^{\overline{\theta}} \delta(t)C(q(t))dt. \tag{15}$$

*In praticular, if $\delta(\theta) = 1$, then*

$$r(\theta) = \pi(\overline{\theta}) + \theta C(q(\theta)) + \int_{\theta}^{\overline{\theta}} \delta(t)C(q(t))\,dt \geq 0, \text{ all } \theta \in \Theta. \tag{16}$$

PROOF: The function $\pi(\hat{\theta}, \theta)$ has bounded partial derivative $C(q(\theta))$ with respect to $\theta$, so by the envelope theorem (cf. e.g.Milgrom and Segal [2002]), (13) implies that $\pi(\theta)$ can be written as

$$\pi(\theta) = \pi(\overline{\theta}) + \int_{\theta}^{\overline{\theta}} \delta(t)C(q(t))dt$$

for each $\theta$. Now (16) follows after insertion of (12). $\qquad\square$

What constitutes an optimal regulatory policy clearly depends on the objective of the regulator.

*Expected welfare maximization.* In the simplest conceivable case, where only aggregate welfare matters, the regulator will seek to maximize

$$\int_{\Theta} \delta(\theta) \left[ V(q(\theta)) - \theta C(q(\theta)) \right] f(\theta) d\theta \tag{17}$$

over all regulation policies $(\delta, q, r)$. Since the size of the subsidy does not matter for welfare, which depends only on allocation, the regulation should be such that

$$q(\theta) = \theta C'(q(\theta)),$$

with $\delta(\theta) = 1$ for each $\theta$ such that $[V(q(\theta)) - \theta C(q(\theta))] \geq 0$ and $\delta(\theta) = 0$ otherwise. This is the case of pure marginal cost pricing already considered, and the present reconsideration adds only the size of the subsidy to be paid for each given value of $\theta$, namely $r(\theta) - P(q(\theta))q(\theta)$ with $r(\theta)$ as given in Proposition 6.

*Expected consumer surplus optimization with a subsidy constraint.* If the regulator's objective takes into account that subsidy payment $s(\theta) = r(\theta) - P(q(\theta))q(\theta)$ has a negative influence on welfare, then the regulatory policy should be chosen so as to maximize

$$\int_{\Theta} \delta(\theta) \left[ S(q(\theta)) - s(\theta) \right] f(\theta) d\theta$$

subject to a constraint on the payoff of the firm,

$$\int_{\Theta} \pi(\theta) f(\theta) d\theta \geq \Pi$$

for a constant $\Pi \geq 0$. Suppose that $(\delta, q, r)$ solves this problem. The Lagrangian of this maximization problem, after inserting the expressions for $S(q(\theta))$ and $s(\theta)$, can be written as

$$\int_{\Theta} \delta(\theta) \left[ V(q(\theta)) - \theta C(q(\theta)) - \pi(\theta) \right] f(\theta) d\theta + \lambda \int_{\Theta} \pi(\theta) f(\theta) d\theta. \tag{18}$$

Using (15) of Proposition 6, we have

$$\int_{\Theta} \delta(\theta) \pi(\theta) f(\theta) d\theta = \int_{\Theta} \left[ \pi(\bar{\theta}) + \int_{\theta}^{\bar{\theta}} \delta(t) C(q(t)) dt \right] f(\theta) d\theta$$

$$= \pi(\bar{\theta}) + \int_{\Theta} \delta(\theta) C(q(\theta)) \left[ \int_{\underline{\theta}}^{\theta} f(t) dt \right] d\theta = \pi(\bar{\theta}) + \int_{\Theta} \delta(\theta) C(q(\theta)) F(\theta) d\theta, \tag{19}$$

where we have changed the order of integration in the second line of the expression. Inserting into the Lagrangian, we obtain that $(\delta, q, r)$ maximizes

$$\int_{\Theta} \delta(\theta) \left[ V(q(\theta)) - v(\theta)C(q(\theta)) \right] f(\theta)d\theta - (1 - \lambda)\pi(\bar{\theta}), \qquad (20)$$

where

$$v(\theta) = \theta + (1 - \lambda)\frac{F(\theta)}{f(\theta)}.$$

We may think of $v(\theta)$ as a *virtual* productivity parameter, and maximizing (20) would then imply that production should be determined in such a way that $V'(q(\theta)) = P(q(\theta)) = vC'(q(\theta))$ and $\delta(\theta) = 1$ if and only if $V(q(\theta) - v(\theta)C(q(\theta)) \geq 0$, and the intuition holds at least for well-behaved parameter distributions $F$. For a more detailed description of optimal policies we refer to Baron and Myerson [1982].

*Welfare maximization under a no-subsidies constraint.* This corresponds to the setup which led to Ramsey pricing in the full information case, cf. Greve and Keiding [2016]. A feasible regulatory policy is optimal if it maximizes expected net welfare

$$\int_{\Theta} W(q(\theta), \theta)\delta(\theta)dF(\theta) \qquad (21)$$

subject to the no-subsidy condition

$$r(\theta) \leq P(q(\theta))q(\theta). \qquad (22)$$

Some properties of optimal regulatory policies are listed below.

LEMMA 1 *Let $(\delta, q, r)$ be an optimal regulatory policy. Then*
  (i) $\delta(\theta) \in \{0, 1\}$ *for all $\theta \in \Theta$,*
  (ii) *there is $\theta^0 \in \Theta$, such that $\{\theta \mid \delta(\theta) = 1\} = [\underline{\theta}, \theta^0]$,*
  (iii) *for each $\theta$ with $\delta(\theta) = 1$, $q(\theta) \in [q^0, q^1]$, where $q^0$ is defined by $P(q^0)q^0 = \theta^0C(q^0)$ and $q^1 = \sup\{q \mid P(q)q - \theta C(q) \geq (\theta^0 - \theta)C(q^0), \theta \leq \theta^0\}$.*

PROOF: (i) An optimal regulatory policy $(\delta, q, r)$ maximizes $\int_{\Theta} W(q(\theta), \theta)\delta(\theta) dF(\theta)$ subject to the constraint in (16). Suppose that $0 < \delta(\theta) < 1$ is some small interval. Then increasing $\delta(\theta)$ will increase expected welfare without violating the constraint, a contradiction, so that $\delta(\theta)$ must be either 0 or 1. If $\theta^0 = \inf\{\theta \mid \delta(\theta) = 1\}$ we get from continuity of objective and constraint that also $\delta(\theta^0) = 1$.

(ii) Suppose that $\delta(\theta) = 0$ and that $\delta(\theta') = 1$ for some $\theta' > \theta$. Then $r(\theta') \geq \theta'C(q(\theta')) > \theta C(q(\theta'))$, and we would have a violation of incentive compatibility. Thus, $\{\theta \mid \delta(\theta) = 0\}$ is an interval in $\Theta$ containing $\bar{\theta}$, and by (i), its complement is an interval containing $\underline{\theta}$.

(iii) Let $q^0 = q(\theta^0)$. Since $P(\theta^0)q(\theta^0) \geq \theta^0 C(q^0)$ and $(\delta, q, r)$ is optimal, we have that $P(\theta^0)q^0 = \theta^0 C(q^0)$. For $\theta' < \theta^0$, $q(\theta') \geq q(\theta^0)$ by incentive compatibility, and clearly $q(\theta') \leq q^1$, where $q^1$ is such that $P(q^1)q^1 - \theta C(q^1)$ is at least equal to the profit to be obtained by stating $\theta^0$ instead of the true type $\theta$, all $\theta \leq \theta^0$. ☐

As shown by the lemma, in an optimal regulatory policy either production is not carried out at all or the firm will be asked to produce in the interval $[q^0, q^1]$ defined in part (iii). The absence of subsidies means that production will be suspended for large values of $\theta$, and also that production when carried out will differ from the one where marginal cost intersects demand. The difference can be assessed using the following result.

PROPOSITION 7 *Let $(\delta, q, r)$ be a feasible regulatory policy which maximizes (21) subject to (22). Then*

$$P(q(\theta)) - \theta C'(q(\theta)) \geq \frac{\theta^0 - \theta}{q^1} C(q^0) \tag{23}$$

*for each $\theta$ with $\delta(\theta) = 1$.*

PROOF: For each $\theta \in \Theta$, the welfare maximizing production $q^*(\theta)$ satisfies $P(q^*(\theta)) = \theta C'(q^*(\theta))$, whereas $q(\theta)$ must be such that profits $P(q(\theta))q(\theta) \geq r(\theta) \geq \theta C(q(\theta))$ whenever $\delta(\theta) \neq 0$, since $(\delta, q, r)$ is individually rational.

By Proposition 6,

$$P(q(\theta))q(\theta) - \theta C(q(\theta)) \geq r(\theta) - \theta C(q(\theta)) = \pi(\theta^0) + \int_{\theta}^{\theta^0} \delta(t)C(q(t))dt > (\theta^0 - \theta)C(q^\delta),$$

where we have used that $\pi(\theta^0) \geq 0$ and assessed the integral by the length of the interval for which $\delta(\theta) = 1$, multiplied by a value $C(q)$, which is as small as any value $C(q(\theta))$ taken in this interval. Dividing on both sides by $q(\theta) \neq 0$, we get

$$P(q(\theta)) - \theta \frac{C(q(\theta))}{q(\theta)} \geq \frac{\theta^0 - \theta}{q(\theta)} C(q^0) \geq \frac{\theta^0 - \theta}{q^1} C(q^0), \tag{24}$$

where $q^1 \geq q^0$ are defined in Lemma 1. Since $C'(q) \leq \dfrac{C(q)}{q}$ for all $q$ on the left-hand side (the inequality holds due to the non-decreasing returns to scale), one gets (23). ☐

In the case of constant marginal cost $c$, the expression in (23) reduces to

$$\frac{P(q(\theta)) - \theta c}{\theta c} \geq \left( \frac{\theta^0}{\theta} - 1 \right) \frac{q^0}{q^1}.$$

On the left hand side, we have if not the Lerner index, then an approximation, showing that the markup on marginal cost becomes larger when the productivity parameter gets smaller.

## 6.2   Healthcare contracts under physician agency

In the models of regulation with asymmetric information considered so far, the producer was seen as a usual profit maximizing agent. In line with our considerations of supply decisions in the previous chapter, we should also consider the case of a healthcare provider with a more subtle objective, involving the perceived welfare of the patient. This regulation aspect considered above is relevant since it adds to a long discussion of the optimal remuneration structure for physicians (by healthcare organizations or health insurers). An important contribution to this discussion is the model proposed by Choné and Ma [2011], which is outlined below.

We consider a physician providing treatment to the amount of $q$ to patients, who will obtain a benefit $\alpha V(q)$ from this. Here the benefit function $V$, assumed to be increasing in $q$, is common knowledge, whereas the parameter $\alpha$ is known only to the physicist. The physician has cost $C(q)$ and is paid a remuneration $r$, so that the profit is $r - C(q)$. But since the physician also takes the patient's welfare into consideration, the objective is $r - C(q) + \beta V(q)$, where $\beta$, the weight put on patients' benefit, is private information. The two parameters $\alpha$ and $\beta$ may not be identical.

We assume that a healthcare organization wants to design a policy so as to regulate the provision of care through the remuneration. We have now two unknown parameters $\alpha$ and $\beta$, each with possible values in some intervals $\left[\underline{\alpha}, \overline{\alpha}\right]$ and $\left[\underline{\beta}, \overline{\beta}\right]$, and the regulator knows only the joint distribution of $(\alpha, \beta)$, which has density function $f$. A mechanism is now a pair $(q, r)$, where $q(\alpha, \beta)$ determines the quantity delivered given the values of $\alpha$ and $\beta$, and $r(\alpha, \beta)$ is the remuneration paid to the doctor. As previously, we assume that the doctor states some values of $\alpha$ and $\beta$, after which $q$ and $r$ determines the outcome. To obtain truthful signaling of the parameters, the mechanism should be *incentive compatible* in the sense that

$$r(\alpha, \beta) - C(q(\alpha, \beta)) + \beta V(q(\alpha, \beta)) \geq r(\alpha', \beta') - C(q(\alpha', \beta')) + \beta V(q(\alpha', \beta')) \qquad (25)$$

for all $(\alpha, \beta), (\alpha', \beta') \in \left[\underline{\alpha}, \overline{\alpha}\right] \times \left[\underline{\beta}, \overline{\beta}\right]$, and individually rational in the sense that profit should be nonnegative,

$$r(\alpha, \beta) - C(q(\alpha, \beta)) \geq 0 \qquad (26)$$

for all $(\alpha, \beta) \in \left[\underline{\alpha}, \overline{\alpha}\right] \times \left[\underline{\beta}, \overline{\beta}\right]$. The mechanism as described may look strange if compared to real-life situations, but as previously, we rely on the revelation principle telling us that if there is some mechanism, where the physician sends different signals and outcome is determined depending on these signals, such that the regulator's objectives (which have not yet been described) are satisfied when the physician chooses what is optimal according to her objective, then there is also a direct mechanism such that truth-telling is optimal, and we investigate this mechanism.

We first take another look at the incentive compatibility constraint (25), which can also be written as

$$r(\alpha, \beta) - C(q(\alpha, \beta)) + \beta V(q(\alpha, \beta)) = \pi(\beta) \tag{27}$$

for all $(\alpha, \beta) \in [\underline{\alpha}, \overline{\alpha}] \times [\underline{\beta}, \overline{\beta}]$, with

$$\pi(\beta) = \max_{\alpha', \beta'} r(\alpha', \beta') - C(q(\alpha', \beta')) + \beta V(q(\alpha', \beta')). \tag{28}$$

It may be noticed that the incentive compatible payoff $\pi$ does not depend on $\alpha$. Actually, this independence of the competence parameter can be extended also the regulatory policy.

PROPOSITION 8 *Let $(q, r)$ be a regulatory policy which is incentive compatible, and let $\alpha, \alpha' \in [\underline{\alpha}, \overline{\alpha}]$. Then*

$$r(\alpha, \beta) = r(\alpha', \beta), \quad q(\alpha, \beta) = q(\alpha', \beta)$$

*for almost all $\beta \in [\underline{\beta}, \overline{\beta}]$.*

PROOF: Let $\alpha, \alpha' \in [\underline{\alpha}, \overline{\alpha}]$ be arbitrary. Using the same reasoning as in the proof of Proposition 6, we have that

$$\pi(\beta) = \pi\left(\underline{\beta}\right) + \int_{\underline{\beta}}^{\beta} V(q(\alpha, \beta)) dt = \pi\left(\underline{\beta}\right) + \int_{\underline{\beta}}^{\beta} V(q(\alpha', \beta)) dt \tag{29}$$

from which we get that $V(q(\alpha, \beta)) = V(q(\alpha', \beta))$ for almost all $\beta$. Since $V$ is assumed to be an increasing function of $q$, we get that $q(\alpha, \beta) = q(\alpha', \beta)$ for almost all $\beta$. Using that

$$r(\alpha, \beta) = \pi(\beta) + C(q(\alpha, \beta)) - \beta V(q(\alpha, \beta)), \tag{30}$$

we obtain that $r(\alpha, \beta) = r(\alpha', \beta)$ for almost all $\beta$. $\square$

Given the result of the proposition, we may restrict ourselves to regulatory policies which are independent of $\alpha$, and we write $r(\beta), q(\beta)$ in the sequel. We now turn to the regulator, which in the present context may be thought of as a health insurance company or a government healthcare institution. We assume that the objective of the regulator is given by expected value of $aV(q) - r$, patient satisfaction minus payment to the doctor. Expected value of the regulation $(q, r)$ is then

$$W = \int_{\underline{\alpha}}^{\overline{\alpha}} \int_{\underline{\beta}}^{\overline{\beta}} [\alpha V(q(\beta)) - r(\beta)] f(\alpha, \beta) d\alpha d\beta = \int_{\underline{\beta}}^{\overline{\beta}} [\alpha_0(\beta) V(q(\beta)) - r(\beta)] g(\beta) d\beta,$$

where $\alpha_0(\beta) = \int_{\underline{\alpha}}^{\overline{\alpha}} \alpha h(\alpha, \beta) d\alpha$ is the conditional mean of $\alpha$ and $g$ is the density function of the marginal distribution over $\beta$.

Assuming now that the regulation is incentive compatible, so that $r(\beta)$ has the form given in (30), we may rewrite the regulator's objective as

$$W = \int_{\underline{\beta}}^{\bar{\beta}} [\alpha_0(\beta) + \beta V(q(\beta)) - \pi(\beta) - C(q(\beta))]\, g(\beta)\mathrm{d}\beta,$$

which should be maximized under the constraint (26). Here we notice that if $\beta$ is large enough, then the physician care so much for the patient that she is willing to accept zero profits, and assuming that this occurs for some $\widehat{\beta}$ with $\underline{\beta} < \widehat{\beta} < \bar{\beta}$, the regulator may choose $q(\beta) = \hat{q}$, that is a constant, for $\beta \geq \hat{q}$. We therefore split the integral in two parts and further insert the expression for $\pi(\beta)$ given in (29); reorganizing in the same way as we did above in (15)–(20), we obtain that

$$W = \int_{\underline{\beta}}^{\widehat{\beta}} [v^*(\beta)V(q(\beta)) - C(q(\beta))]\, g(\beta)\mathrm{d}\beta - G(\widehat{\beta})\widehat{\beta}V(q(\widehat{\beta})) \qquad (31)$$

$$+ \int_{\widehat{\beta}}^{\bar{\beta}} [\alpha_0(\beta)V(\hat{q}) - C(\hat{q})]\, g(\beta)\mathrm{d}\beta,$$

where we have introduced the virtual competence level $v^*(\beta) = \alpha_0(\beta) + \beta + \dfrac{G(\beta)}{g(\beta)}$, which differs from the true competence level due to the lack of information of the regulator. We can use the expression in (31) to obtain som qualitative information about the structure of the optimal regulation. Assuming that $v^*$ is nondecreasing in $\beta$, we see that

- for $\underline{\beta} \leq \beta \leq \widehat{\beta}$, the quantity $q(\beta)$ should be such that

  $$v^*(\beta)V'(q(\beta)) = C'(q(\beta)),$$

  so that virtual marginal patient satisfaction, which may be seen as the price, including informational rent, that the regulator is willing to pay for an additional unit of care, should equal the marginal cost of delivering this additional unit, and
- for $\widehat{\beta} \leq \beta \leq \bar{\beta}$, the quantity $\hat{q}$ should satisfy

  $$\alpha_0 V'(\hat{q}) = C'(\hat{q}),$$

  equating the (true) average marginal patient satisfaction to marginal cost. The informational rent is absent since the physician accepts zero profits.

The remuneration part of the optimal regulation is found using (30).

It may be argued that the optimal regulation found here has very little to do with the fee-for-service or capitation rules that was our point of departure. Also, implementing the optimal regulation in a literal sense would mean that the

doctor should state her tradeoff between own money gain and patient satisfaction, which would not be the kind of information that could be easily transmitted.
On the other hand, it seems right that this tradeoff matters, and it could be obtained by asking in other ways (as always, we have considered truth-telling in
direct mechanisms, but we could have obtained the same equilibrium in other
contexts).

What emerges from our considerations is that the optimal regulation determines
the amount of services to be delivered and then remunerates the doctor accordingly,
and for both decisions the information about $\beta$ matters. This may be seen as a an
alternative to fee-for-service and capitation. Here the doctor will be assigned a
certain number of services and paid for delivering exactly this number of services.
The assignment and payment will depend on the character of the doctor as revealed
by the information collected.

## 7   Paying the hospital

In the previous sections we have discussed pricing under various circumstances,
all of which could be said to occur in the healthcare sector of an economy, and in
doing so we focussed on the way in which price and quantity of a good or service
would be determined. Without explicitly saying so, we have clearly assumed that
the goods and services to be priced were well-defined and identifiable. In some
cases, such as the services of a medical doctor, this would be a gross simplification,
but still one that could be defended referring to the need for a simple model. But
there are cases where such a simplification becomes untenable: if we consider
the activities of a hospital, it is next to meaningless to describe output by a one-
dimensional variable "treatment" (we have done so, alas, in our discussion of the
Newhouse model, but here our focus was on the quantity-quality tradeoff rather
than determining output and prices), and in any case it does not fit with practical
needs for the determination of how to pay the hospital.

### 7.1   *Prospective pricing and DRG*

The traditional payment for hospital treatments would either be a detailed billing
of all services offered during a treatment, or alternatively – in countries with a tax-
financed healthcare system – a fixed payment per day independent of the illness

treated. These systems became increasingly deficient as healthcare cost arose in the second half of the last century: If the hospital is paid for each procedure initiated during a hospital stay, there will be no incentive towards efficiency in patient treatments, and similarly arguments can be raised against the common per diem payment.

The increase in Medicare's expenses on hospital treatments led to the introduction in 1983 of *prospective payment* of hospitals in the US. In a prospective payment system, there will be a fixed payment for a given treatment, so that the payment does not depend on whether the treatment of a particular patient is more or less costly for the hospital. In order for such a system to work, one needs a definition of the type of hospital treatments that give rise to a particular payment, and this was achieved by the introduction of DRGs, Diagnosis-Related Groups.

The DRG system is one of many possible realizations of *case-mix*, understood as an aggregation of types of cases, diagnostic or procedural, into clinically meaningful categories (cf. e.g. Goldfield [2010]). Thus, in a case-mix one operates with categories or groups, each containing many members which are different from each other. If the payment is the same for all these different cases, it is unavoidable that the net payment (payment minus cost) may be smaller for some than for others. In order to make the system viable, the groups cannot be too large. Traditionally, it has been stressed that the groups should be

(1) clinically meaningful, so that all the treatments in the group are related to the same kind of illness or diagnosis, and

(2) resource homogeneous, meaning that the cost of the treatments should have largely the same size,

To this is often added a third condition related to the system as a whole rather than to the individual categories, namely that it should be

(3) manageable, in the sense that there should not be too many categories.

This third condition has to do with the practical implementation, since the placement of a given treatment in the right category should be a routine activity. However, such problems were more relevant at the time of the introduction of the system than it is today. As a response to (1) the DRG system has been set up so as to correspond closely to ICD-10, the WHO system for classification of diseases, so that the DRG of a treatment can be found automatically from the disease data. In the first versions, the systems would contain around 500 groups, and the number has been slowly increasing over the years.

Once the DRG system has been set up, the next step is to find *DRG prices* so as to pay the hospital this price for a treatment in the relevant DRG. Traditionally, this has been done by assigning the aggregate cost of the hospitals which are involved in the payment system, to each of the DRGs actually produced by the hospitals (thus by a procedure of the type mentioned in Section 5.4 above). Since this is a rather demanding task, it is done only with irregular time intervals, and in the meantime the results of the last calculation are used as *DRG weights* and updated by an index for overall hospital cost.

Since the use of DRG prices means that pricing is prospective – the payment for a hospital treatment does not depend on the specific cost of treating the patient, only on the DRG of this treatment – it matters much to the hospital that the DRG price does not systematically fall short of the cost. Practical experience has shown that the rigidity of the DRG system would have to be broken in several directions: additional payment is given when patients stay in hospital much longer than what is expected for this category, and also for patients with special background making their cases more severe. However, with these revisions payment according to DRG has survived and even spread from the initial case of Medicare payment to US hospitals to the situation today where DRG prices are used partially or fully in several European countries.[2]

### 7.2   *Case-mix and quality*

When different goods or services are paid according to a single common price, as it happens for treatments belonging to the same DRG, the providers will adapt, not only – as intended – by avoiding possible inefficiencies connected with delivering more than necessary in some cases, but possibly also by selecting another level of quality of the service delivered. This is supported by the following simple model of Allen and Gertler [1991].

We consider a firm producing two commodities 1 and 2 with demand functions

$$q_1 = d_1(p_1, s_1), \quad q_2 = d_2(p_2, s_2),$$

where for $i = 1, 2$, $q_i$ is quantity delivered, $p_i$ the price of commodity $i$, $s_i$ its quality. The firm has linear costs $c(q_1 s_1 + q_2 s_2)$ and profits are

$$\Pi = p_1 d_1(p_1, s_1) + p_2 d_2(p_2, s_2) - c(q_1 s_1 + q_2 s_2).$$

---

[2]The system has however not been taken up by the US health insurance companies, cf. Reinhardt [2006].

There is a regulator maximizing welfare, expressed as the sum of consumers' surplus and profits,

$$W = \int_{p_1}^{\infty} d_1(z, s_1) dz + \int_{p_2}^{\infty} d_2(z, s_2) dz + \Pi.$$

The first order conditions for a welfare maximum with respect to the price are

$$\frac{\partial W}{\partial p_i} = (p_i - cs_i)\frac{\partial d_i}{\partial p_i} = 0, \ i = 1, 2$$

from which, assuming that demand is decreasing in price, we get that

$$p_i = cs_i, \ i = 1, 2. \tag{32}$$

First order conditions with respect to quality take the form

$$\frac{\partial W}{\partial s_i} = \int_{p_i}^{\infty} \frac{\partial d_i}{\partial s_i}(x, s_i) dx + (p_i - cs_i)\frac{\partial d_i}{\partial s_i}(p_i, s_i) - cq_i, \ i = 1, 2,$$

which after insertion of (32) reduces to

$$\int_{p_i}^{\infty} \frac{\partial d_i}{\partial s_i}(x, s_i) dx = cq_i, \ i = 1, 2. \tag{33}$$

The conditions derived are not surprising – in a welfare maximum, quantities are such that the demand and the marginal cost curves intersect, and quality is found where average willingness-to-pay equals cost. We are not principally so much interested in this optimum with differential pricing as in what occurs when the two commodities are grouped into one and paid with the same price $p$. But for later comparison we look a little closer at the welfare optimum. First of all we notice that by (32), the optimal price-quality combinations $(s_1^0, p_1^0)$ and $(s_2^0, p_2^0)$ are situated on the same ray from the origin in an $(s, q)$-diagram, cf. Fig. 4.2. We may also find all the $(s_i, p_i)$-combinations which satisfy (33), $i = 1, 2$, giving us two curves in the diagram, and the optimum is found where these curves intersect the ray through the origin.

Using the implicit function theorem, we have that the curve determined by (33) has slope

$$\frac{\mathrm{d}p_i}{\mathrm{d}s_i} = -\frac{\int_{p_i}^{\infty} \frac{\partial^2 d_i}{(\partial s_i)^2}(x, s_i) dx}{\frac{\partial d_i}{\partial s_i}(p_i, s_i)}, i = 1, 2.$$

If we assume that the second partial derivatives are negative but numerically small, then $\frac{\mathrm{d}p_i}{\mathrm{d}s_i}$ is positive and larger than $c$ for $i = 1, 2$, so that at the intersection points the curves determined by (33) intersect the ray given by (32) from below.

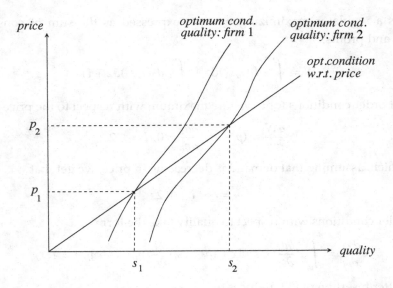

Fig. 4.2   Social optimum and equilibrium in a market with two goods. In the optimum one good will be delivered in better quality and at a higher price. Introducing a common fixed price will increase the quality differences.

Assume that for each level of the prices , the quality matters more to the consumers of commodity 2 than to those of the first commodity. We may think of the second commodity as a service directed towards patients more afflicted by illness than those demanding commodity one. If the quantities demanded are roughly of the same magnitude, then the curve determined by (33) for commodity 2 is positioned below that of commodity 1, as depicted in Fig. 4.2, and in the optimum it is commodity 2 that has higher price and larger value of $s$.

*A fixed common price paid by the patients.* The introduction of a case-mix system in our simple model takes the form of one price $\hat{p}$ which the providers must charge for delivering any of the two commodities. Maximizing $W$ under the constraint $p_1 = p_2 = \hat{p}$ gives the first order conditions

$$\hat{p} = c\left(s_1 \frac{\partial d_1}{\partial p} + s_2 \frac{\partial d_2}{\partial p}\right), \; i = 1,2 \tag{34}$$

with respect to the common price and

$$\int_{\hat{p}}^{\infty} \frac{\partial d_i}{\partial s_i}(x, s_i)dx + (\hat{p} - cs_i)\frac{\partial d_i}{\partial s_i}(\hat{p}, s_i) = cq_i, \; i = 1,2, \tag{35}$$

for the quality variables $s_1$ and $s_2$. Now the optimal price-quality combinations $(s_i, \hat{p})$, $i = 1, 2$, are found at the intersection of the horizontal line $p = \hat{p}$ with the curves defined by (35), which however are not the same as those given by (33). Assuming that the quantities have changed rather little, from $p_1$ to $\hat{p}$ we have that $s_1$ must be smaller in the common price optimum than in the first-best case, and similarly $s_2$ must have increased. Thus quality differences have increased as compared to the welfare optimum, a consequence of the provider choices, since the quality variable now is the only instrument for influencing demand and thereby profits.

*Fixed common price paid by a third party.* If the price charged is paid by a health insurance company or a government healthcare organization, then the demand of patients will be influenced only by the quality choices of the providers, so that demand will be equal to $d_1(0, s_1)$ and $d_2(0, s_2)$ for the two commodities given the quality levels $s_1$ and $s_2$. The welfare function takes the form

$$W = \int_0^\infty [d_1(z, s_1) + d_2(z, s_2)]\, dz + \bar{p} d_1(0, s_1) + \bar{p} d_2(0, s_2) - c(q_1 s_1 + q_2 s_2),$$

where $\bar{p}$ is the price paid by the insurer to the provider. The first order conditions for a welfare maximum under this additional constraint is

$$\int_0^\infty \frac{\partial d_i}{\partial s_i}(x, s_i)\, dx + (\bar{p} - cs_i)\frac{\partial d_i}{\partial s_i}(0, s_i) = cq_i, \quad i = 1, 2, \tag{36}$$

(we consider here only the quality aspects) which looks much like that in (35), but there are differences: the quantity demanded has increased considerably, so for the equality in (36) to hold, both $s_1$ and $s_2$ must decrease. As a consequence, quality levels in this last case turns out to be lower than in the previous two cases.

The results of the analysis show that aggregating different commodities into a single one has consequences for the quality aspects of the production. It should be emphasized that we have only scratched the surface of the problems, treating so far only socially optimal allocation under the different circumstances. A more thorough analysis would go into the maximization problems of the providers in the present context as well,.

## 8 Problems

**1.** Suppose that the citizens in a country subscribe to the Samaritan principle in the sense that they are want to have a healthcare service taking care of people hit by illness and accidents. Show that such a well-specified healthcare service can be considered as a public good which can be produced and made available to the citizens.

Sketch the implications for the decisions about the size of the healthcare sector and the way in which citizens should pay for it. Does this approach – converting externalities to public goods – work for all kinds of externalities?

**2.** A number of lifestyle related diseases can be seen as caused by previous acts of the individual concerned. Explain how this can be formulated as an *external effect* caused by consumption of particular goods (tobacco, fast-food etc.) and resulting in disutility for the population as a whole having to look at the disease-hidden person or alternatively pay for her treatment.

In general, externalities may be remedied either by creating artificial markets or by taxes or subsidies. How should the two types of intervention be constructed in the case considered?

It is decided to avoid taxes and subsidies. Instead, it is contemplated to set up a system of *medical savings accounts* for treatment of lifestyle diseases, whereby all individuals are allowed to deduct transfers to these accounts from their income, and all treatment has to be paid from these individual accounts. Give an assessment of this system in relation to efficient financing of lifestyle related diseases.

For type 2 diabetes, it is possible to measure the progression of the disease and therefore also to give an estimate of the probability of reaching the stage where serious illness needing costly treatment occurs. It is therefore proposed to introduce a scheme where each individual pays the yearly change in expected cost of treatment if positive, or alternatively receives this amount if it is negative. Give an assessment of this scheme; which advantages does it have from the point of view of prevention, and what are the disadvantages?

**3.** A small community of $n$ individuals contemplates to set up a scheme which provides members with a three-day cure at a health resort. All members pay an equal membership contribution $n$. Since not all members can be treated each year, the members should be treated according to their health needs stated. It is proposed to use the so-called Vickrey-Clark-Groves mechanism working as follows:

Members state their health needs $u_i$ (in terms of subjective willingness to pay), and the healthcare provision is found by selecting the $k$ members with highest health needs. An additional payment $t_i$ is then collected from each member $i$, determined as the difference between sum of the $k$ highest of the stated needs, for all except $i$, minus the sum of the $u_i$ who are actually selected, except possibly $i$.

Write up this rule and show that the individuals have no incentive to cheat, since that stating the true health needs will always be as good for individual $i$ as stating any other value.

**4.** Monetary evaluations of the benefits of health care programmes that reduce the risk of premature death are often used to inform healthcare providers.

How can willingness-to-pay for a reduction in risk of death can be measured empirically? Discuss how to use such willingness-to-pay data for economic evaluation of health care programmes that reduce the risk of premature death.

Consider a model in which an individual's utility depends on whether he survives a given period or dies right away and on the size of his wealth (or his estate in case of death) $y$. Survival is expressed by a dummy variable $L$, which takes the values 0 or 1 (to indicate "death" or "life"). Suppose that his preferences are in accordance with expected utility theory, and let $u(L, y)$ denote the (von Neumann Morgenstern) utility function.

How does a person's willingness-to-pay for a given absolute risk reduction change with his level of initial risk? How does willingness-to-pay for a given absolute risk reduction change with initial income?

In a cost-benefit analysis, is it reasonable that the health care provider takes into account persons' initial risks? What about their initial incomes?

**5.** A pharmaceutical company is specialized in producing of a particular cholesterol-lowering drug, where it has obtained an acceptable market share. It now turns out that this drug can be used to achieve weight reduction for persons suffering from overweight independent of their level of cholesterol, and the company wants to market the drug for this purpose under another brand name. It is expected that there is a considerable market for this product, which can be sold as OTC (over-the-counter) medicine without prescription.

The company is non-for-profit, and the production costs of the drug are very low, but it has a large and costly research department, something which is considered as necessary in order to be leading in the market for cholesterol-lowering drugs.

Before marketing the new brand, the company manager suggests that the price of the two types of medicine should be the same, since it is basically the same product. Give an assessment of this suggestion and suggest an improvement.

# Chapter 5

# Health insurance

The theory of health insurance, to which we turn in this chapter, is one of the central parts of health economics, and most of it applies to healthcare systems in all countries, independent of whether it is organized as voluntary or mandatory insurance or as a tax-financed government healthcare system. The same problems occur, since they are related to fundamental market failures rather than to the way in which people pay for their future care.

In the chapter, we begin by considering the fundamentals of insurance, assuming full information, so that both insurer and insured can observe it when the event which gives a right to a reimbursement has occurred. Unfortunately, this is not always – actually very seldom – the case, and we must consider the various cases of asymmetric information, taking the form of either moral hazard or adverse selection. We proceed to a discussion of the ways in which health insurers, whether formally organized as insurance companies or not, can keep down the cost which arises from these market failures.

## 1 Insurance under full information

In this section, we discuss the special case of insurance under full information, Êwhich in this case means that both the insurer and the insured observe the event (loss) that the insurance covers. The results obtained are due to Arrow [1963a]. We assume that there are several different states describing possible illnesses, occurring with known probabilities $p_s$, $s = 1,\ldots,S$, and that the individuals have von Neumann-Morgenstern utilities of the form

$$U(x_1,\ldots,x_S) = \sum_{s=1}^{S} p_s u(x_s),$$

where $x_s$ is the amount of money available in state $s$, and $u(x_s)$ is the utility of the amount of money $x_s$ obtained with certainty.

In the following we consider contracts of the form $(\phi, P)$, where $P$ is the premium, to be paid independently of state $s$, and $\phi$ is the reimbursement function of the contract. In our present model, the events are described by a money loss $L_s$ happening in state $s$ with probability $p_s$, $s = 1, \ldots, S$. We assume that all $L_s$ are different (otherwise we merge states with the same loss). Then the function $\phi$ describes what the insured gets from the insurer at the different losses. We may assume that the reimbursement function depends only on the size of the loss. We are interested in the functional form of $\phi$; at the outset, we may assume $\phi(L_s) \leq L_s$ but there are no other immediate properties.

The expected utility of the insured derived from the contract $(\phi, P)$ is

$$U(W - P - (L - \phi(L))),$$

where $W$ is initial wealth (here considered as an $S$-vector with all coordinates equal to $W$; the quantity $P$ is treated in the same way). We may now state the first result.

PROPOSITION 1 *Assume that the insurer is risk averse, and that the insurance company offers all contracts with equal expected loss* $\mathbf{E} \, \phi(L)$ *at the same premium. Then the insured will choose a contract will full coverage* $\phi(L) = L$.

PROOF: Assume to the contrary that the contract $(\phi^0, P^0)$ is optimal, but that the net loss of the insured satisfies

$$L_s - \phi^0(L_s) > L_t - \phi^0(L_t)$$

for two states $s \neq t, s, t \in \{1, \ldots, S\}$, such that it is bigger in $s$ than in $t$. Let $\delta > 0$ be a number with

$$L_s - \phi^0(L_s) - \delta > L_t - \phi^0(L_t) + \delta$$

and consider the contract $\phi^1$ which satisfies

$$\phi^1(L_s) = \phi^0(L_s) + p_t \delta$$
$$\phi^1(L_t) = \phi^0(L_t) - p_s \delta$$
$$\phi^1(L_{s'}) = \phi^0(L_{s'}), \; s' \neq s, t;$$

This new contract $\phi^1$ is unchanged in all states except $s$ and $t$, where it reduces the difference between the net losses, see Fig. 5.1. We show that the insured prefers the contract $\phi^1$ to $\phi^0$.

First of all we notice that the mean value of the reimbursements of the two contracts is the same:

$$E\,\phi^1(L) = \sum_{s'=1}^{S} p_{s'}\phi(L_{s'})$$

$$= E\,\phi^0(L) + p_s(p_t\delta) - p_t(p_s\delta) = E\,\phi^0(L).$$

By our assumptions the insured can buy $\phi^1$ at the same premium as $\phi^0$. It remains only to check the change in the expected utility of the insured. We have

$$E\,[u(W - P - (L - \phi^1(L)) - u(W - P - (L - \phi^0(L)))]$$

$$= \sum_{s'=1}^{S} p_{s'}[u(W - P - (L_{s'} - \psi^1(L_{s'})) - u(W - P - (L_{s'} - \psi^0(L_{s'})))]$$

$$= p_s[u(W - P - (L_s - \psi^1(L_s)) - u(W - P - (L_s - \psi^0(L_s)))]$$

$$+ p_t[u(W - P - (L_t - \psi^1(L_t)) - u(W - P - (L_t - \psi^0(L_t)))],$$

so the difference in expected utility is determined solely by what happens in the states $s$ and $t$.

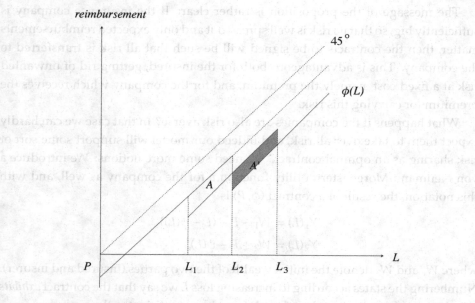

Fig. 5.1 Arrow's theorem on health insurance: If the graph of the loss reimbursement $\phi(L)$ is *not* a straight line parallel to the 45° line, then it is possible to design an improvement, as in the graph where reimbursement is increased from $L_2$ to $L_3$ and decreased from $L_1$ to $L_2$, so that expected reimbursement is unchanged but the insured is better off.

We take a closer look at the relevant two members in the expression: Denote the incomes using contract $\phi^0$ in state $s$ by $z_s^0$ and similarly in state $t$ by $z_t^0$. We have that $z_s^0 < z_t^0$. If we introduce the quantity

$$K = \frac{u(z_t^0) - u(z_s^0)}{z_t^0 - z_s^0},$$

then we get from concavity of $u$ that

$$u(z_t^0 - p_s\delta) \geq u(z_t^0) - Kp_s\delta,$$

and similarly

$$u(z_s^0 + p_t\delta) \geq u(z_s^0) + Kp_t\delta$$

(in both cases we move from the interval endpoints into the interval and compare the graph of the function to the straight line). Inserting in the expression for expected income, we get

$$\mathsf{E}\,[u(W - P - (L - \phi^1(L))) - u(W - P - (L - \phi^0(L)))] > p_t p_s\delta - p_s p_t\delta > 0,$$

from which it follows that $(\phi^1, P)$ is better than $(\phi^0, P)$, a contradiction. $\qquad\square$

The message of the proposition is rather clear: If the insurance company is sufficiently big, so that its risk is well spread out and only expected reimbursements matter, then the contracts to be signed will be such that all risk is transferred to the company. This is advantageous both for the insured, getting rid of unwanted risk at a fixed cost, namely the premium, and for the company which receives the premium for carrying this risk.

What happens if the companies are also risk averse? In that case we can hardly expect them to take over all risk, and indeed our model will support some sort of risk sharing as an optimal contract. We need some more notions: We introduce a von Neumann-Morgenstern utility function $v$ for the company as well, and with this notation, the result of a contract $(\phi, P)$ is

$$Y_1(L) = W_1 - P - (L - \psi(L))$$
$$Y_2(L) = W_2 + P - \psi(L),$$

where $W_1$ and $W_2$ denote the initial wealth of the two parties (insured and insurer). Numbering the states according to increasing loss $L$ we say that the contract *exhibits risk sharing* if for states $s$ and $s + 1$ with $L_s$ and $L_{s+1}$ sufficiently close

$$\psi(L_{s+1}) - \psi(L_s) < L_{s+1} - L_s, \text{ all } s.$$

**Proposition 2** *Assume that both insured and insurer are risk averse with concave (von Neumann-Morgenstern) utility functions. Then the optimal contract will exhibit risk sharing.*

PROOF: Consider the set of pairs $(u^*, v^*)$ such that

$$u^* = u(Y_1(L)), \; v^* = v(Y_2(L)),$$

where $Y_1, Y_2$ are derived from some contract $(\phi, P)$. It is easily seen that the set of such $(u^*, v^*)$ is convex. If $(u^0, v^0)$ in this set belongs to a Pareto-optimal contract, then there must be a linear function, given by positive numbers $\lambda_1, \lambda_2$, so that $(u^0, v^0)$ maximizes $\lambda_1 u^* + \lambda_2 v^*$ over all feasible $(u^*, v^*)$.

If the $\lambda$-weighted sum

$$\lambda_1 \sum_{s=1}^{S} p_s u(Y_1(L_s)) + \lambda_2 \sum_{s=1}^{S} p_s v(Y_2(L_s)) = \sum_{s=1}^{S} p_s[\lambda_1 u(Y_1(L_s)) + \lambda_2 v(Y_2(L_s))]$$

is maximal, then for each $s$ we must have

$$\lambda_1 u'(Y_1(L_s))\frac{dY_1}{dz} + \lambda_2 v'(Y_s(L_s))\frac{dY_2}{dz} = 0,$$

where $z$ represents change in insurance reimbursement. Clearly

$$\frac{dY_1}{dz} = -\frac{dY_2}{dz},$$

so our expression takes the form

$$\lambda_1 u'(Y_1(L_s)) - \lambda_2 v'(Y_s(L_s)) = 0.$$

This expression gives us $\phi$ as implicit function of $L$.

Using the implicit function theorem, we get that $\phi$ is a differentiable function af $L$ with derivative

$$\frac{d\phi}{dL} = -\frac{F'_L}{F'_\phi}.$$

Here

$$F'_L = \frac{\partial F}{\partial L} = -\lambda_1 u'',$$

and

$$F'_\phi = \frac{\partial F}{\partial \phi} = \lambda_1 u'' + \lambda_2 v'',$$

so that we obtain

$$\frac{d\phi}{dL} = \frac{\lambda_1 u''}{\lambda_1 u'' + \lambda_2 v''},$$

which is between 0 and 1. The statement in the proposition follows immediately. $\qquad\square$

So far the consideration of optimal functional forms have led to either full reimbursement, or to risk sharing in the rather special case of a risk averse insurance company, something which might occur in connection with very expensive treatments of rare but spectacular illnesses. There seems to be little room for user payments in an optimally functioning system of health insurance.

However, what has been considered so far pertains to insurance under full information. If the losses cannot be observed by both parties, insured *and* insurer, then the insurer must expect the reported loss to exceed the actual loss. Or, in the context of health insurance, if the objective need for treatment is not observed by the insurer, the insured may claim higher reimbursement, corresponding to more treatment, than what was considered as reasonable given the objective needs of the patient. We are thus led to the basic problem of health insurance, namely moral hazard, to be considered in the sequel.

## 2   Health insurance and moral hazard

Moral hazard has been called "the original sin of health insurance". In the ideal world of full information, risk averse individuals can be offered full coverage of risky outlays so that the risk is eliminated. However, once the illness occurs and the treatment is necessary, the fact that such treatment is provided without a cost to the insured may encourage a use of scarce ressources which differs from what would have occurred if healthcare had to be bought in the market and weighted against all other goods and services.

Moral hazard occurs when relevant *actions* of the insured cannot be observed by the insurer, making it a case of *hidden action*. Several forms of moral hazard can be distinguished: there is *ex ante* moral hazard, pertaining to actions taken either before the event happens (usually in the form of neglecting loss-preventing activities) or when it happens (loss-reducing activities), and there is *ex post* moral hazard, where the actions take place after the event has happened. The latter form of moral hazard is clearly the most important in the context of health insurance, so this is where we begin.

### 2.1   *Optimal insurance with health dependent preferences*

We consider a situation which is closer to health insurance than was the general model of the previous section. We introduce *state-dependent preferences*, so that the utility of consumption depends on the state (health). This produces an obvious case for *ex-post moral hazard:* One being in a particular health state, the need for medical attention as compared to other types of consumption changes drastically from what it was originally, with the result that if medical attention is available without payment in this state (due to insurance), there will be almost no limit to its demand. Nevertheless, we shall see that much of what was established in the previous section can still be carried over, at least with some modifications. The most important of these is that we need to allow for *coinsurance* in the sense that the outlays to medical attention are shared in a fixed ratio between insured and insurer. In the language of health insurance, this is the theoretical justification of *cost sharing*, the out-of-pocket payments of the patient having an insurance.

The model considered is that of Drèze [2002]. We assume now that there are $S+1$ states of nature, whereby we have introduced a specific state $s = 0$, interpreted as full health where no medical attention is needed. Individuals demand pairs $(M_s, C_s)$ in state $s$, where $M_s$ is medical attention and $C_s$ is consumption, both measured in money units. Expected utility of the $(S + 1)$-tuple $(M_s, C_s)_{s=0}^{S}$ is

$$U((M_0, C_0), (M_1, C_1), \ldots, (M_S, C_S)) = \sum_{s=0}^{S} p_s u^s(M_s, C_s),$$

where $u^s$ is the state-dependent utility function on sure outcome pairs $(M_s, C_s)$ in state $s$, $s = 0, \ldots, S$. Given initial wealth $W_s$ (which is also taken to be state-dependent) and the reimbursements $I = (I_0, I_1, \ldots, I_S)$ provided by the insurance company against the premium $\pi(I)$, the individual has expected utility

$$\sum_{s=0}^{S} p_s u^s(M_s, W_s - M_s - \pi + I_s), \tag{1}$$

and optimal insurance design, for given functional relationship $\pi(\cdot)$ between premium and reimbursements, is found by maximizing expected utility in $M = (0, M_1, \ldots, M_S)$ and $I$ under the constraint $\pi = \pi(I)$. The first-order conditions for a maximum are

$$\frac{\partial U}{\partial M_s} = p_s(u_1^s - u_2^s) = 0$$

$$\frac{\partial U}{\partial I_s} = p_s u_2^s - \sum_{t=0}^{S} p_t u_2^t \frac{\partial \pi}{\partial I_s} = 0,$$

where $u_1^s$ and $u_2^s$ are the partial derivatives of $u^s$ w.r.t. first and second argument, respectively.

To use the first order conditions, it is helpful to specify the premium-reimbursement relationship in more detail. Suppose for example that

$$\pi(I) = (1 + \lambda) \sum_{s=0}^{S} p_s I_s,$$

so that the premium equals the expected reimbursements plus a percentage $\lambda$, known as the *loading factor*. As we are interested in coinsurance, we write the reimbursements as $I_s = \alpha_s M_s$, where $\alpha_s$ is the (state-dependent) coinsurance rate, and $C_s = W_s - \pi - M_s(1 - \alpha_s)$. In this formulation, the maximization problem considered above reduces to maximizing the Lagrangian

$$\sum_{s=0}^{S} p_s u^s(M_s, W_s - \pi - M_s(1-\alpha_s)) - \mu^1\Big((1+\lambda)\sum_{s=0}^{S} p_s \alpha_s M_s - \pi\Big) + \sum_{s=0}^{S} \mu_s^2 M_s + \sum_{s=0}^{S} \mu_s^3 \alpha_s,$$

where $\mu_1$ is a Lagrangian multiplier for the premium-reimbursement relationship, and $\mu_s^2$, $\mu_s^3$ are multipliers belonging to the non-negativity constraints on $M_s$ and $\alpha_s$ for each $s$. Using Kuhn-Tucker, we get first order conditions

$$p_s\big[u_1^s - (1 - \alpha_s)u_2^s\big] - \mu^1(1 + \lambda)p_s\alpha_s \leq 0,$$

$$-p_s u_2^s M_s - \mu^1(1 + \lambda)p_s M_s \leq 0$$

for $s = 0, \ldots, S$ (to which should be added the complementary slackness conditions that either $M_s = 0$ or the first inequality is an equality, and similarly either $\alpha_s = 0$ or the second inequality is an equality). Assuming $M_s > 0$ for all $s \geq 1$ we get from the second equation that $u_2^s = \mu^1(1 + \lambda)$ and using this in the first equation we get that $u_1^s = \mu^1(1 + \lambda)$ as well, so that

$$u_1^s = u_2^s = u_2^t, \text{ all } s, t = 0, \ldots, S, \, s \neq t.$$

It shows that marginal rates of substitution between medical care and consumption is 1 at each health state, so that there is no over-consumption of medical care. Also the marginal rate of substitution between consumption at any two health states is equal, showing that risk and consumption has been spread over states in the best possible way.

## 2.2   *The second-best solution and the implicit deductible*

Unfortunately, the maximization problem still ignores ex-post moral hazard. When the premium has been paid, it becomes irrelevant for the consumer, who therefore maximizes without consideration of the link between expected reimbursements and premium. Consequently, the individual will choose so that

$$u_1^s = (1 - \alpha_s)u_2^s, \tag{2}$$

which with reimbursement rate $\alpha_s$ close to 1 will give that $u_1^s$ is close to 0, meaning that there is overconsumption of health care.

If we take the individual ex-post optimizing behavior into account, we get another constraint in our maximization problem, namely that in each state, the

---

**Box 5.1 The access motive for insurance and efficient moral hazard.** The standard treatment of the theory of health insurance (including the one presented in this book) usually abstracts from questions of budget constraints when dealing with choices under risk. Consequently health insurance is presented as a way of dealing with risk aversion, allowing risk averse individuals to avoid risk, or at least to reduce risk, at a cost which is a gain to the less risk averse insurer.

Clearly, a much more straightforward reason that a health insurance is useful comes from the fact that without insurance, many individuals could not afford a treatment for health problems that might occur. This *access motive* for health insurance, pointed out by Nyman [1999], seems to be more fundamental than the more subtle risk sharing motives considered in theory. It might be argued that such problems could be taken care of by a suitable income redistribution, but such an argument tends to overlook that health insurance is *in itself* a method of redistributing income, and this may indeed be its more fundamental role in the economy,

This alternative viewpoint on health insurance has consequences also for the approach to moral hazard, cf. Nyman [2004]. Intuitively, moral hazard in health insurance occurs when the patient consumes healthcare paid by the insurance which she would not have chosen if paid by the patient from her own money. The test for moral hazard is here that the particular service would not be chosen if the insurance pays a lump sum to the patient rather than paying for services delivered.

In the models of the present section, moral hazard is genuine since there the individual is not budget constrained, and the effect arises as a result of a change in relative prices. But with budget constrained individuals, what appears as over-consumption may not be so but instead an effect of the correction in income distribution provided by health insurance.

---

individual has chosen $M_s$ and $C_s$ best possible given $\alpha_s$. The first order condition for this problem (assuming interior solution) is

$$\frac{du^s}{dM_s} = u_1^s - (1 - \alpha_s)u_2^s = 0,$$

which defines $M_s$ as a function of $\alpha_s$. The derivative of this function can be found by the implicit function theorem as

$$\frac{dM_s}{d\alpha_s} = -\frac{M_s[u_{21}^s - (1 - \alpha_s)u_{22}^s] + u_2^s}{\dfrac{d^2u^s}{dM_s^2}}, \tag{3}$$

where we have used that $u^s$, and therefore $u_1^s$ and $u_2^s$, depend on $\alpha_s$ through the formulation in (1). The derivative is positive since the denominator is negative (this follows from second-order conditions for maximum), and the numerator can be written as

$$M_s \frac{du_2^s}{dM_s} + u_2^s > 0. \tag{4}$$

We now consider the problem of finding an optimal insurance contract subject to incentive compatibility constraint (in the first-order form) (2), so that we search for $(\alpha_s)_{s=0}^S$ maximizing the Lagrangian

$$L = \sum_{s=0}^{S} p_s u^s(M_s, W_s - \pi - (1 - \alpha_s)M_s) - \mu^1\Big[(1 + \lambda) \sum_{s=0}^{S} p_s \alpha_s M_s - \pi\Big]$$

$$- \sum_{s=0}^{S} \mu_s^2 M_s[u_1^s - (1 - \alpha)u_2^s] + \sum_{s=0}^{S} \mu_s^3 \alpha_s + \sum_{s=0}^{S} \mu_s^4(1 - \alpha_s).$$

The first-order conditions are

$$\frac{\partial L}{\partial M_s} = -\mu^1(1 + \lambda)p_s \alpha_s - \mu_s^2 M_s \frac{d^2 U}{dM_s^2} \le 0, \ M_s \frac{\partial L}{\partial M_s} = 0,$$

$$\frac{\partial L}{\partial \alpha_s} = p_s u_2^s M_s - \mu^1(1 + \lambda)p_s M_s - \mu_s^2 M_s\Big[M_s \frac{du_2^s}{dM_s} + u_2^s\Big] - \mu_s^4 \le 0, \ \alpha_s \frac{\partial L}{\partial \alpha_s} = 0.$$

We obtain the following characterization of the second-best optimum.

PROPOSITION 3 *There is a partition of the set of states* $S = \{0, 1, \ldots, S\}$ *in three subsets* $\{S_0, S_\alpha, S_1\}$, *such that*
   (i) *for* $s \in S_0$, $\alpha = 0$ *and* $u_2^s < \mu^1(1 + \lambda)(1 + \eta_s)$,
   (ii) *for* $s \in S_\alpha$, $0 < \alpha_s < 1$ *and* $u_2^s = \mu^1(1 + \lambda)(1 + \eta_s)$, *and*
   (iii) *for* $s \in S_1$, $\alpha_s = 1$ *and* $u_2^s > \mu^1(1 + \lambda)(1 + \eta_s)$,
*where* $\eta_s = \dfrac{\alpha_s}{M} \dfrac{dM_s}{d\alpha_s}$ *is the elasticity of medical expenditure with respect to coverage rate.*

PROOF: Assuming $0 < \alpha_s < 1$, solving the first-order condition

$$-\mu^1(1 + \lambda)p_s \alpha_s - \mu_s^2 M_s \frac{d^2 U}{dM_s^2} = 0$$

for $\mu_s^2$ and inserting in the other first-order condition, we get after inserting from (3) and (4) that

$$u_2^s = \mu^1(1 + \lambda)\left[1 - \frac{\alpha_s}{M_s} \frac{M_s \dfrac{du_2^s}{dM_s} + u_2^s}{\dfrac{d^2 u^s}{dM_s^2}}\right] = \mu^1(1 + \lambda)(1 + \eta_s).$$

The statements in (i) and (iii) follow easily.   □

The result may not look of much, but with few additional assumptions it turns out to be quite useful. Consider the case of state-independent wealth, and let the utility functions $u^s$ be additively separable in the form

$$u^s(M_s, C_s) = f^s(M_s) + g(C_s),$$

so that the preferences over healthcare changes with state but preferences over consumption stays as it was. Then the optimal contract gives the same reimbursements as a contract with full coverage except for a deductible which is an increasing function of $\eta_s$, the elasticity of medical expenditures w.r.t. $\alpha_s$. Indeed, in this case $u_2^s$ depends only on $(1 - \alpha_s)M_s$, the net medical expenditure, which can also be considered as the state-dependent deductible from full coverage. When $\eta_s$ increases, then so does the expression $\mu^1(1 + \lambda)(1 + \eta_s)$, and for $u_2^s$. From concavity of $g$ (risk aversion), we get that $u_{22}^s < 0$, so in order to have the left-hand side increase, the consumption must decrease, which with fixed wealth implies that the net spending on health (equal to the deductible) has increased.

We also see that there are no states $s$ with $\alpha_s = 1$ (that is $S_0 = \emptyset$), since otherwise we would have $u_2^s > u_2^t$ for any $t \in S_\alpha$. Then the consumption spending in state $s$ must be smaller than that in state $t$, contradicting that wealth is the same and nothing is used on healthcare, since there is full coverage.

The implicit deductible can be found as follows: For all states such that $\eta_s$ has a given value $\bar{\eta}$, there should be a fixed deductible $\bar{k}$, and then healthcare outlays are $M_s(1-\alpha_s) = \min\{M_s, \bar{k}\}$ for all such states. This is obtained by fixing coverage rates as

$$\alpha_s = \max\left\{0, 1 - \frac{\bar{k}}{M_s}\right\}.$$

How can the insights obtained be used in practice? Clearly the relevant deductibles are not easily implementable since they depend on elasticities which are personal information. The usefulness should be seen in the qualitative statements about the role of deductibles. Thus, we have shown that the practice of higher coverage rates (not only higher reimbursements) for large medical expenses is reasonable from a welfare point of view: For very serious afflictions the elasticity of health expenses w.r.t. coverage is low – healthcare is needed whether reimbursed or not – and therefore the deductible is small.

As pointed out in Drèze [2002], the results suggest a system of reimbursement where medical expenditures are classified according to *amount* and *type of treatment*, with the ultimate goal of capturing the variation of elasticity w.r.t. coinsurance rate. Once a classification has been found such that elasticities seem reasonably constant in the population for each of the relevant subclasses, then a system of deductibles can be introduced which at least approximates the second-best system studied here.

## 3   Health insurance and adverse selection

While moral hazard may be considered the most important case of market failure that has to be dealt with in the context of health insurance, there is another classical problem connected with insurance which, even if perhaps less important, has significant impact on the structure of insurance. This is the case of *adverse selection* which will be discussed in this section. The treatment of adverse selection was initiated by Rothschild and Stiglitz [1976] with health insurance as the prominent case.

### 3.1   *A model of insurance with adverse selection*

We consider a model of insurance against the expenses caused by illness which is a simple versioon of the classical health insurance model considered in Section 2. All cases of illness and subsequent treatments are subsumed in a single uncertain loss of the size $L > 0$. There is an insurance scheme where the individual pays a premium and is then reimbursed, fully or partially, in the case of loss. We let $B$ denote the reimbursement, $0 \le B \le L$. In the context of health insurance, the reimbursement may be in kind, consisting of free medical treatment.

Individuals are characterized by their individual risk and their utility function on income, which describes the attitude towards risk. Individual risks are given by the probability $\pi$ of incurring the loss $L$; $\pi$ belongs to an interval $[\pi_{min}, \pi_{max}]$, and individual risk parameters are distributed in this interval in accordance with a distribution function $F$, so that the frequency of consumers with illness risk in any interval $[\pi_1, \pi_2]$ is given by $F(\pi_2) - F(\pi_1)$. Let $\bar{\pi}$ denote the mean of this distribution, $\bar{\pi} = \int_{\pi_{min}}^{\pi_{max}} \pi \, dF(\pi)$.

A crucial feature of our model is the presence of asymmetric information: The individual risk is private knowledge of the individual concerned, at it cannot be observed by an insurance company.

Assume now that there is an insurance which reimburse the outlays to the amount of $B$ in the case of illness of all citizens with a risk greater than or equal to some $\pi'$; then the average outlays of the insurer per insured individual is

$$C(\pi', B) = \frac{1}{1 - F(\pi')} \int_{\pi'}^{\pi_{max}} \pi B \, dF(\pi); \tag{5}$$

the integral gives the total outlays as the probability of illness times outlays of the firm in case of illness, averaged over all the indicated costumers, and this is divided by the number of costumers.

---

**Box 5.2  Blue Cross and Blue Shield.** These two organizations, introducing pre-paid healthcare to the US citizens, were for many years the backbone of healthcare financing in the US, being also initiators of healthcare for the elderly and as such precursors of Medicare.

The beginning of Blue Cross is an example of entrepreneurship: A university hospital in Dallas was experiencing lack of patients in 1929 and found that in order to get patients who could afford paying for the treatment, they should propose employers to introduce prepaid treatment for their employees, in the original plan (for Dallas school teachers) a payment of $ 6 would give right to 21 days of hospital treatment per year. The concept was a success and it spread to other states in the 1930s, in particular after the original health plans related to a single hospital were extended to cover a network of hospitals.

Some of the characteristic features of Blue Cross was *community rating*, meaning that all paid the same price for participating in a hospital treatment plan, and non-for-profit operation, giving Blue Cross the character of a charitable organization. In the late 1930s, a parallel organization for treatment by general practitioners was developed under the name of Blue Shield, and the two organizations were gradually becoming a single one, providing health plans covering all aspects of healthcare. In the years following World War II, Blue Cross Blue Shield (BCBS) was the most used healthcare financing organization in the USA.

In the 1960s, the BCBS organization was contemplating an extension of their activity so as to cover also healthcare for the elderly, which generally falling out of the system, since health insurance was organized on an employment basis, and when Medicare was initiated, the organization participated in the administration of the health plans.

In the years following, BCBS lost ground to other types of health insurance, not bound by the principle of community rating, and when in the 1990s the legislation permitted some of the member organizations to change from non-profit to profitable organizations, the traditional character of the system was also changed and became less easily distinguishable from the commercial insurers, leading to a further fall in the number of customers.

A detailed historical account of BCBS can be found in Cunningham and Cunningham [1997].

---

For later use we notice that $C$ is differentiable in the second variable, and the (partial) derivative of $C$ w.r.t. $B$ is

$$\frac{\partial C(\pi', B)}{\partial B} = \frac{1}{1 - F(\pi')} \int_{\pi'}^{\pi_{\max}} \pi \, dF(\pi),$$

which does not depend on $B$; the value of the derivative taken at $(\pi_{\min}, B)$ is $\overline{\pi}$, the mathematical expectation of $\pi$. This is obvious from intuitive reasoning as well: The average cost for the insurance company of reimbursing one dollar more, when all individuals participate, equals the average (over all individuals) risk of loss which triggers the reimbursement.

Now we turn to the risk assessments of the individual consumers. We assume that each consumer is endowed with a von Neumann-Morgenstern utility function $u$ on alternative levels of wealth; the utility of a risky prospect is defined as the expected utility of its outcomes. Thus, the utility of a risky prospect, where the initial wealth of $W$ is modified by a loss of $K$ with probability $\pi$, is expressed as

$$\pi u(W - K) + (1 - \pi)u(W).$$

Under these assumptions we can find the amount $P$ that an individual with utility function $u$ and individual risk parameter $\pi$ is willing to pay in order to obtain the amount $B$ as (partial) reimbursement of losses, namely as solution to the equation

$$\pi u(W - P - (L - B)) + (1 - \pi)u(W - P) = \pi u(W - L) + (1 - \pi)u(W). \qquad (6)$$

If utility is monotonic and the consumers are assumed to be risk averse (the function $u$ is concave), then the solution to (6) is nonnegative. Clearly, it defines the insurance premium which the consumer will pay in order to have the amount $B$ covered in the case of illness.

Since equation (6) defines $P = P(\pi, B)$ as a function of $\pi$ and $B$, we can find its derivatives using the implicit function theorem: writing (6) as

$$F(\pi, P, B) = \pi u(W - P - (L - B)) \qquad (7)$$
$$+ (1 - \pi)u(W - P) - \pi u(W - L) - (1 - \pi)u(W) = 0,$$

we find

$$\frac{\partial P}{\partial B} = -\frac{F'_B}{F'_P} = -\frac{\pi u'(W - P - (L - B))}{-\pi u'(W - P - (L - B)) - (1 - \pi)u'(W - P)}$$
$$= \left[ 1 + \frac{1 - \pi}{\pi} \frac{u'(W - P)}{u'(W - P - (L - B))} \right]^{-1}. \qquad (8)$$

where e.g. $F'_B$ is the partial derivative of $F$ w.r.t. $B$. In the case where $B = L$ that this expression simplifies to

$$\frac{\partial P}{\partial B} = \pi.$$

Differentiating once more in (8) we find that

$$\frac{\partial^2 P}{\partial B^2} \leq 0$$

so that $P(\pi, \cdot)$ is a concave function in $B$. Together with $P(\pi, 0) = 0$, this gives us that $P(\pi, kL) \geq kP(\pi, L)$ for $0 \leq k \leq 1$.

The partial derivative of $P$ w.r.t. $\pi$ is found as in (8) and easily seen to be non-negative; the higher risk, the higher is the willingness to pay for a given insurance.

For later use, we take a closer look at the quantity

$$\frac{(1-\pi)}{\pi} \frac{u'(W-P)}{u'(W-P-(L-B))}$$

in (8). Clearly, it represents a marginal rate of substitution (of the individual with risk parameter $\pi$); if wealth is reduced by a small unit in the case of no loss, then the individual will need exactly this increase in wealth in the case of a loss. If we consider the particular case of no insurance, so that $B = 0$ and $P = 0$, then

$$\kappa = \min \left\{ \frac{(1-\pi)}{\pi} \frac{u'(W)}{u'(W-L)} \middle| \pi \in [\pi_{\min}, \pi_{\max}] \right\} \tag{9}$$

is the upper bound for the relation between a reimbursement of loss (net of premium) and the associated premium that will make any citizen just as well off as with no insurance. We shall need an assumption on $\kappa$, namely

$$\kappa > \frac{1}{\pi} - 1; \tag{10}$$

This assumption says that the utility function $u$ is sufficiently curved so that $u'(W)$ is much smaller than $u'(W - L)$; it tells us something about the risk aversion which should be sufficiently large.

We have now introduced all the ingredients of the model, and we pause to look briefly at the geometry of the model. In Fig. 5.2 we have drawn indifference curves of an individual with loss probability $\pi$. Letting $x_1$ and $x_2$ denote the net wealth in case of a loss and in case of no loss, respectively, we have that indifference curves have slope

$$\frac{dx_2}{dx_1} = -\frac{\pi}{1-\pi} \frac{u'(x_1)}{u'(x_2)}. \tag{11}$$

One sees that indifference curves get steeper with smaller loss probability $\pi$.

In the figure the indifference curves have been drawn corresponding to best and worst cases (in terms of loss probability), and the average. In the point where the indifference curve of the average individual intersects the diagonal, we have no risk removal on the average; the average individual gets full coverage of loss against payment of the premium $P$ to the insurance company.

If this contract is offered, the average individual will be indifferent between insurance or no insurance. But the more-than-average risky individuals will be better off by taking insurance, whereas worse-than-average individuals will be worse off. The latter individuals will not take insurance, even though they in principle are risk averse. We have a case of *adverse selection*.

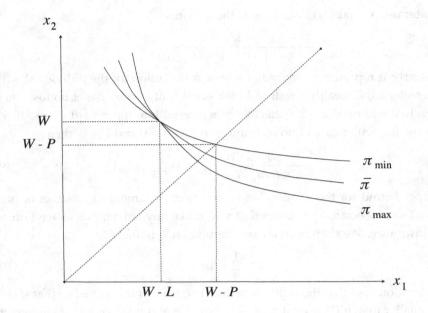

Fig. 5.2   Adverse selection. The indifference curves of the low-risk individuals are less steep than those of the high-risk individuals, reflecting that the bad outcome occurs less often for the former.

## 3.2   *Equilibrium with community rating*

We introduce now a notion of an equilibrium which may be considered as the outcome of a decentralized insurance market with a no-profit condition. The reason why some care must be taken in the formulation will become clearer later.

Assume that there are one or several insurance companies proposing insurance contracts to the public. All contracts must satisfy the community rating principle, in our case taking the form of equal premium to all costumers. Since the individual risk parameter is unobservable, the contracts can depend only on the premium and the reimbursement level $B$. If contracts must stipulate full reimbursement, that is $B = L$, then an equilibrium under the zero-profit condition is defined as a premium level $P$ such that

$$P = \frac{\int_{\{\pi : P \leq P(\pi, L)\}} \pi L \, dF(\pi)}{\int_{\{\pi : P \leq P(\pi, L)\}} dF(\pi)},$$

so that the premium equals average cost of insurance over all individuals of type $\pi$ taking insurance.

In our model the equilibrium is then defined as a parameter value $\pi^0$ such that

$$P(\pi^0, L) = C(\pi^0, L); \tag{12}$$

indeed, individuals with risk parameter $\pi \geq \pi^0$ satisfy $P(\pi, L) \geq P(\pi^0, L)$ (since $P(\cdot, L)$ is non-decreasing) so that they will want to take insurance at premium $P(\pi, L)$; and the average cost of having all these individuals is $C(\pi^0, L)$.

The problem of existence of an equilibrium is resolved rather trivially: Since $P(\pi_{max}, L) > \pi_{max} = C(\pi_{max}, L)$ (individuals are risk averse), at least some individuals will be insured in equilibrium, and if $P(\pi, L) > C(\pi, L)$ for all $\pi$, then takes insurance ($\pi^0 = \pi_{min}$), and we have a market equilibrium with premium $C(\pi_{max}, L)$. Otherwise, there is $\pi^0$ with $\pi_{min} < \pi^0 < \pi_{max}$ satisfying (12). It is not excluded that there can be several equilibria, so that the sets $\{\pi \mid P(\pi, L) > C(\pi, L)\}$ and $\{\pi \mid P(\pi, L) < C(\pi, L)\}$ are not intervals.

Following Hirshleifer and Riley [1992], the geometry of the equilibrium can be illustrated is shown in Fig. 5.3. In the diagram, we have the loss probability along the horizontal axis and various payment rates along the vertical axis, and we have inserted three different graphs. The first of these shows the average reimbursement to the individual of type $\pi$, which is $\pi L$. But due to asymmetric information we get all individuals with loss probability $> \pi$ if we get the individual of type $\pi$, so average reimbursements when the individual $\pi$ is among the costumers is bigger, as illustrated by the curve $C(\pi, L)$, which equals $\pi L$ only in the case where $\pi = \pi_{max}$. The third of the curves shows what an individual of type $\pi$ will pay for insurance, that is $P(\pi, L)$. Again this curve is above $\pi L$, since individuals are risk averse.

If the insurance premium is set so that all individuals have insurance and reimbursements are covered by premium payments, the relevant premium should be $P_1 = C(\pi_{min}, L)$. Unfortunately this premium is so big that many individuals do not want to take insurance (namely all those for which willingness to pay is below $P_1$, and then reimbursements will not be covered. It is easily seen that equilibrium occurs at $\pi_0$ and that only those individuals for which $\pi \geq \pi_0$ will take insurance.

## 3.3 *Equilibrium with self-selection*

One of the classical ways of solving the adverse selection is to consider extensions of the insurance contract, where individuals can choose from a menu of contracts, each of these specified by premium *and* deductible. We shall consider a situation with only two types, with loss probabilities $\pi_1 < \pi_2$. Corresponding to the two types, we have two contracts with different sizes of the premium. We use the notation $R$ for premium reduction (relative to a level to be defined below), and $Z$ for deductible, and intuitively we expect a tradeoff between premium and deductible so that

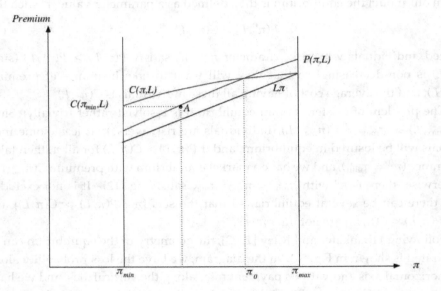

Fig. 5.3 Adverse selection. To the average cost to the insurer of having a given type as costumer must be added the cost of having all the more risky individuals. To break even, the insurer must set a premium which is larger than the willingness to pay of the less risky.

greater $R$ entails greater $Z$. The value of $R$ cannot exceed the highest premium to be paid by any type, and $Z$ must be $\leq L$. The point $(L, G)$ is shown in Fig. 5.4; it corresponds to no insurance (premium reduction is maximal but the deductible equals the loss).

We find the net wealth in the two states (loss and no loss) as

$$x_1 = W - (G - R) - Z = (W - G) + R - Z$$
$$x_2 = W - (G - R) = (W - G) + R,$$

and expected utility of the type $\pi \in \{\pi_1, \pi_2\}$ is

$$U_\pi = (1 - \pi)u((W - G) + R) + \pi u((W - G) + R - Z).$$

The slope of the indifference curve through a point $(Z, R)$ is

$$\frac{dR}{dZ} = \frac{\pi u'((W - G) + R - Z)}{\pi u'((W - G) + R - Z) + (1 - \pi)u'((W - G) + R)}.$$

We may use this to see that for $Z = 0$ the slope equals $\pi$, and for other values of $Z$ it is greater. This means that the indifference curves are steeper than the isoprofit lines of the insurance company which are given by

$$G - R - \pi(L - Z) = \pi Z - R + (G - \pi L).$$

We assume here that the company maximizes profit, so that lower isoprofit lines are better for the insurer.

Consider now the indifference curves of two types which both contain the point through $(L, G)$. Clearly the indifference curve for type $\pi_1$ is below that of type $\pi_2$. We are looking for a pair of contracts $((R_1, Z_1), (R_2, Z_2))$ such that type $\pi_i$ does not prefer contract $(R_j, Z_j)$ to $(R_i, Z_i)$, $i = 1, 2$, $i \neq j$ (incentive compatibility), and such that the profit of the insurance company is maximal. In addition, the contracts must be such that type $\pi_i$ is as well off with insurance than without insurance (individual rationality).

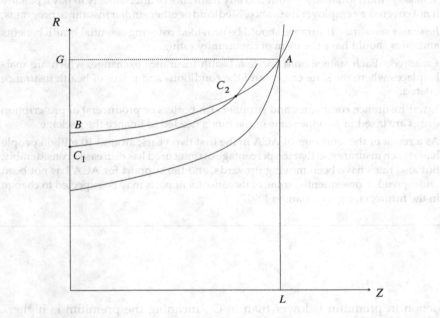

Fig. 5.4 Adverse selection with price discrimination. The insurance company proposes the contract $C_1$ to the risky individuals and a contract $C_2$ to the less risky, such that the risky individuals will not prefer the contract given to the less risky.

To find this optimal pair, we choose a point $C_2$ on the upper indifference curve through $(L, G)$. If type $\pi_2$ is offered the corresponding contract, she is exactly as well off as with no insurance, so incentive compatibility is satisfied. Given $C_2$ we can now find the other contract $C_1$ at the intersection of the $\pi_1$-indifference curve through $C_2$ with the horizontal axis. This contract has no deductible but the

**Box 5.3 Obamacare.** The Patient Protection and Affordable Care Act (ACA), more commonly known to as Obamacare, was introduced from 2014 and onwards in the USA. It is a series of measures which had the purpose of extending the number of people in the US having an health insurance.

The ACA has several different provisions, touching upon almost all aspects of the health insurance market:

*Coverage:* Insurers are no longer allowed to deny individuals coverage due to pre-existing conditions, and states are required to expand Medicaid eligibility above the poverty line (currently to 133%). This leaves out as uninsured mainly illegal immigrants (since they cannot obtain insurance subsidies or join Medicaid), and people who choose not to have insurance, paying the resulting penalty (see below).

*Subsidies:* Households with not too large incomes can obtain subsidies in the form of tax credits when buying health insurance.

*Mandates:* Individuals are required to buy insurance or alternatively to pay a penalty if not covered by employer insurance, Medicaid or other similar insurance programs.

*Insurance standards:* Insurance should be provided covering essential health benefits and rates should have the form of community rating.

*Exchanges:* Each state should create a health insurance exchange, which are marketplaces where the state can control the conditions and prices of health insurance offered.

*Taxes:* Insurance companies and suppliers (importers or producers) of prescription drugs are taxed to provide some of the funds needed to finance the package.

As a result of the workings of ACA in the first two years, around 10 million people have taken insurance so that the percentage of uninsured has decreased considerably. But also rates have been moving upwards, and the support for ACA has not been widespread. Consequently, some of its constituent parts may be expected to change in the future, cf. e.g. Oberlander [2017].

reduction in premium is lower than in $C_1$, meaning the premium is higher. By the very construction, the contract $C_1$ is individually rational for type $\pi_1$ (actually better than no insurance) *and* incentive compatible. Intuitively, the types will by their own free will pick the contracts that were intended for them.

We cannot be sure that the pair of contracts selected in this way maximizes the profit of the insurance company among all such pairs. However, we see that if $C_2$ is moved along the $\pi_2$ indifference curve from $A$ to $B$, composition of the profits earned on the two types of costumers change. In $A$ everything is earned on the high-risk costumers, whereas in $B$ the low-risk costumers are the most important. The optimal choice depends on the distribution of high and low risks in the population.

### 3.4 *Mandatory insurance and political equilibrium*

The suboptimality of the equilibrium considered above was to some extent caused by the fact that the individual has freedom of choice (of whether or not to take insurance). It might therefore be conjectured that the problems could be overcome by making health insurance compulsory. Improvement of the market solution by the introduction of a compulsory scheme has been considered by several authors, cf. Akerlof [1970], Pauly [1974], Johnson [1977]. In this section, we consider a compulsory insurance scheme where the coverage is chosen by majority decision and compare it to the market equilibrium of the previous section. The model considered was introduced in Hansen and Keiding [2001].

A compulsory insurance scheme has the obvious advantage that universal participation gives a lower premium than when some individuals stay outside the scheme. However, the low-risk consumers may still not be satisfied with it; when insurance costs too much compared to what it gives, the unsatisfied individuals will presumably want as little as possible of it, as expressed by a small value of the reimbursement level $B$. For a given value of $B$, the individuals who regard the compulsory insurance scheme as too expensive have risk parameters in the set

$$E_B = \{\pi \mid P(\pi, B) < C(\pi_{\min}, B)\}.$$

Remaining individuals find the insurance scheme advantageous.

Since insurance is no more a matter of individual decisions in the market, it seems reasonable that the forces regulating the contract should be subject to political control. We formulate this in a very simplistic way by the assumption that the insurance scheme should not be rejected by a majority,

$$\int_{E_B} \mathrm{d}F(\pi) \leq \frac{1}{2}. \tag{13}$$

Formally, we define a political equilibrium of our model as a reimbursement level $B^*$ satisfying (13) and maximal with this property. The maximality property of the equilibrium seems intuitive in view of the risk averseness of the public and assures that the market equilibrium with full participation (if it exists) defines a unique political equilibrium.

The existence question has now become less trivial than with market equilibria, so we need a special argumentation; also, we are interested in cases where the political equilibrium satisfies $B^* < L$.

PROPOSITION 4 *A political equilibrium always exists. Moreover, if $P(\pi_m, L) < C(\pi_{\min}, L)$, where $\pi_m$ is the median of the distribution of $\pi$, then $B^* < L$ in equilibrium.*

Proof: If $C(\pi_{\min}, L) \leq P(\pi_m, L)$, then $L$ is a political equilibrium; indeed, since $P(\pi, L)$ is nondecreasing in $\pi$, we have $C(\pi_{\min}, L) \leq P(\pi_m, L)$ for $\pi_m \leq \pi \leq \pi_{\min}$, so that weight of the set of individuals belonging to $E_L = \{\pi \mid P(\pi, L) < C(\pi_{\min}, L)\}$ is at most $1/2$.

Suppose now that $C(\pi_{\min}, L) > P(\pi_m, L)$. The function $\Phi$ defined by

$$\Phi(B) = C(\pi_{\min}, B) - P(\pi_m, B)$$

is defined and differentiable for all $B$ in an open interval containing $[0, L]$, and by our assumption, $\Phi(L) > 0$. Moreover, $\Phi(0) = 0$.

For $B = 0$, we have

$$\Phi'(0) = \left.\frac{\partial C(\pi_{\min}, \cdot)}{\partial B}\right|_{B=0} - \left.\frac{\partial P(\pi_m, \cdot)}{\partial B}\right|_{B=0}.$$

We know already that the derivative of $C(\pi_{\min}, B)$ w.r.t. $B$ is $\overline{\pi}$ independently of the value of $B$. For the second term, we have that

$$\left.\frac{\partial P(\pi_m, \cdot)}{\partial B}\right|_{B=0} = \left[1 + \frac{1 - \pi_m}{\pi_m} \frac{u'(W - P)}{u'(W - P - (L - B))}\right]^{-1} > \frac{1}{1 + \kappa} > \overline{\pi},$$

where we have used our assumption in (9) on risk aversion. It follows that $\Phi'(0) < 0$.

Now we have that the differentiable function $\Phi$ satisfies $\Phi(0) = 0$ and $\Phi'(0) < 0$, so there must be some $\tilde{B} > 0$ such that $\Phi(\tilde{B}) < 0$. Since $\Phi(L) > 0$, there must be some $B^*$ with $B' < B^* < L$ such that $\Phi(B^*) = 0$ or $C(\pi_{\min}, B^*) = P(\pi_m, B)$, giving a political equilibrium with the desired properties.                                                                    □

The condition for the political equilibrium to be smaller than $L$ implies that the median $\pi_m$ is smaller than any market equilibrium $\pi^0$. Indeed, suppose that $\pi_m$ exceeds the smallest market equilibrium $\pi^0$, for which we must have $C(\pi^0, L) = P(\pi^0, L)$; using monotonicity in $\pi$ of both functions we get that

$$C(\pi_{\min}, L) \leq C(\pi^0, L) = P(\pi^0, L) \leq P(\pi_m, L)$$

contradicting the condition $C(\pi_{\min}, L) > P(\pi_m, L)$, so $\pi_m \leq \pi^0$.

It is possible to get some intuitive feeling for what goes on in the model by elaborating slightly the graphical representation given above, as shown in Fig. 5.5. We have the parameter space on the horizontal axis and premiums or average costs along the vertical axis. The density function of the distribution is not shown in the figure; in view of our remarks above this density could hardly be rectangular – the median of the distribution is situated well to the left of the middle of the interval (the reason for this will become clear immediately).

If there is no coinsurance, the average reimbursements to individuals with risk parameter $\pi$ is given by the straight line $L\pi$; the average reimbursement to

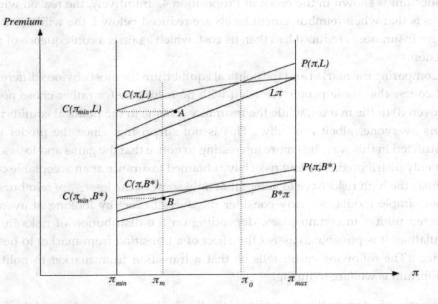

Fig. 5.5 Political equilibrium. At the reduced reimbursement level $B^*$, there is no longer a majority of individuals unsatisfied with the insurance scheme.

individuals with risk $\leq \pi$ is the curve $C(\pi, L)$, and finally, willingness to pay for the individual of type $\pi$ is given by $P(\pi, L)$. The market equilibrium case obtains at the intersection between $P(\cdot, L)$ and $C(\cdot, L)$, which occurs at $\pi^0$. Agents with risk parameter below $\pi^0$ do not insure, agents with risk parameter above $\pi^0$ get full coverage. We assume in the figure that $\pi^0$ is situated between the median and the mean.

Consider now the political equilibrium. Since with full coverage we have $P(\pi_m, L) < C(\pi_{\min}, L)$, there is a majority which considers this reimbursement level to be too large (this is seen from the fact that the premium $C(\pi_m, L)$ is greater than the willingness to pay for all $\pi$ smaller than the value at corresponding to the point $A$ in the figure). Consequently it will be reduced to some $B^* < L$, such that

$$P(\pi_m, B^*) = C(\pi_{\min}, B^*).$$

In the figure, the straight line $L\pi$ becomes $B^*\pi$, the reimbursement $C(\pi, L)$ is changed to $C(\pi, B^*)$, and willingness to pay reduces to $P(\pi, B^*)$. The reimbursement level $B^*$ is determined in such a way that the horizontal line at $C(\pi_{\min}, B^*)$ and $P(\cdot, B^*)$ intersects in the point $B$ at $\pi = \pi_m$. Clearly, $B^*$ is then a political equilibrium.

To achieve this equilibrium, the $P$- and $C$-curves had to move downwards from the situation with full reimbursement. That this will eventually take us to an equilibrium is shown in the proof of Proposition 4. Intuitively, the reason why it works is that when reimbursement levels are reduced below $L$ the willingness to pay for insurance is reduced less than its cost, which again is a consequence of risk aversion.

Comparing the market and the political equilibrium the most obvious difference is of course that some people were left with no insurance (or rather chose not to be covered) in the market, while the insurance scheme in the political equilibrium covers everyone, albeit not fully. This is not surprising, since the model was constructed in this way. It is more interesting to notice that the gains and losses are unevenly distributed: The low risks have obtained insurance at an acceptable cost, whereas the high risks have to accept that only some of the losses are reimbursed. In our simple model, we may consider the overall effect by looking at average expected utility; in certain cases, depending on the distribution of risks in the population, it is possible to assess the effect of a transition from market to health service. The following result tells us that a transition from market to political equilibrium is welfare reducing.

PROPOSITION 5 *Assume that the median of the distribution of $\pi$ does not exceed the mean; then average expected utility is higher in any market equilibrium than in the political equilibrium.*

Proof: In the political equilibrium with reimbursement level $B^*$, the average expected utility is

$$\int_{\pi_{min}}^{\pi_{max}} [\pi u(W - P(\pi_m, B^*) - (L - B^*)) + (1 - \pi)u(W - P(\pi_m, B^*))] \, dF(\pi) \tag{14}$$

$$= \overline{\pi} u(W - P(\pi_m, B^*) - (L - B^*)) + (1 - \overline{\pi})u(W - P(\pi_m, B^*)).$$

By our assumption, we have that $\pi_m \leq \overline{\pi}$; it follows that $P(\pi_m, B^*) \leq P(\overline{\pi}, B^*)$ since $P(\cdot, B^*)$ is non-decreasing, and by monotonicity of $u$, we conclude that

$$\overline{\pi} u(W - P(\pi_m, B^*) - (L - B^*)) + (1 - \overline{\pi})u(W - P(\pi_m, B^*))$$

$$\leq \overline{\pi} u(W - P(\overline{\pi}, B^*) - (L - B^*)) + (1 - \overline{\pi})u(W - P(\overline{\pi}, B^*)) \tag{15}$$

$$= \overline{\pi} u(W - L) + (1 - \overline{\pi})u(W),$$

where the last equality sign follows from the definition of $P(\overline{\pi}, B^*)$. Now the last expression may alternatively be written as

$$\int_{\pi_{min}}^{\pi_{max}} [\pi u(W - L) + (1 - \pi)u(W)] \, dF(\pi), \tag{16}$$

which is the average expected utility without any insurance. However, in the market solution part of the consumers choose insurance, which therefore must leave them better off than if they had no insurance at all. This means that average expected utility in the market solution is greater than (16), and consequently greater than the left hand side of (14). □

REMARKS. (1) It can be seen from the proof of Proposition 5 that the result holds even if $\pi_m$ slightly exceeds $\overline{\pi}$: If $\pi_m \leq \overline{\pi}$, then any market equilibrium gives higher average utility than the political equilibrium. By continuity, there is $\varepsilon > 0$ such that the result remains true when $\|\pi_m - \overline{\pi}\| < \varepsilon$.

(2) In the case of a symmetric distribution ($\pi_m = \overline{\pi}$), we have equality in (13), so that aggregate utility in the political equilibrium equals aggregate utility without any insurance. Intuitively, the gain which an individual with higher-than average risk obtains by having some insurance in the political equilibrium is exactly offset by loss of the symmetric low-risk individual paying too much for the insurance.

(3) If $\pi_m$ exceeds $\overline{\pi}$, then the political equilibrium is better (on the average) than no insurance, but not necessarily better than the market equilibrium; however, for $\pi_m$ large enough, this will obviously be the case.

Thus, in cases where the distribution of risk parameters in the population is such that the mean and the median are close, we can show that the insurance scheme belonging to the political equilibrium is inferior to that given by a competitive market. The result may hold for other distributions as well but it will depend on the exact form of the distribution. It is however remarkable that the attempt to solve allocation problems by what could be considered as democratic decision (majority voting) may be rather unsatisfactory from a welfare point of view.

## 4 Health insurance and prevention

The discussion in Section 3 of moral hazard in health insurance dealt with ex-post moral hazard, the effect of the behavior of the insured *after* the event against which insurance is taken, has happened. This is the most obvious form of moral hazard in the context of health insurance, so it a natural starting point. In other fields of insurance, dealing with losses caused by damage or theft, the ex-ante moral hazard, which has to do with either damage prevention or damage reduction (the terminology is in Ehrlich and Becker [1972], is more important, and insurance theory has much to say about this. It may also be relevant for the discussion of prevention and the role of insurance, and therefore we consider this case in the present section. The model is adapted from Shavell [1979] and Winter [1992].

## 4.1 *The standard insurance model of ex-ante moral hazard*

We consider a simple situation, where the insured has initial wealth $W$ and is exposed to a loss to the amount $L$ (in the applications, the loss is caused by illness and may consist of treatment cost, lost income etc.). The probability of the loss is $\pi(e)$, where $e$ is the effort level of the insured. We assume that the effort is not observable by the insurer; following the usual approach, we assume that there is a fixed cost measured in money terms of $r$ per unit of effort.

Assume now that insurance is offered at the premium $P$, giving a reimbursement $Q$ of the loss. If the insured have a common (von Neumann-Morgenstern) utility function $U$ defined on wealth, we have that the optimal insurance contract (from the point of view of the insured) should be found my choosing $P$, $Q$, and $e$ such that

$$\pi(e)U(W - P - re - L + Q) + (1 - \pi(e))U(W - P - re)$$

is maximized under the constraints

$$\pi(e)U(W_L(e)) + (1 - \pi(e))U(W_N(e))$$
$$\geq \pi(e')U(W_L(e')) + (1 - \pi(e'))U(W_N(e')), \text{ all } e', \tag{17}$$
$$P \geq \pi(e)Q,$$

where we have used notation $W_L(e) = W - P - re - L + Q$ for wealth in the case of loss when effort is $e$, and correspondingly $W_N(e) = W - P - re$ for wealth in the case of no loss when effort is $e$; the dependence on $e$ is made explicit in the notation since it shall play a main role in the sequel, but $W_L$ and $W_N$ depend of course also on the other parameters of the problem, in particular the premium $P$. The first constraint is the incentive compatibility condition: The effort chosen by the insured should be that which is most advantageous for her given the other conditions of the contract (premium and reimbursement level). The second constraint is a break-even-condition – it expresses that the insurance contract should balance in the average.

Rewriting the incentive compatibility constraint, which demands that $e$ should maximize expected utility given $P$ and $Q$ using Kuhn-Tucker, we get that either

$$\frac{1}{r}\pi'(e)[U(W_L(e)) - U(W_N(e))] = (1 - \pi(e))U'(W_N(e)) + \pi(e)U'(W_L(e)) \tag{18}$$

and $e > 0$, or

$$\frac{1}{r}\pi'(0)[U(W_L(0)) - U(W_N(0))] < (1 - \pi(0))U'(W_N(0)) + \pi(0)U'(W_L(0)) \tag{19}$$

and $e = 0$ must hold. We can use this to define the individually optimal effort level as a function $e(Q)$ of $Q$, which together with $P = \pi(e)Q$ may be inserted in the expression for expected utility, which then will depend only on $Q$. First order conditions for a maximum now becomes

$$\frac{\partial}{\partial Q}EU = -e'\pi'Q[(1-\pi)U'(W_N) + \pi U'(W_L)]$$

$$-\pi[(1-\pi)U'(W_N) + \pi U'(W_L)] + \pi U'(W_L) = 0, \tag{20}$$

the right-hand side of which contains three members expressing expected utility gain from marginal increase in coverage arising from (i) change in premium caused by change of premium-coverage relation, (ii) change in premuim due to increased coverage, and (iii) "pure" change in coverage.

The optimal level of coverage will of course depend on the parameters; if the cost $r$ of reducing risk is large, it might not be optimal to choose effort levels different from 0; thus, even if risk may be influenced by the behavior of the insured, this is too costly to be practically important, and moral hazard will not be a matter of relevance for the optimal contract, which then should display full coverage as in the classical situation of full information. But for suitably low unit cost $r$ the optimal coverage may well be less than $L$. This means that the reimbursement will not cover the full loss, giving the insured the desired incentive to reduce risk and thereby the expected outlays. The balance is one between risk reduction on the one side and risk sharing on the other side, and it is not apriori obvious that different organizational implementations of health insurance will strike the right balance. Indeed, they tend to arrive at suboptimal solutions as we shall see in the following.

*Budget constrained public health insurance.* The optimal solution considered above is important as a benchmark, but it does not necessarily come about by itself. Actually, health care financing tends to put obstacles in the way of realizing the optimum. We consider here one such case, namely that of a budget constrained healthcare system. If the public organization providing coverage for health expenditures is financed by taxes, it seems reasonable that it would operate under a fixed budget,

$$\pi(e)Q \leq \overline{P}.$$

Adding the constraint to the maximization problem considered above, we can find a second-best insurance coverage such that expected cost does not exceed the budget $\overline{P}$. The interesting case is of course that where $\pi(e^*)Q^* > \overline{P}$ corresponding to a greater demand for coverage than what can be achieved at the budget available. The solution to the second best optimization problem will be an effort level $e^0$ and a coverage $Q^0$ which solve either

$$\frac{1}{r}\pi'(e)[U(\overline{W}_L(e)) - U(\overline{W}_N(e))] = (1-\pi(e))U'(\overline{W}_N(e)) + \pi(e)U'(\overline{W}_L(e))$$

and $e > 0$, or

$$\frac{1}{r}\pi'(0)[U(\overline{W}_L(0)) - U(\overline{W}_N(0))] < (1 - \pi(0))U'(\overline{W}_N(0)) + \pi(0)U'(\overline{W}_L(0))$$

and $e = 0$, where $\overline{W}_L(e) = W - \bar{\pi} - re - L + Q$, $W_N(e) = W - \bar{\pi} - re$, together with the budget constraint

$$\pi(e)Q = \overline{P}.$$

Since the solution differs from the social optimum in having a smaller coverage ($Q^0 < Q^*$ by our assumption), it might be conjectured that we will have $e^0 > e^*$: Since the insured gets less coverage than she desired due to the budget constraint of the insurer, she substitutes risk sharing by risk reduction. We can check this intuition in our model by considering a small reduction in premium from its optimal level $P^* = \pi(e^*)$.

PROPOSITION 6 *If the insurance company is budget constrained away from the second-best optimum, then optimal risk reduction of the insured exceeds the level attained at the first-best optimum.*

PROOF: Consider the function

$$f(e, P) = \frac{1}{r}\pi'(e)[U(W_L(e, P)) - U(W_N(e, P)) - (1 - \pi(e))U'(W_N(e, P)) - \pi(e)U'(W_L(e, P));$$

we have that $f(e, P) = 0$ when $e$ satisfies the incentive compatibility constraint at premium $P$ and coverage $P/\pi(e)$. The partial derivative of $f$ w.r.t. $P$ is

$$\frac{\partial f}{\partial P} = -\frac{1}{r}\frac{\pi'(e)}{\pi(e)}[(1 - \pi(e))U'(W_L) + \pi(e)U'(W_N)] + (1 - \pi(e))[U''(W_N) - U''(W_L)]$$

where the first member on the right hand side is positive since $\pi'(e) < 0$ and the second since $U'' < 0$ ($U$ is concave) and $|U''|$ is decreasing in $W$.

Correspondingly the partial derivative w.r.t. $e$ is

$$\frac{\partial f}{\partial e} = \frac{1}{r}\pi''[U_L - U_N] + \frac{1}{r}\pi'\left[U_L'(-r - P\frac{\pi'}{\pi^2}) - U_N'(-r)\right]$$

$$- \pi'(U_L' - U_N') - (1 - \pi)U_N''(-r) - \pi U_L''(-r - P\frac{\pi'}{\pi^2})$$  (21)

where each member on the right hand side is $< 0$. Using the implicit function theorem we get that there in a neighborhood of $e^*$ the effort level $e$ can be written as a decreasing function of $P$ (assuming that coverage is given by $P/\pi(e)$). It follows that the optimal effort level $e^0$ at the budget constrained solution is greater than that of the second-best optimum $e^*$.                                                        □

The result points to a gain from budget constraints in the form of improved health. This however presupposes that 'effort' can be interpreted as more healthy ways of living, which may not always be the case.

### 4.2 The case of additional insurance providers

While the situation treated in the previous subsection was a typical second-best problem which could arise in many other situations, the following one is more specific for health insurance. It is becoming increasingly widespread that a public health care system is supplemented by privately contracted insurance, either for services which can only be delivered by the public system after a long waiting time or for payment of services for which the public reimbursement is insufficient. In the present section, we therefore consider a situation where this kind of *topping up* is possible, in the sense that private insurance companies may contract for additional reimbursement of losses, not covered by the public system.

Thus, we consider a situation where the individual is receiving public insurance with coverage $Q_0$ at a premium $\pi_0$, presumably not attaining the first-best optimum because of a budget restriction as considered in the previous section, and we open up for the possibility of alternative private insurance companies offering additional contracts for partial reimbursement of the residual loss $L - Q_0$. There are several cases to consider:

*Free entry* of insurance companies: New insurers may enter the market, offering contracts of arbitrary size, competing in *premium-coverage ratio* $p = P/Q$. The agent may choose any amount of total coverage combining the public contract with an arbitrary number of supplementary insurance contracts. In an optimum, the individual maximizes

$$\pi(e)U(W - (\pi_0 + pQ_1) - re - L + (Q_0 + Q_1)) + (1 - \pi(e))U(W - (Q_0 + pQ_1) - re)$$

with respect to $e$ and $Q_1$, the total coverage obtained in private insurance. Assuming interior optimum, we get a first-order condition

$$\pi U_L'(1 - p) - (1 - \pi)U_N'p = 0,$$

which may be rewritten as

$$\frac{\pi}{1 - \pi}\frac{U_L'}{U_N'} = \frac{p}{1 - p}.$$

If coverage is less than full, the quantity $U_L'/U_N'$ is greater than 1, and then $p > \pi$, that is premium-coverage ratio exceeds the probability of loss. But then insurance companies earn positive profits, which contradicts free entry. We conclude that total coverage must be full; this means that the individually optimal effort level will be lower than $e^*$, the effort level of the optimum. We conclude that this optimum cannot be obtained under free entry.

*A single private company maximizing profits:* If access to the market for additional insurance is restricted, so that individuals may contract with only one company, we have a situation of one monopolistic insurance company offering a contract $(\pi_1, Q_1)$ with $Q_1 \leq L - Q_0$, subject to the condition

$$\pi_1 \geq \pi(e)Q_1,$$

where $e$ is the effort level chosen by the individual, given that she is insured by both the original and the new company. In an equilibrium, the individual chooses effort level $e$ maximizing expected utility given the premium $\pi_0 + \pi_1$ and the coverage $Q_0 + Q_1$. The insurance company chooses $(\pi_1, Q_1)$ such that $\pi_1 - \pi(e)Q_1$ is maximal given that the consumer accepts the contract and chooses $e$ as stipulated above, and finally, the public insurance is assumed to set $(\pi_0, Q_0)$ in such a way that expected utility is maximal given the budget constraint $\pi(e)Q_0 \leq \pi_0$ and the incentive compatibility constraint with $P = \pi_0 + \pi_1$ and $Q = Q_0 + Q_1$. Note that we retain the previous assumption of a benevolent public insurance company which maximizes social welfare but which however is constrained, both by its budget and by the choices of the private insurance company. Also, we have assumed that the private company, being alone in the market, is aware of the moral hazard problem underlying the insurance contracts and takes the individual choice of effort into account.

If the optimum can be obtained in equilibrium, then we would have $\pi_0 + \pi_1 = P^* = \pi(e^*)Q^* = \pi(e^*)(Q_0+Q_1)$, and since the public insurance company would satisfy the budget constraint with equality in equilibrium, we get that $\pi_1 = \pi(e^*)Q_1$, so that the private company would earn zero profits in equilibrium. We now exhibit an alternative insurance contract which would be accepted by the individual but which would yield positive profit to the company, thus showing that the first-best optimum cannot be an equilibrium.

To find a contract which is better for the monopolist, one may try increasing the premium from $\pi_1$ while keeping the reimbursement fixed at $Q = Q_0 + Q_1$. It may be shown that this will result in an increase in the optimal level of effort of the individual, and if this is so we have that the change in the profit of the monopolist $\pi_1 - \pi(e)Q_1$ is

$$1 - \pi' \frac{de}{d\pi_1} Q_1 > 0$$

showing that profits were not maximal at the first-best optimum. To see this, one can use implicit function theorem on the incentive compatibility constraint (18) formulated as

$$F(e, \pi_1) = \frac{1}{r}[U_L - U_N] - (1 - \pi)U'_N - \pi U'_L,$$

with $U_L = U(W - (\pi_0 + \pi_1) - re - L + (Q_0 + \pi^{-1}\pi_0))$, $U_N = U(W - (\pi_0 + \pi_1) - re)$. Writing partial derivatives of $F$ as $F'_{\pi_1}$ and $F'_e(e, \pi_1)$, it can be shown that

$$\frac{de}{d\pi_1} = -\frac{F'_{\pi_1}}{F'_e} > 0$$

showing that effort does indeed increase.

*A single, non-profit insurance company.* Our treatment of the monopoly case, where the zero-profit property of the first-best optimum prevented its attainment as an equilibrium, points to a possible solution, consisting in opening up for topping-up of public insurance by a single, non-profit company. If the non-profit company offers additional coverage and sets the premium such that average reimbursements are exactly covered, taking into account the choice of effort level of the individual, then the first-best optimum will indeed be sustained in an equilibrium. This is, however, rather trivial, since the non-profit insurance company takes over the role of the public insurance company while not being subject to the budget constraint (and indeed the division between public and non-public insurance becomes arbitrary). Therefore, it does not add anything new to the treatment of our basic problem.

### 4.3  Health insurance with multiple risks

In our discussion hitherto there has been a single well-defined loss, the probability of which could be influenced by the effort of the insured. Though simple and reasonably tractable, the assumption of a simple well-defined event seems quite remote from the realities of health insurance; illness and its consequences tend to take many different forms, often even difficult to identify for both patient and doctor. Therefore, a realistic model of health insurance and moral hazard needs to take into account the heterogeneity of events on which insurance payments are contingent. A way of doing this while keeping the model simple is to allow for several different events, indiced by $i \in \{1, \ldots, n\}$, with associated losses $L_i$ and effort-determined probabilities $\pi_i(e)$, $i = 1, \ldots, n$. We assume that the probabilities are so small that we may neglect cases of two or more simultaneous events.

In our first approach we will assume that efforts are independent in the sense that total effort $e$ has the form $e = (e_1, \ldots, e_n)$ and that $\pi_i$ depends only on $e_i$. Letting the cost of effort be given by $r = (r_1, \ldots, r_n)$ we have that expected utility is

$$\sum_{i=1}^{n} \pi_i(e_i)U(W - P - r \cdot e - L_i + Q_i) + \left(1 - \sum_{i=1}^{n} \pi_i(e_i)\right)U(W_N(e)), \qquad (22)$$

where, as previously, $P$ is the premium paid to the insurance company.

As above we look for a social optimum taking into consideration the incentive compatibility constraint for the insured and budget balance for the insurance company. The necessary conditions derived from the incentive compatibility constraints is

$$\frac{1}{r}\pi_i'(e_i)[U(W_{L_i}(e)) - U(W_N(e))]$$

$$= \left(1 - \sum_{i=1}^{n} \pi_i(e_i)\right)U'(W_N(e)) + \sum_{i=1}^{n} \pi_i(e_i)U'(W_{L_i}(e)), \qquad (23)$$

(where we assume that $e_i \neq 0$) for each $i$ which is the counterparts of (18) for our present case. The solution to these equations gives us optimal effort levels $e_i(Q)$ as functions of $Q = (Q_1, \ldots, Q_n)$, and the first-best inurance contract maximizes $EU$ over $Q_1, \ldots, Q_n$ given that the premium is connected with the coverages by

$$P = \sum_{i=1}^{n} \pi_i(e_i)Q_i. \qquad (24)$$

For a characterization of the optimum, we seek an expression generalizing (15) to the case of multiple risks. Even with independent moral hazards, the optimal effort level for risk $i$ depends on the coverage of *all* the risks; however, since this dependence works only through the general levels of utility of the individual, we may assume that the partial derivatives $\partial e_i / \partial Q_j$ are so small that they may be neglected. Then we get from (22) and (23) that the optimum is characterized by

$$\frac{\partial}{\partial Q_i}EU(Q) = -e_i'\pi_i'(e_i)Q_i\left[\sum_{j=1}^{n} \pi_j(e_j)U'(W_{L_j}) + \left(1 - \sum_{j=1}^{n} \pi_j(e_j)\right)U'(W_N)\right]$$

$$- \pi_i(e_i)\left[\sum_{j=1}^{n} \pi_j(e_j)U'(W_{L_j}) + \left(1 - \sum_{j=1}^{n} \pi_j(e_j)\right)U'(W_N)\right] \qquad (25)$$

$$+ \pi_i(e_i)U'(W_{L_i}) = 0,$$

where the three terms on the right hand side have interpretations corresponding to those of (15) (the notation $\frac{\partial}{\partial Q_i}EU(Q)$ is used to emphasize that expected utility is considered as a function *only* of $Q$, since the dependence of $e_i$ has been eliminated by inserting $e_i(Q)$, $i = 1, \ldots, n$.

Proceeding as in previous subsections, we compare the optimum to the case where the public insurance company is budget constrained, so that instead of (24) we have $\sum_{i=1}^n \pi_i(e_i)Q_i \leq \overline{P}$. We assume that the public insurance company has determined the reimbursements $Q_i$ optimally under the budget constraint but without taking into consideration the effects on $\pi_i$ from shifting reimbursements from one risk to another. Technically, we assume that marginal expected utility of a small change in coverage,

$$\frac{\partial}{\partial Q_i}EU(e, Q) = \pi_i(e_i)U'(W_{L_i}), \tag{26}$$

is the same for all risks $i = 1, \ldots, n$. The public insurance company is assumed to use its budget fully,

$$\sum_{i=1}^n \pi_i(e_i) = \overline{P}, \tag{27}$$

distributing its reimbursements between the risks according to (26).

PROPOSITION 7 *In an equilibrium with only public insurance, where the company is restricted by a budget $\overline{P} < P^*$, the outcome is welfare inferior to the second-best optimum obtained by maximizing expected utility under the budget constraint.*

PROOF: In the second best optimum, the reimbursements $Q_1^0, \ldots, Q_n^0$ would satisfy

$$\frac{\partial}{\partial Q_1}EU(Q^0) = \cdots = \frac{\partial}{\partial Q_i}EU(Q_n^0),$$

whereas the equilibrium conditions are

$$\frac{\partial}{\partial Q_i}EU(e, Q) = \cdots = \frac{\partial}{\partial Q_i}\partial EU(e, Q).$$

It follows that the equilibrium will only be a second best optimum if

$$(-e_i'\pi_i'(e_i)Q_i - \pi_i(e_i))\left[\sum_{j=1}^n \pi_j(e_j)U'(W_{L_j}) + \left(1 - \sum_{j=1}^n \pi_j(e_j)\right)U'(W_N)\right]$$

does not depend on $i$, or equivalently

$$e_1'\pi_1'(e_1)Q_1 + \pi_1(e_1) = \cdots = e_n'\pi_n'(e_n)Q_i + \pi_n(e_n),$$

so that changes in the coverages must have the identical effects on the budget when individual risk reduction is taken into account, something that will is fulfilled only accidentally in the equilibrium. $\square$

The result is not surprising and it doesn't take us very far. However, it emphasizes that dividing tasks between a public and a private sector may not always lead to superior outcomes, since the possible positive effects on prevention of greater individual effort may be offset by the supplementary contracts obtained elsewhere. The healthcare system must necessarily be seen in its totality if it should perform optimally. This points to the need for a consideration of individual health plans and comprehensive healthcare packages, which is the topic of the next section.

## 5   Health plans, managed care

In the previous sections, we have repeatedly found that asymmetric information cannot be done away with entirely, and in the second best optima there will be some form of *cost sharing* of the individual. Otherwise put, there will be restrictions on the free access to healthcare. Once we introduce such restrictions, it might also be worthwhile to consider other constraints than those pertaining to the payment, and indeed such constraints are very widespread, ranging from health plans to gatekeeper systems. Such systems were often introduced with other purposes such as cost saving through special contracts with providers, or intentions to provide a better choice of care for patients, but in the context of asymmetric information they fulfill a function of limiting what may otherwise have been an undesirable consumption of healthcare from the part of the insured.

In the following, we consider some of this arrangements, among which the health maintenance organizations which were introduced in the US in the 1990s but in a similar form had existed in Europe for decades, and the gatekeeper system.

### 5.1   *Cost sharing*

When asymmetric information occurs, health insurance reimbursements will include some aspects of patient cost sharing, either as coinsurance or as deductibles. The notion of *cost sharing* presupposes that the payer (insurer or national health service) should in principle cover the cost of treating the patient for the relevant health problem, but due to the different forms of market failure, this principle cannot be upheld fully. It might however be a possibility that not only the patient but also the provider could cover some of this cost, and this idea lies behind the considerations of *provider cost sharing*.

Strictly speaking, cost of treatment is a cost occurring with the provider, so sharing this cost can be consistent with individual rationality only if the provider is remunerated in a way which does not depend on cost, for example by a lump sum payment. As a consequent, the problems of provider cost sharing arises only in the context of paying providers, with which we were concerned in Chapter 4. On the other hand, it may be useful to reconsider the contractual relationship

**Box 5.4 Fundholding GPs.** The system of *fundholding general practitioners* was introduced by the English NHS in 1991 as an attempt to create a market-like environment in the healthcare sector. The basic idea was that the family doctor would receive the healthcare budget of all the individuals in the practice, and all the subsequent dispositions connected to a treatment and delivered by other providers – specialist consultations, medicine, hospitals – would be made and paid for by the doctor. Any surplus arising in the course of the year would remain with the doctor (in principle to be invested in the clinic but in the long run as an increase in wealth).

The system was part of the conservative political program, and the Labour party opposed it from the very beginning, promising to abolish it when assuming power.

After a somewhat slow beginning (where the possibility of becoming fundholders were limited to GPs with more than 9000 patients) the share of fundholders rose, amounting to 57% of all GPs in 1997 [Kay, 2002], the year where the scheme was abolished.

Since it had been in work only for a short period, out of which the first years constituted a period of adaptation to the new rules, it is difficult to assess the pros and cons of this scheme. Some tendencies in the direction of improving the functioning of healthcare were noticed [Klein, 1999],

- fewer referrals to hospitals,
- shorter waiting time for emergency treatment,
- more GP engagement in patients' care,

but also some disadvantages made themselves felt, thus

- less patient satisfaction,
- higher cost of management and transactions.

Some of the fundholders were very successful in the sense of achieving a surplus above £200,000, but there were also fundholders with large deficits leading to a termination of the status as fundholder. After its abolition, some of the ideas of fundholding, such as creating a special budget for the general practitioner, were reintroduced in subsequent reforms of the NHS system.

between payer and provider in the light of the previous discussion of insurance related market failures. We have seen that patient co-payment plays an important role in reducing the distortions which may arise from a possibly unlimited use of healthcare resources by the patient, and it seems logical to involve also the provider, given that patient and provider have a common interest in the use of services which are paid by a third party.

Provider cost sharing is explicitly considered in Eggleston [2005]. The model treated contains a principal which is a payer (either a health insurance company or a national healthcare organisation) and an agent, which in this case is a provider. The provider may choose different levels of effort, and this choice matters for patient

---

**Box 5.5 The German 'Arzneimittelbudget': A budget constraint for the prescriptions of medicine.** The German healthcare reform of 1993 introduced the concept of a *drugs budget* for the general practitioner, essentially amounting to an upper bound on the total cost of prescriptions handled by the doctor. If the limit was surpassed, the payment to the doctor from the healthcare organizations would be correspondingly reduced.

The system can be seen as an example of provider cost sharing, since a larger-than-allowed level of prescription will result in a smaller remuneration of the doctor, provided that the constraint is set sufficiently low and is enforced by the payer organisations ('Krankenkassen').

The system was resented by the doctors and it was abandoned in 2003.

---

benefits. We may think of effort as a quality choice made by the provider. However, these choices are only partially observable to the principal.

The provider can deliver several different forms of healthcare to the patients, denoted by $j = 1, \ldots, r$. The amount of service $j$ delivered is $m_j$ (assumed to be measured in money terms) so that $m_j$ is also the cost of this service, and patients' benefit from the service is $v_j(m_j, e_j)$, where $e_j$ is the effort of the provider in delivering service $j$. In the simple case of $r = 2$, provider cost sharing occurs when the contract specifies a prepayment $r$ for each patient and shares $s_j$ with $0 \leq s_j \leq 1$ of service cost to be covered by the provider, together with incentive payments $\rho_j$ per unit of effort in service $j$, $j = 1, 2$.

For a provider caring to some extent $\alpha$ for the patients, payoff is

$$U = \pi + \alpha \left[ v_1(m_1, e_1) + v_2(m_2, e_2) \right] - c(e_1, e_2),$$

where $c(e_1, e_2)$ is the cost to the provider of delivering effort levels $e_1$ and $e_2$ in the two services, and

$$\pi = r - s_1 m_1 - s_2 m_2 + \rho_1 e_1 + \rho_2 e_2$$

is the net payment to the provider. Maximization of $U$ gives rise to first order conditions

$$\alpha \frac{\partial v_j}{\partial m_j} = s_j, \quad \alpha \frac{\partial v_j}{\partial e_j} + \rho_j = \frac{\partial c}{\partial e_j}, \quad j = 1, 2. \tag{28}$$

Using implicit function theorem on the first order conditions, one may investigate how the optimum choices of $m_j, e_j$ for $j = 1, 2$ depend on the parameters $s_j, \rho_j$ for $j = 1, 2$ (for details, see Eggleston [2005], p.219). Here we shall be satisfied with an intuitive argumentation in a particular case.

We consider a situation where $e_1$ is unobservable (or, strictly speaking, non-contractible in the sense that binding agreements cannot be made on the size of $e_1$), so that $\rho_1 = 0$, and we further assume that $s_2$ is kept fixed, so that only $s_1$ and $\rho_2$ can be changed.

Suppose now that the quality payment $\rho_2$ is increased. Then we get from (28) that $\dfrac{\partial v_2}{\partial e_2}$ must decrease, or marginal cost of effort must increase. Assuming that marginal patient benefit from agent effort is decreasing in $e_2$, equality is reestablished by increasing $e_2$. However, this change will influence also the marginal cost of delivering $e_1$, which reasonably may be assumed also to increase, and to counterbalance this effect, the level of $e_1$ must be reduced. We see therefore that increased effort in the service where it is observable will be obtained at the cost of reduced effort in the sector where it cannot be observed.

If effort in the delivery of the first service matters, the incentives must go via cost sharing. Indeed, decreasing $s_1$ will according to (28) give rise to a reduction in marginal benefit of service delivered in order to reestablish equality. This reduction can be obtained either by increasing the amount of service at constant effort, which however would upset first order condition in $e_1$, or by increasing $e_1$, which can be done without upsetting the other first order condition since both marginal benefit and marginal cost is increasing in $e_1$. We conclude that lowering the provider cost sharing will give increased quality in this case.

As indicated above, the model and its conclusions focus on contract structure rather than on the role of provider cost sharing in restricting the possible damage caused by moral hazard. However, it does show that contracts with a fixed payment *and* a cost-sharing element may be useful for several purposes.

## 5.2 Managed care and HMOs

The connection between provider contracts and medical treatment delivered, both with regard to quantity and quality, has been considered in theory, as it was indicated repeatedly in this book, and it has been exploited in practice for a long time. Since a specific contractual agreement with the provider is called for, it is natural that the insurer selects the providers with which such a contract can be agreed upon, and that the patients subsequently are to be served by these and only these providers.

However, managed care goes beyond this, and it has other theoretical justification than just selecting the providers with which to enter in contractual relationship. In a system of managed care, and in particular in the subsequent organizational

---

**Box 5.6 Health insurance: Kaiser Permanente.** One of the most important health insurance organizations in the USA is Kaiser Permanente, which actually is much more than an insurance company, considering itself as a *managed care organization* involving health plan groups and even hospitals. The health plans are non-profit organizations of employers and employees offering prepaid healthcare and insurance. The medical groups are physician-owned and profit-oriented, and they get their funding from the health plans. In addition, Kaiser operates hospitals in several states as well as out-patient facilities.

The history of the organization goes back to the 1930s, where an industrialist Henry J. Kaiser initiated the formation of an insurance company to offer compensation to his workers. At the same time, a medical doctor S. Garfield had experimented with providing treatment for workers injured in the construction of the large infrastructure projects of this period, growing into the so-called Permanente Health Plan. All this was subsequently consolidated into the Kaiser Permanente organization.

From its beginning, the emphasis on health plans and later on the concept of managed care meant that the organization differed sharply from Blue Cross and Blue Shield, which were more actively promoted by the medical doctors' association, and it expanded more rapidly in the postwar decades. Subsequently this trend reversed, as the idea of managed care was coming to the forefront.

By 2015 Kaiser Permanente had around 10 million health plan members, 186,500 employees, 38 medical centers and 622 medical offices [Kaiser Permanente, 2015]. It is particularly active in California but not present in many other states.

In the European context, Kaiser Permanente became widely known in the beginning of the 21st century, since its organization and efficiency was considered as being in many respects superior to the national healthcare systems in Europe.

---

form of a *health maintenance organization* (HMO), the patient (that is, the insured) is limited in her choice of provider, of treatments and medicine, having to use those providers who belong to the plan if the cost is to be covered. IThis partial suspension of the free choice of the insured has not received widespread attention in the literature. In Chalkley and Malcolmson [1998], a model is considered where payer preferences differ from patient preferences, and since contracts are made between providers and the payer, it will be the preferences of the latter which matter the most. If the payer selects the treatment according to these preferences, the optimal contract between payer and provider will reflect this, resulting in a less expensive treatment than might otherwise have occurred.

The partial elimination of the choice of the patient – such as the possibility of a "second opinion" – comes at a cost, and it has been argued that managed care and quality in health care are largely irreconcilable, see e.g. Litvak and Long [2000]. The theoretical aspects of this are however yet unexplored.

### 5.3 *The family doctor as gatekeeper*

The particular institution of a *gatekeeper* in healthcare, taken on by the general practitioner as family doctor, is a basic part of the system in tax-financed healthcare systems of the NHS type but has also been introduced in countries with other methods of financing. The function of the gatekeeper is usually presented as one of directing the patient to the right treatment in the system as a whole, but it is clear that this can also be seen as a way of preventing the patient from involving the payer (government or insurance organization) in expenditures which the latter considers as unnecessary. The possibility of seeking treatment from other providers than the family doctor will then be restricted to varying extent (see Box 7), directing the patients to a particular selection of type of service. If combined with a method of regulation which puts limitations on the number of referrals that the family doctor is allowed to make without being met with sanctions of some kind, the outlays of the payer can be rather effectively curtailed.

Notwithstanding its widespread use, the gatekeeper role in healthcare and health insurance has not been much investigated. One of the contributions is by Godager et al. [2015] who set up a model of the gatekeeper function, to be briefly outlined below.

We consider a case where the healthcare organization (either a national healthcare system or a health insurance), uses the general practitioner (GP) as gatekeeper, so that for any given patient, the GP may either treat the patient himself or refer to a specialist. The benefit $u \in [0, K]$ to the patient of being treated by the GP, which is observed immediately, but the benefit that the patient obtains by being treated by the specialist is unobservable to the GP, so it is considered as a random variable $v$ with probability distribution $F$ over $[0, K]$ and density function $f$.

If the patient is referred to a specialist, the latter will know $u$ from the patient notes sent by the GP, and moreover, the specialist will also observe the value of $v$. Since the referral implies a delay in the patient's treatment, both the benefit of treatment and payment are multiplied by a discount factor $\delta \in [0, 1]$.

Following Godager et al. [2015], we assume that the GP can choose between a public and a private specialist. Both the GP and the private specialist are paid on a fee-for-service basis, whereby the GP gets a profit of $p$ and the specialist $q$. The public specialist is public employee and gets a fixed salary.

It is assumed that the specialist has the possibility of sending the patient back to the GP upon an assessment of the patient's benefit of being treated in primary care. This possibility must be taken into account by the GP before a decision on referral is made. It is assumed that the physicians care for profits but do also care for patients' benefit, so the GP gets a utility of $p + \alpha u$ if treating the patient himself,

**Box 5.7 The use of family doctors as gatekeepers is increasing.** Reidling and Wendt [2012] give a survey of the use of gatekeeping in the healthcare systems of OECD countries and provide a brief overview as reproduced in Table 5.1 below.

Table 5.1. Use of gatekeeping and access to providers in selected OECD countries.

| | Gatekeeping: | | | Provider choice: | | |
|---|---|---|---|---|---|---|
| | Reg. with GP | Access to specialist | Re-form | Choice of GP | Choice of specialist | Choice of hospital |
| Austria | Obligatory | Free | | Limited | Limited | Limited |
| Belgium | Incentive | Skip & pay | 2002 | Free | Fee | Free |
| Denmark | Obligatory | Referral | | Limited | Free | Free |
| Finland | None | Referral | | Limited | Limited | Limited |
| France | Incentive | Skip & pay | 2006 | Free | Free | Free |
| Germany | Incentive | Skip & pay | 2004 | Free | Free | Free |
| Ireland | Obligatory | Referral | | Free | Free | Free |
| Italy | Obligatory | Referral | | Free | Free | Free |
| Nether-lands | Obligatory | Referral | | Limited | Free/limited | Free/limited |
| Norway | Obligatory | Referral | 2001 | Free | Free | Free |
| Portugal | Obligatory | Referral | | Free | Free | Free |
| Spain | Obligatory | Referral | | Free | Free | Free |
| Sweden | None/ | Free/ | | Free | Free | Free |
| Switzer-land | None | Free | | Free | Free/limited | Free/limited |
| UK | Obligatory | Referral | | Limited | Free | Free |
| US(conv,) | None | Free | | Free | Free | Free |
| US(man.care) | Obligatory | Referral | 1993 | Limited | Limited | Limited |

Source: Reidling and Wendt [2012], Table 3

The overall picture is one of increasing use of gatekeepers, even though the extent to which referral by GP is necessary is still rather small. The expression "skip & pay" means that the patient may circumvent the gatekeeper, going directly to a specialist, but this will be reflected in a higher payment for the service.

In some countries, several systems coexist, allowing for patients who choose to have free access to all healthcare providers, while those accepting the gatekeeper system will have a limited choice but also a smaller payment.

and similarly, the specialist treating the patient will get a utility of $q + \beta v$, Here $\alpha$ and $\beta$ are the weights assigned to the patient by the GP and the specialist respectively.

When deciding upon the question of treating the patient or using a specialist, private or public, the GP considers expected utility of either decisions. If the GP treats the patient, utility is

$$p + \alpha u, \tag{29}$$

and no randomness occurs. If a public specialist is used, then the patient is rejected and returned to the GP in the case that $v < u$ and otherwise treated by the specialist, given an expected utility of

$$\int_{v<u} \delta(p + \alpha u) f(v) \, dv + \int_{v \geq u} \delta \alpha v f(v) \, dv, \tag{30}$$

since the specialist will reject the patient if the benefit is higher when treated by the GP. A private specialist paid $q$ to treat the patient will accept this patient if the utility payoff of treating is higher than the utility payoff of rejecting, that is if

$$q + \beta v > \beta u,$$

or $v > u - \dfrac{q}{\beta}$, so the GP expected utility of referral to the private specialist is

$$\int_{v<u-\frac{q}{\beta}} \delta(p + \alpha u) f(v) \, dv + \int_{v \geq u-\frac{q}{\beta}} \delta \alpha v f(v) \, dv. \tag{31}$$

It can be seen that for small values of $u$ (or, strictly speaking, for $u \to 0$, the probability that $v \leq u$ becomes very small, so that if $\delta < 1$, the utility of treating the patient (29) exceeds that of referring to a specialist, public or private. A similar reasoning shows that referral to a specialist is better for the GP than own treatment when $u$ is very large.

In the model specified so far, the public specialist will be a better choice than the private specialist, independent of $u$. Indeed, for the function

$$v \mapsto 1_{\{v>u\}} \delta(p + \alpha u) + 1_{\{v \geq u\}} \delta \alpha v$$

(where $1_A$ is the indicator function of the set $A$, i.e. the function which has values $1_A(x) = 1$ for $x \in A$ and $1_A(x) = 0$ for $x \notin A$) has values which are always $\geq$ the values taken by

$$v \mapsto 1_{\{v>u-\frac{v}{\beta}\}} \delta(p + \alpha u) + 1_{\{v \geq u-\frac{v}{\beta}\}} \delta \alpha v,$$

since the values are either identical or $u - \dfrac{v}{\beta} \leq v \leq u$, in which case

$$p + \alpha u > \alpha v.$$

To make the private specialist an attractive alternative for some values of $u$, we may assume that the weight put on treatment by a private specialist is some $\alpha' > \alpha$, or alternatively – and perhaps more in line with intuition – that the weight put on treatment by a public specialist is smaller, some $\alpha'' < \alpha$. In this case the we may have that the GP will treat the patients himself for small $u$, refer to public specialists for intermediate values of $u$ and to a private specialist for large values of $u$.

If the GP is restricted in the referral, so that too extensive a referral to specialist might trigger some negative respons from the payer organization, then there would be a fixed (subjective) cost to add in both (31) and (30), and the payoff maximizing GP will choose to treat more patients himself. This reaction is not surprising and is indeed what was intended by imposing the restriction. It is of more interesting to consider the health effects on the patient of such policies.

For this, we need to introduce the patient, which has been largely absent so far. In order to do this in a simple way, we shall assume that the condition of a patient is given by a pair $(u, v)$ and randomly distributed in $[0, K]^2$, with distribution function $H$ and density $h$. The patient does not know $(u, v)$ but can get to know them by consulting the GP and the specialist.

If the patient is unrestricted, she may consult both and choose the largest of them, giving a patient payoff of

$$\pi^1(u, v) = \delta \max\{u, v\},$$

where in the spirit of the model we have assumed that the initial consultation phase causes a delay in the treatment. The expected gain is then

$$\int_{[0,K]^2} \delta \max\{u, v\} h(u, v) \, du dv, \tag{32}$$

were $g$ is the density function of $G$. This should be compared to the expected patient payoff in the gatekeeper system. Assuming for simplicity that there are only private specialists, patient payoff has the form

$$\pi^2(u, v) = \begin{cases} u & p + \alpha u \geq \int_{v<u} \delta(p + \alpha u) h(v|u) \, dv + \int_{v \geq u} \delta \alpha v h(v|u) \, dv, \\ \delta u & p + \alpha u < \int_{v<u} \delta(p + \alpha u) h(v|u) \, dv + \int_{v \geq u} \delta \alpha v h(v|u) \, dv, \text{ and } v < u, \\ v & \text{otherwise,} \end{cases}$$

since the patient will be treated by the GP if the latter originally decides to do so, or if the GP refers to a specialist but the specialist rejects, giving rise to a delay in treatment. Notice that in our new setup, the GP observes $u$ and forms a conditional distribution on $v$ with density $h(u|v)$, which corresponds to the density $f$ considered in the beginning.

The expected value is

$$\int_0^K \int_0^k \pi^2(u, v) h(u, v) \, du dv, \tag{33}$$

and the two expressions (32) and (33) must now be compared in order to assess the advantages or disadvantages of the two approaches.

The outcome of this comparison depends on parameter values and on the overall distribution, more specifically on the correlation of $u$ and $v$. Intuitively, the size of the region consisting of $(u, v)$, for which $v > u$ but the GP prefers to treat the patient himself, contributes negatively to the expected value of the gatekeeper system, whereas the delay in treatment using the patient's free choice counts in the other direction.

## 6  Problems

**1.** In loss insurance subject to ex post moral hazard, the size of a loss may often be verified by the insurer, but this verifcation is costly. Show that if the contract is such that the insured has an incentive to report truthfully, then the reported losses will be controlled only if they exceed a certain limit.

How can this be applied to the functioning of the GP as a gatekeeper verifying the symptoms claimed by the patient before sending to a specialist or a hospital?

**2.** We consider a country with a tax-financed public healthcare system. After several years of budget cuts, involving also expenditure on healthcare, there are capacity problems in the sector, and in particular the waiting time in emergency wards has incrased dramatically.

In this situation is is proposed to introduce a special category of Premium-Class patients, to which all have access against a yearly payment. Membership gives right to preferential treatment in emergency wards, circumventing the queue of non-acute patients. The payment is used for increasing the staff of the emergency ward, and its size should be such that it covers the treatment of the patients in the Premium Class.

It is argued that the arrangement creates inequality in the access to healthcare, but it is pointed out that the Premium Class patients essentially pay for their own treatment, thereby relieving the pressure on the emergency ward for the treatment of ordinary patients. Give an assessment of this argument.

As a partial concession to the public opinion, it is suggested that patients with more than five visits to emergency wards in the course of the last 2 years become Premium Class patients without payment of membership fee. How will the arrangement be influenced by this?

**3.** A travel agency arranging skiing tours in Europe for young people offers an additional health insurance covering out-of-pocket payment for treatment in European countries, where the costumers are covered only by the common European card. The insurance is a non-profit arrangement, and the premium is based on previous outlays of the costumers.

After the first year it turns out that fewer than expected have bought insurance, and there is a minor deficit. Give an explanation and a suggestion for further action.

A closer scrutiny of the first season shows that there have been large outlays for some major accidents, and it is known that these accidents have happened when the insured have moved outside the marked ski runs. This can however not be verified, so the insurer cannot deny reimbursement. How should problems of this type be handled?

It is proposed to offer the costumers a choice between two insurance contracts, both reimbursing all outlays, but one with a fixed premium, the other one twice as high premium, but where 90% of the premium is reimbursed in the case of no losses. Comment this arrangement.

**4.** In a country where the healthcare system is under financial strain, it has been decided to separate all healthcare related to salmonella infections and their treatment and to set up a special insurance scheme for this illness. Participation is voluntary, but the insurance scheme should be such that all costs are covered by the premium payments of the participants. There is an additional cost of administrating the scheme, and due to capacity limitations unit cost of administration increases with number of participants.

At the outset, it is decided that the insurance premium must be equal for all. It is known, however, that the individuals in the country concerned have almost identical probability of becoming infected, but they differ considerably in their attitude towards risk. Give a formalized presentation of this situation and show that there may be adverse selection in the sense that some individuals who basically want insurance nevertheless choose not to participate.

Give a suggestion to what the new insurance organization could do in order to increase as much as possible the welfare of the population, given that it may introduce other elements than the common premium in the contract. What will happen if it is decided that several insurance companies may offer this type of insurance?

Since participation in the scheme turns out to be small, so that a considerable part of the population remains uninsured, it is decided that participation shall be mandatory. It is however accepted that the insurance organization offers a contract (the same for all) which has less than full coverage and therefore also a lower premium. What will be the equilibrium in this case?

**5.** A country with a predominantly public system of healthcare, which however does not cover immigrants, has introduced a voluntary health insurance scheme for the latter; the scheme must satisfy the community rating principle in the sense that the premium should be the same for all. It turns out that immigrants from countries with poor health conditions have a higher risk of illness, but at the same time these immigrants are much less risk averse than the immigrants from countries with good health conditions.

Give an assessment, based on the theory of health insurance, of how this situation may affect the number of immigrants holding a health insurance, and describe the general consequences.

It is proposed that the insurance scheme should have a premium which is common for all but a deductible which depends on country of origin. Will such a scheme constitute an improvement of the previous one?

**6.** In an attempt to reduce government spending on healthcare it has been proposed that injuries and diseases which are inflicted as a result of recreational activities (sports, cultural events etc.) will not be covered by free healthcare services, but should be paid by the patients themselves. Give a suggestion as to how it can be determined what the patients should pay for treatment in hospital and with the general practitioner.

It is further proposed that a government insurance scheme should be created to cover patients' cost. Participation in the insurance scheme should however be voluntary, and the premium to be paid should cover the cost of the scheme. Give an explanation of the specific problems to be faced by such insurance schemes due to asymmetric information. How should the insurance contracts be formulated to reduce such problems as far as possible.

**7.** A private insurance company offers two different insurance contracts covering treatment of diabetes 2 and its consequences, namely (a) an expensive insurance with full coverage, and (b) a cheap insurance with reduced coverage of treatment for diseases related to obesity and lifestyle. Explain how this double system of contracts may give incentives to taking voluntary insurance.

Following new biological discoveries a test method has been introduced, which with a very high degree of precision can show whether a patient is predisposed for developing type 2 diabetes. The insurance company offers to its costumers a free test, where the result is given only to the costumer, not to the company. Could this be profitable for the insurance company?

# Chapter 6
# Cost-effectiveness analysis

## 1 Introduction

The increasing concern about the cost of healthcare in most countries has led to a greater concern about new medical technologies, which in many cases are spectacularly expensive. Since most healthcare organizations find it difficult to step back on treatments which are already being offered, a careful scrutiny of cost and effect of a new treatment is correspondingly important. Such calculations of cost and effects of new treatments – big or small – have become standard procedure in many countries, in for particular treatments related to use of drugs, since in this case the result of such an analysis may have an impact on market permits or decisions about reimbursement of patients' outlays when buying the drug.

Parallel to the development of cost-effectiveness analysis in practice, there has been a growing interest among theorists in the field, often initiated by practical questions such as whether particular items should figure as a cost or possibly as effects and if so, by which amount. The theoretical foundations of what is done in practice have been discussed at length in recent years, and some conclusions seem to have emerged from this discussion. In addition, the debate has led to new methods of economic appraisal and to an informal and partial consensus about how such appraisals should be carried out.

There is, however, not general agreement about very much in this field, even the name of what is being done may be subject to some disagreement. There is a textbook tradition of distinguishing between at least three types of appraisals, namely *cost-effectiveness* analyses measuring the cost of achieving a particular effect measured in units that are relevant in the medical context, *cost-utility* for evaluations which use an index of health related quality of life as measure of the effect, and *cost-benefit*, where the effects are evaluated in money terms. This distinction makes sense but is of little practical importance since the way in which effect is measured will anyway be obvious from the outset in any practical analysis, and it has no bearing on what should be done in the course of the evaluation (except of course with respect to measuring effects). In the present book, we follow the American tradition where every economic appraisal of medical interventions is called a *cost-effectiveness analysis* [Gold et al., 1966].

It should be added that there is a fourth type of economic evaluation which is somewhat different from those mentioned, namely the *cost-of-illness* analysis, finding the cost to society of a given disease (such as e.g. diabetes mellitus). There has been a tendency among specialists to downgrade such evaluations, since they do not show the consequences of any specific action (it is not realistic to assume that diabetes mellitus can be removed from society from one year to another), and therefore the cost as computed is not an amount which society could save in some way or another. On the other hand, cost-of-illness analyses may be useful as input to cost-effectiveness analysis, since the latter often need an assessment of what society could save by having one patient less suffering from the given illness. We shall not treat cost-of-illness assessments in this chapter; the methods used are however the same as those that we discuss.

The chapter is organized as follows: We begin in Section 2 with a discussion of the theoretical background for cost-effectiveness analysis, a field which is still somewhat controversial, and where several alternative approaches can be found in the literature, pointing to some relativity in the conclusions to be obtained. We then discuss the details of an appraisal in Section 3 treating the underlying computational model and dealing with the evaluation of cost and effects. In the following Section 4, we discuss the way in which the underlying uncertainty can be incorporated in the analysis. Section 5 is a digression into a field not yet developed very far, dealing with the assessment of what has been called "watchful waiting". In the final Section 6, we discuss guidelines, taking us back to the foundational considerations of Section 2.

## 2  Foundations of cost-effectiveness analysis

### 2.1  *The welfarist approach*

The classical – in terms of a recent discussion to be commented on below, *welfarist* – approach to cost-effectiveness analysis takes as its point of departure the derivation of cost-benefit analysis from economic welfare theory, e.g. in Varian [1992]. Here one considers projects which give rise to a displacement in the consumption bundles of some or all individuals in society, and assuming that the initial, pre-project state of the economy was an equilibrium supported by prices, one may deduce that the aggregate value (at these prices) of the displacements of individual consumption is a measure of desirability of the project for society. Increased aggregate value indicates that society is better off, and if aggregate value decreases, society is worse off after the project has been implemented.

However, the setup to be considered when the abstract "project" is related to health differs somewhat from the textbook case. The effects of such an intervention cannot reasonably be restricted to changes in individual consumptions of marketed goods and services. Indeed, in most cases the very reason for considering medical interventions is that they are expected to give rise to improvements in individual health states, presumably at a cost in terms of resources, which again means consumption foregone. Restricting the analysis to goods and services therefore means neglecting the main aspects of the intervention, giving obviously misleading conclusions.

We now extend the classical approach to project evaluation so as to take account of effects not confined to marketable goods and services. We consider a society with $m$ individuals, each endowed with a utility function $u_i(x_i, h_i)$, which assigns a number, the utility, to pairs consisting of vectors $x_i$ describing the consumption of the $l$ available goods and services, and vectors $h_i$ consisting of $k$ additional variables, $h_i = (h_{ik}, \ldots, h_{ik})$. As on previous occasions (in Chapters 1,2 and 4), we shall refer to these variables as health characteristics, and for the interpretation we may think of them as health state measures. In accordance with our previous discussions, we consider health status as many-dimensional, at least at the present, introductory state of our analysis.

We assume that society's preferences can be represented by a social welfare function of the form

$$S(u_1(x_1, h_1), \ldots, u_m(x_m, h_m)).$$

A more elaborate setup (involving non-traded consumption goods and other desiderata) is possible, cf. e.g. Canning [2013], but the present one will do for our purposes. An *intervention* is described by its consequences with regard to each of the individuals concerned in terms of changes in consumption $dx_i = (dx_{i1}, \ldots, dx_{il})$ and health $dh_i = (dh_{i1}, \ldots, dh_{ik})$. The resulting change in social welfare is then

$$dS = \sum_{i=1}^{m} S_i' \sum_{h=1}^{l} u_{ih}' dx_{ih} + \sum_{i=1}^{m} S_i' \sum_{j=1}^{k} u_{ij}' dh_{ij}, \tag{1}$$

where $S_i'$ is marginal social utility of individual $i$'s well-being, $u_{ih}'$ and $u_{ik}'$ individual $i$'s marginal utility of commiodity $h$ and health characteristic $k$, respectively. Unfortunately, most of the quantities in this expression are unobservable, so that it cannot be used for deciding upon the desirability for society of the intervention.

To proceed, we need some assumptions connecting unobservable marginal utilities with other economic variables which may be observed.

The first of our assumptions relates marginal utilities to market prices:

ASSUMPTION 1 *In the initial allocation, consumers obtain their commodity bundles by trading in the market.*

The assumption says that there is some price $p \in \mathbb{R}_+^l$ such that for each individual $i$, the consumption bundle $x_i$ maximizes $u_i$ over all bundles $x_i'$ satisfying the budget constraint

$$p \cdot x_i' \le p \cdot x_i = w_i,$$

where $w_i$ is the income of the individual $i$, for $i = 1, \ldots, m$. From consumer theory (see, e.g., Varian [1992], p.100), we get that

$$u_{ih}' = \lambda_i p_h$$

for each commodity $h$, where $\lambda_i > 0$ is the individual $i$'s marginal utility of income. Inserting this expression in (1), we get

$$dS = \sum_{i=1}^m S_i' \lambda_i \sum_{h=1}^l p_h dx_{ih} + \sum_{i=1}^m S_i' \sum_{j=1}^k u_{ij}' dh_{ij}.$$

The (unknown) quantities $S_i' \lambda_i$ may be interpreted as society's marginal utility of assigning income to individual $i$. We may eliminate them from the expression by assuming that $S_i' \lambda_i = K$, all $i$, where $K$ is a constant not depending on $i$. This assumption may be formulated as follows:

ASSUMPTION 2 *The distribution of incomes with which consumers obtain their commodity bundles in the initial allocation is optimal as measured by the social welfare function.*

The assumption that society is indifferent as to which of its individuals get an additional unit of income seems quite strong. However, not having this assumption would open up for situations where an intervention which produced less health than status and at the same cost could nevertheless be considered as an improvement simply because it shifted society's income distribution in a desirable direction. Thus we may consider the assumption as one which allow us to focus on the cost- and health-related aspects of the intervention at hand without being distracted by other more standard aspects.

So far, the expression (1) has been reformulated as

$$dS = K \sum_{h=1}^{l} p_h \sum_{i=1}^{m} dx_{ih} + \sum_{i=1}^{m} S_i' \sum_{j=1}^{k} u_{ij}' dh_{ij}.$$ (2)

Proceeding in the same way (but reversing the order of the assumptions) with the second member on the right of (1), we may assume that the initial distribution of health is optimal from the point of view of society:

ASSUMPTION 3 *For each health characteristic* $j$, *health is optimally distributed among individuals in the sense that*

$$S_1' u_{1j}' = \cdots = S_m' u_{mj}' = H_j > 0.$$

Also in this case, the assumption that society is indifferent as to which individual achieves an additional unit of health may be open to criticism. Moreover, in the case of health it is less obvious that the assumption can be justified as concentrating upon essential aspects of the intervention. While redistribution of income is easy to achieve (at least in principle) by taking money from one individual and giving it to another, the same simplicity is no longer there when we consider health. Although it makes sense to speak about distribution of health, redistributing health is a much more complicated process since health cannot be transferred directly between individuals.

Using Assumption 3, we get that welfare gains for society can be expressed as

$$dS = K \sum_{h=1}^{l} p_h \sum_{i=1}^{m} dx_{ih} + \sum_{j=1}^{r} H_j \sum_{i=1}^{m} dh_{ij},$$ (3)

so that the welfare gains of society are expressed as a weighted sum of the health gains and the changes in value of consumption.

The expression in (3) still contains the unknown constants $H_1, \ldots, H_j$ and $K$, so that even if the change in value of total consumption $\sum_{h=1}^{l} p_h \sum_{i=1}^{m} dx_{ih}$ may be observed, as well as the aggregate change in each of the health characteristics, $\sum_{i=1}^{m} dh_{ij}$, the sign of $dS$ cannot be unambiguously determined. But we still lack a counterpart of Assumption 1 which allowed us to perform aggregation of $l$ different commodities into a single one.

ASSUMPTION 4 *There exists an aggregated health state measure* $Q(h_1, \ldots, h_k)$ *such that for each* $i$, $u_i(x_i, h_i) = u_i(x_i, h_i')$ *if and only if* $Q(h_i) = Q(h_i')$.

The assumption is trivially satisfied if health can be measured by a single characteristic, and this is the case if we can make sure that all characteristics except a single one remains unaffected by the intervention. If this is not the case, we are back in the problems of aggregating health state measures which we discussed in Chapter 1.

With the last assumption, we may rewrite utility functions as $v_i(x_i, q_i) = u_i(x_i, h_i)$ with $h_i$ such that $Q(h_i) = q_i$. We then get that

$$\sum_{i=1}^{m} S_i' \sum_{k=1}^{r} u_{ik}' dh_{ik} = \sum_{i=1}^{m} S_i' \frac{\partial v_i}{\partial q_i} \sum_{j=1}^{k} \frac{\partial Q}{\partial h_{ij}} dh_{ij} = H \sum_{i=1}^{m} dQ_i,$$

where in the last equality we have used Assumption 3 and expressed the change in individual aggregated health measure of individual $i$ as $dQ_i = \sum_{j=1}^{k} \frac{\partial Q}{\partial h_{ij}} dh_{ij}$. In the interpretation, the quantity $dQ_i$ is assumed to be observable as e.g. the QALY change obtained through the intervention.

Summing up, we have been able to reduce the original expression (1) to

$$dS = K \sum_{h=1}^{l} p_h \sum_{i=1}^{m} dx_{ih} + H \sum_{i=1}^{m} dQ_i, \tag{4}$$

where only the constants $K$ and $H$ are unknown. This may seem quite much still, and indeed, in the (typical) case where one of the members of the right-hand side of (4) is positive and the other negative, the sign of $dS$ may change when the values of the constants change. However, it is still good enough for making *comparisons* of two interventions, as shown in the following proposition.

PROPOSITION 1 *Under Assumptions 1 – 4, if $P^r = (dx_1^r, \ldots, dx_m^r, dh_1^r, \ldots, dh_m^r)$, $r = 1, 2$ are two interventions with*

$$c^r = -\sum_{h=1}^{l} p_h \sum_{i=1}^{m} x_{ih}^r > 0, \text{ each } r,$$

*then $P^1$ implemented at some scale $\lambda > 0$ is preferred to $P^2$ if and only if its cost-effectiveness ratio is smaller than that of $P^2$, that is if*

$$\frac{dc^1}{dQ^1} < \frac{dc^2}{dQ^2}, \tag{5}$$

*where $Q^j = \sum_{i=1}^{m} dQ_i$, $i = 1, 2$.*

PROOF: Let $dS^r$ be the change in $S$ caused by $P^r$, $r = 1, 2$, so that by (4),

$$dS = -Kdc^r + HdQ^r,$$

and $dS^1 > dS^2$ if and only if $Hdh^1 - Kdc^1 > Jdh^2 - Kdc^2$, which, since $dc^2 > 0$, is equivalent to

$$\frac{H}{K}\frac{dh^1}{dc^2} - \frac{dc^1}{dc^2} > \frac{H}{K}\frac{dh^2}{dc^2} - 1. \tag{6}$$

If $\hat{P}^1$ is the project $P^1$ carried out at a scale $\lambda > 0$, that is $\hat{P}^1 = (\lambda dx_1^1, \ldots, \lambda dx_m^1, \lambda dh_1^1, \ldots, \lambda dh_m^1)$, where $\lambda$ is such that $d\hat{c}^1 = \lambda dc^1 = dc^2$, then since $d\hat{Q}^1 = \frac{dc^2}{dc^1}dQ^1$, the expression (6) transforms to

$$\frac{H}{K}\frac{d\hat{Q}^1}{d\hat{c}^1} - 1 > \frac{H}{K}\frac{dQ^2}{dc^2} - 1,$$

which is equivalent to (5). □

The cost-effectiveness ratio which emerges from Proposition 1 is usually called the *incremental* cost-effectiveness ratio (ICER) since both numerator and denominator are given by small changes (in value of consumption and in health). The quantity in the numerator is the value of consumption foregone and can therefore be considered as a cost of the intervention.

*The search for a benchmark case.* As shown above, comparisons of interventions with respect to their desirability for society may be carried out using the cost-effectiveness ratio. However, in practice we may be more interested in the question of whether or not to implement a given intervention. This may follow if it has a smaller cost-effectiveness ratio than another one actually implemented, and indeed such an argumentation is often used in practice. It would however facilitate the applications considerably if one could point to a benchmark case, an intervention which constitutes a limiting case of what society may want.

An intuitive approach to this problem could be as follows: Assume that all the interventions currently adopted are ordered according to their cost-effectiveness ratios. Then it seems right to assume that the interventions with lowest cost-effectiveness ratio have been adopted first, followed by interventions with higher cost-effectiveness ratio, up to the intervention with highest cost-effectiveness ratio among those adopted. It may then be inferred that interventions with a cost-effectiveness ratio lower than this maximal one would have been adopted if they had been available, and conversely interventions with higher cost-effectiveness ratios are not acceptable. Thus, we have a candidate for a benchmark case; the argument is illustrated in Fig. 6.1.

The argumentation has drawbacks: It presupposes that choices in the health-care sector have been made by a rational and consistent decision maker, putting together the national health service according to traditional marginalistic thinking, something which hardly corresponds to reality. On the other hand, a benchmark

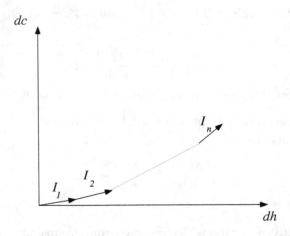

Fig. 6.1 The $n$ interventions actually used in healthcare ordered by increasing cost-effectiveness ratio. The last acceptable intervention determines the benchmark ratio.

cost-effectiveness ratio may of course emerge as a shadow price of health whenever the production of health is considered as a maximization problem.

To see this, assume as before that society's welfare is represented by

$$S(u_1(x_1, h_1), \ldots, u_m(x_m, h_m)), \tag{7}$$

where $x_i$ and $h_i$ are the commodity and health characteristics vectors achieved by individual $i$, for $i = 1, \ldots, m$. Now we add a technological constraint on all allocations $((x_1, h_1), \ldots, (x_m, h_m))$ which can be made available, assuming that they must satisfy the equation

$$G(x_1, \ldots, x_m, h_1, \ldots, h_m) = 0. \tag{8}$$

We may view (8) as a transformation curve specifying the combinations of commodity and health consumption which are technologically feasible and efficient.

PROPOSITION 2 *Assume that Assumptions 1 – 4 are satisfied, and that the aggregation index $Q$ is affine. If the allocation of commodities and health in society has been chosen so as to maximize social welfare (7) under the feasibility constraint (8), then there is a benchmark cost-effectivity ratio $z^0$ such that interventions are desirable (undesirable) for society (in the sense of Proposition 1) if their cost-effectiveness ratio $dc/dQ$ is $< z^0$ ($> z^0$).*

PROOF: We use Assumption 4 to introduce the utilities $v_i(x_i, q_i)$ depending only on aggregated health. From the first order conditions for a maximum, we get for each $i$,

$$S_i' \frac{\partial v_i}{\partial x_{ih}} = \lambda \frac{\partial G}{\partial x_{ih}}, \ h = 1, \ldots, l,$$

$$S_i' \frac{\partial v_i}{\partial q_i} \frac{\partial Q}{\partial h_{ij}} = \lambda \frac{\partial G}{\partial h_{ij}}, \ j = 1, \ldots, k,$$

where $\lambda$ is the Lagrangian multiplier associated with the constraint (8). By Assumptions 1, 2 and 3, these equations may be rewritten as

$$K p_h = \lambda \frac{\partial G}{\partial x_{ih}}, \ h = 1, \ldots, l,$$

$$M \frac{\partial Q}{\partial h_{ij}} = \lambda \frac{\partial G}{\partial h_{ij}}, \ j = 1, \ldots, k.$$

Since the health aggregator $Q(h_1, \ldots, h_k)$ is affine, its partial derivatives $Q_k'$ are constant, so the left-hand sides in the equations above are the same for all $i$. It is now easily seen that the vector $(K p_1, \ldots, K p_l, M Q_1', \ldots, M Q_k')$ separates feasible allocations from preferred allocations, in the sense that

$$K \sum_{h=1}^{l} p_h \sum_{i=1}^{m} dx_{ih}^0 + M \sum_{i=1}^{m} \sum_{j=1}^{k} Q_j' dh_{ij}^0 = 0$$

for a small displacement $(dx_1^0, \ldots, dx_m^0, dh_1^0, \ldots, dh_m^0)$ such that $dG = 0$.

Let

$$z^0 = -\frac{\sum_{i=1}^{m} \sum_{h=1}^{l} p_h dx_{ih}^0}{\sum_{i=1}^{m} \sum_{j=1}^{k} Q_k' dh_{ij}^0} = \frac{M}{K}.$$

Then $z^0$ is the desired benchmark cost-effectiveness ratio. □

## 2.2 *The decision maker's approach*

In several contributions to the literature on cost-effectiveness analysis, most distinctly in Brouwer and Koopmanschap [2000], it has been argued that the approach outlined above, called the welfarist approach, which takes as point of departure the existence of a social welfare function to be maximized by the choices of medical interventions made available to the population, is ill-founded and over-theoretical. Instead the basic principles of the analysis should be found in the reality-oriented consideration of the actual decision problem for which the cost-effectiveness analysis is undertaken, namely the choice by the decision maker in the healthcare organization of whether or not to adopt a given intervention, a choice which is made under the objective of getting as much health as possible within the limits set by the budget made available for the decision maker.

Since the approach explicitly rejects the idea of an underlying social welfare function, a formalization of the decision maker's approach must start elsewhere. Focussing on the situation of the hypothetical decision maker, we may view his situation as choosing a health status vector $(h_1, \ldots, h_m)$ (where as before, each $h_i = (h_{i1}, \ldots, h_{ir})$ describes the level attained for each of the $r$ available health characteristics) within the limits of a given budget $B$. To describe the trade-offs of the decision maker between health of different types and of different individuals, we assume that the decision maker has an objective function $U(h_1, \ldots, h_m)$ defined on all health status vectors. We assume that the function $U$ is nondecreasing in all its arguments.

Now we may formulate the decision maker's problem as maximizing $U(h_1, \ldots, h_m)$ under the constraint that the cost of attaining $(h_1, \ldots, h_m)$ must not exceed $B$. To make the latter notion precise we need to introduce a notion of the cost of achieving a given health status; to keep the approach as general as possible, and also to make it comparable with the above approach, we let the technology for obtaining health be given by a subset $H$ of $\mathbb{R}^{l+km}$, where an element of $H$, written as

$$(x, h_1, \ldots, h_m) = (x_1, \ldots, x_l, (h_{11}, \ldots, h_{1k}), \ldots, (h_{m1}, \ldots, h_{mk})),$$

indicates that the decision maker can achieve the health allocation $(h_1, \ldots, h_m)$ for the citizens of society if she can dispose of the vector $x$ of commodities. For simplicity we assume that the set $H$ can be described by a (differentiable) function $F : \mathbb{R}^{l+rm} \to \mathbb{R}$ in the sense that $F(x, h_1, \ldots, h_m) \leq 0$ if and only if $(x, h_1, \ldots, h_m) \in H$, and $F(x, h_1, \ldots, h_m) = 0$ if, in addition, $(x, h_1, \ldots, h_m)$ is efficient in the sense that no other array $(x', h'_1, \ldots, h'_m)$ can give as much health of any type and for any individual without either reducing health of some other type or individual or using more of some commodity.

We can now formulate the decision maker's problem as

$$\max U(h_1, \ldots, h_m)$$
$$F(x, h_1, \ldots, h_m) = 0, \tag{9}$$
$$B = -p \cdot x,$$

where $p = (p_1, \ldots, p_l)$ denotes the prices at which the decision maker can buy the commodities.

From here we proceeding to the analysis of an intervention, which in the present context may be formulated as a $(dx, dh_1, \ldots, dh_m)$, where $dx$ denotes the change in consumption of society caused by the intervention, whereas $dh_i$ as before denotes the vector of changes in individual health status, $i = 1, \ldots, m$. In contrast with the previous approach, assessing the value to the decision maker of the intervention is in principle straightforward, since all that is needed is to solve the problem (7) with the new intervention (which changes $H$ and $F$ taken into account). Since the functions in the problem are not fully known in practice, it might however be preferable to assess the intervention indirectly, by computing a suitable cost-effectiveness ratio.

To do this, some additional assumptions are needed, here numbered in accordance with the corresponding assumptions as stated above:

ASSUMPTION 1*. *The decision maker buys commodities at market prices, and in the initial situation, she has maximized the problem (9).*

Under this assumption, we have that the following first order conditions for constrained maximization must be satisfied,

$$\mu \frac{\partial F}{\partial x_h} = -v p_h, \ h = 1, \ldots, l,$$
$$\frac{\partial U}{\partial h_{ij}} = \mu \frac{\partial F}{\partial h_{ij}}, \ i = 1, \ldots, m, \ j = 1, \ldots, k, \tag{10}$$

together with the constraint $F(x, h_1, \ldots, h_m) = 0$, where $\mu$ and $v$ are Lagrangian multipliers of the first and second constraint in (9). To evaluate the intervention by changes d$c$ in aggregate consumption $c = p \cdot x$ and in the health characteristics of each individual, $(dh_1, \ldots, dh_m)$, the decision maker must check whether the increase in her objective function,

$$dU = \sum_{i=1}^{m} \sum_{j=1}^{k} \frac{\partial U}{\partial h_{ij}} dh_{ij},$$

arising from the health changes in the population, is greater than the fall in the objective function which is caused by reduction in other activities necessary so that the budget can contain the cost of the new intervention; this loss in $U$ is equal to $-vp \cdot x$ (where we have used that the Lagrangian multiplier $v$ equals the marginal value of changes in the relevant constraint). Inserting from (10), we may write this condition as

$$\sum_{i=1}^{m} \sum_{j=1}^{k} \mu \frac{\partial F}{\partial h_{ij}} dh_{ij} > -v \sum_{h=1}^{l} p_h dx_h,$$

or, alternatively, as

$$\frac{-\sum_{h=1}^{l} p_h dx_h}{\sum_{i=1}^{m} \sum_{j=1}^{k} \mu (\partial F / \partial h_{ij}) dh_{ij}} < \frac{1}{v}. \tag{11}$$

Once again we have a criterion which takes the form of a cost-effectiveness ratio. The right-hand side of the expression may be interpreted as the marginal cost of health for the decision maker in the initial situation, the cost of the most expensive intervention contained in the budget at the initial situation.

To facilitate comparison, we add another assumption corresponding to Assumption 3 above (the counterpart of Assumption 2 has been incorporated in the approach since the decision maker worries only about total cost but not about who bears it):

ASSUMPTION 3*. *The decision maker considers health (of a given type) of each individual as equally important,*

$$\frac{\partial U}{\partial h_{ij}} = H_j, \ i = 1, \ldots, m, \ each \ j.$$

Under Assumption 3*, the expression in (11) simplifies to

$$\frac{-\sum_{h=1}^{l} p_h dx_h}{\sum_{k=1}^{r} H_k \sum_{i=1}^{m} dh_{ik}} < \frac{1}{\nu}$$

which is more tractable than (11) but still not quite good enough, in the sense that the quantities $H_k$ remain observable (for all except the decision maker), much like the case considered above. Once again we need to aggregate across health characteristics, and to do this we invoke Assumption 4 introduced above.

As previously, we may rewrite the objective function as $V(x, q_1, \ldots, q_m) = U(x, h_1, \ldots, h_m)$ with $h_i$ such that $Q(h_i) = q_i$, and we get that

$$\sum_{j=1}^{k} H_j \sum_{i=1}^{m} dh_{ij} = \sum_{j=1}^{k} \frac{\partial U}{\partial h_{ij}} \sum_{i=1}^{m} dh_{ij} = \sum_{i=1}^{m} \frac{\partial V}{\partial q_i} \sum_{j=1}^{k} \frac{\partial Q}{\partial h_{ij}} dh_{ij} = \sum_{i=1}^{m} dQ_i,$$

where we have used that $V$ may be chosen so that $\frac{\partial V}{\partial q_i} = 1$ for all $i$, and as before have set $dQ_i = \sum_{j=1}^{k} \frac{\partial Q}{\partial h_{ij}} dh_{ij}$. Again, we may think of $dQ_i$ as the QALY change obtained through the intervention. With this addition, the criterion in (9) takes the form

$$\frac{-\sum_{h=1}^{l} p_h dx_h}{\sum_{i=1}^{m} dQ_i} < \frac{1}{\nu}. \tag{12}$$

This expression may be exploited to obtain the following counterpart of Proposition 1. Its first part is proved in the same way as Proposition 1, and the second part follows directly from (12)

PROPOSITION 3 *Assume that Assumptions $1^*$, $3^*$ and 4 are fulfilled, and let $P^r = (dx^r, dh_1^r, \ldots, dh_m^r)$ with $dc^r = \sum_{h=1}^l p_h dx_h$ for $j = 1, 2$ be two interventions. Then $P^1$ carried out at some scale is preferred to $P^2$ by the decision maker if and only if*

$$\frac{dc^1}{dQ^1} < \frac{dc^2}{dQ^2}.$$

*Moreover, there exists a benchmark cost-effectiveness ratio $\sigma$ such that a project $P = (dx, dh_1, \ldots, dh_m)$ improves the criterion of the decision maker if and only if*

$$\frac{dc}{dQ} \leq \sigma.$$

Although the decision maker's approach has the appearance of being very different from our initial one, it leads to the same kind of decision rule. However, the fact that one uses a cost-effectiveness ratio in both does not necessarily mean that the value of this ratio will be the same. Indeed, looking back to the derivations, it may be observed that the way in which cost and effects are measured may differ considerably. The prices used by the decision maker need not be prices at which consumers in society buy their consumption bundles; and the criterion of the decision maker may not be consistent with a social welfare function (provided that such one exists).

While the decision maker's approach as outlined here seems easier to use, since it depends on fewer assumptions on what happens in society, it may be considered as deficient in other ways, notably in the lack of connection between what the budget constrained decision maker finds optimal, and what society wants. Lack of correspondence between the two objectives may occur both due to inadequate budgets and to misconceptions of society's needs from the point of view of the decision maker (and the recent political history in countries with a single, budget-constrained healthcare organization provides examples of both). Nevertheless, in practice the tendency seems to move towards the decision maker's approach; countries or healthcare organizations impose more and more detailed restrictions on the method of constructing a cost-effectiveness ratio, thereby establishing their own criteria for optimality of interventions. We shall return to this problem below.

## 2.3 *Production instead of consumption*

Our first problem when confronting reality is that assessing the change in consumption connected with an intervention is principally possible but in practice quite a complicated task, since it involves a rather large number of consumers, also many who are not directly involved in the medical intervention. However, neglecting transfers from outside or depletion of inventories which would seem irrelevant in our context, the total change in consumption of the $l$ goods must be equal to the change in their net production. Consequently, the value of the change in consumption equals value in change of net production,

$$\sum_{i=1}^{m} dx_{ih} = \sum_{j=1}^{n} dy_{jh}, \quad h = 1, \ldots, r,$$

where $dy_{jh}$ denotes the change of net production of the $h$th commodity in firm $j$, for $j = 1, \ldots, n$ (where we have assumed that there are $n$ productive firms in the country). It follows that

$$c = \sum_{h=1}^{l} p_h \sum_{i=1}^{m} dx_{ih} = \sum_{h=1}^{l} p_h \sum_{j=1}^{n} dy_{jh},$$

so that $c$ can be evaluated from observation of the production changes.

The obvious advantage of an assessment from the production side is that in a medical intervention, the changes of net production usually are confined to the medical sector in a wide sense, including pharmaceutical production. Assessing the value of $\sum_{h=1}^{l} p_h \sum_{j=1}^{n} dy_{jh}$ therefore amounts to assessing the *cost* of the intervention, although in a sense which is somewhat broader than what one is used to, as we shall see in the next section.

## 3  The stages of a cost-effectiveness analysis

### 3.1  *The structure of a CEA in practice*

*The "reference case".* Having dealt at length with foundational questions, it is time to turn to the practical aspects of cost-effectiveness analysis. Although it is intuitively clear – and sustained by our theoretical analysis – that the purpose of a CEA is to exhibit the costs and effects of an intervention, so that an cost-effectiveness ratio, or can be produced, there may still be many cases, where cost or effect can be assessed in different ways, and for the users of CEAs, it is important that the ICERs computed do not display too much variation which has to do with the method rather than with the underlying factual circumstances. Therefore, some *standardizing* is called for: The results of a CEA is needed for decision support, to facilitate the choice of one medical intervention rather than another one, and the users should be reasonably confident that the results presented in the form of an ICER is obtained in a reliable way, so that different CEAs can be compared before a decision is made. As it happens, the search for a unified and standardized method may have unwanted side effects, as there may be situations where the one-size-fits-all approach becomes unsatisfactory from a theoretical point of view. We shall see several such instances below.

Box 6.1 **NICE** was initiated in 1999 as the National Institute of Clinical Excellence, an institution belonging to NHS, the English healthcare system. Its original purpose was to promote a unified offer of treatment for all patients, and the main tool to achieve this is the use of *guidelines* for medical interventions. Such guidelines have widespread use in medical practice, not only in England but in other countries as well. A specific feature of the approach of NICE was that guidelines were elaborated also for other activities than purely medical, in particular since 2005 when its field of activity was extended to cover problems of public health as well. A reorganisation in 2013 meant that also the social sector was included, and its name was changed to the National Institute for Health and Care Excellence (fortunately allowing it to keep the original abbreviation).

Since NICE has as its main purpose to propose methods of treatment in healthcare, the institution is by its very nature a main user of CEAs. These CEAs are not elaborated by NICE itself but are produced either in the industry (if the intervention considered is the use of a particular pharmaceutical drug) or in research institutions. The main role of NICE is to collect the analyses and to reach a consensus among relevant stakeholders about their conclusions, so that the final recommendation is acceptable for all the involved parties.

As a user of CEAs, NICE has had an obvious interest in specifying, how the analysis should be performed, and consequently it has produced detailed prescriptions for this at least since 2013. These guidelines are revised from time to another, the latest version is [NICE, 2013].

The movement towards a standardized version of a CEA is somewhat hampered by the absence of a suitable framework, an institution which would encourage and promote such developments, or at least a commonly agreed set of principles. The closest we can come to such a framework is the guideline published by NICE in England. NICE's guidelines, which in principle are only relevant for CEAs elaborated on behalf of the English healthcare system NHS, are often used in other countries as well, possibly supplemented by specific rules in some areas. We shall return to the NICE guidelines several times as we proceed.

A key concept in the guidelines of NICE is *"the reference case."* This concept goes back to the first systematical discussions of cost-effectiveness analysis, namely Gold et al. [1966]. Here the reference case is defined as a standardized set of methods which the analyst is supposed to use when carrying out a cost-effectiveness analysis. In other words, the reference case is a specification of the structure of a cost-effectiveness analysis together with a description of how to carry out the constituent parts of the analysis. These parts have materialized over the years, so that the reference case as it appears in NICE [2013] has become the commonly agreed approach, and it will be followed in main outlines below. However, from time to another, this approach may give rise to doubts if applied in a wider context than that assumed by NICE, and we shall comment on this as we proceed.

*The choice of viewpoint in the analysis.* In our discussion of foundational questions, we assumed, at least at the outset, that the overall objective should be the wellbeing of all involved citizens, patients or not. We did, however, mention the so-called "decision-maker's approach", where the objective is citizens' health but where a budget constraint puts limits to what can be achieved. Under ideal conditions, the size of budget is such that the final assessment will be the same, but in practice, things may be far from ideal, so that decisions which improve health given the budget may turn out to be suboptimal from a social point of view.

In practice, this dilemma shows up in connection with the choice of *viewpoint* for the CEA. This viewpoint may be either that of society (as in our theoretical approach), or it may be that of the healthcare system. In principle, one might have other viewpoints as well, but only these are encountered in the CEA literature. Even though it is straightforward that any other viewpoint than that of society as a whole is unfortunate and potentially harmful, the alternative viewpoint is used in many contexts. There are several reasons for this; CEAs are made to support decisions, and the decision makers, who are usually placed in the healthcare system, prefer an analysis which is tailored to their situation. It has also a practical advantage in many concrete cases, since neglecting patients' contribution to the cost of an intervention (for example a pharmaceutical drug) may improve the ICER quite substantially.

The guidelines of NICE are very clear on this, they want the CEAs to use the healthcare system perspective. As a consequence, all the factors which relate to the patient's role outside the healthcare system (in particular improved or deteriorated ability to work) is considered irrelevant. Since these items are often very difficult to assess in a precise way, it makes life easier for the analyst, but clearly at the cost of allowing for possible misallocation of resources.

*The five stages of a cost-effectiveness analysis.* In accordance with the above-mentioned reference case, and supported by practical common sense, the analysis can be separated into several stages in the following way,

(1) The model: Construction of a stylized version of the intervention, to be used as a basis for the subsequent computations.
(2) Cost: When the model is established, one needs to identify cost items and their size.
(3) Effects: This is perhaps the weakest part of the analysis, where the health gained from the intervention is established.

(4) ICER: The result of the analysis, made on the basis of steps (2) and (3).

(5) Sensitivity analysis: Here is investigated how much the result varies with the underlying conditions of the calculation, both data and mode assumptions.

The numbering matters, in particular it makes sense to consider (2) before (3). In most of the interventions for which a CEA is set up, the health effects are such that patients are no worse off than in the status-quo treatment, and if it turns out during stage (2) that the new intervention saves cost, then (3) might be omitted, and instead of an ICER, which is difficult to interpret when the numerator and the denominator have opposite signs), one says that the intervention *dominates* status-quo. The main advantage is that we avoid to assess the health effects which anyway is the weakest part of the analysis.

## 3.2 *The model of a CEA*

In the previous section, we have been looking at cost-effectiveness analysis from a purely theoretical viewpoint, trying to establish a foundation for the practical assessments to be carried out when dealing with a concrete intervention. The latter problems will concern us more directly in this and the following sections.

*Decision trees.* In order to carry out the necessary assessments and computations, one needs a model, and it is convenient to begin with a graphical representation of what happens as a result of the intervention. For the individual patient, some acton is performed (medication, surgery, other treatment), which, depending on the outcome, may be repeated, after which some other action is taken, etc. If the start is represented by a point (or node), the treatment could be shown as an arrow, or an *edge* pointing away from the point, after which a new action will be taken depending on whether or not the first action had any effect, or whether there were side effects (which will give further arrows or branchings). In many cases the status-quo intervention may be represented as still another arrow from the starting point, with its own subsequent branchings.

The result of this initial analysis will be a graph in the form shown in Fig. 6.2, known as a *decision tree.* Technically the graph is actually a *tree,* namely a connected graph (one can get from any node to any other node following the edges) which is *acyclic* (moving in the direction of the arrows, one will never get back to a node already visited). The decision tree is a simple and intuitive representation of the intervention, and it should be used as often as possible, clearly as long as the tree does not get too complex.

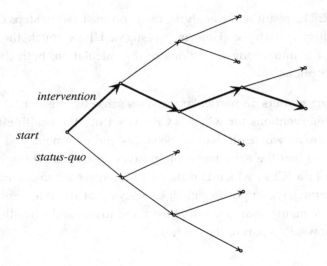

Fig. 6.2  A decision tree. There are two branches going out from start, corresponding to the intervention and to status quo. Subsequent branching reflects what can happen as a result of the intervention, and there will typically be more than indicated in the figure. A possible path through the tree is indicated.

Once the decision tree has been drawn up, the next step consists in assigning cost and effect to each possible pathway through the tree from the root to a terminal node. More specifically, one needs to find (1) the cost which has been incurred while transferring from start to end, (2) the effects obtained, and (3) the probability of moving along this path. The architecture of the tree, as well as the probabilities of going in one or the other direction, comes from the description of the intervention together with the natural history of the underlying disease. When all this is done, one may find the average cost of the intervention by multiplying the cost in each final node with its probability and adding over all the nodes; average effects are found in the same way. Since probabilities enter the computation in this way, what we find are *expected* cost and effect, or, if we can rely on the law of large numbers, the average cost and effect over all the patients treated in accordance with this intervention.

Having assessed the intervention, it remains to assess the status quo treatment in the same way, and from this one may proceed directly to the ICER.

Decision trees are most suited for simple interventions, where the simplicity is connected with possible relapses into earlier states of treatment, of which there should be few, since otherwise the tree get so many branches that it becomes virtually intractable. In such cases it is preferable to use the other main type of model, to which we turn next.

**Box 6.2 Decision tree analysis.** Here is a strongly simplified (and fictive) example of an analysis using a decision tree. The intervention is a drug to be taken in cases of acute headache, and it has shown itself to be effective in 1/10 of the cases. If untreated, the health state will have QALY-value 0.95. The cost of the treatment is €200.

The decision tree looks as follows:

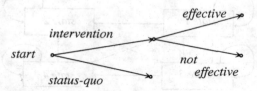

If the treatment works, a QALY-value of 1 is obtained at the cost of €20. If it does not work, one gets only 0.95 as QALY value, and the cost is the same €200, so that on average we have a cost of €20 and a QALY score of

$$\frac{1}{10} \cdot 1 + \frac{9}{10} \cdot 0.95 = 0.955.$$

In the status quo treatment (which here is no treatment at all), cost is 0 and QALY score is 0.95. We find

$$ICER = \frac{20 - 0}{0.955 - 0.95} = \frac{20}{0.005} = 4,000€,$$

a result which is not outstanding, but still reasonably good, for our fictive treatment.

*Markov models.* Depending on the details in the intervention considered, the associated decision tree may be quite simple or it may be a very complex one with a large number of branchings. If the tree gets very large, it may be inconvenient to analyse it in the usual way, and an alternative representation of the intervention should be considered. This is also the case for interventions which change the long-term prospects of patients for whom the periods of good and bad health may change over time, and where a return to a previous state of health is possible. This conflicts with the basic property of a tree, namely acyclicity – one never returns to a node which has already been visited. In such a case another approach must be taken.

This alternative approach is known as a *Markov model*. Here the focus is the different possible states of health of the patient and the transitions from one state of health to another one. Thus, a Markov model is given by a set of *states*, usually but not always characterized by a certain state of health. The patient moves from one state to another (which however may be the same one) with a given *transition probability,* describing the probability of changing state over a fixed time interval, usually one year. The Markov model may be illustrated graphically as shown in Fig. 6.3, where each state has a box and transitions show the possibility of moving from one state to another.

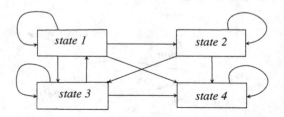

Fig. 6.3   Markov model. The arrows between the states indicate the transitions that have positive probability. It is possible to get into state 4 but not to get out; such a state is called an *absorbing state.* The arrows starting in one state and returning to the same state correspond to the patient staying in this state, and such arrows are often omitted in the graphical representations.

What matters in the Markov model is not its graphical representation but the transition probabilities. If $p_{ij}$ denotes the probability of moving from state $i$ to state $j$, then we can subsume the crucial information of the model in the matrix $P$ of transition probabilities,

$$P = \begin{pmatrix} p_{11} & p_{12} & \cdots & p_{1n} \\ \vdots & \vdots & & \vdots \\ p_{n1} & p_{n2} & \cdots & p_{nn} \end{pmatrix}$$

In the $i$th row we have the probabilities of going from state $i$ to all the other states, including the state $i$ where we are already, and the sum of all these probabilities must therefore be 1.

Knowing the probability of moving from any state to any other state in the course of one period, one may find the probability of moving from $i$ to $j$ in two periods. To get this, consider any state $k$, which may possibly be passed on the way $i$ to $j$. The probability of the particular tour from $i$ over $k$ to $j$ is $p_{ik}p_{kj}$, and adding the probabilities of all the possible tours we get

$$p_{ij}^{(2)} = \sum_{k=1}^{n} p_{ik}p_{kj}.$$

The matrix $P^{(2)}$ consisting of all the two-period transition probabilities can be obtained by multiplying $P$ with itself, something which is convenient in computations.

As it was said already, the transition probabilities are the key features of the Markov model, since they characterize the intervention. To obtain an ICER one needs two matrices of transition probabilities, one characterizing the course of the disease *without* the intervention and the other one *with* the intervention. The

---

**Box 6.3 Markov model, example.** We consider a new treatment which may change the course of a cronical disease. During the patient's lifetime, bad periods where the patient has increased mortality and need of care may be followed by good periods where the patient feels almost perfectly cured. There is a higher mortality rate in each state than in the population at large.

Before the introduction of the new treatment the course of the disease can be described by the transition probabilities

|         | Healthy        | Ill           | Dead          |
|---------|----------------|---------------|---------------|
| Healthy | $\frac{1}{2}$  | $\frac{1}{4}$ | $\frac{1}{4}$ |
| Ill     | $\frac{1}{6}$  | $\frac{1}{2}$ | $\frac{1}{3}$ |
| Dead    | 0              | 0             | 1             |

In the healthy state the patient has a QALY-value of 1 and costs nothing, whereas in the illness state the QALY score is only 0.6, and there are healthcare costs amounting to €5,000. De diseased patients cost nothing, but they do not contribute to the QALY score either.

We assume a very short horizon and want to follow the patients only for 2 years. Starting our observations of the patient in the illness state, in the following year the fractions $\frac{1}{6}$, $\frac{1}{2}$ and $\frac{1}{3}$ of the patients will be healthy, ill, and dead, respectively, and this gives a contribution of

$$\frac{1}{2} \cdot 5000 = 2.500 \text{ €}, \quad \frac{1}{6} \cdot 1 + \frac{1}{2} \cdot 0,6 = 0,67 \text{ QALY}$$

for each patient. In the following year the fraction of patients in the three states are $\frac{1}{6}$, $\frac{7}{24}$ og $\frac{13}{24}$ (check this!), and the contributions therefore

$$\frac{7}{24} \cdot 5000 = 1458 \text{ €}, \quad \frac{1}{6} \cdot 1 + \frac{7}{24} \cdot 0,6 = 0.342 \text{ QALY}.$$

For reasons not yet explained (discounting of future costs and effects), these amounts are reduced by approximately 3%, so that they become 1414 kr. and 0.332 QALY. We add this to the contributions of the first year, so that we get a total cost of 3.914 kr. and a total QALY-score of 1.018.

**Example, continued.** The treatment takes place once and for all, and it costs €30,000. It must be given to patients in the state of illness in order to be effective. It changes the course of the disease, so that after the treatment, the transition probabilities are as follows:

|          | Healthy       | Ill           | Dead          |
|----------|---------------|---------------|---------------|
| Healthy  | $\frac{2}{3}$ | $\frac{1}{6}$ | $\frac{1}{6}$ |
| Ill      | $\frac{1}{3}$ | $\frac{1}{2}$ | $\frac{1}{6}$ |
| Dead     | 0             | 0             | 1             |

We perform the same computations as above, and we get that in the first year costs are €2,500 and effects are 0.633 QALY, and in the second year costs and effects are

$$\frac{11}{36} \cdot 5000 = 1528 \text{ € and } \frac{7}{18} \cdot 1 + \frac{11}{36} \cdot 0,6 = 0.572 \text{ QALY,}$$

respectively, and after reducing by around 3%, this is added to the contributions of the first year, and we get a total of €3982 and 1,188 QALY. To this we should add the cost of treatment, €30.000.

We can now find the ICER as

$$\frac{33982 - 3914}{1.188 - 1.018} = 176.870 \text{ €/QALY.}$$

This is not a very impressive result, considering the improvements that are actually achieved, but then we have looked only at a two-year period. If the analysis is extended to cover a longer span of time, the intervention will appear as more attractive.

probabilities are obtained either from the medical literature or from patient data, if such are available.

Once the transition probabilities are in place, the next step consists in assigning costs and effects to staying one year in each of the states. Having done that, one can find average cost and average effect year by year, and finally, after summation over the years considered, total expected cost and effect over the whole period is obtained. Carrying through this procedure for the intervention as well as for the status-quo, one may finally compute the ICER of the intervention.

*Average or Monte Carlo simulation.* In the approach outlined above, we were interested in averages of cost and effect, so that what we found was a typical or an average lifespan of a patient. Alternatively one might construct individual trajectories, simulating a patient history by randomly choosing the next state according to the transition probabilities. For this, the randomness generator of the computer is applied repeatedly; letting the computer construct e.g. 100,000 of these random trajectories, the result is a detailed set of patient data rather than a simple average. The data may then be used to find averages, but this was known already, so the advantage of this method, known as *Monte-Carlo simulation*, is that it gives some insight into the variation around the average. This may be useful in some cases, for example if the intervention gives a small cost reduction on the average which however may not materialize very often due to the variation around this average.

Since we are dealing with a simulation, no new information is revealed which was not already latently present in the transition probabilities, so what is obtained is only new ways of looking at the same model. But since it is rather straightforward to perform Monte-Carlo simulations (there are ready-made computer programs for this), they will often be encountered in the cost-effectiveness literature.

*Within-trial versus outside-trial analysis.* This distinction, partially inherited from the medical sciences, has to do with the data on which the cost-effectiveness analysis is based. When these data are taken from a clinical trial, basically reporting on how individual patients reacted to treatments, one speaks of a within-trial analysis. In this case, what is computed is based on results from the trial and (at least in principle) nothing else.

As we have already seen and shall see repeatedly in the sequel, what is computed in a cost-effectiveness analysis is in most cases *more* than a recompilation of records made in a trial. In most cases we cannot trace the use of resources at the patient's bedside, since a crucial part of the cost or cost saving connected with an intervention is related to what would have happened if the intervention had not taken place. Clearly, extending the trial (and in particular the observations of the control group on which no intervention is made) so that patients are followed over their remaining life, would take care of this objection. But new problems will show up – how can we include the future participation or lack of participation in ordinary economic activities with subsequent value creation for society in a randomized clinical trial?

As can be seen, insisting on within-trial analyses as "better" in some sense would effectually put an end to cost-effectiveness analyses. That such a ranking would be proposed at all can be seen as a historical circumstance, since cost-effectiveness grew out of purely medical considerations about establishing evidence for the effectiveness of treatments. In economics, we cannot make controlled trials, so we have to rely on other methods.

## 3.3   *Assessing cost (1): Direct cost*

We now turn to the details of the assessment, whereby we – following the insights of the previous section – concentrate on the technological aspects of the intervention. Since an intervention naturally splits into components which have to do with changes in use of marketable goods and services on the one hand, and components relating to individual health and consequently not directly transferable between individuals on the other hand, we must approach these two parts of the assessments – conveniently named as *cost* and *effects* – separately.

*Direct cost.* In the assessment of the cost side of the intervention, it is useful to distinguish between *direct* costs, which are those related to the treatment of the patient, and *indirect* costs, which are the remaining cost items[1]. While the assessment of direct costs do not pose many problems of a fundamental character, there are nevertheless situations where some care is called for. Some such cases are considered below.

*Cost allocation.* As we have seen in previous sections, the relevant cost concept for assessment of interventions is *marginal cost*, the cost of changing activity by a small amount. This means that capacity costs (fixed equipment, administration) should be taken into account only to the extent that they are influenced by the intervention, which however happens reasonably often. On the other hand, if actual production is close to the capacity limit, or if some inputs are in short supply (as in the case of human organs for transplantation), then the resource use should be evaluated at shadow prices which of course are not easily obtained in practice.

*Hospital treatment and DRG prices* In most countries, a system of prices on hospital treatments, based on the classification of such treatments according to Diagnosis Related Groups (DRGs), has been in place since the mid-nineties. The DRG-classification may differ slightly between countries, but agree in general on the number of items, close to 600, and their overall relationship to the medical classification system ICD-10. The basic idea of DRG prices has been to find the average cost in the country of the respective hospital treatments; this cost is found using the reported costs of hospitals, which are then assigned to DRGs.

As is well known from managerial economics, computation of unit costs in enterprises producing several different outputs can be done only on additional assumptions, in most cases of an ad-hoc character. What can be assigned to treatments (DRGs) are those cost items that are directly related to these treatments,

---

[1]In the textbook literature, one may find mention also of *intangible cost*, which are cost items related to anxiety and fear connected with treatment (as distinct from the anxiety and fear itself, which belongs to the effect side of the intervention). Intangible costs are however without practical importance and their magnitude is very difficult to assess (see for this e.g. Larg and Moss [2011].

whereas other cost items, 'overheads', have to do with some or all of the treatments and not any single treatment in particular. This problem is serious in the sense that hospital costs in general have the nature of overheads, and increasingly so with the technological development over time. Even nursing cost tends to take form – cost studies reveal that less than 30% of the nursing cost is directly related to the individual patient with a given diagnosis, whereas the remaining part has to do with general monitoring, instruction etc.

Since DRG prices exist, it seems logical to exploit them as the relevant assignment of cost to hospital treatment, and indeed this is the approach usually taken and recommended in manuals. The use of DRG prices simplifies the analysis and makes it more transparent, and alternative approaches would rely on other ad-hoc assumptions which then would have to be explained. However, DRG prices are artificial, computed for purposes of accounting and for funding of hospital services, and they are not primarily intended to reflect society's cost of an additional DRG. We are pretty far from the prices of a competitive equilibrium which was what we should be looking for according to Section 2 above, and when using the DRG prices we should at least be aware of their shortcomings.

*Taxes.* One of the practical questions facing the analyst is how to treat commodity taxes such as VAT when calculating costs. For an answer to this, one would refer back to the theoretical foundation, according to which prices used should reflect as far as possible those coming from an idealized or simulated market with perfect competition. This approach would suggest that prices should be taken *before* taxes.

It should however be remembered, that the point of view of the analysis does matter here. The above argument assumes implicity that the point of view is that of society – or alternatively a government institution which does not pay taxes. There might well be situations where taxes should be included, namely if they represent a cost to the organization from whose point of view the analysis is set up.

*Discounting future cost.* In accordance with the standard approach to economic assessment of future cash flows, the cost items belonging to future periods should be suitably discounted before being compared to items which are related to the present or to other periods in the future. Although this is rather uncontroversial, it is not easy to find any "correct" rate of interest to use for discounting, a problem which is resolved in practice by the guidelines which set the discount rates, at present typically around 3%. It goes without saying that fixing the discount rate by decree is at best a way of facilitating administrative work, and as such it is a case where the practice of economic appraisals move from scientific research towards administrative procedure. We shall see that this is by no means the only one.

Moving slightly ahead of our story, it should be mentioned at this point that not only cost, but also effects of an intervention may fall in different, often very distant, points of time. Consequently there is a case for discounting effects, however measured. We have a conceptual problem here, since the discounting of for example future blood pressure or future quality of life cannot be justified easily by reference to a market, as it is the case for discounting of cash flows, so we have to use the other standard explanation of discounting, that of subjective time preference, which may or may not be convincing. There are no easy answers, partially since the problem of discounting effects is only a small part of the bigger problem, that of measuring effects in a way which makes sense.

### 3.4  *Assessing cost (2): Indirect cost*

As mentioned already, the indirect cost items are those which are not related to the treatment of the patient but have to do with the way in which the intervention changes the allocation of marketable goods and services. If the patients can be treated so as to return into productive employment rather than lying ill, there is a gain to society – in the form of additional output – over and above the individual gains of the patients that are treated. This is the so-called *production gain,* which has been the object of much debate in the literature on cost-effectiveness. But there are other types of indirect costs which we shall discuss in due course.

For each type of indirect cost, we must consider whether this item should at all be included, and if so, how it should be assessed. As we shall see, controversies may arise at each of these points.

*The production gain.* If the productive efforts of cured patients should count as a reduction in the cost of the intervention, then obviously the objective of the decision maker must take into account not only health obtained within a given budget but also spin-offs in the form of larger production of goods and services elsewhere in the economy. In other words, for answering the question (1) of whether or not to include production cost in the analysis, we must look at the purpose of the analysis. If the analysis is carried out from the point of view of society, it should be included; if the point of view is that of a healthcare organization, big or small, public or private, then it should not; advantages reaped from the intervention outside the realm of the healthcare organization are irrelevant unless the organization can cash them in, and this is typically not the case.

Once we agree that production gain should be taken into account, we shall have to accept that some interventions will appear as having a much lower cost than others due to the fact that average patients in the first are in the productive age groups whereas the patients of the others are retired citizens. Here and in other similar cases, one should not confuse the *cost side* of the analysis with the analysis

**Box 6.4 Example.** Assume that there are two consumption goods and health. The first consumption good can also be used as input in production of good 2 and health. Society has an endowment of 1 unit of good 1 and nothing of the other goods, and the production functions have the form

$$y = \sqrt{z_2}, \quad h = \sqrt{z_3}, \tag{17}$$

where $x_2$ and $x_3$ denote the amount of good 1 used in producing good 2 and health, respectively. We assume that all individuals have utility functions $u(x, y, h) = x + y + \frac{3}{4}h$, so that only goods give rise to utility, and health $h$ produced gives rise to an increase in the endowment of good 1 to of the amount $\frac{h}{2}$. Feasible allocations are then triples $(x, y, h)$ such that

$$x + z_2 + \frac{1}{2}z_3 \leq 1$$

and (17) is satisfied.

Consider now the allocation $\left(\frac{1}{2}, \frac{1}{2}, \frac{1}{2}\right)$, obtained by inserting $\frac{1}{4}$ in the production of commodity 2 and another $\frac{1}{4}$ in production of health. This results in $\frac{\beta}{4}$ units of commodity 1 being unused, and a utility level of $\frac{11}{8}$. If the prices of commodity 1 and 2 are fixed at 1, then the allocation may be sustained if consumers sell the endowment to get an income 1, receive profits $\frac{1}{4}$ from the production of good 2, and pay taxes $\frac{1}{4}$ financing the production of health. With the remaining 1 unit of income, they buy the consumption goods, and they receive the health production as public service. Thus, budget balance and individual optimization of consumers and producers are satisfied. The allocation is, however, not a competitive equilibrium since some of the good 1 is left idle.

Clearly, we might contemplate using some of the good for producing additional health. The direct cost of producing another (small) unit of $h$ is the inverse of the derivative of the production function, that is

$$\text{marginal direct cost of health} = \left(\frac{1}{2}x_3^{-\frac{1}{2}}\right)^{-1} = 2\sqrt{x_3} = 1.$$

To this we must add the production gain which amounts to $\beta$ times the units of health produced, measured in terms of good 1. If good 1 is valued at the prices actually paid, which is $p_1 = 1$, then the (marginal) cost of the intervention is $1 - \frac{1}{2} = \frac{1}{2}$. Since marginal utility of the intervention is $\frac{3}{4}$, this intervention gives a cost-effectiveness ratio of $\frac{3}{8}$.

---

**Example, continued.** On the other hand, assessing the value of additional units of good 1 at the price 1 seems incorrect, since there are unused units of the good already. Therefore, its shadow price is 0, and the additional units of the good do not count any more.

Consequently, the cost-effectiveness ratio becomes $\frac{3}{4}$ instead of $\frac{3}{8}$. This can well make a difference, since an alternative intervention consisting in expanding the production of good 2 rather than of health gives more utility for money if evaluated using this shadow price 0, whereas health would be preferable when the price is set to 1.

---

as a whole. When assessing the *effects* of the intervention, the social position of the patients will play no role, but taking account of the resource use involved in carrying through the intervention, this position matters and must be taken into account.

As always, finding the value of this cost item consists of two parts, namely (1) determining the extent of additional participation in production which is obtained through the intervention, and (2) assessing the value of this participation. While (1) is given by the description of the medical technology (except for a possible correction factor to be mentioned below), the part (2) is a task for the economist. Two approaches are proposed in the literature:

*The human-capital method.* Here we look for the contribution to society's production caused by availability of an additional unit of a factor, in our case labour. This means that we need the *value marginal product* of this factor, and according to standard textbooks, in a perfectly competitive world this marginal product equals the *wage* of the factor in question, as determined in the relevant labour market. Thus, the wage rate gives the right estimate of the contribution the social product, even when the average patient is not a wage earner.

Clearly, for this estimate to be the right one the assumptions underlying it should be at least approximately satisfied, which is not necessarily the case in practice. The labour markets are not smoothly functioning competitive markets but highly organized and regulated. This is not a problem restricted to labour markets, since many other prices taken from the real world markets may be quite far from what would have been equilibrium prices in perfectly competitive markets. However, it is particularly visible when dealing with labour markets, where imbalances in the form of unemployment bear witness to the fact that prices are not adapting so as to balance supply and demand.

*The frictional method.* The fact that considerable unemployment exists in many countries have given rise to an alternative approach to the assessment of the value of labour power, namely valuing by *shadow prices*. The idea of valuation by the economically more satisfactory notion of shadow prices seem well-founded. However, things are more complicated than they seem at a first look, as shown by the following example.

It may also be seen that there is no simple answer as to which method is the best. Actually we have a problem at the very outset, since the initial allocation here is inefficient. This conflicts with our basic assumptions behind cost-effectiveness analysis, which may not cause undue worries by itself, since such conflicts between the ideal and the real are bound to appear sooner or later, but it poses a very simple problem: When allocation is inefficient, then welfare could be improved without any interventions, just by adjusting allocation. Therefore the gains and losses of any intervention include some amount of general efficiency improvement, which cannot be distinguished from the consequences of the interventions. Using the frictional method amounts to keeping possible efficiency gains out of the analysis when considering the production gain; unfortunately, the same distortions of prices are present and hidden in all the other cost components, so that the method arbitrarily corrects one price, leaving the others as they were, something which makes the approach not more correct but rather more arbitrary than it was before.

*Consumption in gained life years.* If an intervention has as its consequence that patients live longer, then the additional life years of patients will give rise to an additional consumption in these years. On the face of it, this extra consumption, which draws on resources previously used for other purposes, is a consequence of the intervention, and therefore it would seem reasonable to include them, just as it was right to take into account the productive efforts of the cured patients in society, as far as there were any. However, production and consumption does not enter into the considerations in a completely symmetric way.

*Unrelated medical cost.* As additional lifeyears give rise to consumption of ordinary goods and services, it will also result in increased demand for healthcare. Some of this is related to the illness against which the intervention was directed in the first place, and as such it should already be figuring among the (direct) costs of the intervention. But other services of the healthcare system may have no relation to the intervention, being healthcare needed for the average person in the age group considered. Such items are known as unrelated medical cost, and one may wonder whether this should be counted as a cost or not.

Since unrelated medical cost is just a single item among many belonging to the general category of consumption in additional life years, the answer is immediate: Unrelated medical cost should *not* count as a cost, at least when the

**Box 6.5 Example:** The following simple example may show the point: A society consists of two persons with a possible lifespan of two years. However, individual 2 has a probability $p$ of dying after the first year. There is only one consumption good, and individuals have utility $u(c)$ of consuming $c$ units of the good in any period; we assume that $u$ is concave so that individuals are risk averse. If there are 2 units of the good available in each period, then the allocation is efficient if the amounts $c_i^t$ consumed by individual $i$ in period $t$ satisfy

$$c_1^1 + c_2^1 = 2,\ c_1^2 = 2 \quad \text{with probability } p,$$
$$c_1^1 + c_2^1 = 2,\ c_1^2 + c_2^2 = 2 \quad \text{with probability } 1 - p.$$

Since we are mainly interested in averages, we may assume that a normal average consumption is $c = 1$ in both years. Expected utilities in this case would be

$$(2 - p)u(1) + pu(2) \text{ for individual 1, } (2 - p)u(1) \text{ for individual 2.}$$

Assume now that a new medical technology is introduced, whereby individual 2 can survive with probability 1 if an amount $z$ of the consumption good is given up in the first period. If the cost of prolonging life of individual 2 does not exceed the expected additional consumption in the last year, $z \le p$, then individual 2 would be better off having the intervention and covering its cost, since average consumption is at worst unchanged and a lottery is now replaced by a sure prospect.

However, this does not exhaust the consequences on the allocation of carrying out the intervention. Indeed, individual 1 is also affected, since due to the survival of individual 2, her consumption in the second year will be reduced from 2 to 1 with probability 1. Notice that this reduction is exactly the consumption of individual 2 in the gained lifeyear.

What is the cost of the intervention? Since ressources to the size of $z$ are given up in order to obtain the effects, this amount should of course figure as a cost. But what about the increased consumption in period 2, or equivalently the consumption loss of individual 1? It is fairly obvious that no consumption goods disappear in period 1, what individual 1 loses (with probability $p$) is exactly what individual 2 gets. So from society's point of view, the resource loss necessary to obtain the longer life is $z$ and nothing more.

cost-effectiveness analysis is carried out from the point of view of society. On the other hand, if the viewpoint is that of the healthcare system, it might be appropriate to include such costs (and indeed all costs of the healthcare system which are a consequence of prolonged life of patients), thus giving us one more case where the point of view of the analysis (or, to be more precise, of the decision maker for whom the analysis is made) matters for the way in which it is carried out.

## 3.5 Assessing effects

*Natural units.* As the cost-effectiveness analysis is often an outgrowth of a clinical trial, the latter will in many cases contain measures of the effect of the intervention which have a direct medical interpretation (stated as so-called 'end points' in the study). If the intervention is about lowering blood pressure, it is natural that consequences of the intervention are stated in terms of blood pressure; cholesterol lowering drugs are assessed according to the decrease in cholesterol that they bring about. Since measures of blood pressure or cholesterol are already well-known and have an exact meaning, it seems straightforward to use them as the measure of effect. In this case, one speaks about effect measurement in natural units.

This approach has the obvious advantage of being meaningful (something which is not quite the case for the alternative approaches to be discussed next), but there is a drawback as well. Measuring the cost of lowering blood pressure is fine as long as the only comparison to be made is with alternative methods of lowering blood pressure; obviously the result of the analysis does not say anything about the merits of lowering blood pressure as compared e.g. to hip replacement. For such comparisons, effects should be measured in something which makes sense also for interventions against very different diseases, pointing to the measuring of effect as change in length as well as quality of life.

There is another, more practical problem connected with measuring effects in natural units, namely that the effects of an intervention only rarely are captured fully be a single measure. Cholesterol, for example, is usually measured by at least two different numbers, and the use of two or more measures to give an adequate picture of the effects of the intervention is the rule rather than the exception. As a consequence, cost-effectiveness *ratios* become less useful, since there will be as many as there are different outcome measures, neither of them giving a full picture of the situation.

*Utility based measures of effect.* Since the situations where the non-monetary consequences of the intervention can be described by a single measure in natural units are so relatively few, there is a need for developing synthetical measures of comprehensive effect, known in the field as *utility based measures*. The most prominent of these measures is the QALY, already discussed at length in Chapter 2, where we also stressed its nature of being an interval measure, a property which is important in the present context where we want to reach a conclusion in terms of cost-effectiveness ratios, relating differences in cost to differences in effect.

*Willingness to pay as effect measure.* The third possibility, namely measuring the effects in money terms, so that the analysis becomes what is known as a *cost-benefit*

**Box 6.6 Endogenous cost-effectivity analysis.** In our approach to cost-effectivity analysis of pharmaceutical drugs, we have taken the price of the drug as given, and the ICER which is obtained in the analysis is then used to decide whether or not treatment with this drug should be implemented, comparing among other things the ICER with the established benchmarks. It should be expected that the producers take this procedure into account when they calculate the price of the drug.

This situation has been investigated by Jena and Philipson [2013] introducing the concept of *endogenous cost-effectiveness analysis*. If unit production cost is $c$, which is private information, and quality (measured in QALYs) is $q$, then the ordinary cost-effectiveness ratio would be $\zeta_c = c/q$. However, in a cost-effectiveness analysis based only on public information, which is the drug price $p$, it would be $\zeta_p = p/q$. This official cost-effectiveness ratio matters for payer decisions about adopting the drug, subsidizing its cost.

Let $P(\zeta_c)$ be the probability that the payer accepts to subsidize the drug, after which the price to the consumer is $s(p)$. If $D(p', q)$ denotes the demand given the consumer price $p'$ and quality $q$, then expected profit of the producer at price $p$ is

$$A(\zeta_p)(p - c)D(s(p), q) + (1 - A(\zeta_p))(p - c)D(p, q), \tag{13}$$

where the second member reflects the situation when the drug is not adopted and the consumers must pay the full price. Assuming that the demand is zero when price is not subsidized (or alternatively, that the drug is not given market permit if not adopted by the payer), then the second member disappears, and first order conditions for a maximum in (13) wrt. $p$ are

$$A'(\zeta_p)\frac{1}{q}(p - c)D(s(p), q) + A(\zeta_p)\left[D(s(p), q) + (p - c)D'(s(p), q)s'(q)\right] = 0. \tag{14}$$

If the subsidization scheme is such that consumers pay the price of the drug if below a certain limit and then pay only this limit price (a stop-loss subsidy), then we may assume that $s'(p) = 0$, and (14) reduces to

$$A'(\zeta_p)\frac{p - c}{q} = -A(\zeta_p),$$

which can also be written as

$$\frac{p - c}{p} = \frac{1}{\varepsilon_A}, \tag{15}$$

where $\varepsilon_A = -A'(\zeta_p)/\zeta_p$ is the elasticity of $A$, the probability of adoption. In optimum, the mark-up, here stated in terms of the Lerner index, should be equal to the reverse elasticity of the adoption probability. The dependence of the optimal price on the probability of acceptance of the drug is not surprising, but in addition to this, the formula, which resembles that of monopoly pricing, gives us the exact nature of this dependence.

*analysis*, runs into problems from the outset, given that effects have been defined exactly as those consequences which cannot readily be valued in money terms. The approach is not altogether excluded by such formal reasons, however. Money measures cannot be delivered by the market or by simulating the market, but there is always a possibility of collecting information directly from the concerned as *willingness-to-pay*. We have already discussed willingness-to-pay in an earlier chapter (see Ch. 6), and we refer to this discussion; in practice, there has been considerable reluctance towards the use of willingness to pay in cost-effectiveness analyses.

## 4 Uncertainty in cost-effectiveness analysis

It is rather obvious that much of what is assessed and computed during a cost-effectiveness analysis is subject to uncertainty. There is a tradition for dividing the different sources of uncertainty, namely *data uncertainty*, the statistical uncertainty originating in data collection, and *method uncertainty* related to the very model and the parameters that have been assessed without statistical estimation. As it will become evident below, there are several quite sophisticated techniques available for treatment of data uncertainty, and not surprisingly this will take up much space in published cost-effectiveness analyses. Unfortunately, method uncertainty, which can be assessed only by rather crude tools, is as important in practical analysis as data uncertainty if not more (it suffices to mention the part played by QALY measures the meaningfulness of which is under increasing debate).

### 4.1 *Methods for assessment of data uncertainty (1): Confidence intervals*

To apply statistical techniques, we must have access to data, typically collected in clinical trials. These data give information on cost $c$ and effect $h$ of treatment, both in the intervention group and the control group, and somewhat simplified, we assume that the data take the form of pairs $(\Delta c, \Delta h)$ of incremental costs and effects

It seems not too unreasonable to assume that $\Delta c$ and $\Delta h$ are (jointly) normally distributed. However, the distribution of the cost-effectiveness ratio is certainly not normal, and indeed in general unknown; there is no simple functional expression of ratios of normal random variables. This means that usual statistical analysis of the cost-effectiveness ratio, including the construction of confidence intervals, must take a roundabout approach, and there are several such approaches available.

**Box 6.7 Confidence intervals.** A standard way of illustrating the uncertainty connected with an estimation is by the way of *confidence intervals*. Suppose that the incremental cost of an intervention is normally distributed. Then the true value of incremental cost is estimated by the *sample mean* $\Delta c^0$, and this estimator is also normally distributed, so if the standard deviation of incremental cost $\sigma_{\Delta c}$ was known, one could find for any preassigned probability $\alpha$ a symmetric interval around $\Delta c^*$ such that the estimation on a sample of the given size would be in this interval with probability $\alpha$.

Suppose that a sample of 9 observations give the following results (in 1,000 €):

| Observation $j$ | 1 | 2 | 3 | 4 | 5 | 6 | 7 | 8 | 9 |
|---|---|---|---|---|---|---|---|---|---|
| $\Delta c_j$ | 11.2 | 10.4 | 10.3 | 10.7 | 10.8 | 11.1 | 10.6 | 10.4 | 10.9 |

Then the sample mean is $\sum_{j=1}^{9} \Delta c_j / 9 = 10.7$, and if we know that $\sigma_{\Delta c} = 0.3$, then we can find a 99% confidence limits as

$$10.7 \pm 1.96 \cdot \frac{0.3}{\sqrt{9}} 0.3$$

giving us the confidence interval $[10.5, 10.9]$. Here we have used the 99%-fractile in the standardized normal distribution, which is 1.96.

Now $\sigma_{\Delta c}$ is usually *not* known, so it must be estimated from the data, giving some value $s_{\Delta c}$. But then the distribution of the estimator is no longer normal but has a $t$-distribution with $N - 1$ degrees of freedom, where $N$ is the sample size, and the confidence limits are found as

$$\Delta c^0 \pm t_{1-\frac{\alpha}{2}, N-1} \frac{s_{\Delta c}}{\sqrt{N}}.$$

where $t_{1-\frac{\alpha}{2}, N-1}$ is the $1 - \frac{\alpha}{2}$ fractile in the $t$-distribution with $N-1$ degrees of freedom. The sample variance in our example is found as $\sum_{j=1}^{9} (\delta c_j - \delta c^0)^2 / 8 = 0.101$, so the sample standard deviation is $0, 318$, and we use the 99%-fractile in the $t$-distribution with 8 degrees of freedom, which is 3.355, to get the confidence limits $\Delta c^0 \pm \frac{0.101}{\sqrt{9}} 3.355$ and the confidence interval $[10.36, 10.92]$.

It is seen that confidence interval is *not* an interval containing the true value of incremental cost with probability $\alpha$ (the true value either is or is not in the interval), but tells us only that out of 100 estimations using a sample size of $N$ the result will be in the interval $100 \cdot \alpha$ of the times. On the other hand, since the sample mean converges to the true value as the sample increases, and the confidence interval shrinks, the interval will eventually catch the true value.

*Box-methods.* This is the simplest possible approach to estimating a confidence interval for the cost-effectiveness ratio given that confidence limits can be established for cost and effect estimates separately. If cost data have mean $\Delta c^0$ and lower and upper confidence limits (say, at level 0.99) $\underline{\Delta c}$ and $\overline{\Delta c}$, respectively, while the effect data result in corresponding estimates $\Delta h^0$, $\underline{\Delta h}$ and $\overline{\Delta h}$, then we may construct the box consisting of all $(\Delta h, \Delta c)$ with

$$\underline{\Delta h} \leq \Delta h \leq \overline{\Delta h}, \; \underline{\Delta c} \leq \Delta c \leq \overline{\Delta c},$$

illustrated in Fig. 6.4. Now a candidate for a confidence interval for the cost-effectiveness ratio $\dfrac{\Delta c}{\Delta h}$ is the range of all ratios $\Delta c/\Delta h$ for points $(\Delta h, \Delta c)$ in the box, geometrically the interval of slopes of rays from the origin that intersect the box (indicated in Fig. 6.4). It goes without saying that this approach is inaccurate; the box does not correspond to the cost-effect combinations that carry 99% probability, not even in the case of independence between cost and effects, and ratios achieved by points in the box could be achieved for many points outside the box as well. Thus, the conceptual simplicity should be weighted against the crudeness of this approach.

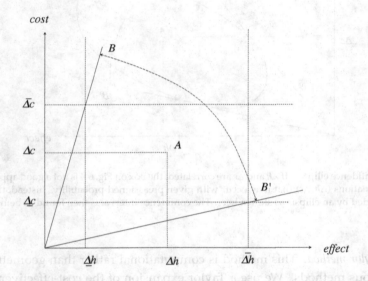

Fig. 6.4   The box method for finding confidence interval. Given upper and lower confidence limits for $\Delta h$ and $\Delta c$, one can find an approximate confidence interval for the ICER as the interval of ratios $\Delta c/\Delta h$ for all points $(\Delta h, \Delta c)$ where both coordinates are in their respective confidence intervals (indicated as $BB'$).

*Confidence ellipses.* The first objection against the box method (that the box does not yield a set of cost-effect points carrying probability of 99%) can be remedied if we know the (joint) probability distribution function $F(\Delta h, \Delta c)$ of $\Delta h$ and $\Delta c$, replacing the box by the set

$$\{(\Delta h, \Delta c) \mid F(\Delta h, \Delta c) \leq 0.99\}$$

as indicated in Fig. 6.5. The confidence interval for the cost-effectiveness ratio is obtained in the same way as before. If $F$ is the normal probability distribution, the set will be bounded by an ellipsis, whence the name of the method. It is easily seen that the method eliminates one source of inaccuracy (at the cost of an assumption on the distribution) but retains the other one, while it looses some of the extreme simplicity of the box method.

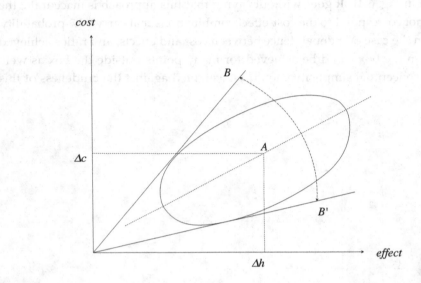

Fig. 6.5   Confidence ellipses. If $\Delta h$ and $\Delta c$ are correlated, the box on Fig. 6.4 is not a good approximation of the combinations $(\Delta h, \Delta c)$ that may occur with given preassigned probability. Instead, these points will be bounded by an ellipsis as shown here. The confidence interval is then found as before.

*The Taylor method.* This method is computational rather than geometric as the two previous methods. We use a Taylor expansion of the cost-effectiveness ratio around $\Delta c^0/\Delta h^0$; writing $z = z(\Delta h, \Delta c)$ for the first order Taylor approximation, we have that

$$\mathsf{E}z = \frac{\Delta c^0}{\Delta h^0} - \frac{\Delta c^0}{(\Delta h^0)^2}\left[\mathsf{E}\,\Delta h - \Delta h^0\right] + \frac{1}{\Delta h^0}\left[\mathsf{E}\,\Delta c - \Delta c^0\right] = \frac{\Delta c^0}{\Delta h^0},$$

and

$$\sigma^2(z) = \mathsf{E}\left[\,z(\Delta c, \Delta h) - \mathsf{E}\,z(\Delta c, \Delta h)\,\right]^2.$$

Inserting and using standard formula for the variance, this reduces to

$$\sigma^2(z) = \frac{(\Delta c^0)^2}{(\Delta h^0)^4}\sigma^2(\Delta h) + \frac{1}{(\Delta h^0)^2}\sigma^2(\Delta c) - \frac{2}{(\Delta h^0)^2}\sigma(\Delta c, \Delta h).$$

We thus get an estimate of the variance using only the variances of the cost and the effect side, respectively, together with their covariance.

Knowing the variance of a random variable does not immediately provide us with confidence limits, unless of course the variable is normally distributed. On this assumption (with which there is much good reason to be unhappy) we finally get confidence limits

$$\frac{\Delta c^0}{\Delta h^0} \pm N_\alpha \sigma \left( \frac{\Delta c}{\Delta h} \right),$$

where $N_\alpha$ is the $(1 - \alpha/2)$-fractile in the normal distribution $N(0, 1)$ with mean 0 and variance 1.

The Taylor method introduces inaccuracies in the approximation (by deleting all powers above 1 in the Taylor series) and its implicit assumption of normality is not realistic. It has been shown that it works rather poorly in computer experiments.

*Fieller's method.* Here we do not work directly with the cost-effectiveness ratio, but instead we consider

$$Y = \Delta c - \Phi \Delta h,$$

where $\Phi$ is the ('true') cost-effectiveness ratio. The random variable $\Phi$ is normally distributed with $E\,Y = 0$ and $\sigma^2(Y) = \sigma^2(\Delta c) + \Phi^2 \sigma^2(\Delta h) - 2\Phi\sigma(\Delta c, \Delta h)$. We divide it by its standard deviation to get a variable which is $N(0, 1)$, and then consider its square,

$$Y^* = \frac{(\Delta c - \Phi \Delta h)^2}{\sigma^2(\Delta c) + \Phi^2 \sigma^2(\Delta h) - 2\Phi\sigma(\Delta c, \Delta h)}.$$

We have then that $Y^*$ has a $\chi^2$ distribution with 1 degree of freedom, and if $k_{1-\alpha}$ is the $(1 - \alpha)$-fractile in this distribution, then

$$\text{Prob} \left\{ \frac{(\Delta c - \Phi \Delta h)^2}{\sigma^2(\Delta c) + \Phi^2 \sigma^2(\Delta h) - 2\Phi\sigma(\Delta c, \Delta h)} \leq k_{1-\alpha} \right\} = 1 - \alpha,$$

which reduces to

$$\text{Prob}\{Q(\Phi) \leq 0\} = 1 - \alpha,$$

where $Q(\Phi) = a_2 \Phi^2 + a_1 \Phi + a_0$ is a second degree polynomium in $\Phi$ with coefficients

$$a_2 = \Delta h^2 - k_{1-\alpha} \sigma^2(\Delta h),$$
$$a_1 = 2(\sigma(\Delta c, \Delta h) k_{1-\alpha} - \Delta h \Delta c),$$
$$a_0 = \Delta c^2 - k_{1-\alpha} \sigma^2(\Delta c).$$

Intuitively, the result obtained tells us that if we repeat the trial many times and compute $\Delta c \Delta h$, using the given value of $\Phi$, then in $(1 - \alpha)$ of the cases the quantity $Q(\phi)$ will be negative. But this means that $\{\Phi \mid Q(\Phi) \leq 0\}$ will contain the true $\Phi$ in $(1 - \alpha)$ of the cases, and this is just what we are looking for in terms of a confidence interval for the true $\Phi$. Thus we solve $Q(\Phi) = 0$ for $\Phi$, getting (in well-behaved cases) two roots defining the confidence limits (for the calculations, unknown quantities are replaced by estimates, meaning that the number of degrees of freedom of the relevant $\chi^2$-distribution is changed correspondingly).

*Marginal net gain.* This method looks much like the previous one, and indeed it will give the same result when suitably elaborated. We start with the quantity

$$\Pi(\lambda) = \lambda \Delta h - \Delta c,$$

the *marginal net gain* from the new treatment compared to the standard treatment, given that the effect can be assessed in money terms as $\lambda$ money units per unit of effects. Given this exchange rate, the new treatment will be preferred if $\Pi(\lambda) > 0$ and rejected if $\Pi(\lambda) < 0$. And – still assuming that the exchange rate $\lambda$ of the decision maker is given – we may construct confidence limits for $\Pi(\lambda)$ which is normally distributed.

Unfortunately, this approach depends crucially on the value of $\lambda$, which may not be easily determined. In this case it is recommended to report the result for several values of $\lambda$, which increases the chance of getting a reasonably good result but on the other hand makes reporting less simple. Therefore the analyst might help the decision maker by finding the set of values of $\lambda$ for which 0 belongs to the constructed confidence interval for $\Pi(\lambda)$ (if the decision maker's $\lambda$ is not in this set, then the confidence interval contains only positive or only negative values, and the decision to be taken is obvious). Constructing this interval turns out to be the same problem as determining the confidence interval using Fieller's method, reinforcing the impression that the two methods are closely related.

## 4.2  *Methods for assessment of data uncertainty (2): Other approaches*

In the preceding subsections, we have been concerned with the problem of establishing confidence limits for the empirical distribution of the cost-effectiveness ratio. We did not, however, worry about whether confidence limits are at all appropriate for our purpose, or indeed what the purpose would be in the first place. We may well be excused for this, since the idea of establishing a confidence interval for the estimated cost-effectiveness ratio is one which presents itself in a routine manner, by analogy with other empirical procedures.

On the other hand, it may well be argued – and indeed it has been argued by Claxton [1999] – that confidence limits are largely irrelevant for the *decision problem*

**Box 6.8 Example.** Assume that the cost-effectiveness ratio $z$ has an exponential distribution on $\mathbb{R}_+$ with density $\lambda e^{-\lambda z}$ with parameter $\lambda = 1/15.000$ (corresponding to a mean value of 15.000 €/QALY for the cost-effectiveness ratio), so that the one-sided 5% confidence limit $\bar{z}$ is given by

$$\bar{z} = \inf\{z' \mid P\{z > z'\} \leq 0.05\},$$

which can be found by solving $e^{-\lambda \bar{z}} = 0.05$ to give that $\bar{z} = -\ln 0.05/\lambda \sim 44,900$. Applying benchmark rule-of-thumb to the confidence limit, we see that the intervention should not be adopted, since it goes far beyond the acceptable limit of 30,000 €/QALY.

Whether this decision is right or wrong depends of course on the objective of the decision maker (or society). To keep things as simple as possible, assume that there is another intervention which for each and every patient gives exactly the same health effect as would the intervention considered, and which has a deterministic cost of 20,000 €/QALY. In this – admittedly not very realistic – situation, the uncertainty is restricted to the cost component.

Assume that the objective function of the decision maker takes the form

$$U(z) = (30,000 - z) - e^{\alpha \max\{z-30,000,0\}}$$

in the present situation (where it expresses the utility of the cost savings connected with shifting from the existing to the new technology); the function is concave showing that the decision maker is risk averse, and we assume that $\alpha < \lambda$. Then expected utility of adopting the intervention is

$$E[U(z)] = \int_0^\infty [(30,000 - z) - e^{\alpha \max\{z-30,000,0\}}]\lambda e^{-\lambda z}\,dz$$

$$> 30,000 - \bar{z} - \int_{30,000}^\infty \lambda e^{-(\lambda-\alpha)z}\,dz$$

$$> 15,000 - \frac{\lambda}{\lambda - \alpha},$$

which is positive when $\alpha$ is not too close to $\lambda$. This shows that rejecting the intervention on the basis of the confidence limit is an irrational decision in the present case.

(of whether or not to adopt a given new medical technology). The following example illustrates the argument.

It should be stressed that the above argumentation does not lead to abolishing the computation of confidence limits. What has been pointed out is that confidence limits cannot be used as criteria for deciding whether or not to adopt a treatment. For this, expected gain according to the decision maker's objective function remains the ultimate criterion. However, quantifying the underlying uncertainty, possibly by confidence limits, does still have a purpose, since it may be useful in decisions on whether or not to collect additional information, cf. Claxton [1999].

The following methods of assessing the data uncertainty are not directly oriented towards finding confidence intervals.

*Bootstrapping.* Instead of computing distributions of quantities related to the cost-effectiveness ratio, the *non-parametric bootstrapping*[2] approach sets out to find the distribution of the estimator directly from data: Taking subsamples (with replacement) of the given sample many times, and computing the cost-effectiveness ratio in each of these subsamples, one can construct an empirical distribution of the cost-effectiveness ratio. This distribution may then be used either for estimating the sample variance, which then can be used to compute confidence ratios assuming normality, or for determining confidence limits directly from the distribution. Simple as this sounds, the bootstrapping methods have additional complications since the direct approach is known to work poorly in small samples, calling for correction terms in the statistical estimation.

*Bayesian analysis.* Constructing the relevant distributions directly from data as one does in the bootstrapping approach points to using a Bayesian approach. Here one starts with a *prior* distribution of the cost-effectiveness ratio (which may be uniform in the case that no prior knowledge is available), and updates it using the data from the clinical study to obtain a *posterior* distribution of the cost-effectiveness ratio. Letting $h^0$ be the density of the prior distribution, then density $h^1$ of the posterior distribution is found using Bayes' formula as

$$h^1(\Phi \mid \Delta h, \Delta c) = \frac{h^0(\Phi) f(\Delta h, \Delta c \mid \Phi)}{\int h^0(\phi) f(\Delta h, \Delta c \mid \phi) \, d\phi},$$

where $f(\Delta h, \Delta c \mid \Phi)$ is the density of the probability distribution for the data conditional on $\Phi$. Even if the distributions of cost and effect are assumed to be normal, the posterior distribution must usually be obtained by numerical methods.

Having found a distribution for the cost-effectiveness ratio, the next question is how to report it, whether as a whole or by choosing suitable characteristics (mean, variance, median etc.). However, it is more in the spirit of Bayesian analysis to see the posterior distribution not as an end result but as an input for further analysis with the aim of finding the best decision (maximizing the decision maker's expected utility). We shall return to this viewpoint below.

*Cost-effectiveness acceptability curves* have some resemblance to Bayesian analysis but represents still another approach. As in many cases before, we assume

---

[2]The term *bootstrapping* is taken from the expression 'to pull oneself up by the bootstraps', referring to the construction of the distribution of the estimator from the very data used in the estimation. Bootstrapping as a statistical technique has application also in other fields.

momentarily that $\lambda$, the subjective exchange rate between cost and effect of the decision maker, is given. We may then use the calculate the probability that the decision maker will accept the new treatment, as

$$CE_{acc}(\lambda) = \text{Prob}\left[\left\{\hat{\Phi} > \lambda \mid \Delta h > 0\right\} \cup \left\{\hat{\Phi} > \lambda \mid \Delta h < 0\right\}\right],$$

which actually can be written with the notation introduced earlier as

$$CE_{acc}(\lambda) = \text{Prob}\{\Pi(\lambda) > 0\}.$$

This is reported as a graph, showing $CE_{acc}(\lambda)$ as a function of $\lambda$.

It should be noted that the cost-effectiveness acceptability at some $\lambda$ strictly speaking is *not* the probability that the true cost-effectiveness ratio is below $\lambda$ (cf. Fenwick et al. [2004]); rather it is connected with the significance level of a test of whether the new treatment should be considered as superior to the old one. However, for practical purposes, the first interpretation is more appealing.

*Expected value of perfect information:* With this method one tries to assess the imperfectness of current information by the gain to be obtained if this information was perfect. The underlying principles are as follows: Suppose that a decision $d$ must be made out of a set $D$ of possible ones, and that the payoff to the decision maker $u(d, s)$ depends on an uncertain event taking values $s_1, \ldots, s_n$ with probabilities $p_1, \ldots, p_n$. If $s$ can be observed, then the optimal decision would be the one achieving

$$u^*(s) = \max_{d \in D} u(d, s).$$

However, if states $s$ cannot be observed, and only the probabilities are known, then the decision maker can do no better than maximizing expected utility, getting

$$u^0 = \max_{d \in D} \sum_{i=1}^{n} p_i u(d, s_i).$$

The difference between what can be obtained with or without information, assessed before any information is sampled, is then

$$\sum_{i=1}^{n} p_i u^*(s_i) - u^0.$$

Clearly, this quantity is nonnegative reflecting that with full information, the decision can be made dependent on what is observed, whereas it must be made once and for all if this information is not available. It is known as the *expected value of perfect information*.

In practical applications, the probability distribution is not known, and the final decision to be made is usually whether or not to implement the new intervention in current medical practice. Even so, it is possible to compute an expected gain either in terms of money saved or QALYs obtained if full information of relevant parameters was available, given the posterior distribution of the relevant parameter. For examples, see e.g. Claxton et al. [2002].

### 4.3 *Method uncertainty*

In the previous sections, we have been concerned almost exclusively with data uncertainty, and the extent of the discussion may well lead to the impression that this type of uncertainty is the most important one for the average cost-effectiveness analysis. This is however not the case; in most of the analyses performed, the modelling and the choices of functional forms and parameters in describing the consequences of the intervention causes a higher degree of uncertainty than the data collected. Unfortunately, there is little to be said on systematical approaches towards documenting this uncertainty. The standard approach consists in *sensitivity analysis,* computation of cost-effectiveness ratios with other assumptions on the value of the crucial parameters than those used in the base computation. There is a tendency towards adding more and more such alternative computations in the presentations of the cost-effectiveness analyses performed, not only involving many alternative values of each of the parameters, but also two- or even three-sided sensitivity analyses, where several parameters at a time are assigned values different from the base computations.

The advantages of having an impressive amount of alternative computations documented in the final report should not be overstated. On most cases they give at best a second-hand impression of the possible sources of imprecision in the given cost-effectiveness analysis. There are other important choices made during the analysis which do not lend themselves easily to sensitivity computation, in particular the modelling aspects which go beyond the simple choice of some numerical parameters. The expansion of the sensitivity analysis part of a cost-effectiveness analysis which can be observed in recent years is perhaps as much an effect of the competition among consultants performing this work, where the final product is given an ever more "technical" or "specialist" appearance. The value added by the technicalities are never debated, but should probably be.

## 5 The value of waiting and cost-effectiveness

In the previous sections, we have been concerned with a decision about using or not using a particular treatment or drug. There are however situations where the decision about treating a patient should not be taken right away but should be postponed. This corresponds to the case of an investment, which may be initiated right away but may also be postponed. We consider one such situation below, where the intervention is a major one (such as an organ transplantation) which however can be postponed as long as the situation of the patient allows it, and the conservative treatment does not become too costly. We will then have a case of "watchful waiting", and the analysis aims at deciding when to abandon the conservative treatment and perform the intervention.

Let $C_t$ denote the cost of treating the patient at time $t$; we consider $(C_t)_{t \in \mathbb{R}_+}$ as a stochastic process, the outlays over time is determined by some underlying randomness. More specifically, there is given a probability space $(\Omega, \mathcal{F}, P)$, where $\Omega$ is a set of states of nature, $\mathcal{F}$ a family (technically: a $\sigma$-algebra) of subsets (measurable events) of $\Omega$, and $P$ a probability measure on $(\Omega, \mathcal{F})$, together with a filtration $(\mathcal{F}_t)_{t \geq \infty}$ which is an increasing family of sub-$\sigma$-algebras of $\mathcal{F}$ (the events measurable at $t$), and each $C_t$ is a $\mathcal{F}_t$-measurable function from $\Omega$ to $\mathbb{R}_+$. We shall simplify further, assuming that $(C_t)_{t \in \mathbb{R}_+}$ has a well-behaved functional form, where relative changes in $C_t$, written as $\dfrac{dC_t}{C_t}$, follows a Brownian motion, so that at each $t$ they are normally distributed with a mean $\alpha$ and standard deviation $\sigma$. We write this as

$$\frac{dC_t}{C_t} = \alpha dt + \sigma dW_t$$

where $dW_t$ denotes the standardized Wiener process. This is alternatively written as

$$dC_t = \alpha C_t \, dt + \sigma C_t \, dW_t, \tag{16}$$

and written out in more detail (16) means that at each $t$

$$C_t = \int_0^t \alpha C_s \, ds + \int_0^t \sigma C_s \, dW_s,$$

where the last member on the right-hand side is the stochastic integral w.r.t. Brownian motion.

Clearly the formalization of treatment cost and its change over time as a geometric Brownian motion is a drastical simplification, ignoring all the details of the underlying illness. However, it can be argued that there are cases where it may be a reasonable approximation: In the geometric Brownian motion, both the drift (the non-stochastic part of the process) and the randomness are considered as relative changes from a given level, here the actual cost of treatment. When the health of the patient deteriorates, the random ups and downs tend also to increase in amplitude.

In the decision problem to be considered here, at any $t$ there is a choice between two treatments, a conservative treatment $A_0$ which is the one giving rise to the process $(C_t)_{t \in \mathbb{R}_+}$ introduced above, and an operative intervention $A_1$. It is assumed that once decision $A_1$ is made, it is irreversible, so that a return to the conservative treatment is impossible. The decision may be a transplantation of an organ or a similarly radical intervention. For the purpose of our analysis, we assume that once the decision $A_1$ is made, the treatment cost is non-random. This simplifies our formalism since we may now consider $A_1$ as an investment to be carried out at some date $t$ of our choice, and the costs after having made this decision can be discounted to a fixed amount $I$.

Let $V(C_t)$ be the present value at date $t$ of future patient cost in the conservative treatment. Alternatively, this can be seen as the savings obtained by choosing the alternative decision. If at some $t$, this value exceeds the cost $I$ of the decision $A_1$, then this decision should be taken. It remains to find an expression for $V(C_t)$.

In any small interval of time $dt$, the value at $t$ is composed of the expenses in $dt$, which are $C_t\, dt$, and their value (positive or negative) at $t + dt$, or rather their expected value, since they are random. Thus,

$$V(C_t) = C_t\, dt + \mathsf{E}[V(C_t + dC_t)e^{-\rho\, dt}], \tag{17}$$

where the value at $t+dt$ is discounted with a factor representing the time preferences of the decision maker. We take a closer look at $V(C_t + dC_t)$. Using Ito's lemma and (16), we get that

$$V(C_t + dC_t) = V(C_t) + [\alpha C_t V'(C_t)s + \frac{1}{2}\sigma^2 C_t^2 V''(C_t) - \rho V(C_t)]\, dt$$

Here all variables are referring to date $t$, so that there is no need for taking expectations. We now insert (17) and let $dt$ tend to zero, giving us the equation

$$\frac{1}{2}\sigma^2 C_t^2 V''(C_t) + \alpha C_t V'(C_t) - \rho V(C_t) + C_t = 0, \tag{18}$$

which is an ordinary second degree differential equation determining $V(\cdot)$. To find solutions to (18), we look first at the homogenous equation

$$\frac{1}{2}\sigma^2 C_t^2 V''(C_t) + \alpha C_t V'(C_t) - \rho V(C_t) = 0, \tag{19}$$

The characteristic equation of (19) is

$$\frac{1}{2}\sigma^2 \beta(\beta - 1) + \alpha\beta - \rho = 0,$$

Since the value of the left-hand side goes to infinity when $\beta$ becomes numerically large, and is negative for $\beta = 0$, we get that the characteristic equation has two real roots $\beta_1$ and $\beta_2$ with $\beta_2 < 0 < \beta_1$. We may assume that $\beta_1 > 1$, at least when $\alpha < \rho$, since $\beta_1 \leq 1$ would result in a negative left-hand side.

The solution to the homogeneous equation is then

$$V(C_t) = K_1 C_t^{\beta_1} + K_2 C_t^{\beta_2}$$

with $K_1$ and $K_2$ arbitrary constants. To get the full solution to (18) we need to add a particular solution to (18). It is easy to see that $C/(\rho - \alpha)$ is such a solution, so that the general family of solutions as

$$V(C_t) = K_1 C_t^{\beta_1} + K_2 C_t^{\beta_2} + \frac{C_t}{\rho - \alpha}. \qquad (20)$$

with $K_1, K_2 \in \mathbb{R}$.

To find the values of the constants $K_1$ and $K_2$ we need to introduce boundary conditions for our problem. A reasonable assumption in our present context is that $V(0) = 0$: if the cost of treating a patient is zero, there seems to be no reason to expect other cost in the future. Given this assumption, we must have $K_2 = 0$, since otherwise $V(C_t)$ would tend to infinity for $C_t \to 0$. Also the other constant can be done away with: Using Ito's lemma on $C_t^{\beta_1}$, we get

$$\frac{dC_t^{\beta_1}}{C_t^{\beta_1}} = [\beta_1 C_t^{\beta_1 - 1} \, dC_t + \frac{1}{2}\beta_1(\beta_1 - 1)C_t^{\beta_1 - 2}\sigma^2 C_t^2 \, dt]/C_t^{\beta_1},$$

and inserting $dC_t$ from (16), we get

$$\frac{dC_t^{\beta}}{C_t^{\beta_1}} = [\beta_1\alpha + \frac{1}{2}\beta_1(\beta_1 - 1)\sigma^2] \, dt + \beta_1\sigma \, dW_t = \rho \, dt + \beta\sigma \, dW_t.$$

It is seen that the drift in this stochastic process depends only on $\rho$, the subjective discount rate, so that it does not matter for the discounted future value, which will be determined alone by the fluctuations. Assessing a future cash flow in this way can be thought of as a speculative bubble, and it would not seem reasonable in the present context. Therefore, the first constant $K_1$, can be set equal to 0 as well, and the solution becomes

$$V(C_t) = \frac{C_t}{\rho - \alpha}. \qquad (21)$$

It may be noticed that the solution is surprisingly simple, particularly in view of the trouble we have taken in deriving it: It means that future cost is assessed as observed present cost growing at the rate $\alpha$ and then discounted according to the subjective rate $\rho$. This simple form of discounted future values was however not entirely obvious from the beginning, and it does depend on our assumptions.

We may now turn to what was the real problem, namely the assessment of the treatment program which begins with a conservative treatment $A_0$ but shifts to $A_1$ when this becomes advantageous. Let $F(C_t)$ denote the value of the option of shifting from $A_0$ to $A_1$, assessed at time $t$ given observed cost $C_t$. To find an expression for $F(C_t)$, we use the same type of reasoning as before: The connection between the values of the option at date $t$ and $t + dt$ is given by

$$F(C_t) = E[F(C_t + dC_t)e^{-\rho\,dt}],$$

where the right-hand side is as that in (17) except for its first member. The analysis of this equation leads to a differential equation

$$\frac{1}{2}\sigma^2 C_t^2 F''(C_t) + \alpha C_t F'(C_t) - \rho F(C_t) = 0, \tag{22}$$

which is now homogeneous. The characteristic equation of (22) is

$$\frac{1}{2}\sigma^2 \gamma(\gamma - 1) + \alpha\gamma - \rho = 0.$$

As before, we find that this equation has two real roots $\gamma_2 < 0 < \gamma_1$, with $\gamma_1 > 1$ when $\rho > \alpha$, and using again the plausible boundary condition $F(0) = 0$, we get that (22) has solutions

$$F(C_t) = H C_t^{\gamma_1}$$

for $H \in \mathbb{R}$.

In order to find $H$, we need other further boundary conditions. Let $C_t^*$ be the value of current cost at which the shift from $A_0$ to $A_1$ takes place. It seems clear that at this point we must have

$$F(C_t^*) = V(C_t^*) - I,$$

the value of having the possibility of shifting to $A_1$ equals the value of $A_1$. We may then insert the expression for $V(C_t^*)$ to get

$$H(C_t^*)^{\gamma_1} = \frac{C_t^*}{\rho - \alpha} - I. \tag{23}$$

Next, assuming that $F$ is differentiable at $C_t^*$ (and this is actually the case, cf. Brekke and Øksendal [1991]), we also have that

$$\gamma_1 H(C_t^*)^{\gamma_1 - 1} = \frac{1}{\rho - \alpha}. \tag{24}$$

Together, (23) and (24) yield that

$$C_t^* = \frac{\gamma_1}{\gamma_1 - 1}(\rho - \alpha)I, \tag{25}$$

and $H$ can be determined, so that

$$F(C_t) = \left[ \frac{(\gamma_1 - 1)^{\gamma_1 - 1} I^{-(\gamma_1 - 1)}}{(\rho - \alpha)\gamma_1^{\gamma_1}} \right] C_t^{\gamma_1}.$$

The important result is that of (25), showing that it is optimal to shift to $A_1$ when current cost has reached a level corresponding to the capital cost derived from $I$, which is $\rho$ minus $\alpha$, the average growth rate of cost, multiplied by a correction term $\gamma_1/(\gamma_1 - 1) > 1$, which gives a numerical expression of the savings which may be obtained by postponing the shift to $A_1$.

The analysis given here depends heavily on the functional form of the stochastic process for $C_t$, and even though a similar analysis could be carried out if $C_t$ follows some other process, the computations become less simple. We should not expect that this type of methods will be implemented in practice to any large degree. For other applications of the option method, see e.g. Palmer and Smith [2000].

## 6 Guidelines and evidence-based health economics

### 6.1 *Evidence-based decision making*

Since the discipline that we consider has originated in the need for adding economic considerations to the analysis of effectiveness of an intervention as shown by the results of a clinical study, it is not surprising that on many aspects, the approaches taken are inspired by similar approaches in purely medical research. The need for a standardized research design, spelling out what can be considered as the "best" or "most scientific" approach, has led to the establishment of *guidelines* for the correct procedures in a variety of different contexts, among which also economic appraisal of medical interventions. The first guidelines were set up in Australia around 1990, followed by similar events in other countries. In the beginning, guidelines were rather short documents, set up by healthcare organizations and specifying certain approaches that would not be considered as proper (the Australian guidelines excluded indirect cost). Lately, the trend has gone in the direction of more specifications of what should be done. The guidelines set up by NICE in the UK [NICE, 2013] gives detailed indications about data collection and data processing.

The trend towards more elaborate guidelines has met some opposition from academical circles (notably Gafni and Birch [2004]), but there have been few if any objections from the industry which is responsible for the preparation of cost-effectiveness analysis satisfying the demands of the guidelines. This may have several reasons, one being that industry prefers detailed instructions from the authorities, where compliance gives some assurance that the marketing permit or reimbursement rate applied for will also be granted. A more subtle reason may be that increasing the cost of preparing the cost-effectiveness analyses will add an advantage to the bigger and more consolidated firms against smaller competitors in the drugs market, for which the procedure will be relatively more burdensome. The fact that cost-effectiveness analysis of medical intervention has opened a new and very lucrative line of activity for the economic profession, represented on each side of the table in the bargaining for markets and reimbursements, cannot probably be discarded altogether as a contributing factor.

Guidelines, short or detailed, fulfill a specific need, namely the specification of the objectives of the relevant authority or decision maker. This relevance of the viewpoint for the analysis has been mentioned repeatedly in this chapter. Below we present another approach to the problem of objectives, showing that the idea of guidelines that are objectively correct cannot be upheld. There are no scientifically correct guidelines, the way of performing cost-effectiveness analysis depends on the objectives of the decision maker. The model considered is an elaborated version of work by Demski [1973] on rules for proper accounting, a problem which is formally very close to ours.

### 6.2   *The impossibility of universal guidelines*

We consider a situation where a decision maker – society or a health care organization – has to make a choice subject to some uncertainty. In the model, there is a finite set $S = \{s_1, \ldots, s_n\}$ of uncertain states, each of which affect the results of the decision. The choices are formalized as a set $A$ of functions $a : S \to X$ mapping state $s \in S$ to outcomes $a(s)$ in a set $X$ of possible consequences. In our present case, a decision is the adoption of a certain treatment or intervention. The consequences of the treatment (in terms of cost and effect) are not known fully, since they are subject to randomness.

Following the usual approach in this field, we assume that the decision maker has some initial beliefs about the likelihood of each of the underlying states $s_1, \ldots, s_n$ influencing outcome of the decisions, formulated as a ("prior") probability distribution $(P(s_1), \ldots, P(s_n))$. Also, we assume that the decision maker has a utility function $U : X \to \mathbb{R}$ assigning utility or degree of satisfaction to each possible outcome. Relying only on the initial beliefs, we would expect the decision maker to maximize expected utility

$$\mathsf{E}_P[U \circ a] = \sum_{i=1}^{n} P(\sigma_i)U(a(s_i))$$

over all decisions $a \in A$.

To introduce "evidence-based medicine" in our model, we add the possibility of *collecting and processing* information before the decision is made. The way in which this should be done is what guidelines are concerned with. In our simplified formal world, an *information method* is a pair $(\Sigma, p)$, where $\Sigma = \{\sigma_1, \ldots, \sigma_m\}$ is a finite set of *signals*, and $p$ is a system of conditional probabilities $p(\sigma_j|s_i)$, for $j = 1, \ldots, m$, $i = 1, \ldots, n$, interpreted as the probability that signal $\sigma_j$ is reported given that the true state of nature is $s_i$. Thus, the information method tells us *what to observe* and *how to make inference* about the true state of nature from our observations.

Given an observed signal $\sigma_j$, the decision maker may compute posterior probabilities $P^*(\cdot|\sigma_j)$ of states using Bayes' formula,

$$P^*(s_i|\sigma_j) = \frac{p(\sigma_j|s_i)P(s_i)}{P(\sigma_j)},$$

where $P(\sigma_j) = \sum_{h=1}^{n} p(\sigma_j|s_h)P(s_h)$ is the probability of observing the signal $\sigma_j$. Given the observed signal $\sigma_j$, the decision maker must now maximize expected utility with respect to posterior probabilities,

$$\mathsf{E}_{P^*(\cdot|\sigma_j)}[U \circ a] = \sum_{i=1}^{n} P^*(s_i|\sigma_j)U(a(s_i)),$$

over all $a \in A$. The optimal decision, given the signal $\sigma_j$, is denoted $a[\sigma_j]$, and the expected utility of this decision will typically be greater than what could be achieved without this observation.

We may now evaluate expected utility obtained using the given information method by taking expectation over signals observed, and from this we get the *value of the information method*

$$V(\Sigma, p; U) = \sum_{j=1}^{m} P(\sigma_j)\mathsf{E}_{P(\cdot|\sigma_j)}[U \circ a[\sigma_j]] - \mathsf{E}_P[U \circ a],$$

as the difference between the ex ante expected utility with and without the information method.

The value of information, as defined above, depends on the utility function $U$ of the decision maker. The natural next question is whether information methods can be ranked in a way which is *independent* of the (utility function of the) decision maker. In our case this amounts to ranking different methodological approaches to medical technology appraisal in a way which is independent of the final user of the analysis.

To obtain an answer, we need to be more precise about the meaning of "ranking": We shall understand this as a *partial order*, accepting that some information methods may not be comparable.

**Box 6.9 Example.** The following simple example may serve to illustrate the approach. Suppose that we have to decide about the use of a medical drug in another country; there are three different brands, to be denoted I, II and III, all produced locally. Each of these drugs may turn out to be cheap or expensive, effective or ineffective. These attributes are connected with the industrial environment in the country, so all the brands share the condition. However, the consequences of the conditions differ among the brands.

We have four possible states (combinations of cheap versus expensive and effective versus ineffective), and there are three decisions (choice of brand). It is assumed that the utility function of the decision maker has the following form:

|  | (effective,expensive) | (effective,cheap) | (ineffective,expensive) | (ineffective,cheap) |
|---|---|---|---|---|
| I | 10 | 10 | 10 | 10 |
| II | 20 | 5 | 15 | 0 |
| III | 12 | 14 | 8 | 6 |

Furthermore, it is known that each state has the same prior probability 1/4.

Now the expected utility of each decision can be computed. For brand I it is

$$\frac{1}{4} \cdot 10 + \frac{1}{4} \cdot 10 + \frac{1}{4} \cdot 10 + \frac{1}{4} \cdot 10 = 10,$$

and by the same method the expected utility of the other decisions are computed to be also 10, so that all decisions are equally good *a priori*.

Suppose that the decision maker is offered the information method which consists in revealing (with no error) whether drugs are cheap or expensive. We check the decision for each of the two possible signals: If the signal is "expensive", then only the first and the third columns matter, each having (conditional) probability 1/2, so expected utility of I remains 10, but II becomes

$$\frac{1}{2} \cdot 20 + \frac{1}{2} \cdot 15 = 17.5$$

which is the best possible.

If the signal is "cheap", expected utilities are [I: 10, II: 2.5, III: 10], and best decisions are I and III. The value of the information method is found as the expected value of the best result at each possible signal,

$$\frac{1}{2} \cdot 17,5 + \frac{1}{2} \cdot 10 = 13.75$$

minus expected utility of the best choice without information, which was 10; we have therefore that the value of this information method is 13.75 − 10 = 3.75.

**Example, continued.** In a similar way, we may compute the value of other possible information methods, for example the method which exactly reveals whether medicin produced in the country is effective or ineffective. We may also compute the value of complete revelation of state, for which expected utility becomes

$$\frac{1}{4} \cdot 20 + \frac{1}{4} \cdot 14 + \frac{1}{4} \cdot 15 + \frac{1}{4} \cdot 10 = 17.25,$$

so that the value of complete information is 7.25.

An example of partial orders of information methods is the following: For $(\Sigma, p), (\widehat{\Sigma}, \hat{p})$ information methods with $|\Sigma| = m, |\widehat{\Sigma}| = \widehat{m}$, we say that $(\Sigma, p)$ is *more informative than* $(\widehat{\Sigma}, \hat{p})$ if for each signal $\hat{\sigma}_{\hat{j}} \in \widehat{\Sigma}$ such that $\widehat{P}(\cdot | \hat{\sigma}_{\hat{j}}) \neq 0$, there are nonnegative numbers $r_{\hat{j},1}, \ldots, r_{\hat{j},m}$ with $\sum_{j=1}^{m} r_{\hat{j},j} = 1$ such that

$$\widehat{P}(\cdot | \hat{\sigma}_{\hat{j}}) = \sum_{j=1}^{m} r_{\hat{j},j} P(\cdot | \sigma_j).$$

An equivalent formulation of this condition is that there is an $(\widehat{m} \times m)$ matrix $R$ with all column sums equal to 1 such that

$$\widehat{P} = RP,$$

where $\widehat{P}$ is the $(n \times \widehat{m})$-matrix with characteristic element $\widehat{P}(s_i | \hat{\sigma}_{\hat{j}})$, $P$ the $(n \times m)$ matrix with characteristic element $P(s_i | \sigma_j)$, and $R$ is $(\widehat{m} \times m)$ with elements $r_{\hat{j},j}$, $\hat{j} = 1, \ldots, \widehat{m}$, $j = 1, \ldots, m$. If one information method is more informative than another, then every signal obtained in the latter can be obtained in the former, possible after some recoding of signals.

The following is a formulation of the classical result by Blackwell [1951] adapted to our situation. We work with classes of acceptable utility functions which are more restricted than what is usually seen in the formulations of Blackwell's theorem, where it is usual to allow all possible utility functions. The proof of the theorem is postponed to the next subsection.

PROPOSITION 4 (Blackwell's theorem) *Let* $(\Sigma, p), (\widehat{\Sigma}, \hat{p})$ *be information methods, let* $\mathcal{U}$ *be a set of utility functions, $A$ a set of actions such that for all vectors* $q \in \mathbb{R}^n$, *there are* $U \in \mathcal{U}, a, a' \in A$ *such that* $U(a(s_i)) = q_i$, $U(a'(s_i)) = 0$, $i = 1, \ldots, n$. *Then the following are equivalent:*

*(i)* $(\Sigma, p)$ *is more informative than* $(\widehat{\Sigma}, \hat{p})$,

*(ii) $V(\Sigma, p; U) \geq V(\widehat{\Sigma}, \hat{p}; U)$ for all $U \in \mathcal{U}$.*

What Blackwell's theorem tells us is that when we search for a ranking of information methods that does *not* depend on the preferences of a given decision maker, but is valid for a reasonably large class of possible decision makers with their evaluation of consequences, then the only ranking which remains is the trivial one: More observation is better than less observation. All other rankings are relative in the sense that only some decision makers agree on them, while other decision makers may disagree.

Since information methods, and translated to our case, methods for collecting and processing observations on interventions, can be judged upon only with reference to particular decision makers, the idea of scientifically founded guidelines for cost-effectiveness analyses is too ambitious. What can be established is at most guidelines for performing cost-effectiveness in the interest of a particular decision maker. Incidentally, this is also what has been the more or less directly stated intent of most guidelines elaborated in the past, so our new insight does not challenge past experience, to the contrary it provides the established practice with a theoretical underpinning.

On the other hand, it may lead to some afterthought in the academic world. Here cost-effectiveness analysis has been considered as scientific research on the same footing as the reports on the medical aspects of clinical trials, to be published in scientific journals and collected in research databases. Given the relativity of objectives established by Blackwell's theorem, we should be aware that any given cost-effectiveness analysis can at best illustrate the point of view of some specific decision maker and may therefore be irrelevant or even misleading for another decision maker. Cost-effectiveness analysis can be considered as decision support and very useful as such. It is more questionable whether it is "pure" science.

### 6.3   *Appendix: A proof of Blackwell's theorem*

Below we give a proof of the version of Blackwell's theorem used above. The method of proof is that of Bielinska-Kwapisz [2003].

PROOF OF BLACKWELL'S THEOREM: (ii)$\Rightarrow$(i): Suppose on the contrary that $V(\Sigma, p; U) \geq V(\widehat{\Sigma}, \hat{p}; U)$ for all $U \in \mathcal{U}$ but that $(\Sigma, p)$ is not more informative than $(\widehat{\Sigma}, \hat{p})$; then by definition we have that there is a signal $\hat{\sigma}_{\hat{j}}$ of the information method $(\widehat{\Sigma}, \hat{p})$ with $\widehat{P}(\cdot|\hat{\sigma}_{\hat{j}}) \neq 0$ such that

$$\widehat{P}(\cdot|\hat{\sigma}_{\hat{j}}) \notin \mathrm{conv}(\{P(\cdot|\sigma_j)|j = 1, \ldots, m\}).$$

By separation of convex sets, there must then be $q \in \mathbb{R}^n$, $q \neq 0$, such that

$$q \cdot \widehat{P}(\cdot|\hat{\sigma}_{j^*}) = \sum_{i=1}^{n} q_i \widehat{P}(s_i|\hat{\sigma}_{j^*}) = \lambda > 0, \quad q \cdot P(\cdot|\sigma_j) \leq 0, \quad \text{all } \sigma \in \Sigma.$$

Now we use the assumption on $\mathcal{U}$ and $A$ to find $U \in \mathcal{U}$ and $a_1, a_2 \in A$ such that $U(a_1(s_i)) = q_i$, $U(a_2(s_i)) = 0$, $i = 1, \ldots, n$; in the following we assume that $A$ contains only these two acts. Then for each $\sigma \in \Sigma$ we have that

$$\max_{a \in A} \mathsf{E}_{P(\cdot|\sigma)}[U \circ a] = \max\{P(\cdot|\sigma) \cdot q, P(\cdot|\sigma) \cdot 0\} = P(\cdot|\sigma) \cdot 0 = 0$$

since $P(\cdot|\sigma) \cdot q \leq 0$ for each $\sigma$. It follows that

$$V(\Sigma, p; U) + \max_{a \in A} \mathsf{E}_P[U \circ a] = \sum_{j=1}^{m} P(\sigma_j) \max_{a \in A} \mathsf{E}_{P(\cdot|\sigma_j)}[U \circ a] = 0.$$

Assessing the value of the information method $(\widehat{\Sigma}, \hat{p})$ similarly, we get

$$V(\widehat{\Sigma}, \hat{p}; U) + \max_{a \in A} \mathsf{E}_P[U \circ a] =$$

$$= \sum_{j=1}^{\widehat{m}} \widehat{P}(\hat{\sigma}_j) \max_{a \in A} \mathsf{E}_{\widehat{P}(\cdot|\hat{\sigma}_j)}[U \circ a] = \sum_{j=1}^{\widehat{m}} \widehat{P}(\hat{\sigma}_j) \max\{\widehat{P}(\cdot|\hat{\sigma}_j) \cdot q, \widehat{P}(\cdot|\hat{\sigma}_j) \cdot 0\}$$

$$\geq \widehat{P}(\hat{\sigma}_{j^*})(\widehat{P}(\cdot|\hat{\sigma}_{j^*}) \cdot q) + \sum_{j \neq j^*} \widehat{P}(\hat{\sigma}_j)[\widehat{P}(\cdot|\hat{\sigma}_j) \cdot 0] = \widehat{P}(\hat{\sigma}_{j^*})\lambda > 0.$$

It follows that $V(\widehat{\Sigma}, \hat{p}; U) > V(\Sigma, p; U)$, a contradiction, showing that (i) must hold.

(i)$\Rightarrow$(ii): We have that for each signal $\hat{\sigma}_j \in \widehat{\Sigma}$ such that $\widehat{P}(\cdot|\hat{\sigma}_j) \neq 0$, there are nonnegative numbers $r_{j,1}, \ldots, r_{j,m}$ with $\sum_{j=1}^{m} r_{j,j} = 1$ such that

$$\widehat{P}(\cdot|\hat{\sigma}_j) = \sum_{j=1}^{m} r_{j,j} P(\cdot|\sigma_j).$$

Therefore, if $a[\hat{\sigma}_j]$ is the optimal decision given $\hat{\sigma}_j$, then

$$\mathsf{E}_{\widehat{P}(\cdot|\hat{\sigma}_j)} U(a[\hat{\sigma}_j]) = \sum_{i=1}^{n} \widehat{P}(s_i|\hat{\sigma}_j) U(a[\hat{\sigma}_j](s_i)) = \sum_{i=1}^{n} \sum_{j=1}^{m} r_{j,j} P(s_i|\sigma_j) U(a[\hat{\sigma}_j](s_i))$$

$$= \sum_{j=1}^{m} r_{j,j} \sum_{i=1}^{n} P(s_i|\sigma_j) U(a[\hat{\sigma}_j](s_i)) \leq \sum_{j=1}^{m} r_{j,j} \sum_{i=1}^{n} P(s_i|\sigma_j) U(a[\sigma_j](s_i))$$

$$= \sum_{j=1}^{m} r_{j,j} \mathsf{E}_{P(\cdot|\sigma_j)} U(a[\sigma_j])$$

where we have used that $a[\sigma_j]$ maximizes $E_{P(\cdot|\sigma_j)}[U \circ a]$. Multiplying by $\widehat{P}(\hat{\sigma}_j) = \sum_{i=1}^{n} \hat{p}(\hat{\sigma}_j|s_i)P(s_i)$, and summing over $\hat{j}$, we get that

$$\sum_{j=1}^{\widehat{m}} \sum_{i=1}^{n} \hat{p}(\hat{\sigma}_j|s_i)P(s_i)E_{\widehat{P}(\cdot|\hat{\sigma}_j)}U(a[\hat{\sigma}_j])$$

$$\leq \sum_{j=1}^{\widehat{m}} \sum_{i=1}^{n} \hat{p}(\hat{\sigma}_j|s_i)P(s_i) \sum_{j=1}^{m} r_{\hat{j},j}E_{P(\cdot|\sigma_j)}U(a[\sigma_j])$$

$$= \sum_{j=1}^{\widehat{m}} \sum_{i=1}^{n} \sum_{j=1}^{m} \text{Prob}\{\sigma_j, \sigma_{\hat{j}}|s_i\}P(\sigma_i)E_{P(\cdot|\sigma_j)}U(a[\sigma_j])$$

$$= \sum_{j=1}^{m} \sum_{i=1}^{n} p(\sigma_j|s_i)P(\sigma_i)E_{P(\cdot|\sigma_j)}U(a[\sigma_j]) = \sum_{j=1}^{m} P(\sigma_j)E_{P(\cdot|\sigma_j)}U(a[\sigma_j]),$$

and it follows that $V(\Sigma, p; U) \geq V(\widehat{\Sigma}, \hat{p}; U)$.                                  □

## 7   Problems

**1.** A newly developed drug can shorten the duration of all the known instances of influenza by 2 days. It is contemplated to introduce a subsidy of 80% of the price for this medicine which is expected to reduce the sickness absence of the workforce. It is assumed that this loss of working days due to influenza is high for workers with wages below €25.

The producer sets the price so that the society's savings from reduced sick leave exactly corresponds to the cost of the drug, given that 20% of the population is hit by the influenza. Give a sketch of the cost-effectiveness analysis carried out before marketing.

From the clinical trials it is learned that the medicine is much less effective than expected with regard to shortening the duration of the sickness period, but it reduces the subjective discomfort of influenze, corresponding to a gain of 0.1 QALY over the 7 days. Will this change the conclusions of the cost-effectiveness analysis?

**2.** For patients suffering from extreme obesity, surgical intervention may be an alternative to standard dietary treatments. The effectivity of this intervention is well-documented and better than that of other treatments, but there is a certain, though small, risk of adverse effects, including death, under surgery.

Explain how a cost-effectiveness analysis of this intervention should be organized, and discuss the way in which the analysis takes into account the risk of death during surgery.

**3.** It is a well-established fact that a diet containing fish has a preventive effect on the development of heart problems. In order to improve the treatment of patients with diagnosed heart diseases, it is proposed to increase the use of fish in the diet of these patients. The main objective of the proposal is to prevent a further deterioration of the conditions and in particular to avoid premature death, based on the results of several studies which show that in particular fat fish with a high content of omega-3 fatty acids have a positive effect on heart disease.

Since previous campaigns for increased use of fish in the diet have had limited effects, a more direct method is proposed, in which frish fish is delivered directly to the home of the relevant patients once a week. To take care of this arrangement, it is suggested to contract with one of commercial operators already active in direct delivery to consumers. The project will run over 6 months, and it is expected that a majority of the involved patients (more precisely, 65%) will carry on also when the free delivery of fish is terminated.

Initial consultations with the commercial catering services has indicated, that it is possible to obtain a discount of around 50% compared to the price paid by ordinary consumers.

Give a cost-effectiveness analysis of this project (using data available on the internet). How does it compare to an alternative approach in which the same patients are given omega 3 fish oil capsules?

**4.** In connection with a debate about public support for smoke cessation it is decided to carry out an cost-effectiveness analysis for each of three different approaches to smoke cessation, namely

    (1) Courses in smoking cessation

    (2) Nicotine patches

    (3) Tablets for smoking cessation (varenicline)

It has been decided, that the smoking cessation campaign should have a duration of at most 3 months, and full public payment for a treatment will be given only once.

Give a sketch of the procedure to be following when carrying out the CEA, and give a preliminary result (using generally available data) for each of the three alternatives.

**5.** A pilot study of a new intervention had 9 patients, and the data delivered can be summarized in the following table, where $\Delta h$ is measured in QALYs and $\Delta c$ in €:

| Patient | 1 | 2 | 3 | 4 | 5 | 6 | 7 | 8 | 9 |
|---------|------|------|------|------|------|------|------|------|------|
| $\Delta h$ | 0.021 | 0.018 | 0.022 | 0.020 | 0.018 | 0.016 | 0.019 | 0.022 | 0.020 |
| $\Delta c$ | 150 | 138 | 174 | 156 | 149 | 161 | 171 | 167 | 159 |

Find the incremental cost-effectiveness ratio and carry out suitable sensitivity analysis (geometric methods, Fieller's method, cost-effectivity acceptability curves and bootstrapping).

Assume that the prior distribution over cost-effectiveness ratios was uniform, and find the posterior distribution using Bayes' rule.

# Chapter 7

# Regulating the healthcare sector

## 1 On the need for regulation of healthcare provision

Throughout the discussions in the previous chapters, government interference in the economic activities has been a recurrent theme. Indeed, government is directly involved in healthcare in most countries, and the reason for this involvement has been outlined. Thus, there is no compelling need for explaining why the healthcare sector must be the object of government regulation.

Nevertheless, there are some fields of regulation which have yet not been touched upon, but which are of principal importance. We have been concerned with *efficiency* in health, but we have so far largely neglected questions of *equity*, which may be as important, perhaps even more important than efficiency. And we still need to discuss the role of government in setting priorities, determining health policy and the relative importance of healthcare as compared to other sectors of the economy.

It is now time to consider these problems in more detail. We begin with a discussion of equity, in general terms and in relation to healthcare, and we conclude the chapter with the problems of priority setting in healthcare. In between, we insert a treatment of a topic which is more oriented towards microeconomics than the other two, namely that of regulating competition in drug markets through the policies of drug subsidization.

## 2 Equality in health and healthcare

Questions of equality – or rather equity as it is usually called in the literature, we return to terminology in a moment – in health have not taken up much space so far, and time has come to pay some attention to them. Equity considerations play a considerable role in the medical profession, and this could not go unnoticed in health economics.

## 2.1   *Equality or equity*

Unfortunately, equality and inequality is a topic where economic theory tradition-ally has had little to say, being mainly concerned with clarifying the very concept of inequality, a task which is still far from being completed. Given this not quite satisfactory state of affairs in economics as a general discipline, it is not surprising that inequalities in health is confronting many challenges, and that it is far from ob-vious what equality in health actually means, and there have been several attempts to clarify the situation, e.g. Williams and Cookson [2000].

Before going into detail, there is a detail of terminology which needs some attention. Following Whitehead [1991], a distinction can be made between *inequal-ity of health,* which covers all kinds of health inequalities, including such that is a consequence of biological differences or a result of a free choice, and *inequity* in health, which deal only with inequalities that are considered as *unjust,* such as differences due to income, social status, education, possibilities of treatment etc. In what follows, we shall be interested in the latter concept, so we are dealing with equity rather than equality. The distinction is specific for considerations related to health. Since the theoretical tools to be discussed below were developed with purely economic equality or inequality in mind, the additional ethical dimension was absent or at least much less important.

Turning now to the discussion of what is meant by equity in health, it may be useful to take as starting point the idea that there is a feasible set of health outcomes for the citizens of society (illustrated by the area below the transformation curve in Fig. 7.1), and that society chooses from this set according to some criterion for social welfare. This approach has been used repeatedly already, and it has been assumed that society's welfare could be measured as the sum of the outcomes of its individuals. This condition, known as *utilitarianism* is not specific for health economics but shows up in almost all forms of applied economics, for example whenever society's performance is measured in terms of aggregate production or value added, and the implicit assumption is that when the sum of the individual achievements is maximal, then other problems could be subsequently solved by suitable redistributions.

Clearly, redistributing health is less straightforward than redistributing con-sumption goods, and the utilitarian criterion of maximal achievement may there-fore be questioned, as it indeed has been. Actually, even the redistribution of ordinary consumption goods is no simple matter, and it is therefore quite reason-able that other criteria for an optimal allocation (of goods, of health, etc.) should be contemplated. Among these, the most frequently encountered is the *maximin* criterion, according to which the achievement of a society should be judged by the

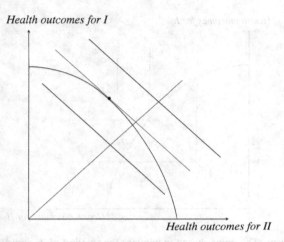

Fig. 7.1 Utilitarianism. The point chosen maximizes the sum of the coordinates (level curves of the maximand are parallel lines as shown).

outcome for the least favored individual. This criterion is often associated with the name of Rawls, who forcefully argued that it should be taken as the foundation for establishing a just society (justice as fairness, see Rawls [1971]).

Maximizing the outcome of least favored points in the direction of treating everyone in the same way (egalitarianism), since in an allocation which is unequal there must be one individual who is worst off, and if the allocation was chosen using maximin, there would be no other allocation treating this individual in a better way. If the set of feasible allocations is well-behaved (see the exercises for more precise conditions), this cannot be the case, and the allocation must indeed be egalitarian, cf. Fig. 7.2.

It goes without saying that the two alternatives mentioned here are in no way an exhaustive listing of criteria for how health should be allocated in society. It is not even clear whether the concept of equity can be satisfactorily treated in the context outlined so far, which also has been rather loosely defined. What should be understood by "health outcomes" for an individual and how these outcomes should be measured remains to be specified, and this is by no means uncontroversial. We therefore step back for another approach from a somewhat different angle.

## 2.2 *Welfarism: Preference aggregation*

In the discussion so far, we have introduced a set of technically feasible arrays of individual health outcomes, being however deliberately unspecific about the nature

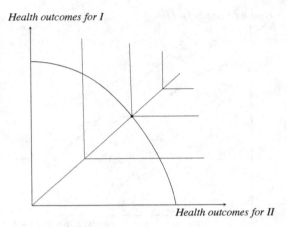

*Health outcomes for I*

*Health outcomes for II*

Fig. 7.2   Egalitarianism. The point chosen maximizes the smallest of its coordinates (level curves of the maximand are broken lines as shown).

of these health outcomes, which may be outcomes measured in natural units or in QALYs. In the latter case, the set of feasible outcomes would incorporate possible externalities, whereby the health of one individual depends on the health of other persons. It seems better – and it is in accordance with the standard approach in the literature – to work with a given set of *alternatives* X, which could be the set of all arrays of attainable health outcome vectors measured in natural units, from which a choice must be made, and then to consider the problem of determining a criterion for this choice as one of *preference aggregation* – if each individual ranks the alternatives in a particular way, how should they then be ranked by society?

*Ordinal preference aggregation.* The point of departure for such considerations is the array $(\succsim_1, \ldots, \succsim_n)$ of preference relations of the individuals $1, \ldots, n$ comprising the society in question. Such an array, which formally is a map from the set $\{1, \ldots, n\}$ of (indices of) individuals to preference relations on X, is called a *profile*. To aggregate the profile $(\succsim_1, \ldots, \succsim_n)$ means to find a single preference relation $\succsim$ representing the profile in some sense yet to be specified. In particular, we are interested in *systematical* ways of aggregating profiles, applicable not only to a single given profile but to a large class or even to all conceivable profiles. In other words we are looking for a *function* assigning (societal) preference relations to profile. Such a function will be called a *social welfare function* (SWF).

It is quite easy to give examples of SWFs: A constant map assigning a given fixed relation $\succsim$ to every profile will do. But obviously this is not what we had in mind, since society's preference relation is *imposed* on the individuals. Another example, still quite unsatisfactory, is a *dictatorial* SWF. For $i \in \{1, \ldots, n\}$ an individual, the

$i$-dictatorial SWF assigns to every profile $(\succsim_1,\ldots,\succsim_n)$ the preference relation $\succsim_i$, i.e. that of individual $i$. Again it is debatable whether such a procedure can be considered as an aggregation.

Turning to SWFs displaying some features of democracy, we may consider the idea of aggregation by voting. This can be done in several ways; one possibility is to construct society's preference relation by a series of votings, each one deciding for a given pair $x, y$ whether a majority has $x > y$ or $y > x$.

This procedure goes further in satisfying our demands to an aggregation since it pays attention to the individual preference relations, but again it has some unattractive features. Suppose that the set of individuals can be partitioned in three disjoint subsets $A, B, C$ of equal size, and that preferences on $\{x, y, z\} \subset X$ are such that

$$x \succ_i y \succ_i z \quad \text{for all } i \in A$$
$$y \succ_i z \succ_i x \quad \text{for all } i \in B$$
$$z \succ_i x \succ_i y \quad \text{for all } i \in C.$$

It is easily seen that society will have $x > y$, $y > z$, $z > x$, so that society's preference relation is cyclic, making it difficult to interpret it as a "ranking" of alternatives open for society. Also, such a cyclic ranking may present difficulties when we want to pick a maximal element, since it may not have any.

The above examples suggest that the problem of finding a simple, yet reasonable, aggregation procedure may not be easily solved. Actually, it may have no solution at all, depending of course on the precise content of words as "simple" and "reasonable", which can be understood in many different ways. Below we specify our demands to an aggregation procedure as the family of properties proposed by Arrow [1963b]:

(1) *Unrestricted domain:* The aggregation procedure (SWF) applies to all profiles $(\succsim_1,\ldots,\succsim_n)$ where each $\succsim_i$ is a total preorder.
(2) *Regularity:* The aggregation results in a total preorder.
(3) *Pareto-compatibility:* If the profile $(\succsim_1,\ldots,\succsim_n)$ is such that $x \succ_i y$ for all $i$, then society has $x > y$.
(4) *Binariness:* If for two profiles $(\succsim_1,\ldots,\succsim_n)$ and $(\succsim_1',\ldots,\succsim_n')$ and alternatives $x, y \in X$ we have $x \succ_i y \Leftrightarrow x \succ_i' y$, and $y \succ_i x \Leftrightarrow y \succ_i' x$ for all $i$, and the profiles result in $\succsim$ and $\succsim'$, respectively, then $x > y \Leftrightarrow x >' y$, $y > x \Leftrightarrow y >' x$.
(5) No dictatorship: There is no individual $i$, who is a dictator in the sense that for every profile $(\succsim_1,\ldots,\succsim_n)$ and pair $x, y \in X$ of alternatives, if $x \succ_i y$ then $x > y$.

We comment briefly upon the individual properties: (1) is a rather obvious demand of an aggregation procedure if no profiles in society can be ruled out a priori; (2) says that the outcome of the aggregation should be well-behaved so that we avoid situations as that in the voting example. Property (3) says that unanimity among individuals should be respected in the aggregation; in particular, it rules out imposed SWFs.

Property (4) is a little less transparent than the remaining ones, and it is also this property which is most open to criticism. What it says is that society's preferences for $x$ against $y$ should depend on individual preferences *only* for $x$ against $y$, that is, the individual preferences for $x$ or $y$ against some $z$ and for $z$ against $w$ should be irrelevant for society's valuation of $x$ against $y$. The property is also called "Independence of irrelevant alternatives".

Whether or not binariness of aggregation procedures is acceptable must depend on the situations considered. It may be violated if aggregation is to take into account also intensities of preferences, and in general it may be considered as the least convincing of the properties. Finally, property (5) is reasonable enough and needs no further comments.

Even though property (4) may give rise to some reservations, the conditions in system (1)-(5) seem fairly weak. It is therefore rather surprising that the following holds true:

PROPOSITION 1 ("Arrow's impossibility theorem") *If X has at least 3 elements then there is no SWF which satisfies properties (1)-(5).*

Thus, preferences cannot be aggregated in a "reasonable" way if by reasonable we understand the restrictions on the aggregation procedures given by our properties. This should not be taken as a statement that preferences cannot be aggregated at all – some such aggregation is performed all the time in practical life – but only that it is impossible to find a theoretically "true" or "just" way of doing this.

We shall not give a full proof of Proposition 1 but since the proof gives some impression of what is going on, we shall do it for the special case of $n = 2$.

PROOF OF PROPOSITION 1 (for $n = 2$): We say that an individual $i$ is *decisive for $x \in X$ over $y \in X$* if in every profile in which $x >_i y$ and $y >_j x$, $j \neq i$, results in $x > y$. By property (4) the above needs to hold only in one profile.

First of all we show that there is one agent who is decisive for some $x$ over some $y$: Choose a profile $(\succsim_1, \succsim_2)$ with $x >_1 y, y >_2 x$ for some $x, y \in X$. If society has $x > y$ ($y > x$) then 1(2) is decisive for $x$ over $y$ ($y$ over $x$). If society has $x \sim y$, then we consider another profile with

$$x >_1 y >_1 z \qquad y >_2 z >_2 x.$$

We know that society has $x \sim y$ (by property (4)). By property (3) it has $y > z$, and then application of property (2) yields that $x > z$, so that 1 is decisive for $x$ over $z$.

Next, we show that if some individual, say 1, is decisive for $x$ over $y$, then she is decisive for $x$ over $w$, for $w$ an arbitrary alternative. Indeed, consider a profile with

$$x \succ_1 y \succ_1 w \qquad y \succ_2 w \succ_2 x.$$

Here society has $x > y$ (since 1 is decisive for $x$ over $y$) and $y > w$ by property (3), and then property (2) yields that $x > w$. We see that 1 is decisive for $x$ over $w$.

But she is also decisive for $y$ over $w$: Consider a profile with

$$y \succ_1 x \succ_1 w \qquad w \succ_2 y \succ_2 x.$$

Society has $x > w$ (since 1 is decisive for $x$ over $w$), $y > x$, hence $y > w$.

Summing up, we have shown that if individual 1 is decisive for $x$ over $y$, then he is decisive for both $x$ and $y$ over any third alternative. It follows that he is decisive for any $z$ over any $w$.

We have shown now that for any $x, y \in X$, if $x \succ_1 y$ and $y \succ_2 x$, then society will agree with individual 1 in its ranking of $x$ and $y$. To finish the argument, consider a profile with

$$x \succ_1 w \succ_1 y \qquad w \succ_2 y \sim_2 x.$$

Society has $x > w$ (1 is decisive for $x$ over $w$) and $w > y$ by property (3), consequently $x > y$. But this shows that society has $x > y$ whenever $x \succ_1 y$, for all alternatives $x, y \in X$, i.e. individual 1 is a dictator, violating property (5). □

*Aggregation of cardinal preferences: utilitarianism and leximin.* The somewhat discouraging result of the impossibility theorem sets severe limits for what can be derived as an overall criterion for ranking outcomes for society. However, this may be a result of its very general nature – the procedure must work on all conceivable preference profiles and give a consistent result. We have already seen that individual preferences over health outcomes for most purposes need to have some additional properties, for example the meaningfulness of utility differences (an increase in QALY score is indeed assumed to be something which can be weighed against an increase in treatment cost). Technically, this means that we should reduce the domain of our aggregation quite drastically.

We therefore reconsider the framework for preference aggregation somewhat, following Deschamps and Gevers [1978]: As before, $X$ is the set of all alternative social (health) states, and we have a set $N = \{1, \ldots, n\}$ of individuals. The preference profiles of the individuals will be introduced as a set $U$ of maps $u : X \times N \to \mathbb{R}$ with the interpretation that for each $i \in N$ and $x, y \in X$, $u(x, i) \geq u(y, i)$ if and only if $i$ is at least as well off with $x$ as with $y$. An SWF is now a map $f : U \to \mathcal{R}$, where $\mathcal{R}$ is the set of all total preorders on $X$.

As in the general case treated above, we consider a list of properties which should be satisfied. The first one is *binariness* which has already been introduced and needs no comment.

B: *Binaryness:* For all $u, u' \in U$ and each two-element subset $Y$ of $X$, if $u = u'$ on $Y \times N$, then $f(u) = f(u')$ on $Y$.

The next property is also well-known from before, at least in a weaker version:

SP: *Strong Pareto principle:* For $x, y \in X$, if $u(x, i) \geq u(y, i)$ all $i$, and $u(x, j) > u(y, j)$ for some $j$, then $x$ is strictly preferred to $y$ in $f(u)$.

Now we come to a property not encountered previously, namely that of anonymity:

A: *Anonymity:* If $\sigma$ is a permutation of $N$, and $u, u' \in U$ are such that $u(x, i) = u'(x, \sigma(i))$ for all $x$ and $i$, then $f(u) = f(u')$.

Since profiles of individual preferences are given in the form of utility functions, we want to use this information also in the aggregation, meaning that we have to compare utility levels of different individuals. The following property reflects this:

ME: *Minimal Equity:* There is $u \in U$, $x, y \in X$, and $j \in N$, such that for all $i \neq j$, $u(y, i) < u(x, i) < u(x, j) < u(x, j)$ *and $x$ is at least as good as $y$ in $f(u)$.*

The minimal equity property precludes that the individuals who are better off than all the others will always determine what society should prefer, there is at least one utility profile where this does not happen. Being far from proposing equality, this property only guarantees that the most favored should not dictate the preferences of society.

The following property can be seen as following up on the possibility of interpersonal utility comparisons, which were already introduced in ME. Essentially it says that utilities are cardinal, but the cardinality holds for all individuals simultaneously.

CC "*Co-Cardinality*": For every $u, u' \in U$, if $a$ and $b > 0$ are such that $u(x, i) = a + bu'(x, i)$ for all $x$ and $i$, then $f(u) = f(u')$.

Now we need to add only one more property to our list, which has to do with *unconcerned* individuals: If two alternatives are considered as equally good by a subset of the individuals, then these individuals should have no influence on society's ordering.

SE *Separability:* If $u, u' \in U$ and $\{N_1, N_2\}$ is a partition of $N$ such that $u(x, j) = u(y, j), u'(x, j) = u'(y, j)$ for all $x, y \in X$ and $j \in N_1$, and $u(x, i) = u'(x, i)$ for all $x \in X$ and $i \in N_2$, then $f(u) = f(u')$.

Put in this way, the separability property seems rather reasonable, but it carries a good deal of power, being essentially a version of the independence properties which are used to establish additive or multiplicative functional forms of utility functions defined on product spaces.

With this list of properties, we obtain a first result on cardinal preference aggregation:

PROPOSITION 2 *If f is a social welfare function which satisfies B, SP, A, ME, CC and SE, then f is either the leximin principle or the utilitarian rule.*

Here the *leximin* principle is defined as follows: For each $u \in U$ and $x \in X$, define $i_x(h)$ for $h = 1, \ldots, n$ by the condition $u(x, i_x(h)) < u(x, i_x(k)) \Rightarrow h < k$, so that $i_x(h)$ is the $h$th worst off individual if $x$ is chosen. Now, the leximin principle says that for each $u \in U$ and $x, y \in X$ if there is $m$ such that for all $h < m, u(x, i_x(h)) = u(y, i_y(h))$ and $u(y, i_y(m)) = u(x, i_x(m))$, then $x$ is preferred to $y$. The leximin principle is the formal version of what we have described more intuitively as maximin; in the present version it takes into account also the case where several individuals share the position of being worst off.

For a proof of Proposition 2, we refer to Deschamps and Gevers [1978]. The result is important, since it shows that the two seemingly opposite ways of aggregating preferences, or – in a terminology closer to applications in health economics – of determining priorities, have the same roots, sharing a great deal of common properties. In order to characterize either utilitarian or leximin rules, additional properties are needed. At this point such properties are very close to being a statement of the rule which is searched for, and therefore they present only limited interest in our context.

Clearly, once it is realized that maximizing the sum of utilities may give a result very different from that obtained maximizing the utility of the worst situated, it might seem to be only of academic interest that the two rules share a large number of basic properties. However, there is a point in knowing this, namely that the seemingly inherent conflict between the approaches should not detract attention from the shared properties, which may very well be violated in practice, so that the real world problems of setting priorities may differ from both rules.

## 2.3 *The extra-welfarism approach and capabilities*

The difficulties arising in the attempts to find a method of ranking health alloca-tions based on individual rankings naturally leads to consideration of alternative approaches, and there is indeed a tradition in health economics of challenging classical welfare economics. The latter is characterized as 'welfarist', based on individual utilities, an approach considered as unsatisfactory, and an alternative 'extra-welfarist' approach is called for to replace it.

The exact nature of this extra-welfarist approach – apart from being oriented towards other aspects of healthcare than individual perceptions of their quality of life – is in general not very well described, and the very notion of extra-welfarism may have different meanings and consequences. In Coast [2009] not only utili-ties but also the very idea of maximization is considered as misleading, whereas Brouwer et al. [2008] do not discard utilities but argues that other types of infor-mation than the preferences of society's citizens should enter as arguments in the social utility function. The latter situation is actually not excluded in the classi-cal approach to social choice, as all types of aggregations of preferences may be studied, and indeed should be, as there are no theoretically valid arguments for restricting attention to particular functional forms of the SWFs. Here and in other similar cases, it seems that the contradictions are more apparent than real, and that the traditional approach easily encompasses the extra-welfarist ideas as well, cf. Birch and Donaldson [2003].

Among the concepts which the extra-welfarists introduce into the assessment of healthcare programmes is that of *capabilities*. The capability approach suggested by Sen (1980, 1985) has been applied in several different fields of economics, including research in poverty and inequality and health related quality of life. To introduce capabilities, one has to start with Sen's notion of functionings. Sen distinguishes between several forms of relationship between an individual and a good (such as for example a car): a good is an item (the car), utility is the benefit derived from using this item (pleasure from driving), characteristics are qualities of the goods (transport), and the functioning relates to use of the car (moving around). Functionings are important, but what matters more is the capability, the extent to which the individual can function in a particular way, or whether or not she chooses a particular functioning.

As stated in Anand [2005], the capability approach has some advantages when compared to the traditional approach, in particular

– making explicit the options that individuals have rather than the activities they choose,

- allowing for a wide variety of capabilities gives a broader approach to well-being,
- capabilities make it easier to perform interpersonal comparisons,
- allowing for adaptive preferences, that is preferences that change if some of the options are exercised.

These properties are clearly attractive, and it is only natural that many researchers – and in particular those subscribing to extra-welfarism, see e.g. Coast et al. [2008] – consider the capability approach as a new and qualitatively superior way of treating the problems related to prioritization in healthcare. It has also been observed that capabilities are well adapted to questions of health, where the characterization always return to a description of activities which the individual is able to perform. It would seem that a reformulation of health measurement and of aggregating profiles of individual health states should be performed using the notion of capabilities.

The literature is however less abundant in practically oriented applications of the capability approach than in general descriptions of its potential. It has been emphasized repeatedly that the traditional, utility based approach is too narrow and must eventually be superseded by a non-utility approach, and that capability would present such an approach. We consider this argument in a simple framework, checking whether it can be substantiated using a straightforward formalization of the notion of capabilities.

In the following we assume that functionings can be formalized as vectors in $\mathbb{R}_{++}^L$, and that capabilities are subsets $C$ of $\mathbb{R}_+^L$ with some additional properties. Indeed, we assume that they belong to a given family $\mathfrak{C}$ of subsets, which are compact, convex, and comprehensive (meaning that if $x \in C$ and $y \in \mathbb{R}_+^L$ satisfies $y_h \leq x_h$ for $h = 1, \ldots, L$, then $y \in C$) subsets of characteristics (interpreted as sets of functionings open to an individual in different health states). For our subsequent reasoning, it is convenient to assume that $\mathfrak{C}$ is rich enough to contain some distinguished sets, in particular $\mathfrak{C}$ contains $\{0\}$ and permits the operation of (Minkowski) weighted averages, i.e. if $C, C' \in \mathfrak{C}$ and $\lambda \in [0, 1]$, then the set

$$\lambda C + (1 - \lambda)C' = \{y \in \mathbb{R}_+^L \mid y = \lambda x + (1 - \lambda)x', x \in C, x' \in C'\}$$

belongs to $\mathfrak{C}$ as well. We shall say that a family $\mathfrak{C}$ with these properties is *regular*.

In our present setup, the capabilities approach to QALY measurement would imply that there is a complete preorder $\succsim$ on the sets $C \in \mathfrak{C}$; we let $\succ$ and $\sim$ denote the associated strict order and indifference, respectively. One capabilitiy (= set of functioning) may be considered by an individual to be better or worse than another capability, or the individual may be indifferent between the two. For completeness of exposition, we state this as a first axiom.

AXIOM 1 *The preference relation* $\succsim$ *on the family* $\mathfrak{C}$ *is a complete preorder, and it is continuous in the sense that* $\{C' \in \mathfrak{C} \mid C \succsim C'\}$ *and* $\{C'' \in \mathfrak{C} \mid C'' \succsim C\}$ *are closed in the topology on* $\mathfrak{C}$ *induced by the Hausdorff distance[1] for all* $C \in \mathfrak{C}$.

We shall consider in some more details the properties of this preorder which seem reasonable if it is to be represented by an index with QALY-like properties. First of all, we assume that averages make sense and that the indifference relation is stable under such averages:

AXIOM 2 *Let* $(C_1, C_2)$ *and* $(C'_1, C'_2)$ *be pairs of elements of* $\mathfrak{C}$ *with* $C_1 \sim C_2$, $C'_1 \sim C'_2$, *and let* $\lambda \in [0, 1]$. *Then*

$$\lambda C_1 + (1 - \lambda)C'_1 \sim \lambda C_2 + (1 - \lambda)C'_2.$$

This property is a strong one, inducing some linearity into the preferences over capabilities. On the other hand it seems no more restrictive than what is usually assumed when considering preferences over health states, where indifference between suitable lotteries are instrumental for assessing the values of the utility indices.

For the intuitive interpretation of a QALY score as size of the set of available functionings, we would like to have the following monotonicity axiom:

AXIOM 3 *If* $C_1 \subset \operatorname{int} C_2$, *then* $C_2 > C_1$.

In its present form, this axiom can hardly be controversial, stating that if there are strictly less functionings available, then the resulting smaller capability set is less desired than the large one. We shall later have to consider modifications of this axiom which are perhaps less immediately acceptable.

AXIOM 4 *For each* $C \in \mathfrak{C}$, *there exists* $x \in C$ *such that* $\{x\} - \mathbb{R}^L_+ \in \mathfrak{C}$ *and* $\{x\} - \mathbb{R}^L_+ \sim C$.

This axiom can be recognized as a version of the celebrated IIA principle (Independence of Irrelevant Alternatives). If preferences over capabilities can be rationalized by a utility function, then the utility-maximizing element of the availability set (extended by free disposal to satisfy comprehensiveness) should be exactly as good as the larger choice set containing options that will not be chosen anyway. Thus, an IIA axiom of some type (and we shall consider another type of IIA axiom later) seems to be a necessary ingredient in any system of axioms for preferences on availability sets which can be rationalized by utility maximization.

---

[1]The Hausdorff distance $d_H$ between two compact sets $X$ and $Y$ in $\mathbb{R}^L$ is defined as $d_H(X, Y) = \max\{d(X, Y), d(Y, X)\}$, where $d(X, Y) = \max_{x \in X} \min_{y \in Y} d(x, y)$ and $d(\cdot, \cdot)$ is the ordinary Euclidean distance in $\mathbb{R}^L$. The Hausdorff distance induces the structure of a metric space on the set of all compact subsets of $\mathbb{R}^L$, and this metric space is compact.

For ease of notation in the sequel, we introduce the notation $\{x\} - \mathbb{R}_+^L$ for $\{x\} - \mathbb{R}_+^L$. We note that if Axiom 3 holds, then the vector $x$ of Axiom 4 must belong to the boundary of $C$.

PROPOSITION 3 *Let $\mathfrak{C}$ be a regular family of subsets of $\mathbb{R}_+^L$, and let $\succsim$ be relation on $\mathfrak{C}$. Then the following are equivalent:*

*(i) $(\mathfrak{C}, \succsim)$ satisfies Axioms 1 − 4,*

*(ii) there is a linear map $u : \mathbb{R}_+^L \to \mathbb{R}$ such that*

$$C \succsim C' \Leftrightarrow \max_{x \in C} u(x) \geq \max_{x \in C'} u(x).$$

PROOF: The proof of the implication (ii)⇒(i) is straightforward and left to the reader. Define the set

$$D = \left\{x \in \mathbb{R}_+^L \mid \{x\} - \mathbb{R}_+^L \in \mathfrak{C}, \{x\} - \mathbb{R}_+^L \succsim C', \text{ all } C' \in \mathfrak{C}\right\}.$$

By Axiom 1 there are maximal elements for $\succsim$ on $\mathfrak{C}$, and by Axiom 4, we get that $D$ is nonempty.

Next, choose any $x^* \in D$ and define for each $\lambda \in [0, 1]$ the set

$$D^\lambda = \left\{x \in \mathbb{R}_+^L \mid \{x\} - \mathbb{R}_+^L \sim \{\lambda x^*\} - \mathbb{R}_+^L\right\}.$$

By Axiom 2, each set $D^\lambda$ is convex, and we have that $\lambda' \lambda^{-1} D^\lambda \subseteq D^{\lambda'}$ whenever $\lambda' \leq \lambda$. Letting $\widehat{D} = \{x \mid \lambda x \in D^\lambda \text{ for some } \lambda \in [0,1]\}$ we get that $\widehat{D}$ is convex and that for each $x \in \widehat{D}$, the sets $\{x' \mid x' < x\}$ and $\widehat{D}$ are disjoint. Consequently, by separation of convex sets there is $c \in \mathbb{R}_+^L$, $c \neq 0$, such that $D \subset \{x' \mid c \cdot x' = 1\}$. It follows that $D^\lambda \subset \{x' \mid c \cdot x' = \lambda\}$ for each $\lambda \in [0, 1]$.

Define the map $u : \mathbb{R}_+^L \to \mathbb{R}$ by $u(x) = c \cdot x$ for each $x$. We show that $u$ satisfies the conditions in (ii). Let $C$ be arbitrary, and assume that $C \sim \{x\} - \mathbb{R}_+^L$ for some $x \in D^\lambda$. Then there is $y \in C$ with $\{y\} - \mathbb{R}_+^L \sim \{x\} - \mathbb{R}_+^L$, and since $u(y) = u(x) = \lambda$, we have that $\max_{z \in C} u(z) \geq \lambda$. Suppose that $\max_{z \in C} u(z) = \lambda' > \lambda$; then $C$ contains some vector $z \in D^{\lambda'}$, meaning that $z' = \lambda(\lambda')^{-1} z$ must belong to $D^\lambda$. But since $\{z'\} - \mathbb{R}_+^L$ is contained in the interior of $C$, Axiom 3 gives a contradiction. □

The proposition says that if an individuals ranks capabilities in a particular way, and this ranking is consistent in the sense of the Axioms 1-4, then it this ranking is actually derived from an underlying utility on functionings. In this sense capabilities add little new if we want to find a social ranking based on how individuals rank alternative capabilities. Clearly the result pertains mainly to our formalization of capabilities, not to the capability approach aa such, and the problem of finding an exact framework in which to treat capabilities must be regarded is still open.

## 2.4   The 'fair innings' argument

In the discussion on equity and its meaning, the 'fair innings' approach to inter-generational equity has achieved much attention. Originally formulated in Harris [1985], it was elaborated upon by Williams [1997]. The point of departure is society's assessment of life years or quality adjusted life years for different types of individuals. Assuming that the current situation, with its resulting distribution of life expectations, is efficient in the sense that it is on the boundary of the production possibilities, an optimum would imply that the set of socially preferred distributions does not intersect the production possibility set (Fig. 7.3). Casual observations, supported by systematically collected interview data, suggest that the egalitarian distribution (all have the same life expectancy) is not achieved and not even desired, meaning that a simplistic interpretation of equity is not a widespread desideratum in health policies.

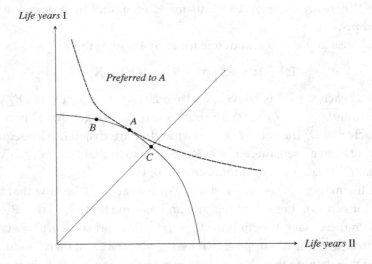

Fig. 7.3   The 'fair innings' argument in a society with two individuals: If current distribution of life expectation is represented by *B* and society wants a more equitable distribution, in this case *A*, even if not the egalitarian one *C*, then society is willing to give up some life years of I against more life years for II, and in this sense it is considered that I has got his fair share of life.

Next, noticing that the actual distribution of life expectation in most countries favors the wealthier parts of the population, one can see that exchanging some months of life of the most fortunate against longer life of the less fortunate might be in accordance with social welfare, pointing towards a concept of a reasonable length of lifespan to be supported by the healthcare system.

Pushing the argument further, it might also be possible that such tradeoffs can be observed between additional life years of elderly and life years of younger individuals. This fits with ordinary use of language, the death of an old person may be considered as a sad event whereas the death of a young person would be characterized as a tragedy. Whether this could be sustained by existing data to show that society as a whole subscribes to the idea of a certain length of life as fair and justified and additional years as less, is yet another matter.

It may be noticed that the discussion is phrased in terms of life expectations and as such are not easily translated to something operational. Also, a reasoning which depends on the concept of a social utility function must necessarily remain rather abstract. Finally, while discussing the tradeoff between life years of different persons, other tradeoffs, notably between life years and other goods enjoyed in life, is absent. Given the close relation between inequalities in health and inequalities in consumption possibilities, this remains a serious drawback of the approach.

## 3 The role of government: healthcare policy

Throughout the discussion of health economics, government has been present, often in a very direct way as participant in the economic activities, either as the insurer or payment organisation, or directly as healthcare provider through state-owned hospitals, medical centers etc. This role of government, which for our purpose is less essential, since it could have been, and in many countries actually is, performed by non-government entities, has been taken care of as we proceeded, and at present we are more interested in the traditional government role as regulator of the economic activity.

### 3.1 *Government as regulator*

Setting apart direct government intervention and participation in the market, the classical role is that of a regulator, the main aspects of which are:

   (i) securing that competition will prevail whenever possible,
   (ii) setting rules for the activity of the market participants if competition is insufficient,
  (iii) preventing abuses by the enforcement of standards for providers,
  (iv) facilitating entry of market participants.

In a broader view on regulation, it may also include activities which are related to the future workings of the markets,

   (v) supporting innovations in the market.

The way in which this regulation is carried out will depend on the overall objectives, which are not always explicit (and even when they are, they may be difficult to interpret in terms of concrete action to be taken, as for example when government subscribing to a 'Samaritan principle' as mentioned in Chapter 4). For a discussion related to US healthcare, cf. Box 7.1.

The exact way in which these activities materialize will differ from one healthcare system to another, and the examples have been discussed already in connection with the different fields of healthcare provision and payment. Also, some of them are on the margin of economics proper and pertain to the legal aspects of healthcare. We shall therefore restrict attention to a particular case which was left untouched in the previous chapters, namely that of drug subsidization and its use in fostering competition among producers of pharmaceutical drugs.

Drug subsidization is introduced mainly to facilitate access to medicine for low income consumers, as well as in order to increase the overall fairness healthcare provision, exempting the sick from the additional burden of paying for the treatment. Since drug subsidies must be financed from the budget, an additional purpose of reducing overall cost of pharmaceutical drugs comes in, and in pursuing this objective it becomes important to secure competition on the supply side. There are of course other important government policies which have impact on the market for pharmaceutical drugs, such as the rules about orphan drugs (cf. Box 3.3.3) which opens up for innovations in the market which otherwise might not have been forthcoming.

### 3.2   *Using drug subsidies to improve competition*

There are several methods for providing incentives to the drug producers for price reductions. The general idea is to direct the demand of the consumers (patients) towards the producer charging the lowest price. If the system is one of 100% subsidization (except possibly for a fixed price-independent fee), then government essentially acquires a monopsony.

*Generic substitution* means that the drug which was prescribed by the physician is replaced at the pharmacy by another drug in the same generic group, which in practice means that the active component (molecule) should be the same, and that the concentration and way of administering the drug should also be identical. In principle, there should be no difference between what the doctor writes in the prescription and what the patient gets. But even if the molecule is the same, generic drugs are not absolutely identical. First of all, the additional content needed to produce a pill may differ from one brand to another, and secondly, the method of production can also have some impact on the final product. Consequently, the principle that generic drugs are absolutely identical cannot be upheld in practice.

---

**Box 7.1** The roles of competition policy in US healthcare. According to Porter and Teisberg [2004], the healthcare regulation policy in the United States has changed over time as a consequence of changing objectives as shown below:

**Past objectives: reduce cost, avoid cost**

- Focus on cost, bargaining power and rationing:
    - cost shifting among patients, providers, physicians, payers, employers, government
    - limits on access to services
    - bargained down prices for drugs and services
    - prices unrelating to the economics of delivering care
- Focus on legal recourse and regulation:
    - patient rights
    - detailed rules for system participants
    - increased reliance on the legal system

**Present objectives: enable choice, reduce errors**

- Focus on cost of health plan:
    - competition among health plans
    - information on health plans
    - financial incentives for patients
- Focus on provider and hospital practices
    - online order entry
    - appropriate staffing
    - mandatory guidelines
    - 'pay for performance' when standard of care are used

As argued in Porter and Teisberg [2004], the objectives of healthcare regulation are under continuous evolution, and the objectives are expected to change:

**Future objective: increase value**

- Focus on the nature of competition:
    - competition on the level of specific diseases and conditions
    - distinctive strategies by payers and providers
    - incentives to increase value rather than shift costs
    - information on providers' experience, outcomes, and prices
    - consumer choice

Since government regulation is considered here from a management point of view (and takes into consideration the structure of US healthcare financing, where health insurance is contracted by employers), it does not necessarily cover all aspects of regulation, not even of regulating competition in healthcare.

---

From an economic point of view, the idea of treating two versions of the same product as identical should give rise to almost automatical skepticism, even in the case where they are truly indistinguishable from a physical point of view. In economic analysis, two versions of a product should be treated as different as

soon as some consumer perceives them as different. It may be reasonable for a
regulating authority to treat them as identical, but in our analysis they remain
different commodities.

The workings of generic substitution can be studied in a simple model of monopolistic competition in price and quality. It is assumed that the individual patient
has a subjective evaluation of ideal quality and that she will evaluate each given
product according to its distance from this ideal. In order to use the model, we
must assume that quality can be measured on a one-dimensional scale, which
of course is a rather far shot from the complicated situation which was sketched
above. Moreover, this measure of quality is objective in the sense that it is the same
for all individuals, who differ only in their assessment of the ideal.

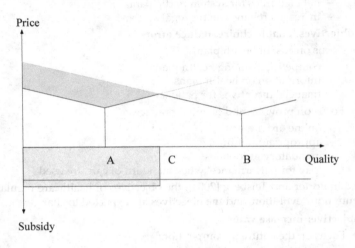

Fig. 7.4   The effects of regulating by generic substitution. Assuming 50% cost reimbursement, the payer
organization faces the same prices as the patient before regulation, so that subsidizing $A$ gives rise to a
cost shown as the shaded area below the axis. After introducing generic substitution, both parties pay
only the price of $B$, so subsidies are reduced slightly. Consumer disutility are however increased by the
shaded area in the first quadrant.

In Fig. 7.4 the situation is illustrated for two medical drugs with different prices.
One has quality $A$ and its price $p_A$ is bigger than that of the other one, which has
quality $B$ and price $p_B$. Assuming a 50% subsidy or reimbursement from a third-
party payer, the amount paid by the latter will have the same magnitude as the
price seen by the patient and shown on the vertical axis. The subsidy is depicted
downwards from the origin, so that the price to the industry for quality $A$ should
be found as the sum of the two. The costumer with an ideal far away from $A$ will
in addition experience a (subjective) cost in the form of a utility loss, indicated by

the upwards sloping line from *A* (or *B*). The dividing point between costumers choosing *A* and *B* can be found as *C*.

Under generic substitution everybody must choose quality *B*. The third-party payer will save an amount corresponding to the reduction in the rectangular area indicated in the figure – costumers to the left of *C*, who got a 50% subsidy for *A*, are now buying quality *B* and get a correspondingly smaller subsidy.

While the savings of the third-party payer can be read off the figure, it is perhaps less immediately seen that there is a welfare loss connected with the restrictions of the free choice. In the figure this loss can be found as the area indicated above *A*: Each of the former purchasers of *A* has a higher cost in terms of payment and utility loss due a more distant quality of the new variant. That this area is greater than that indicating savings of the third-party payer is a feature of our illustration (or ultimately, the parameters chosen in the model) and does not represent a general result. However, the point which may be obtained from the analysis is that a method of regulation which gives rise to a cost saving to some party, perhaps the government in the case of a tax-financed healthcare system, does not necessarily bring increased welfare and may occasionally give the opposite, namely a welfare loss.

*Reference pricing.* While generic substitution aims at minimizing reimbursement through direct intervention in consumer choices, other methods of regulation reaches the same goal by different methods. If a system of reference prices is used, reimbursement will be *as if* the patient has bought a specific drug (typically the cheapest drug of the same kind) rather than the one prescribed. The effect is illustrated in Fig. 7.5 using the same simple model as above: If the subsidy is computed as 50% of the price of the cheapest drug, this will have the same effect for the consumer as if the price of the drug of quality *A* has increased. The consequence is certain change in consumption patterns (point *C* moves to the left) and increased expenditure for those still choosing *A*.

It is seen that the welfare loss for patients cannot exceed the one experienced under generic substitution, since the loss of the individual can be separated into increased payment for the medicin plus inconvenience from not getting the right brand, and the latter will be unaffected by reference pricing as compared with no regulation, while generic substitution entails an increase in misallocation.

Both generic substitution and reference pricing will have a positive effect on competition in the market. This is obvious for generic substitution, since only the cheapest drug will stay in the market if substitution is 100% effective (which is only rarely the case). But also reference pricing has the effect that differences in prices charged by the industry are magnified since the subsidy is independent of the price of all except the cheapest drug in the market

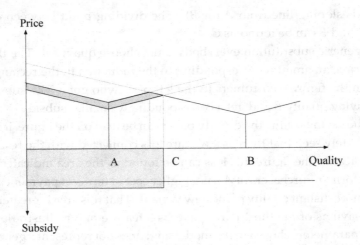

Fig. 7.5   Reference pricing: The patient preferring *A* must pay its price minus the subsidy paid to the other quality *B*, giving rise to a rise in cost and disutility. The payer organization saves the additional subsidy paid to *A*.

For the assessment of reference pricing in a more general context than that of our simple benchmark model, we should also consider the *choice of reference price*. A straightforward choice would be the cheapest drug (of the same type) in the market, but since national markets often have few suppliers and the risk of tacit collusion is high, it may be better to extend the reference to a family of countries which are otherwise compatible, and this is what has eventually happened in most European countries.

*Parallel imports.*   The previously discussed regulations have basically only shifted the payment from third-party payer back to the patient. The effects on industry pricing has at best been marginal. There is however another method which aims directly at industry prices. This is the method of *parallel imports*, which uses the well-known phenomenon of *arbitrage* trade: If a commodity is sold cheaper in one market than in another, then in principle there is money to be earned at little or no cost buying up the commodity where it is cheap and selling it where it is expensive. It is a fundamental aspect of well-functioning markets that all possibilities of arbitrage has already been ruled out.

On the other hand, drug markets are far from smooth and well-functioning. As we have discussed above, marketing a drug in a given country is a time-consuming procedure so that setting up new business just to exploit temporary price differences seems out of the question. But when it comes to import and sale of brands which are already marketed in the country in question, European rules allow immediate marketing of the packages bought abroad, only the documentation should be in native language.

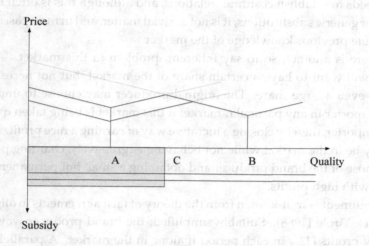

Fig. 7.6 Parallel imports: If quality A is sold abroad at a price lower than quality B, then opening up for parallel imports means that both patient and payer organization saves on the price reduction. If also reference other regulations are in force, the subsidy paid to all qualities may decrease.

Given that price differences between European countries are substantial, this opens up for considerable economic activity with a resulting increased price competition in high-price countries. Consequently, the expectations were high when parallel imports were set into system in around 1990.

In our basic model we assume that quality A is bought abroad by a parallel importer, who sells the drug at a price below those of both A and B. The total effects in the market will depend on the other regulations used in the country considered, but in any case the result will be a reduced outlay for the third-party payer. In Fig. 7.6 it is seen that with no other regulation the purchasers of A (in the imported version) is increased to the right, which will give rise to a considerable reduction in subsidies. If there is also generic substitution, the quality B will be replaced by A, giving a further reduction in outlays for the third-party payer.

In the analysis so far, parallel imports increases competition and reduces the reimbursement costs of the healthcare system. The story is not complete yet – and in practice, these positive effects of parallel import did not fulfill expectations. Increased competition may reduce prices but all too often, textbook results on *perfect* competitions are invoked in situations where the number of firms changes from one to two or three, which is usually not the same as creating perfect competition.

It is comparatively easy to enter the market as a parallel importer, in the sense that there are no administrative barriers – market permit has already been given to the product which was fully documented by the brand producer. But even so, the entrant needs to establish costumer relations, and although this is often facilitated by rules for generic substitutions, it is not a trivial matter, and in most cases demand considerable previous knowledge of the market.

But there is another, so to say inherent, problem in this market. A parallel importer will want to have a certain share of the market, but not necessarily the largest or even a large share: The original producer may choose to underprice a parallel importer in any particular market if this market is being taken over by the parallel importer, thereby closing a lucrative way of earning a nice profit. It is much better stay be in the market while not behaving aggressively, charging prices very close to those of the brand producer and obtaining a small but permanent share of a market with high profits.

The argument is well-known from the theory of tacit agreements in oligopolistic markets, cf. Tirole [1988]. Suitably simplified, the brand producer would obtain monopoly profits $\Pi_{mon}$ in each period if alone in the market. A parallel importer has the possibility of taking over the market completely by charging lower prices, obtaining a one-shot profit which would amount to at most $\Pi_{mon}$. However, the consequence might be the loss of this market from next period and onwards due to undercutting by the brand producer. With a discount rate of $\delta$, the total loss is then

$$\delta(s\Pi_{mon}) + \delta^2(s\Pi_{mon}) + \cdots + \delta^t(s\Pi_{mon}) + \cdots = \frac{\delta}{1-\delta}(s\Pi_{mon}),$$

where $s < 1$ is permanent market share of the non-aggressive parallel importer. For discount rates and market shares such that

$$s > \frac{1}{\delta} - 1$$

the loss exceeds the possible gains so that the parallel importer refrains from aggressive price competition. This seems to fit quite well with what is observed in countries where parallel importers set their prices in such a way that they capture a not too spectacular share of the market, charging prices only slightly below that of the brand producer. In this way they obtain a solid stable profit which still is not large enough to force the brand producers into countermeasures. The unfortunate by-product is that the price to the consumer and the subsidizer remains largely unchanged.

# 4   Setting priorities in healthcare

In most countries, healthcare is an object of political concern, and government policy makers are invariably involved in the workings of the healthcare sector, either in preparing or implementing comprehensive healthcare reforms, or in formulating detailed policies, regulating particular sectors or reacting upon public worries about particular diseases and their treatment. It is commonplace that experts, either medical or economic, will get involved in this process, and this is quite reasonable.

As it has been seen in the preceding sections, deriving an objective for government regulation from underlying principles is not a simple matter. This means that attempts to find general principles for solving the day-to-day problems in healthcare allocation should be handled with care. There is general consensus about the need for prioritization in healthcare, since the limited ressources cannot cover all health needs, but the question of *who* should do this prioritization should be handled with care.

## 4.1   *The Oregon experiment*

As an example of the problems of prioritization in healthcare, and of the revisions and changes which must be made when transforming abstract principles to real-world political decisions, one usually refers to the experience of Medicaid in Oregon in 1992–93 when attempting to formulate a decision about the treatments which should be supported, see e.g. Blumstein [1997]. The point of departure was an experienced budgetary deficit (Medicaid is financed by federal as well as state budgets), and a decision to save money on organ transplants, using instead the funds in maternal care, had resulted in a public outcry when a seven-year-old boy was denied support for a bone marrow transplant.

Medicaid provides health insurance coverage for indigent citizens, and it was earlier decided, that all persons below the poverty limit should be eligible, and also that these persons should be treated equally. Since funds were limited, it was decided to set up a prioritized list and then contract for prices, including as many treatments as the budget allowed. It remained then to construct the prioritization list.

In the initial stage, a list of 709 condition-treatment (CT) pairs was created. For each of these CT pairs, information was collected about the outcomes of the interventions, relying mainly on professional societies, in order to determine the medical benefit. In the first approach to prioritization, Oregon's planners tried to supplement the purely scientific terms of medical benefits by determining a net benefit from intervention. For this, they used the Quality-of-Well-Being (QWB) scale [Kaplan et al., 1993], a health state index mainly based on professional assessments, and found cost-effectiveness ratios of each CT pair. The 709 CT pairs were then ranked according to the results of these cost-effectiveness ratios to constitute an *interim* proposal of the planners.

This proposal was however rejected by the commission appointed by Oregon's governor, and a second approach was initiated. Here, 17 service categories were set up, which in their turn were divided in three groups,

- essential services (9 of the 17, given rank 1 – 9),
- very important services (4 categories, ranked as numbers 10 – 13)
- services that are valuable to certain individuals (4 categories, numbers 14 – 17).

Each CT pair was then placed in one of the categories, and inside the category they were ranked according to "net benefit", the increment in the well-being according to the QWB scale. Having done that the result was submitted to the commission, where the rankings were revised on a pure subjective basis. It turned out that in the final ranking, the "net benefit" had little influence on the position of the CT pairs, and also the cost played a very limited role.

The final ranking was then submitted to the federal administration for approval, but it was turned down, partially due to legal shortcomings. A new proposal was produced. Here the list was somewhat reduced (from 709 to 688), quality-of-life information was completely disregarded, and the category approach was abandoned. Instead, the CT pairs were assessed on what could be considered as "objective" criteria, namely (1) probability of death, (2) probability of returning to a stable asymptotic state, and (3) cost of avoiding death. This proposal was accepted by the federal administration, but only after som revision, in particular the criterion (2) was abandoned in ranking the CT pairs.

As it can be seen, what came out of the procedure was very far from what was planned at the beginning. The idea of ranking treatments according to cost-effectiveness had to be given up, and what remained was a ranking which relied only on the medical profession and the politicians dealing with healthcare. The point here is not whether this ranking is more or less reliable or desirable than one based on the standard tools of health economics, but that the latter was not accepted by the decision makers. Otherwise put, the tools that we have developed may be useful and even indispensable as *decision support*, but they cannot replace decisions. A prioritization list is such a replacement, and it should not be too surprising that it cannot be left to technicians to prepare such a list.

## 4.2  *Prioritization as rationing: accountability*

In most countries, the need for prioritization in healthcare has been generally accepted, but the actual attempts at carrying out prioritizations have been much debated and have had only limited success. It should be realized that in practice, prioritization will result in rationing of healthcare; some services will not be delivered to those having a well-documented need for them. Decisions about rationing particular services will invariably produce cases which can be seen as unjust and unreasonable. On the other hand, the rationing is in most cases based on well-argued reasoning and collected evidence about medical effects and cost.

While individual rationing decisions may be reasonable based on the particular professional knowledge which is relevant for the case, they may be less reasonable to the general public, and moreover, the rationing decided based on local criteria may produce wide variation in the severity of rationing even within a country (as it is the case e.g. in England, cf. Gray [2016]). Some of these problems could be reduced or even removed if more emphasis could be made on *accountability* for reasonableness of rationing criteria. That the reasonableness of a given rationing decision may not be a simple matter has already been mentioned in the previous chapters, and it can be seen also from Table 7.1, taken from Daniels [2016].

**Table 7.1.** CEA vs. fair distribution

|  | CEA | Fairness |
|---|---|---|
| Best outcome vs. fair chances | Best outcome | Weighted chances |
| Priority to worst off | None | Some |
| Aggregation | Full | Some |

Indeed, cost-effectiveness based decisions will always favor the best alternative, but this may conflict with a widespread attitude in the general public, wanting to give people a fair chance of a considerable benefit, even if it is not the best. Clearly, cost-effectiveness pays attention to the patients which are worst off, and in the bottom row, it will incorporate all benefits, however small, so that very small benefits given to a large number of people can outweigh spectacular benefits (life-saving) to a few. Clearly, these differences should be taken with some reservation, since they depend on the application of either cost-effectiveness analysis or fairness considerations to particular patients or groups of patients rather than to interventions as such, but it serves to highlight the different criteria for rationing that may occur given the approach taken.

Since there is no simple way of solving such problems, the best that can be done is to insist on openness and accountability with respect to the criteria used when deciding upon a given rationing.

## 5   Problems

**1.** A well-known graphical way of displaying inequality is by the way of *Lorenz curves*. If a quantity (income, health state measured in QALYs, amount of healthcare received) can be measured as values in an interval, one can depict its distribution function $F$ on this interval normalized as $[0, 1]$. In the special case where the variable is income level, then we get the standard Lorenz curve: Explain how to use this

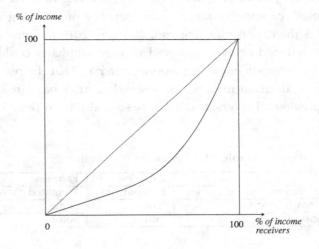

construction to illustrate inequality in health and inequality of healthcare received. Will the curves always be situated below the diagonal (which corresponds to a uniform distribution)?

**2.** In order to obtain information about the preferences of a decision maker, responsible for rationing access to life-saving health care, she has been confronted with 3 hypothetical dilemmas (cases A – C below). In each case, two patients in a specified age and health state both suffer from an acute life threatening disease. If a patient is not treated, he or she will die immediately. If a patient is treated, he or she can expect a specified amount of additional life years (in unchanged health state.

| Patient | Health state | Age (years) | Life years gained |
|---------|--------------|-------------|-------------------|
| A1 | No health problems | 40 | 5 |
| A2 | Confined to bed | 40 | 5 |
|  | Unable to wash or dress self |  |  |
|  | Moderate pain or discomfort |  |  |
|  | Moderately anxious or depressed |  |  |

| Patient | Health state | Age (years) | Life years gained |
|---------|--------------|-------------|-------------------|
| B1 | No health problems | 30 | 15 |
| B2 | No health problems | 40 | 20 |

| Patient | Health state | Age (years) | Life years gained |
|---------|--------------|-------------|-------------------|
| C1 | No health problems | 50 | 10 |
| C2 | No health problems | 70 | 10 |

In case A, the decision maker prefers to treat A1, in case B patient B2 is treated, and in case C, the decision maker is indifferent between treating any of the two.

Discuss the potential (in)compatibility of the social preferences of the decision maker with relevant fairness and efficiency concerns.

Write up a population health evaluation function (a "health-related social welfare function") for assessment of health distributions compatible with the decision maker's choices below. Discuss the model.

**3.** A government wants to subsidize the patients' purchase of pharmaceutical drugs in such a way that patient utility is maximal, but there is only a fixed budget available for this purpose. Show that this situation can be considered as one of a government sale of drugs purchased at the pharmacies, with prices paid by patients are set so as to maximize utility.

Explain that in this case Ramsey pricing (Chapter 4, Section 5.3) applies, so that inverse elasticity determines the size of the subsidy.

Compare with subsidization schemes used in European countries. How does it fit with a graduation of subsidies depending on the degree of necessity for the patient of the drug?

# Bibliography

D. Acemoglu and J. Linn. Market size in innovation: theory and evidence from the pharmaceutical industry. Technical Report 10038, NBER, 2003.

P. Aghion, P. Howitt, and F. Murtin. The relationship between health and growth: when Lucas meets Nelson-Phelps. *Review of Economics and Institutions*, 2:1–24, 2011.

G.A. Akerlof. The market for "lemons": Quality uncertainty and the market mechanism. *Quarterly Journal of Economics*, 84:488–500, 1970.

M. Allais. Le comportement de l'homme rationnel devant le risque: critique des postulats et axiomes de l'ecole Americain. *Econometrica*, 21:503–546, 1953.

R. Allen and P. Gertler. Regulation and the provision of quality to heterogeneous consumers: The case of prospective pricing of medical services. *Journal of Regulatory Economics*, 3: 361–375, 1991.

P. Anand. Capabilities and health. *Journal of Medican Ethics*, 31:299–303, 2005.

S. Anand and K. Hanson. Disability-adjusted life years: a critical review. *Journal of Health Economics*, 16:685–702, 1997.

K.J. Arrow. Uncertainty and the welfare economics of medical care. *American Economic Review*, 53:941–973, 1963a.

K.J. Arrow. *Social choice and individual values*. Yale University Press, 1963b.

K.J. Arrow. Political and economic evaluation of social effects and externalities. In J. Margolis, editor, *The analysis of public output*, pages 1–30. NBER, 1970.

D.P. Baron and R.B. Myerson. Regulating a monopolist with unknown costs. *Econometrica*, 50:911–930, 1982.

W.J. Baumol. Macroeconomics of unbalanced growth: the anatomy of urban crisis. *American Economic Review*, 57:415–436, 1967.

G.S. Becker and K.M. Murphy. A theory of rational addiction. *Journal of Political Economy*, 96:675–700, 1988.

B.D. Bernheim and M.D. Whinston. Common agency. *Econometrica*, 54:923–942, 1986.

A. Bielinska-Kwapisz. Sufficiency in Blackwell's theorem. *Mathematical Social Sciences*, 46: 21–25, 2003.

S. Birch and C. Donaldson. Valuing the benefits and costs of health care programmes: where's the 'extra' in extra-welfarism? *Social Science & Medicine*, 56:1121–1133, 2003.

A. Björnberg. Euro health consumer index 2015 report. Technical report, Health Consumer Powerhouse, 2016.

D. Blackwell. Comparison of experiments. In *Proceedings of the Second Berkeley Symposium on Mathematical Statistics and Probability*, pages 99–102. University of California Press, 1951.

H. Bleichrodt, P. Wakker, and M. Johannesson. Characterizing QALYs by risk neutrality. *Journal of Risk and Uncertainty*, 15:107–114, 1997.

J.F. Blumstein. The Oregon experiment: the role of cost-benefit analysis in the allocation of medicaid funds. *Social Science & Medicine*, 45:545–554, 1997.

J.H. Boyd and J.P. Conley. Fundamental nonconvexities in arrowian markets and a coasian solution to the problem of externalities. *Journal of Economic Theory*, 72:388–407, 1997.

K.A. Brekke and B. Øksendal. The high contact principle as sufficiency condition for optimal stopping. In D. Lund and B. Øksendal, editors, *Stochastic models and option values*. Elsevier Science, 1991.

W.B.F. Brouwer and M.A. Koopmanschap. On the economic foundations of CEA. ladies and gentlemen, take your positions! *Journal of Health Economics*, pages 439–459, 2000.

W.B.F. Brouwer, A.J, N.J.A. van Exel, and F.F.H. Rutten. Welfarism vs. extra-welfarism. *Journal of Health Economics*, 27:325–338, 2008.

D. Canning. Axiomatic foundations for cost-effectiveness analysis. *Health Economics*, 22: 1405–1416, 2013.

M. Chalkley and J.M. Malcolmson. Contracting for health services when patient demand does not reflect quality. *Journal of Health Economics*, 17:1–19, 1998.

P. Choné and C.A. Ma. Optimal health care contract under physician agency. *Annals of Economics and Statistics*, 101/102:229–256, 2011.

F. Christensen, J.L. Hougaard, and H. Keiding. An axiomatic characterization of efficiency indices. *Economic Letters*, 63:33–37, 1999.

K. Claxton. The irrelevance of inference: a decision-making approach to the stochastic evaluation of health care technologies. *Journal of Health Economics*, 18:341–364, 1999.

K. Claxton, M. Sculpher, and M. Drummond. A rational framework for decision making by the National Institute For Clinical Excellende (NICE). *The Lancet*, 360:711–715, 2002.

J. Coast. Maximisation in extra-welfarism: A critique of the current position in health economics. *Social Science & Medicine*, 69:786–792, 2009.

J. Coast, R.D. Smith, and P. Lorgelly. Welfarism, extra.welfarism and capability: The spread if ideas in health economics. *Social Science & Medicine*, 67:1190–1198, 2008.

R. Cunningham and R.M. Cunningham. *The blues: A history of the Blue Cross and Blue Shield system*. Northern Illinois University Press, 1997.

J. Cylus, E. Nolte, J. Figuera, and M. McKee. What, if anything, does the eurohealth consumer index actually tell us? *BMJ Blogs*, 2016. URL http://eprints.lse.ac.uk/68241/.

N. Daniels. Accountability for reasonableness and priority setting in health. In E. Nagel, M. Lauerer, and V. Schätzlein, editors, *Prioritization in healthcare: An international dialogue*, pages 47–56. Springer, 2016.

P.M. Danzon and L.-W. Chao. Cross-national price differences for pharmaceuticals: how large, and why? *Journal of Health Economics*, 19:159–195, 2000.

P.M. Danzon and J.D. Kim. International price comparisons for pharmaceuticals: measurement and policy issues. *Pharmacoeconomics*, 14(Suppl.1):115–128, 1998.

G. Debreu. The coefficient of resource utilization. *Econometrica*, 19:273–292, 1951.

G. Debreu. *Theory of value*. Wiley, New York, 1959.

J.S. Demski. The general impossibility of normative accounting standards. *The Accounting Review*, 48:718–723, 1973.

R. Deschamps and L. Gevers. Leximin and utilitarian rules: a joint characterization. *Journal of Economic Theory*, 17:143–163, 1978.

J.A. DiMasi and C. Paquette. The economics of follow-on drug research and development. *Pharmacoeconomics*, 22 Suppl.2:1–14, 2004.

A. Dixon. Are medical savings accounts a viable option for funding health care? *Croation Medical Journal*, 43:408–416, 2002.

J.N. Doctor, H. Bleichrodt, J. Miyamoto, N.R. Temkin, and S. Dikmen. A new and more robust test of QALYs. *Journal of Health Economics*, 23:353–367, 2004.

R. Dortman and P.O. Steiner. Optimal advertising and optimal quality. *American Economic Review*, 44:826–836, 1954.

J.H. Drèze. Loss reduction and implicit deductibles in medical insurance. Discussion Paper 5, CORE, 2002.

K. Eggleston. Multitasking and mixed systems for provider payments. *Journal of Health Economics*, 24:211–223, 2005.

I. Ehrlich and G.S. Becker. Market insurance, self-insurance, and self-protection. *Journal of Political Economy*, 80:623–648, 1972.

I. Ehrlich and H. Chuma. A model of the demand for longevity and the value of life extension. *Journal of Political Economy*, 98:761–782, 1990.

P.J. Farley. Theories of the price and quantity of physician services. *Journal of Health Economics*, 5:315–333, 1986.

M.J. Farrell. The measurement of productive efficiency. *Journal of the Royal Statistical Society*, 120(3):253–290, 1957.

E. Fenwick, B.J. O'Brien, and A. Briggs. Cost-effectiveness acceptability curves - facts, fallacies and frequently asked questions. *Health Economics*, 13:405–415, 2004.

D.K. Foley. Lindahl's solution and the core of an economy with public goods. *Econometrica*, 38:66–72, 1970.

A. Gafni. Alternatives to the QALY measure for economic evaluations. *Support Care Cancer*, 5:105–111, 1997.

A. Gafni and S. Birch. The NICE reference case requirement: more pain for what, if any, gain? *Pharmacoeconomics*, 22:271–273, 2004.

G. Godager, T. Iversen, and C.A. Ma. Competition, gatekeeping, and health care access. *Journal of Health Economics*, 39:159–170, 2015.

M.R. Gold, J.E. Siegel, L.B. Russell, and M.C. Weinstein. *Cost-effectiveness in health and medicine*. Oxford University Press, New York, 1966.

N. Goldfield. The evolution of diagnosis-related groups (DRGs): From its beginnings in case-mix and resource use theory, to its implementation for payment and now for its current utilization for quality within and outside the hospital. *Quality Management in Health Care*, 19:3–16, 2010.

J.A. Muir Gray. Hellish decisions in healthcare. In E. Nagel, M. Lauerer, and V. Schätzlein, editors, *Prioritization in healthcare: An international dialogue*, pages 39–43. Springer, 2016.

T. Greve and H. Keiding. Regulated competition under increasing returns to scale. *Journal of Public Economic Theory*, pages 327–345, 2016.

M. Grossman. On the concept of health capital and the demand for health. *Journal of Political Economy*, 80:223–255, 1972.

T. Groves and J. Ledyard. Optimal allocation with public goods: a solution to the "free rider" problem. *Econometrica*, 45:783–809, 1977.

J. Gruber and B. Kőszegi. Is addiction "rational?" Theory and evidence. *Quarterly Journal of Economics*, 116:1261–1303, 2001.

B.O. Hansen and H. Keiding. Alternative health insurance schemes: A welfare comparison. *Journal of Health Economics*, 21:739–756, 2001.

J. Harris. *The value of life*. Routledge and Kegan Paul, London, 1985.

J. Hartwig. What drives health care expenditure? – Baumol's model of 'unbalanced growth' revisited. *Journal of Health Economics*, 27:603–623, 2008.

J. Hirshleifer and J.G. Riley. *The analytics of uncertainty and information*. Cambridge University Press, Cambridge, 1992.

J.L. Hougaard and H. Keiding. Representation of preferences on fuzzy measures by a fuzzy integral. *Mathematical Social Sciences*, 31(1-17), 1996.

J.L. Hougaard and H. Keiding. On the aggregation of health status measures. *Journal of Health Economics*, 24:1154–1173, 2005.

T. Iversen. A theory of hospital waiting lists. *Journal of Health Economics*, 12:55–71, 1993.

K. De Jaegher and Marc Jegers. A model of physician behaviour with demand inducement. *Journal of Health Economics*, 19:231–258, 2000.

A.B. Jena and T.J. Philipson. Endogenous cost-effectiveness analysis and health care technology adoption. *Journal of Health Economics*, 32:172–180, 2013.

P. Joglekar and M.L. Paterson. A closer look at the returns and risks of pharmaceutical R&D. *Journal of Health Economics*, 5:153–177, 1986.

W.R. Johnson. Choice of compulsory insurance schemes under adverse selection. *Public Choice*, 31:23–35, 1977.

C.I. Jones. Why have health expenditures as a share of GDP risen so much? Working Paper 9325, NBER, 2002.

D. Kahneman and J.L. Knetsch. Valuing public goods: The purchase of moral satisfaction. *Journal of Environmental Economics and Management*, 22:57–70, 1992.

D. Kahneman and A. Tversky. Prospect theory: an analysis of decision under risk. *Econometrica*, 47:263–292, 1979.

Kaiser Permanente. Annual report 2015. Technical report, Kaiser Permanente, 2015. URL https://share.kaiserpermanente.org/static/kp_annualreport_2015/#numbers.

K. Kan. Cigarette smoking and self-control. *Journal of Health Economics*, 26:61–81, 2007.

R.M. Kaplan, J.P. Anderson, and T.G. Ganiats. The Quality of Well-being scale: rationale for a single quality of life index. In S.R. Walker and R.M. Rosser, editors, *Quality of life assessment: key issues in the 1990s*, pages 65–94. Springer-Science+Business Media, Dordrecht, 1993.

A. Kay. The abolition of the GP fundholding scheme: a lesson in evidence-based policy making. *British Journal of General Practice*, 52:141–144, 2002.

H. Keiding. *Game theory: a comprehensive introduction*. World Scientific, 2015.

D.G. Kendall. Stochastic processes occuring in the theory of queues and their analysis by means of the imbedded Markov chain. *The Annals of Mathematical Statistics*, 22(73-84), 1953.

R. Klein. Markets, politicians, and the nhs. *British Medical Journal*, 319:1383–1384, 1999.

K. Lancaster. A new approach to consumer theory. *Journal of Political Economy*, 74:132–157, 1966.

A. Larg and J.R. Moss. Cost-of-illness studies: A guide to critical evaluation. *Pharmacoeconomics*, 29:663–671, 2011.

B. Liljas. The demand for health with uncertainty and insurance. *Journal of Health Economics*, 17:153–170, 1998.

E. Lindahl. Positive Lösung, die Gerechtigkeit der Besteuerung. In *Classics in the theory of public finance (1967)*. Macmillan, 1919.

C.M. Lindsay and B. Feigenbaum. Rationing by waiting lists. *American Economic Review*, 74:404–417, 1984.

J. Little. A proof of the theorem $L = \lambda W$. *Operations Research*, 9:383–387, 1961.

S.C. Littlechild and G.T. Thompson. Aircraft landing fees: a game theory approach. *Bell Journal of Economics*, 8:186–204, 1977.

E. Litvak and M.C. Long. Cost and quality under managed care: irreconcilable differences? *The American Journal of Managed Care*, 6:305–312, 2000.

M.J. Machina. "Expected utility" analysis without the independence axiom. *Econometrica*, 50:277–323, 1982.

S. Malmquist. Index numbers and indifference surfaces. *Trabajos de Estadistica*, 4:209–242, 1953.

T.G. McGuire and M.V. Pauly. Physician response to fee changes with multiple payers. *Journal of Health Economics*, 10:385–410, 1991.

P. Milgrom and I. Segal. Envelope theorems for abritrary choice sets. *Econometrica*, 70: 583–601, 2002.

J.M. Miyamoto. Quality-adjusted life years (QALY) utility models under expected utility and rank dependent utility assumptions. *Journal of mathematical psychology*, 43:201–237, 1999.

E.H.M. Moors and J. Faber. Orphan drugs: unmet societal need for non-profitable privately supplied new products. *Research Policy*, 36:336–354, 2007.

C.J.L. Murray. Quantifying the burden of disease: the technical basis for disability-adjusted life years. *Bulletin of the World Health Organization*, 72:429–445, 1994.

C.J.L. Murray and A.K. Acharya. Understanding DALYs. *Journal of Health Economics*, 16: 703–730, 1997.

S. Murty. Externalities and fundamental nonconvexities: a reconciliation of approaches to general equilibrium externality modeling and implications for decentralization. Research Paper 756, University of Warwick, 2006.

J.-M. Muurinen. Demand for health: a generalized Grossman model. *Journal of Health Economics*, 1:5–28, 1982.

R. Myerson. Optimal auction design. *Mathematics of Operations Research*, 6:58–73, 1981.

J.P. Newhouse. Toward a theory of nonprofit institutions: an economic model of a hospital. *American Economic Review*, 60:64–74, 1970a.

J.P. Newhouse. A model of physician pricing. *The Southern Economic Journal*, 37:174–183, 1970b.

NICE. Guide to the methods of technology appraisal. Technical report, NICE, 2013. URL http://nice.org.uk/article/pmg9/chapter/Foreword.

J.A. Nyman. The value of health insurance: the access motive. *Journal of Health Economics*, 18:141–152, 1999.

J.A. Nyman. Is 'moral hazard' inefficient? the policy implications of a new theory. *Health Affairs*, 23:194–199, 2004.

J. Oberlander. The end of Obamacare. *New England Journal of Medicine*, 376, 2017.

OECD. Health at a glance 2015: OECD indicators. Technical report, OECD, Nov 2015.

N. Olekalns and P. Bardsley. Rational addiction to caffeine: an analysis of coffee consumption. *Journal of Political Economy*, 104:1100–1104, 1996.

S. Palmer and P.C. Smith. Incorporating option values into the economic evaluation of health care technologies. *Journal of Health Economics*, 19:755–766, 2000.

M.V. Pauly. Overinsurance and public provision of insurance: The roles of moral hazard of adverse selection. *Quarterly Journal of Economics*, 88:44–62, 1974.

J. Pfanzagl. *Theory of measurement*. Springer-Verlag, Berlin Heidelberg, 1971.

C.E. Phelps and J.P. Newhouse. The price of time, and the demand for medical services. *The Review of Economics and Statistics*, 56:334–342, 1974.

M.E. Porter and E.O. Teisberg. Redefining competition in health care. *Harvard Business Review*, pages 1–14, June 2004.

R. Ramanathan. Operations assessment of hospitals in the Sultanate of Oman. *International Journal of Operations & Production Management*, 25:39–54, 2005.

F.P. Ramsey. A contribution to the theory of taxation. *Economic Journal*, 37:47–61, 1927.

J. Rawls. *A theory of justice*. Harvard University Press, Cambridge, Massachusetts, 1971.

N. Reidling and C. Wendt. Gatekeeping and provider choice in OECD healthcare systems. *Current Sociology*, 60:489–505, 2012.

J.F. Reinganum.  The timing of innovation:  research, development, and diffusion.  In R. Schmalensee and R. Willig, editors, *Handbook of Industrial Organization*, volume 1, pages 849–908. North-Holland, 1989.

U.E. Reinhardt. The pricing of u.s. hospital services: chaos behind a veil of secrecy. *Health Affairs*, 25:57–69, 2006.

D. Retzlaff-Roberts, C.F. Chang, and R.M. Rubin.  Technical efficiency in the use of health care resources: a comparison of OECD countries. *Health Policy*, 69(55-72), 2004.

J. Richardson, J. Wildman, and I.K. Robertson. A critique of the World Health Organisation's evaluation of health system performance. *Health Economics*, 12:355–366, 2003.

V.G. Rodwin.  The health care system under french national health insurance: Lessons for health reform in the United States. *American Journal of Public Health*, 93:31–37, 2003.

M. Rothschild and J. Stiglitz.  Equilibrium in competitive insurance markets: An essay on the economics of imperfect competition. *Quarterly Journal of Economics*, 90:629–649, 1976.

S. Sandier, V. Paris, and D. Polton.  Health care systems in transition:  France.  Technical report, WHO, 2004.

D. Schmeidler. Subjective probability and expected utility without additivity. *Econometrica*, 57:571–587, 1989.

S.O. Schweitzer and J. Rafferty.  Variations in hospital product: a comparative analysis of proprietary and voluntary hospitals. *Inquiry*, 13:158–166, 1976.

G. Sermeus and G. Adriaenssens.  Drug prices and drug legislatioin in europe.  Technical report, Bureau Européen des Union de Consommateurs, Brussels, 1989.

S. Shavell. On moral hazard and insurance. *Ouarterly Journal of Economics*, 11:544–562, 1979.

M. Shubik.  Incentives, decentralized control, the assignment of joint costs and internal pricing. *Management Science*, 8(325-343), 1962.

M. Singer and P. Donoso. Assessing an ambulance service with queuing theory. *Computers & Operations Research*, 35:2549–2560, 2008.

H. Sintonen. An approach to measuring and valuing health states. *Social Science & Medicine. Part C: Medical Economics*, 15:55–65, 1981.

A.M. Spence.  Monopoly, quality, and regulation. *The Bell Journal of Economics*, 6:417–429, 1975.

D.A. Starrett. Fundamental nonconvexities in the theory of externalities. *Journal of Economic Theory*, 4(180-199), 1972.

A. Stevens, J. Raftery, J. Mant, and S. Simpson, editors.  *Health Care Needs Assessment*, volume 1. Radcliffe Publishing, 2 edition, 2004.

G.J. Stigler and G.S. Becker.  De gustibus non est disputandum. *American Economic Review*, 67:76–90, 1977.

S.M. Suranovic, R.S. Goldfarb, and T.C. Leonard. An economic theory of cigarette addiction. *Journal of Health Economics*, 18:1–29, 1999.

J. Tirole. *The theory of industrial organization*. The MIT Press, Cambridge, Massachusetts, 1988.

H. Varian. *Microeconomic Analysis*. Norton & Company, New York, 1992.

J. von Neumann and O. Morgenstern. *Theory of games and economic behavior*. Princeton University Press, Princeton, 1944.

Q. Wang. Modeling and analysis of high risk patient queues. *European Journal of Operational Research*, 155:502–515, 2004.

J.E. Ware. The status of health assessment 1994. *Ann.Rev. Public Health*, 16:327–354, 1995.

M. Whitehead.  The concepts and principles of equity and health. *Health Promot Int*, 6: 217–228, 1991.

WHO, editor. *Preamble to the Constitution of WHO*, volume 2, 1946. Official Records of WHO.

WHO. World health report 2000 – health systems: improving performance. Technical report, WHO, 2000.

A. Williams. Intergenerational equity: An exploration of the 'fair innings' argument. *Health Economics*, 6:117–132, 1997.

A. Williams and R. Cookson. Equity in health. In *Handbook of Health Economics*, volume I. Elsevier Science, 2000.

R.A. Winter. Moral hazard and insurance contracts. In G. Dionne, editor, *Contributions to insurance economics*. Kluwer Academic Publishers, Boston, 1992.

B.D. Wright. The economics of invention incentives: patents, prizes and research contracts. *American Economic Review*, 73:691–707, 1983.

J. Zhang, J. Zhang, and R. Lee. Rising longevity, education, savings, and growth. *Journal of Development Economics*, 70:83–101, 2003.

# Index